Mozart

D1390820

Wolfgang Hildesheimer

MOZART

TRANSLATED FROM THE GERMAN BY
Marion Faber

J. M. Dent & Sons Ltd
London

Translation copyright © 1982 by Farrar, Straus and Giroux, Inc.
Originally published in German, copyright © 1977
by Suhrkamp Verlag, Frankfurt am Main

All rights reserved. No part of this publication
may be reproduced, stored in a retrieval system,
or transmitted, in any form or by any means,
electronic, mechanical, photocopying, recording or
otherwise, without the prior permission of J. M. Dent & Sons Ltd.

This book if bound as a paperback is subject to the condition that it
may not be issued on loan or otherwise except in its original binding.

First published in Great Britain 1983
First paperback edition, 1985
Reprinted 1986, 1988

Made in Great Britain by
The Guernsey Press Co. Ltd, Guernsey, Channel Islands, for
J. M. Dent & Sons Ltd
91 Clapham High Street, London SW4 7TA

British Library Cataloguing in Publication Data

Hildesheimer, Wolfgang
    Mozart.
    I. Mozart, Wolfgang Amadeus   2. Composers
    —Austria—Biography
    I. Title   II. Mozart, *English*
    780'.92'4   ML410.M9

ISBN 0-460-02401-9

ACKNOWLEDGMENTS

For help with this book, the author is grateful to Silvia, Christian Hart-Nibbrig, Dorothea Sessler, Walter Jens (as always), Jacques Wildberger, Ursula Ebbers, and Joseph Heinz Eibl. Further thanks are owed to Carl Bär, Raoul Blahacek, Theo Hasler, Beate Kayser, Alexander Hyatt King, Kurt Kramer, Stefan Kunze, Ann Leiser, Walter Levin, Felix von Mendelssohn, Wilhelm Mohr, Robert Münster, Wolfgang Rehm, Wolf Rosenberg, Hans Rudolf Stalder, Inge Thurner, Daniela Vitali, and Gert Westphal.

W. H.

The translator would like to thank Wolfgang Hildesheimer, Aaron Asher, Michael di Capua, Sara Bershtel, Tamara Glenny, Lynn Warshow, Carmen Gomezplata, Erika Nolan, Olga Termini, and, above all, Stephen Hannaford.

M. F.

CONTENTS

Mozart

THIS BOOK IS the third and much expanded revision of a public lecture given in 1956, the bicentennial of Mozart's birth. Out of the preliminary thoughts for that commissioned work an inner urgency formed, grew, and finally took hold. Although part of its motivation was undeniably escapist, its true roots lie in an unceasing and active reverence for Mozart, which, obviously, I am not alone in feeling. Obviously, too, I am not alone in wishing to document this reverence. We cannot measure Mozart's greatness, but we can surely observe how it affects others; their staggeringly numerous interpretations provide clear examples of an unending failure: the unsuccessful attempt to communicate the extraordinary power of one man's work, to explain its inimitable individuality, to fathom its secret.

This failure, then, is the common element in all attempts to resurrect the figure of Mozart, my own included. Nevertheless, I have taken it into account in this work, which is, after three beginnings, the final product of my desire to contribute to the concert of diverse voices and, admittedly, to alter it with my voice. Having written this last version, I shall now return the theme to the confraternity. I seek to hide neither the repetition of some passages from earlier versions nor the modification or withdrawal of earlier theses. Some changes, often significant, are based on the primary literature, now more widely accessible and more clearly elucidated, others are based on new research and interpretive studies growing out of it. Yet most of these studies elicited the disagreement that is a further motif of my own effort: this is, not least, a book of disagreement, a response to provocation, the attempt to cleanse and restore a fresco which has been painted over repeatedly in the course of centuries. The restorer does not proceed systematically but applies himself bit by bit to any area where some of the previous layers have begun to loosen. It is not always a simple task, for the picture is fragile, whereas the materials painted over it are usually quite sturdy.

At times it was not easy to find the boundary marking off valuable material in a mass of information. Over nearly two centuries, more and more specialized studies have accumulated between the caesuras of the "standard works." Such studies, investigations of subtopics and sub-subtopics, are often of doubtful relevance, yet are worth reading as examples of devoted meticulousness. I have often been tempted to begin an essay on "The Boundaries between Useful and Useless Knowledge"; but these boundaries are staked out, after all, according to each man's individual desire for knowledge and vary with the degree of his personal involvement.

Above all, my revision and expansion of this work were dictated by certain changes in my own conception of Mozart, based only partially on the examination of new sources. No attempt to penetrate the essence of Mozart's genius can entertain the question of success or failure. It can at best lead to convictions which, however firm, must not be mistaken for certainty. The limits to potential understanding are everywhere. If one illuminating factor seems to make them recede, they reappear all the more solidly on its dark opposite side. The task comes to be its own justification and to provide enrichment in itself, though fortified by a hope that others may also be enriched. The more facts brought to light, the more puzzling their undiscovered circumstances and motivations: Mozart's reactions to the external and internal conditions of his life as revealed in the documents are not illuminated by his works. Moreover, they are obscured, unconsciously but systematically, and sometimes by Mozart himself. This is both a thesis of my essay and one of its conclusions.

I would have to wear out the word "perhaps" (I will have to use it often enough as it is) or write entirely in the conditional to be totally accurate in this work. But that would have resulted in tiring writing and tiresome reading. Therefore, I must leave it to the reader to "transpose," to measure and evaluate the subjective element which accompanies the authority of conviction based on fact.

If I switch after this observation from the first person singular to the first person plural, I am emphasizing a goal: we mean neither the *pluralis modestiae* nor (truly) the *pluralis majestatis*, but rather the common standpoint of the author and a reader who can identify with his theses, opinions, and conclusions. True, the reader will have to content himself with a product of the imagination, though by no means with a product of fantasy. It should not be too difficult; after all, no scholar or biographer has ever dealt otherwise with Mozart, in those areas where interpretation went beyond an interlinear or comparative analysis of his works, or beyond the verifiable dates and facts of his life. Biographers have not been altogether honorable in this regard: if everything is presented in a serenely authoritative tone, the boundary between fact and speculation is obscured. For this reason, we usually see Mozart's life as a fictitious chronicle, through which he saunters, a domesticated hero, though a little wild at times, in justified and dignified resistance, yet always comprehensible, because he seems to be comprehended by his respective interpreter. He remains true to the familiar forms of mythifying biographies. But that precisely *he*, the Viennese Mozart, cast a new mold, that *he* is the exemplary case which stretches the sociological vocabulary to include the concept of "artistic genius," this is omitted or suppressed by platitude.

Pluralis concordiae, then. I will, however, return to the singular whenever I feel the reader might not wish to make the leap into speculation immediately but would rather test in cool collectedness the distance separating the new standpoint from the deceptive *terra firma*. We will not get close to Mozart. Nevertheless, the urgent, ever-insistent wish to approach him, a recapitulation of all the verified facts, combined with a systematic involvement with the work itself, will enable us to discern the definitive limits of our imagination, and even to isolate aspects of a possible reality. This is not to say that improbable or unbelievable things will suddenly become probable or certain. Quite the opposite. The contradictions between Mozart's life and his influence, between the demands made on him by others and his relation to these contemporaries, harden into inexorable and conclusive facts. They are recurring facts which cannot be refuted, and we shall have to learn to live with them.

In works of fiction one perceives, among other things, the psychic makeup of the author behind his characters. Here the degree of his objectivity is no measure of quality. We have all noticed that it is often precisely his neurosis which gives the author's work its monomaniacal, often monumental subjectivity, its unique value. In biography, however, this degree of subjectivity must be the decisive criterion. For the reader is interested in the information, not in the informant. But here, too, the reader can learn about the matter only through the subjective eye of the author, whom he can, of course, decide to accept or reject. Where the author is aware of his subjectivity, we should accept him; we should acknowledge his authority based on conviction as a quality and a method. To be sure, the author would have to give us an idea of himself beforehand, some proof of his insight into himself. For it is impossible to understand any figure of the past, let alone a genius, if one has never attempted self-understanding. Since there is surely not much affinity between the psyche of a genius and that of his interpreter, the latter must apply the perceptions of psychoanalysis as he himself has experienced it. For it has

taught him to determine and regulate the degree of his relation *to* and identification *with* his object, and therefore to
eliminate as much emotion as possible, positive or negative. It
has taught him, too, to keep in readiness, as proven tools of
understanding, the typical reactions of the psyche, in all their
possible manifestations, including the deepest traumas, but
not to use the potential reaction of his own soul as a yardstick.
Yet this is what all Mozart biographers *have* done, blurring
thereby the boundaries between wish and truth. The representation of "Mozart the man" fluctuates between eulogy and
apologia. When Bruno Walter says that Mozart was an "open,
trusting soul," a "happy, simplehearted young man,"[1] he is
expressing not only a generally cherished wish (which, in addition, unwittingly shows the limits of his own psychological insight) but also an unthinking concession to the public of which
he is part, a public that would like to have this particular kind
of Mozart. Indeed, this is the kind they have always gotten.

This, precisely, is the sorry nature of trite biographies:
they find easy explanations for everything, within a range of
probability we can comprehend. The primary source and the
motivation are the same: wishful thinking. Given their in-
equality of powers, the writer's identification with the hero,
his fixation on him, makes his effort at representation profoundly untruthful. Mozart's life followed laws different from
those of his interpreters. Until now, everyone has squared accounts by assuming that his wretched and degraded earthly
existence was, in the last analysis, fulfilled in the lofty realms
of creativity. His misery paid off, so to speak. The question
"For whom?" is never put.

To posterity, all past conflicts seem resolved into harmony,
illuminating the age itself with melancholy but soothing
beauty. Thus, for example, Bernhard Paumgartner characterizes Mozart's stay in Vienna after the break with the Archbishop in 1781: "The city on the Danube embraced the storm-

tossed artist with maternal arms, becoming the homeland of his maturity."[2] This sentence is a classic example of extreme repression. It demonstrates the whole anomalous spectrum: the overreaching author who, given his overwhelming topic, wishes to go beyond the simple assertion: "Mozart lived henceforth in Vienna." The sentence shows that attachment to circumstances which grows out of wishful thinking: it is a picture prepared for the reader, in which everything must remain within the author's and reader's limits of the imaginable or, at the least, the possible. We see the mother-impulse of the sentence in its moderation and plausibility, its desire for integration, and the immovable, dominating father-impulse in its didacticism and certainty. We see thought cast in national categories, in this case Austrian. The pathos of diction is a sign of an unconscious wish to be assimilated with the hero. For if we clarify that image of "maternal arms," that "city on the Danube," that "storm-tossed artist" whom they "embrace," and the "homeland of his maturity" (only immaturity has no homeland, apparently), we are left with the implication that Mozart found fulfillment and peace in Vienna. We can only point out in passing that the opposite is known to have been the case.*

"Embracing" seems to be a popular euphemism. In Alfred Orel, though, we read not of "maternal arms" but rather of a total takeover: "And so the city on the Danube embraced Wolfgang Amadeus with its mysterious magic and, like so many others before and since, never let him go."[3] Here we might add that it was not so much "mysterious magic" as lack of money that never let him go, preventing his intended move to England, where it appears he might have done well. If we can speak at all of a city as having a collective will, the city on

---

* A peculiar flowering of double idolatry (Mozart and Austria) : "Thus Mozart is for us prefiguration, completion, and future, an utterly timeless perfection, and, like all great human achievements, he is both near to us and far off in time. He who finds no joy in this teaching does not deserve to be called a human being, and certainly not an Austrian." From Joseph Marx's introduction to an edition of the Köchel Catalogue, revised and edited by Karl Franz Müller (Vienna, 1951).

the Danube would have as gladly let "Wolfgang Amadeus" go in 1786, after *Figaro*, as it later did Gustav Mahler and Arnold Schoenberg. Here the author is compensating for the traumatic fact by turning to inaccuracy, which affects even the actual data and distorts the true state of affairs.

Vienna's troubled relationship to Mozart has given rise to a legion of apologists whose cultural chauvinism does not allow them to acknowledge so irreparable a blot. Their efforts at retouching are merely symptomatic and inconsequential examples of that twofold fixation on the hero and his homeland characteristic of the wishful thinkers. Salzburg, too, claims a share which it does not deserve, for Mozart really hated this city, and referred to its citizens in language verging on the slanderous. Of course, Salzburg has always ignored this and asserted its genealogical claim, which has to suffice where a harmonious relationship between hero and homeland is lacking.

Hugo von Hofmannsthal disguised this claim in obscure language: "Mozart was here, and here on this soil, where the old Europe meets the new, at this crossroads of Roman, Germanic, and Slavic culture; here did that music originate, the true, eternal music of our age, utter fulfillment, as natural as nature, and as innocent."[4] It would be idle to try to understand such a sentence, for its meaning is incomprehensible. Besides, only an unusually small number of Mozart's "great works" originated on Salzburg's "soil." Furthermore, great music does not originate from any mystical obscurity or ethnic attachment; rather it is *made*, in the interaction of unconscious ideas and conscious methodology. It is, therefore, not as natural as nature and certainly not as "innocent," if we may indeed credit nature with attributes such as innocence and guilt. It is our task to cleanse Mozart's image of dodges like these. In this case, I admit, we have the "word of the poet," one who would like to prove himself equal to his hero. But it is also in this case a hero who, in establishing a new category, demands a treatment other than the "poetic license" of the aesthete.

That other body of work which endeavors to stick honorably "to the facts" is usually built on conclusions that not only hide their foundations but also assume that contemporary sources, particularly autobiographical evidence, are reliable and objective. We know that autobiographical statements are not necessarily objective, and Mozart's are anything but. Although they demonstrate the developing verbal facility of a phenomenally active mind, Mozart's deeper intellectual essence is never transmitted through his words. At times they testify to a thoroughly pragmatic adaptability: besides the souls dwelling in the breast of Mozart the writer (unlike Faust, he has far more than two, but he reveals them only rarely), there are various disguises, which he knows how to wear with appropriate conviction when necessary. The mastery of means which made him the greatest and most mysterious musician of all time also stood him in good stead in his verbal statements. He had at his disposal a tremendous synthetic-emotional range, with which he could assume many shapes or hide himself entirely, and he employed the whole range without hypocrisy, but also without any compunction about objective truth. When writing, he assumed one of his many personae. He wrote as he saw himself, as he wished or ought to have seen himself, as he had to or sought to appear to others, and as he imagined that others imagined him. But his own words give us no sure way of knowing him *as he was*.

Although some essential information has been lost, primary autobiographical sources are now in optimal condition.[5] Any additional information that comes to light will hardly change the picture. Thus, everyone is free to interpret Mozart's apparent reactions to the conditions of his life as best he can and draw his own conclusions. Let us table the question of whether this helps our ultimate understanding of Mozart the phenomenon. It is hard enough to form an idea of the subjective life of a genius of our own century; with a genius of the past our powers of imagination shrink in direct proportion to the time elapsed, his historical period, and, not least, his lifespan.

I am, then, fully conscious of my dependence on the reader's power of imagination and willingness to imagine; one cannot convince where an iron will refuses to understand, where an automatic defense mechanism rejects a proposed insight before testing it. Such behavior is allowable only in someone who has already concerned himself with the same material and come to a different conclusion. But it is not valid when it is merely the reaction of someone so used to a different or contradictory idea that he is fixated on it, cannot or will not give it up, and rejects any correction to the old formula. The reader must test not only the veracity of my study but also his own willingness to put aside his preconceptions.

To express it musically: we have before us a score consisting of only two staves—the melodic line (Mozart's music) and the bass (his external life). The connecting middle voices are missing—his unconscious, the dictates and impulses of his inner life, that which governs his motives and behavior. Illuminating verbal confessions are practically nonexistent. A familiar exercise in music is to compose a third, connecting part to two that are given (Mozart had to assign this to his students *ad nauseam*). This is how we must regard the work of biographers. To these two other parts—the life's experience and its (assumed) expression in an *oeuvre*—they compose a connecting line. It is crucial to free the original score of Mozart's existence from these additions in order to restore the enigma that is the man. For we have learned over the years to regard all biographies, indeed all historical writing, with appropriate skepticism.

Our task, then, is to blot out existing ideas, but not to mediate between Mozart and the reader. On the contrary, the intention of this study is to make the distance between both sides even greater, not only the gulf between our epochs (which renders speculative all understanding of figures of the late *ancien régime*), but also the unbridgeable distance between Mozart's inner life and our inadequate conception of its nature and dimensions. No biographer has managed to show the elusiveness of this phenomenon convincingly. All have relied on an image originating in biographical familiarity and inherited habit. They pass over bizarre elements, leave out what seems to them unessential, explain away what is embarrassing. Thus, they stretch the image in every direction, upward and (especially) downward, smooth it out and arrange it until it corresponds to a vague Apollonian ideal and idol, which, of course, keeps tumbling off its pedestal. Alfred Einstein writes that we "must accept the fact that Mozart was 'a man with a man's contradictions,' "[6] exhorting us to understand one of the characteristics which he really does share with all of us but which Einstein apparently will not concede in a genius. Mozart does not correspond to any Apollonian ideal. All his statements, even the look, diction, and punctuation of his verbal documents, the gestures, mimicry, and manners we know of, suggest, rather, a Dionysian type. Of course, Mozart would tumble off that pedestal, too, for even this opaque topology does not really apply to him, and especially not to his work, which is totally beyond such categories. From the manuscripts of his scores we see that sketches of even the grandest musical panoramas must have been executed with total control. Clear, transparent, and legible even to the end, rarely marred by a correction (for the composition itself was usually complete long before he wrote it down), the manuscripts betray subjective emotion only in the vigorous flourish of a dynamic marking. Everything about this work is sublimely elusive, unearthly, and, objectively, everything is essential. His autobiographical statements clarify only the fact that he is withdrawing from us, hiding behind his music, and the music, too, in its deepest meaning, is inaccessible to us, allowing no understanding outside music itself.

THE NAME MOZART, like Beethoven or Haydn, is bound to one single figure and unimaginable apart from it. It is unthinkable that anyone today could live up to such a handicap. But even more markedly than the other two names, Mozart calls forth an especially receptive disposition, a kind of ecstasy, in all those who claim to be musical (whatever that may mean). The unstated basis of their collective feeling is that Mozart is an utterly unique phenomenon, indisputably and forever on the credit side of life's ledger, so sovereign and omnipresent that he reconciles us somewhat to the debit side. Indeed, Mozart seems to be reconciliation itself, a kind of redeeming miracle. Of course, he himself did not have the remotest suspicion of his posthumous power to bring such fulfillment. He never would have stretched that far the "silent approval" he detected in the reaction of the Viennese public to *Die Zauberflöte* at the end of his undeniably arduous life. Even less would he have guessed that his name would become synonymous with everything transcendently beautiful and immanently inspired (to condense the enthusiasts' vocabulary). To be sure, he knew his own worth; perhaps he even stood at the top of his own scale of values; but in accordance with his position in his world and time, this scale was relative. He would hardly have known how to measure in absolutes, nor does he ever do so in his documented statements. He also never uses the superlative of absolute enthusiasm. Mozart thought of himself as a person "of superior talent," which he could not deny "without impiety" (letter of September 11, 1778), and therefore superior to all others except the revered Haydn. His relationship to popularity was ironic, for he knew precisely when it was necessary to be "popular," having been adequately instructed by his father. He became increasingly indifferent to honors from the elite, which he began garnering when still almost a child, on his journeys to Italy. These attitudes certainly contributed to his downfall, but attest also to the supremacy of the truly great man. Neither submissive nor servile, he was uninterested in titles and decorations. Characteristically, he forgot to take along the academic diplomas that were intended to be useful to him on his trip to Mannheim and Paris in 1777–79: they had to be sent after him. He possessed a papal order higher than Gluck's (Orlando di Lasso was the only composer before him to receive it), but he probably never wore it after two insolent young Augsburg patricians abused him because of it on his Paris journey (letter of October 16, 1777). We do not know whether the honors helped him later; probably he forgot them. It would not have occurred to him to call himself Ritter von Mozart, except in those letters where he parodied himself or misused the title, calling himself "Ritter von Sauschwanz" ("the Honorable Pig's Tail"). After the Italian journeys, the seventeen-year-old signed some larger scores "Cavaliere" or "Chevalier," but he soon gave that up and called himself "Wolfgang Amadè (or Amadé) Mozart." He never used "Amadeus," except in jest: "Wolfgangus Amadeus Mozartus." Nor is this name in the baptismal register; it is a product of the biographers' desire to smooth out rough edges. Usually he signed his letters "Mozart"; later he added the title "Royal and Imperial Kapellmeister" to compliments or petitions, not because of its importance (it was a modest post), but rather as a formality. Perhaps he felt he had to write it to be sure that the recipient would have some idea who this Mozart was. Arrogance was alien to him, but he exploited his own superiority, sometimes with malicious emphasis. He needed recognition, at least until the great renunciation of his last years. He placed greatest value on the praise of those he himself esteemed, but they were few—more exactly, it was Haydn alone, the only contemporary Mozart admired. Thus, the man who liked to perform only for experts became the darling of the dilettantes.

We should not despise the enthusiasts. Mozart, the object of their enthusiasm, ennobles it, even if it can only be articulated "from the bottom of their hearts." The theologian Karl Barth, for instance, imagines that the angels, left to themselves, play Mozart, and that the dear Lord likes especially to listen to them then.[7] I am a stranger to those spheres, but can visualize a pretty picture: I see God like Rembrandt's Saul enjoying the music of David's harp, lost in the thought that one ought perhaps to have done something for this divine musician during his earthly life. Musicians, too, have availed themselves of the analogy with divine realms: "Others may reach heaven with their works. But Mozart, he comes, he comes from there!"[8] This exclamation, with its rhetorical repetition, also reveals an emotional relationship to its object rather than a valid statement about it; it supports Alfred Einstein's phrase that Mozart was "only a guest on this earth." And yet we must admit that, on some uncomfortably irrational level, we apprehend what is meant: recognition of the miraculous quality in Mozart, the deepest reason for all work about him, a reason so deep that its premise is beyond thought.

At any rate, we have no wish to dispute statements like these, which blend inextricably emotional, naïvely pious, and mystical responses. As we know, the vocabulary of the "inexpressible" has been nearly as constant as Mozart's undisputed greatness. In describing his music, the "divine," "unearthly" quality of this or that passage, the "otherworldliness" will prevail as long as he does, and make certain that his aura of transcendence remains intact. Even if such words obscure their object, they do not do it harm. For those who read them, they will always be the first definition of Mozart. People who do not hear the music itself hear instead the imagined significance of its sound. However the reverent listener articulates the range of his emotions, it is reverence alone he expresses. But the cause for reverence remains a constant pedal point: Mozart.

Mozart as an object of worship is an invention of the Romantics. The publisher Nikolaus Simrock would bare his head when Mozart's name was mentioned;[9] his contemporary Kierkegaard wanted to start a sect to revere Mozart, not above others, but exclusively.[10] To be sure, he himself characterized this reverence as "adolescent," and we wouldn't want to contradict the great confessor on this point.

Let us suppose that Mozart, worshipped by Kierkegaard's sect, is looking down from Barth's heaven onto his domain, whether this be legitimate or misguided: with subjective emotions, it amounts to the same thing. Let Mozart (who never respected position, rank, or title in the least) observe the use of his works for political ceremonies, official merriment, public mourning, and similar purposes requiring no more understanding of his music than his mother-in-law Cäcilie Weber could muster ("In her case what will probably happen will be that she will *see* the opera, but not *hear* it," Mozart writes on October 9, 1791) . Let's hope all this amuses him. Such nonsensical, bombastically pretentious occasions and their initiators often spurred Mozart to extravagant parodies, verbal excesses that show us how little he sometimes respected people he was forced to get along with.

In Mozart's case the changing relationship between adulation and its object has never been in just proportion. Appreciation, the ability to distinguish and respond, changes over time according to the period, the fashion, the "trend"; it allows us to exchange the object of our appreciation at will. We are not reverent because of commitment or *engagement*, for we need not champion something of the past through personal advocacy, nor do we fear its loss. A timeless collective conscience, which the Freemason Mozart in particular would have had to demand (insofar as he ever concerned himself with the ideals of his order, and if any kind of demand were not alien to him), does not exist. So we can take the liberty of blaming his contemporaries for his misery, as if *we* would have recognized him in his greatness immediately and banished all obstacles from his path. But who *is* to be blamed, if not his contemporaries, and, above all, the Viennese? That share of guilt which is his own remains to be examined.

Absolutism no longer exists, it is true, at least not the formal or official kind; no archbishops as feudal lords, no Maria Theresa, who advised her archduke son not to put himself out for traveling riffraff like Mozart and his cohorts (*"gens inutils . . . courent le monde comme de gueux,"* letter of Maria Theresa, December 12, 1771) and therefore not to engage them at his court in Milan. There are no more Count Arcos: when Mozart, court musician to the Archbishop Colloredo, asked for release from service (letter of June 9, 1781), Arco booted him out of the reception chamber. There should be a kind of negative order of nobility for such behavior, with a visible sign like a mark of Cain, which only the intentional good acts of descendants could erase. Though, if we examine the history of the great Habsburg houses, we must acknowledge that they accumulated their titles and possessions by acts far more shameful than a kick in a great man's rear.

But let us be fair to this Count Arco: he, too, was ultimately only a flunky, "Chief Chamberlain" to the Prince Archbishop of Salzburg. We must understand his unworthy action as a consequence of the fact, however strange, that music, as dinner entertainment, came under the domain of the kitchen. The scene took place during the visit of the Archbishop's household to Vienna; the faux pas was preceded by the Count's intimate confession that he, too, often suffered under their mutual lord (though Arco was quite a bit closer to the lord in rank). Above all, he took this opportunity to issue the famous warning that was to prove prophetic a few years later:

Believe me, you allow yourself to be far too easily dazzled in Vienna. A man's reputation here lasts a very short time. At first, it is true, you are overwhelmed with praises and make a great deal of money into the bargain—but how long does that last? After a few months the Viennese want something new.

So Mozart wrote to his father (June 2, 1781), although passing on this negative prediction was not in his interest at the time. It could hardly have surprised his father, who already had a bad opinion of the Viennese public, as we read in a letter of his from 1768. Still, the Count seems to have addressed Mozart with the formal *"Sie,"* which would speak for the sincerity of his effort to convince him.

But Mozart was not to be persuaded. Doubtless he, too, was possessed by a tendency of the time, one which others followed more consciously and collectively: the spirit of rebellion. Mozart experienced it as an urge to freedom, a freedom no one had deemed possible a few years earlier, except those who had always enjoyed it by robbing others of their freedom. Mozart never commented on the political upheaval of the French Revolution and probably did not recognize it as the beginning of a new age. As far as we can determine, political events never penetrated his consciousness. How should he express his thoughts other than in his music? His response to the spirit of the age was *Figaro*, a work whose story he did not create, but whose possibilities he exploited to the full, as was his custom. It was the beginning of his ruin.

Mozart replied to the Count that he did not intend to remain in Vienna: apparently the "mysterious magic" of the "city on the Danube" did not affect him then or later. He wanted to go to England, and harbored this wish until his last years, when all he wanted was the freedom to pursue his own self-imposed projects. Above all, however, he wanted to leave the service of the Archbishop, the "misanthrope," the "arrogant, conceited cleric" who had called him a "dissolute fellow" and demanded that he "clear out." In a sense, therefore, Mozart was only complying with an order. The Archbishop blustered that he "could get a hundred men who would serve him better." Colloredo might have been right: he probably would have done better with a lesser musician, since music for him was something to be delivered, an ever-ready product from a socially inferior servant whose seat at the domestics' table was a bit above those of the kitchen staff. Colloredo, although theoretically a disciple of the Enlightenment, and no tyrant, was nevertheless a local ruler who firmly insisted on his rights. He was extremely unpopular both in Salzburg and Vienna. In his conduct toward Mozart he seems to have reacted with strangely excessive emotion and constant irritation, probably because Mozart was unable and unwilling to hide his latent rebelliousness, a consequence of his drive to self-development. Certainly he had once been a "genius of obedience" (Friedrich Heer), but after 1781 this part of his genius gave way to a growing sense of his own worth, until he finally became a genius at self-concealment.

In our time, men of business and industry try to create a contrast to their mercenary dealings. Something gnaws on their collective conscience, and so they set up shop in the world of the "beautiful," *pro forma et pro statute,* and do something to further the cause of art and artists. The artist is happy to take their alms with one eye closed and the other dry. Anyone who lives in a garret today does so from his own desire. He knows that if he gives it up for more comfortable living conditions, he will be giving up the aura of the poor-but-free artist, which he radiates as the sign of steadfast nonconformity. Unwittingly, but significantly, Mozart helped create this aura. He was perhaps not the first poor artist, but, sociologically at least, he was the first free one, and poor as a result of his freedom. Ultimately, he was destroyed by this very freedom. Yet even he didn't have to live in a garret. True, his diverse dwellings were three-dimensional symbols of his social fall (one of the first, on Schulerstrasse, now Domgasse, was almost "elegant"), but they also provided room for parties and musicales, even in 1789, a time for him of oppressive poverty. In his homes he celebrated holidays, played chamber music with Haydn for a select audience, and even produced informal little opera recitals, to which he invited, among others, his main creditor, Michael Puchberg (who probably guessed the reason). In his last year, though, he no longer played host to musicians or music lovers. Haydn was in London, Constanze, Mozart's wife, in Baden taking the waters (a practice she continued until her death). Household furnishings gradually made their way to the pawnshop. Mozart himself avoided his house, for he could no longer stand to be alone (this was, incidentally, one of the few behavioral characteristics he was aware of in himself). On the other hand, he was able to satisfy his rather healthy appetite (letter of October 8, 1791, two months before his death) until the end, sometimes even with delicacies he couldn't afford but bought anyway. We must not think of his material misery as outright hunger, even if this lack of hunger was dearly bought with dubious financial transactions. It is possible that the banquet scene in *Don Giovanni* was modeled on his own joviality among friends in Prague in 1787. But in *Die Zauberflöte* of 1791 Tamino and Papageno's richly decked table could hardly have been his own, especially since his silver had long since been pawned (it seems amazing that he ever had any). Still, the bright A major of the three boys' invitation to eat and drink certainly does not reflect (as some critics would have it)[11] a sort of *fata morgana* wish fulfillment, set, with watering mouth, to music. Even at that time Mozart's needs were seen to, though not by Constanze, whose absence was to cost him dear. He was still invited, if grudgingly, to dinner. It is said that Emanuel Schikaneder, perhaps for selfish reasons, took an interest in his well-being. And his lodge brother Puchberg played host to him when the money he lent Mozart had trickled away. Like many great artists, Mozart had the gift of repressing his deep and well-founded despair in an excess of work, with an increasingly hectic desire for company, and probably also with an occasional debauch. At any rate, he managed to repress his insight into his ever more discouraging situation: society's failure to respond, his growing isolation. Late at night, he confronted what he avoided during his busy day, but only for as long as it took to draft a plea for some provisional assistance. In tortured haste, he wrote his requests and entreaties, as if diverting his mind from his misery, hoping to exorcize it by the act of writing, and yet, wallowing in self-deprecation, a slave to it still. The artificial style of these letters reminds us of *opera seria*. Mozart employed it, as we shall see, not only to portray his financial straits, but also when commenting on certain turns of fate which ought to have affected him more deeply than they did. His style reveals, ultimately, grief and devastation. We read these letters almost with a guilty conscience, as if we are invading Mozart's privacy, something he would never have permitted. His friend and (insufficient) redeemer Puchberg was usually the recipient of these letters. Sometimes Mozart had been with him at a little house concert only a few hours before, and would perhaps be with him again the next day at some soirée in their private circle. So Puchberg shared Mozart's double life of misery and art. Very likely, he was a full partner in Mozart's tragicomedy of repression: he did not bring money to the soirées, but had it sent by messenger. We don't know whether he did so because his sense of tact forbade the tainting of a well-attended musical gathering with a show of material assistance. We don't know how "tact" was valued at that time and in those circles. It does seem as if creditors and debtors never spoke about money face to face, but that everything was arranged with averted eyes, so to speak. Or rather, nothing was ever fully arranged: the sums sent were always smaller (usually substantially smaller) than what Mozart requested and originally hoped for. But we can assume that he soon began calculating this difference when stating his needs. Of course, we can also assume that Puchberg, for his part, took Mozart's real expectations into account and reduced his payments accordingly.

Michael Puchberg: let us begin our series of "secondary characters" with him. This essentially peripheral, yet ever-present figure stands quietly behind the scenes of Mozart's last years in Vienna. He is mentioned often, but is ultimately only representative of all those who had a function, sometimes a much less significant one, in Mozart's social life: Schikaneder's actors, the in-laws, lodge brothers, and other members of the scarcely illustrious circle. Mozart probably found it to his liking: he needed no great men around him; he himself was great. But that was something neither he nor his circle knew (though he may have suspected it in his final years). Puchberg, his provider during the times of sorriest distress, has also become the subject of biographical speculation. Sometimes his business sense is emphasized, sometimes his devotion to the helpless debtor (usually one quality at the cost of the other). True, there were some requests he never answered, but it is certain that between 1788 and 1791 he helped Mozart out with sums that today would total around $15,000. If Mozart had had his way, the sum would have been more than twice that. But Puchberg was not his only creditor. Not until several years after Mozart's death did Puchberg ask for repayment of the debt from Constanze, who had ripened into a businesswoman and well-to-do widow. He received the money, though not before he asked for it. He was a respectable businessman (Haydn, too, approached him sometimes) and in 1792 could even afford to seek a title, which was granted. He died in 1822, as Herr von Puchberg, though reduced to poverty.

[Vienna,] July 12th, 1789
Dearest, most beloved Friend and most honorable Br.
Great God! I would not wish my worst enemy to be in my present position. And if you, ·most beloved friend and brother, forsake me, we are altogether lost, *both my unfortunate and blameless self* and my poor sick wife and child. Only the other day when I was with you I was longing to open my heart to you, but I had not the courage to do so— and indeed I should still not have the courage—for, as it is, I only dare to write and I tremble as I do so—and I should not even dare to write, were I not certain that you know me, that you are aware of my circumstances, and that you are wholly convinced of my *innocence* so far as my unfor-

tunate and most distressing situation is concerned. Good God! I am coming to you not with thanks but with fresh entreaties! Instead of paying my debts I am asking for more money! If you really know me, you must sympathize with my anguish in having to do so. I need not tell you once more that owing to my unfortunate illness I have been prevented from earning anything. But I must mention that in spite of my wretched condition I decided to give subscription concerts at home in order to be able to meet at least my present great and frequent expenses, for I was absolutely convinced of your friendly assistance. But even this has failed. Unfortunately Fate is so much against me, *though only in Vienna*, that even when I want to, I cannot make any money. A fortnight ago I sent round a list for subscribers and so far the only name on it is that of Baron van Swieten! Now that (on the 15th) my dear little wife seems to be improving every day, I should be able to set to work again, if this blow, this heavy blow, had not come. At any rate, people are consoling me by telling me that she is better —although yesterday evening she was suffering so much— and I on her account—that I was stunned and despairing. But last night (the 14th), she slept so well and has felt so much easier all the morning that I am very hopeful; and at last I am beginning to feel inclined for work. I am now faced, however, with misfortunes of another kind, though, it is true, only for the moment. Dearest, most beloved friend and brother—you know *my present circumstances*, but you also know *my prospects*. So let things remain as we arranged; that is, *thus or thus*, you understand what I mean. Meanwhile I am composing six easy clavier sonatas for Princess Friederike and six quartets for the King, all of which Kozeluch is engraving at my expense. At the same time the two dedications will bring me in something. In a month or two my fate must be decided *in every detail*. Therefore, most beloved friend, you will not be risking anything so far as I am concerned. So it all depends, my only friend, upon whether you will or can lend me another 500 gulden. Until my affairs are settled, I undertake to pay back ten gulden a month; and then, as this is bound to happen in a few months, I shall pay back the whole sum with whatever interest you may demand, and at the same time acknowledge myself to be your debtor for life. That, alas, I shall have to remain, for I shall never be able to thank you sufficiently for your friendship and affection. Thank God, that is over. Now you know all. Do not be offended by my confiding in you and remember that unless you help me, the honor, the peace of mind, and perhaps the very life of your friend and brother Mason will be ruined.

> Ever your most grateful servant,
> true friend and brother
> W. A. Mozart

> At home, July 14th, 1789

O God!—I can hardly bring myself to dispatch this letter!—and yet I must! If this illness had not befallen me, I should not have been obliged to beg so shamelessly from my only friend. Yet I hope for your forgiveness, for you know both the good and *the bad prospects of my situation.* The bad is temporary; the good will certainly persist, once the momentary evil has been alleviated. Adieu. For God's sake forgive me, only forgive me!—and—Adieu!

This letter is perhaps the most uninhibited and yet the most stylized of the twenty-one extant letters to Puchberg. Its tragic aspects (it is probable that Mozart is dramatizing his wife's suffering, though she may have exaggerated it to him) have the quality of a *recitativo accompagnato.* Only after the prelude, with its double address both to the friend and to the lodge brother, does the curtain rise on the troubled scene. It begins with the exclamation *"Gott!"*, much like the *"Deh!"* of *opera seria.* According to the musical grammar of the Neapolitan school, this would be a G minor chord. It is the heroine innocently plunged into distress. The pain is genuine, but the effect upon the recipient is a calculated one. A few lines later, with confused interjections, the declamatory tone dissolves and gives way to unrhetorical lament, a theme with abundant variations.

The letter is evidence of the classic case of the freelance

artist in all his material dependency. Who would not prefer to get the embarrassing task over with in writing, rather than personally confront the potential savior, who might demand an accounting (it might actually have been useful for his creditor to get some accounting for that portion of the debts owed to him). Furthermore, the redeeming facts, those works which are to earn the money back again, are better enumerated in writing. Of the six easy piano sonatas for Princess Friederike of Prussia, only one, in D, K. 576 (July 1789), was completed—his last piano sonata. It is, incidentally, anything but easy—at least it is hard to imagine any Prussian princess playing the sixteenth-note runs for the left hand in the allegretto as they should be played and as Mozart played them. It wasn't the only time he forgot both the purpose and the recipient of a composition in the course of writing it. In fact, we sometimes guess that the superior man's irony lies behind many of these commissioned pieces: when, for example, he dedicates the C major Sonata, K. 545 (June 26, 1788) to an unknown "beginner," he does so (in light of the allegro, at least) in pure mockery.

Of the six quartets for King Friedrich Wilhelm II of Prussia, himself a cellist, one was already written: K. 575 in D (June 1789). Two others, K. 589 in B-flat and K. 590 in F, were completed in May and June 1790, not until a year after the letter. Perhaps temporary alleviations of the severest distress (including payment for *Così fan tutte*) made completion less urgent. Of this set, only these three quartets were written. We do not know if the King ever received them. The publisher Artaria acquired them for the price of a sandwich. Puchberg probably expected just that of Mozart's promises—he sent nothing. And only when reminded, five days later, did he dispatch 150 gulden.

It is really less a question of the ancillary figure Puchberg himself than of the role he plays as Mozart's partner. It is only a small part at the climax of the tragedy. Though not present at the final catastrophe, he is vitally essential to the hero. We will anticipate the catastrophe in order to establish here for the first, but not the last, time the strange fact that the characters of Mozart's last years will not reveal themselves to us, not even in relation to him. They meet us with silence.

Naturally this also applies to Constanze,* who appears at the turning point, but becomes active, and (to a degree) articulate, only after his death, and then only to expose her depressing banality.

Who were the patrons, the friends? Who, for example, were the two Gottfrieds, van Swieten and von Jacquin, apart from their predetermined social positions and functions, and especially apart from Mozart's references to them as "dearest, most beloved friends," whom he favored with generous dedications? We know it was van Swieten who introduced him to the works of Bach, but that cost nothing. On the contrary, he was rewarded for it with all the arrangements he desired, even complete programs, for his Sunday-afternoon musicales. But what Mozart thought of him personally we do not know. Mozart's reticence about personalities is so striking that it inclines us to think he saw in his fellow man only what was relevant to him, the musical side of the personality. What was the nature of his personal ties—to the extent that we can speak of them? Who *was* this "dearest most beloved friend" Puchberg, about whom we know at least that he helped Mozart modestly, in accordance, perhaps, with his own means? To us he remains the man who replies indirectly to Mozart's voluminous and often degrading and submissive pleas, expressing himself exclusively in notations on the margin of the letters: "Sent 25 florins on April 23," "150 florins on May 17," etc. An automaton, not satisfying exactly, but reliable in that he kept the petitioner going until the next petition. If only to a limited

---

* It is necessary to take into account the arbitrary orthography of names in Mozart's time, and in his own writings. Constanze or Konstanze, Aloisia or Aloysia—there is no right or wrong, even in official nomenclature or christenings. Mozart was registered sometimes as Mozard or Mozhardt or Motzart. It would be a vain task to determine whether the famous tenor, the first Idomeneo, was named Raaff or Raaf or Raf or Raff.

extent, Mozart could count on him. With other friends he could not even do that. How did they respond to Mozart's friendship? We know them only as the recipients of letters, dedications, entries in guest books. He served them with generosity, as was his wont. But there is no evidence that they repaid in kind. The "good friend" Prince Lichnowsky, who later befriended Beethoven, borrowed 100 gulden from Mozart on their journey to Dresden, Leipzig, and Berlin (April to June 1789), perhaps the very same gulden that Mozart had borrowed from the chancery clerk Franz Hofdemel before the journey. Apparently Mozart could not refuse the Prince. "You will know why," he wrote ambiguously to Constanze (May 23, 1789). We do *not* know why, but can hope in retrospect that the Prince repaid him. Nor can we totally exclude the possibility that Mozart invented this loan so that he could spend the money without Constanze's knowledge. As we shall see, it would not have been the first time.

For the clarinetist Anton Stadler, he wrote two of his "major works," the Quintet, K. 581 (September 29, 1789) and—a few weeks before his death, between *Zauberflöte* and the Requiem —the Concerto, K. 622 (October 1791). Stadler probably sold Mozart's pawn tickets behind his back and certainly never repaid the 500 gulden he owed him (we wonder where Mozart had got them in the first place). Apparently Mozart did not hold it against him, both because he disliked acknowledging human failings, and because he esteemed Stadler as an outstanding musician.

We have practically no written records of all these companions, no authentic evidence about the collaboration with his librettists Lorenzo Da Ponte and Schikaneder, hardly a line from his students, nothing from Constanze while she was still Constanze Mozart. So our picture of the Mozart of the final Viennese years is of a man trying, unceasingly, to communicate with a world ever more indifferent to him. Frustrated, his own voice weakens and the world no longer takes any notice of him at all. He disappears from it, and his circle grows smaller. Finally, there remain only the few men with whom, according to tradition, he rehearses on his death bed the "Lacrymosa" from his Requiem, while Constanze and her sister Sophie cut out a nightshirt for him.

Mozart must have been aware of the growing distance between himself and the world around him in the last two years of his life. We do not know how much he brooded over it or repressed it. He made no comment about it, but kept on going, one day after another. Although increasingly perturbed, he continued to work as if nothing were wrong. His behavior became more disturbing, but his inner life remained closed; we have no authenticated word about it. Thus, we can learn nothing from him now, either. His self-control might be instructive, but what we imagine to be self-control was perhaps a totally different characteristic, one we cannot figure out by deduction. He not only came on the scene under a set of rules different from our own, he left it in the same way. We cannot get free of the cliché of Mozart as a totally unique phenomenon. We use the term here, not in the sense of enthusiastic gushing, but in order to show the futility of any narrow attempt at classification. Mozart is not even suitable as a didactic model of heroic self-mastery, like Beethoven: in the score of Mozart's life the voice of assimilated experience and elaboration on it is lacking. His silence is shared by most great artists up to the end of the eighteenth century, but because of the seemingly abundant primary sources, Mozart offers a greater temptation to interpreters. In reality, though, the sources serve only to construct the riddle.

This premature summation of the later period of our protagonist's life did not originate as an antibiographical outburst, nor was it exclusively for antibiographical purposes. True, I wanted to blur chronology and to sketch in points of orientation as a context for the examination of earlier stages. Even though the reader is familiar, more or less, with the conclusion of the tragedy, it will be worthwhile for him to keep this ominous, ever-present signpost in mind as the destination of all the highways and byways of our protagonist. Furthermore, I would like, as far as clarity permits, to pursue free associations without being bound to a formal structure.

It is tempting to find the primary cause of his early death in the exertions of his childhood and youth. But if this were the case, the decades between his physical maturity and his sudden death could not have been so productive and energetic, so seldom interrupted by serious illness or bouts of chronic complaint, or by any symptoms of decline.

Besides, neither father nor son experienced the severity and hardship of the early years as such. Mozart did not consider himself overextended; rather, he felt himself equal to the challenge from the beginning. If his is a case of physical disadvantage, then it was so not only for him but for many thousands of budding young musicians everywhere, training to be instrumentalists or singers. It was not only Haydn's youth that was considerably harsher. So were the lives of the hordes of male and female pupils in Italian boarding schools and orphanages from among whose ranks were recruited eighteenth-century opera choruses, orchestras, and soloists from London and St. Petersburg to Naples. But despite the frequent success of those contemporary (usually clerical) Italian masters, one might have expected a more humane approach from the enlightened and educated Leopold Mozart. And so we do suspect that Mozart may have suffered physically, throughout his life, from the effects of a childhood controlled by his single-minded father. Even in Mozart's time, children played outdoors and had contact with each other in school. But Mozart knew few other children and did not play, except on the piano and violin. Leopold was not the only one responsible for this; Mozart was, too, to the extent that obsessed people can be held responsible for the consequences of their obsession. After the age of six, it would probably have been hard to pry him away from his music, even if anyone had tried to. As a true prodigy, he made it hard for himself, and he had it hard thereafter. In accordance with the educational practice of the time, he was brought up like an adult and soon seemed to be an adult in miniature, outwardly an *objet d'art*. We see "little Mozart" in his costume and makeup, with his trademarks: a little violin, a powdered wig, an ornamental sword. No prop is missing; he is a tiny cavalier, who can be presented, who moves perfectly, like clockwork. "A little man with his wig and sword": so Goethe saw the seven-year-old in Frankfurt in August 1763.

We know of no relations between Mozart and other children, except of course for his sister, four and a half years older than he (called Nannerl in the biographies, a name we, too, will retain), and the English violin virtuoso Thomas Linley, with whom he had a short, intense friendship in Florence during the spring of 1770, when both were aged fourteen. Two half-grown prodigies, powerfully drawn to each other, both "destined for an early death": to posterity such a coincidental configuration is strikingly poetic. From Gainsborough's portrait of Linley and his older sister Elizabeth (who later married the playwright Sheridan), we see that the siblings shared an aristocratic, almost ethereal beauty. Linley died in 1778, at twenty-two.

Let us not give Leopold Mozart more than his share of the blame. He atoned for it. And Wolfgang* was indebted to him for a respectable upbringing, an outstanding education, and all the formative impressions of his early development. Certainly some experiences came too soon, and all too quickly. Too soon, father dragged son all over Western Europe for

---

* I am reluctant to take the biographical liberty of calling Mozart by his Christian name, for it seems to me a forced intimacy, the sign of an alleged equality, as if we would have called him *"du."* If I do it sometimes, nonetheless, it is not for the sake of variety but in order to distinguish Mozart from other members of the family.

years. This continual change of scene would have worn out
even a robust child, and certainly one who also had to perform
everywhere. But these years of travel were a hardship for the
father, too, and even more for the women of the family. Living
on an income that was not all that steady, the children had to
be constantly ready to appear on command at every illustrious
salon. The charge had to be met; indisposition meant material
loss. Of course, permission to perform was dependent on the
mood or caprice of the respective prince, or sometimes only on
a well-disposed courtier. Fine weather, favorable predictions
for a hunt or other amusement—and a concert was abruptly
canceled. The Mozarts had to take the inconvenience and the
loss. In such cases they had to invent alternatives—improvised
concerts, spontaneous performances, adroit presentations in
ballrooms or hotel salons to provide the necessary travel funds.
In March 1765 thirteen-year-old Nannerl and nine-year-old
Wolfgang played four-hand music daily from 12:00 to 3:00 in
Hickford's Great Room on Brewer Street in London (a hotel
salon where Gluck was heard in 1746—playing the glass har-
monica!). Like a coin-operated mechanical clock, the two performed for anyone who handed the entrance fee to Leopold,
the cashier. As a special feature they played on covered keys or
sight-read whatever music a listener might have brought
along. For this there was no extra charge. In order to increase
the sensational aspect of their act, Leopold reduced the children's ages by one year on the announcements. Indeed, these
read like circus posters.

And so the Mozart family traversed Europe for three
and a half years, like a family of acrobats. More respectable, of
course, bound to the morality of their task, yet wanderers still,
dependent on fortune and favor, on weather and health, on
the benevolence of the great, whose privilege it was to determine or at least to influence destinies. Words like "dignity"
and "indignity" had, of necessity, to be rooted out of the

vocabulary of such travelers, although Leopold Mozart knew their meaning all too well, and Wolfgang later learned them so thoroughly that they came to be inherent in him.

All this notwithstanding, no member of the group ever complained of his role in this cooperative quartet. At most, we hear Leopold Mozart sigh in frustration, when, for instance, a prince had deigned to hear the Mozart children play but then confined his reward to words of praise or a little gift for Nannerl. But even such financial disappointments were figured into the budget. Leopold's letters to his Salzburg friend Lorenz Hagenauer (who forwarded him travel funds) inspire in us a certain admiration for the breadth and coolness of these calculations. Leopold Mozart reported to Hagenauer as to a diary, in the expectation that his letters would be preserved (a hope that was justified and fulfilled, to our good fortune). His letters are the testimony of an alert if amateurish polymath, who picks up information as if in passing. This clearheaded man ("intellectual" would be saying too much) reported about the international cultural life he knew, as a member of a class that usually expressed itself in writing only sparingly, if at all. It is a pleasure to read these letters. They have an unbroken, rational quality, asserting, with concise realism, that so it was and so it is and we have to take it as it comes. "Patience," Leopold exhorts himself. Without self-pity, unaffected by moods, the letters reflect not only the strain of travel but also the reward: enjoyment of novelty and change and, above all, satisfaction whenever concerts take place as planned. Even complaints about the discomfort of coach travel are mitigated by the insight that he himself is ultimately accountable for any annoyance. These journeys would seem an unimaginable torture for us today, and lead us to conclude that people then were rather more resilient than we are. Take, for example, the two dauntless Mozart worshippers Vincent and Mary Novello (to whom we shall return later), who, in 1829, traveled from London to Salzburg and Vienna: travel began at daybreak, and ended long after darkness had fallen, which, however, did not keep these assiduous cultural pilgrims from devoting themselves to the enjoyment of music until late into the night, only to travel on as early the next day.

It might be easy to imagine that such journeys, such evenings, when his continual, alert presence was demanded, might have been traumatic for a child like Wolfgang Mozart. But we have no reason to suppose so. On the contrary, he must have felt happy despite all the overexertion. This was true at least during his stay in England, which was so transfigured in his memory that he intended to return there all his life. He later described himself as an "arch-Englishman"; he learned the language and nearly did go to England in 1786–87.

Mozart himself wrote most of his London repertoire, the jewel of which is the C major Sonata for piano, four hands, K. 19d. He probably performed it for the first time with his sister on May 13, 1765, in the Great Room. It is derivative, to be sure—how could it be otherwise? Also, father Leopold apparently demanded musical tricks that would astound an audience: echo effects, hand-crossing, a carefully calculated display. And yet we have here a will to independence—the thematic expansion of a merely *galant* phrase, the rhythmic interruption of the unceasing and monotonous mechanical meter that still rules the allegro. In the trio of the minuet, with its slightly contrasting rhythm, there appears for the first time an element unique to the child Mozart—a touch of a certain creative innocence, which even he could not maintain for long. It appears only during this period; it does not and cannot return (despite those who maintain that Mozart never lost his innocence). It is something inexplicably "early Mozartean"; not omnipresent, surfacing only here and there, like a sudden tenderness, a fleeting characteristic idea, neither learned nor required, differentiating him from his models, even significant ones like Johann Christian Bach, whom he admired. In the rondo of this sonata he begins to cast off these models. A peculiar, gentle, soothing magic—which only a child could summon, and which only this one child ever did summon—envelops this work. For this is the work of a child, however much the Mozart scholar Saint-Foix doubted it,[12] asserting that Wolfgang's father here manipulated the date of composition. He certainly did not, even if we must regard with caution the "honorable" (as Saint-Foix calls him) Leopold's contention that his son was the first in the history of music to compose a sonata for piano, four hands.

Despite the strain of unfamiliar, constantly changing conditions, the eight- and nine-year-old composed prolifically, probably greatly stimulated by his varied new surroundings. In 1764–65 he began writing symphonies in London and The Hague. The first, K. 16, is in E-flat, suggesting that his affinity for this key came early, and not particularly during his Freemason period. Here, too, the beginning of the allegro movement is conventional, the exercise of a beginner who must concentrate on the new problem of instrumentation. But already with the second theme Mozart begins to compose with free originality, in obvious joy at the discovery and simultaneous conquest of orchestration. The middle movement in the relative C minor seems to indicate that this key is not reserved—at least not yet—for "poignant pessimism" (Einstein). Certainly we can, if we wish, hear in it the quality of "gloomy foreboding," but we must admit that the mood is part of our own predisposition toward music in this key: our listening patterns have been established. Even in the earliest Mozart, the andante from the Symphony in B-flat (how soon he outlines his range of keys), for example, composed in December 1765 in The Hague, we find shifts to the relative G minor, affecting us like secret initiations into the main musical revelations of his late period. To be sure, he never wants to "say" anything through choice of key, but the keys will tell us something through him. Some of these early symphonies are lost, but those that exist, especially the D major Symphony, K. 19 (London, early 1765), are composed with an originality of melody and modulation which goes beyond the routine methods of his contemporaries. In fact, Mozart sometimes shows greater freedom during this period than later at Salzburg, when the seventeen-year-old, back from Italy, wrote symphonies in the form of Italian overtures.

The unmistakable Mozartean turn occurs even in the earliest works (we await it like Proust's Monsieur Swann waiting for his "little phrase"), and it comes, unfailingly, even if only as a tiny subsidiary idea or a sudden rhythmic inspiration, like the syncopation in the D major Sonata, K. 7, or the chromatic figures of the G major, K. 9 (both Paris, 1764). Or it comes as an expansive idea of stunning elegance: the second theme of the allegro in the fifteen-year-old's A major Symphony, K. 114 (Salzburg, 1771). These are not so much departures from contemporary musical grammar as changes of mood within conventional forms: the elegiac charm, for example, of the D major andante, and a trio in A minor that casts a fleeting doubt on all later interpretations of Mozart's use of this key.

We are always trying, of course, to put our finger on that quality which makes Mozart different from the others. In the later works it really isn't hard to do so. But what is it, even here, that betrays the true Mozart immediately and exactly, despite the naïve counterpoint, the almost nonexistent polyphony, the often wearying *ostinato* of the bass? Sometimes it seems nothing more than the eruption of a short, sudden inspiration, which sinks away again directly. Perhaps it isn't the inimitable quality yet, but merely a special one? Can we explain it at all, or is it, as Arnold Schoenberg says, "something only musical tones can express"?

If one rejects the notion of "inexplicability" and questions the "creative mystery" (which psychoanalysis acknowledges to be unfathomed still), one is obliged to find a substitute for these ideas or to explain in one's own way the unique element in Mozart. What is this special quality? Why does one continue to be preoccupied with Mozart? Here, once again, we run into the question of why this music and its heritage interests not only scholars on the one hand, popular writers on the other, and the initiates (sometimes a combination of all three), but also why everyone with some musical receptivity is aware of the phenomenon of Mozart. Why do people continue to be fascinated by this universal cultural treasure? He has never yet been fathomed, but remains a topic of interest, either latent or, all too often, open to discussion. How can such a disproportionately large number of people have a definite, and usually positive, relationship to him? (Though not always: Frederick Delius couldn't make much of Mozart. Of course, Mozart probably wouldn't have thought much of him, either. And for Verdi Mozart was no more than *"un quartettista."*)

Freud says: "Thinking in images [*Bildern*] is only a very incomplete form of becoming conscious. It is somehow nearer to unconscious processes than is thinking in words, and it is older than the latter, both ontogenetically and phylogenetically."[13] "Image" (*imago*) is meant here not as "picture" (*tabula*) but as an independently arising representation used as a means of reproduction and communication. Only through a willful creative act does the *imago* become a *tabula* (or *pictura*), sublimated into an artwork. Although this activity is a conscious process, capturing the vision in the artist's product, it does not include conceptual thought. It is rare to find a thinker among painters; even the greatest were less seekers in the abstract than finders in the concrete. Even the inventors among them, the Renaissance artists, were guided less by conceptual speculation than by a drive for knowledge, less by a world view than by an ideal of innovation, if only a technical one.

"Thinking in music," on the other hand, is explicable neither ontogenetically nor phylogenetically. On the one hand, it is further from verbal thought than is thinking in images, since it begins without conceptual, and certainly without material, content; on the other hand, its transposition into a creative act demands not only a craft much more complex than that of all other disciplines but also a dimension of thought *sui generis*. This is the conceptualization of its future realization, i.e., its performance, the process through time of that which the composer has drafted as something static onto the paper before him. Thinking in musical tones is an anticipation of their eventual effect.

In contrast to the imperfection of verbal thought, which painfully encounters its own limits, language being insufficient ("If one cannot say a thing, one must be silent about it": Wittgenstein), musical thought is constructed exclusively on its own material, not upon an abstraction lying outside the discipline, but upon the supply of musical tones, infinitely enriched by timbres. It formulates with the greatest possible differentiation and precision. But *what* does it formulate?

We will of necessity come across this question many more times, without being able to answer it for Mozart. It may not make good sense at this point to touch again on this puzzling area, a playground of suspicions, suppositions, deductions, mystifications. We do so only in order to enrich the mystery, and to add to its facets, not to solve it. How is it that Mozart is the perpetual representative of this riddle? Why is he an eternally relevant subject, kindling discussions and controversies relating not only to interpretations and actual performances but also to himself, "as a person," as flesh and blood, the bearer of will and thought, an intellectual power, a mighty transmuter of ideas, an executor of concepts? How can we explain the heritage of his music, awakening understanding and misunderstanding equally, unabashedly making him into a therapist, if not a savior? The moribund prefer Mozart to all other music; he is considered a comfort, a sedative, a refiner of the spirit, and an aid to childbirth.* Although the forms

---

* "Dr. Eric Bloch, forty-six, senior physician of the women's hospital in Halmstad, Sweden, has discovered a classical aid to childbirth: Wolfgang Amadeus Mozart. When contractions start, a tape of Mozart's Piano Con-

of appreciation may seem strange to us, ranging as they do from trust in its comforting or redeeming effect to faith in miracles, the very fact of their existence points to Mozart's special position. Here music in its effect and suggestive power goes far beyond its normal function, beyond what the "music lover" expects of it, hopes to experience deeply, or actually does experience. Here, it seems, a cult is being celebrated to the point of absurdity or beyond. The reason for it is a mystery. Or is it?

Classicism and Romanticism introduced subjective feeling into music as a conscious element of expression. As we read through music histories or biographies, it would seem that this new equality of form and content is regarded solely as something positive. It is as if we had at last been granted a coveted insight into the artist's inner life, his "human spirit," whereas previously objectivity had prevailed, concealing the creative impulse (Bach's fugues = mathematics, etc.). Although this objectivity has not been elevated to a preclassical principle, or ascribed to a more primitive stage of music's expressive capability, the idea of a greater individual expression persists as an implied truth even into this century. It serves to encourage a viewpoint by which we are to see music history as a large building, like a Gothic cathedral, on which different masters have worked at different times, knowing that they would not live to see the crowning climax, and compelled to reconcile themselves to one part in the work. The high point is generally thought to be Beethoven. Now, we know that his music would not be possible without Haydn and

---

certo, K. 467, is switched on. The mothers-to-be have already practiced their relaxation exercises to this music. The relaxed atmosphere in the labor room is said to make the birth less painful and dangerous. The infant mortality rate in Halmstad is far below the average of other clinics" (*Süddeutsche Zeitung*, 1974). It must be the F major andante that is played, with its virtually uninterrupted *ostinato* beneath the melody, a movement with no significant rhythmical contrasts.

Mozart—he knew it himself—but we are not prepared to accept the idea of Beethoven as the fulfillment of what Mozart began and, because of that, on a qualitatively higher level. For we do not believe that the history of music is the conquest of new territory, making earlier conquests worthless or even slightly less worthy. If that were the case Dufay would be surpassed by Orlando di Lasso, and di Lasso by Sweelinck, etc. One would succeed the other, up to the crowning glory of High Classicism, after which, as most people still agree, everything goes downhill.

So when we hear the exclamation "That almost sounds like Beethoven!" or read the clause "as it was brought to full perfection by Beethoven" (and we read them, quite literally, in nearly all books about Mozart, including Einstein's), we must wonder what supposedly objective criteria determine this opinion. Strictly speaking, it is implied that there exists an objectively perfect solution for musical ideas, waiting in reserve for "the greatest of all composers."

Such impermissible questions would probably not be worth discussing, except that they give us the chance to assert that two great artists of the highest order, from two different periods, are incommensurable, not least because society assigned them different positions and roles, which determined their creative response and thus their entire productive output. That is to say, in addition to differences of individual inner predisposition, of temperament, of the current style (which one may or may not see as "progress"), there can also be a difference in the purpose of music.

One might expect the age of value judgments in musical aesthetics to be over once and for all, but apparently it is not. "Content" still misleads us into looking for a "liberation," where the affirmative intention of a piece of music suggests that kind of conclusion. Concepts like optimism and pessimism enter the picture and become yardsticks. Hermann Abert denies Mozart the "Beethovenesque triumph after struggle": Mozart cannot "master the dark forces of destiny, as Beethoven does." He seems not to speculate whether or not it was Mozart's *intention* to triumph after struggle or to master any particular forces. We can assure Abert that he *didn't* want to, since any such thematic concepts are alien to the absolute nature of his music. Abert speaks of Mozart's late Viennese period: "Now, at the end of his life, the flight of his genius took him to a new country, no longer ruled by the taste of a single stratum of society, however cultured, but only by the artist's own conscience. On the horizon the dawn of *Beethovenesque* art was already shining."[14] Cultured? Can a stratum of society which demanded "something new" every day, which (except for van Swieten) deserted the masters of yesterday for contemporary musicians and didn't even remember the names from the day before yesterday, be cultured? Hardly. Mozart was quite clear on this point: *"Only in Vienna,"* he writes, was "Fate" so hostile that he could "not make any money," whether or not he followed his "artist's conscience," which, according to Abert, he had recognized and developed before Beethoven. Mozart never saw the shining dawn.

The view that Mozart's art, as a product of its time, did not have the expressive power of nineteenth-century art, and the estimation of this power as an absolute advance, still existed in our own time. As late as 1964, the philosopher Ernst Bloch concedes of Mozart's operas: "Certainly there are sections that one remembers,"[15] but in general he finds the music "a seventeen-year-old's," "graceful," yes, but, agreeing with Richard Wagner that this is "enchanting, but not overwhelming, Hellenic music, purifying in a secular sense, but spiritually almost simpleminded." For Bloch, Mozart remains a composer of fairy-tale operas, while the evocation of Beethoven demands another tone: "How the heart swells, O eternal one, when it remembers thee!"[16]

We cannot take this seriously. In Mozart's rather deliberate objectivity we see that unique element, the absolutely puzzling. We don't know how it arises or how it achieves its effect—the awakening and simultaneous stilling of a longing whose nature and origin we become aware of, but not familiar with. Mozart's music reproduces the depth of experience for us without the experience; as the expression of the absolute it does not reach the experience itself, nor does it want to. Everyone understands Mozart's language differently. In reality no one understands it, but the little we do understand is enough to suggest the rest, which we are left to interpret. More than other composers Mozart elicits receptive misunderstanding; it was initiated by his contemporaries, but first given a decisive and important formulation by Goethe.

On February 12, 1829, during one of his conversations with Goethe, Eckermann expressed the hope that *Faust* might someday find a music appropriate to it. We can imagine Goethe replying something like this: "That cannot be. For it is one thing when a figure like Faust gambles his soul in the search for higher knowledge, and another when a figure like Don Juan, for example, loses his soul in the realization of his sensual desires. Music would take away the intellectual content of Faust's words. But Don Juan is no man of intellect. Without his knowing it, music gives him life from the outside; he is manifest only through music."

But Goethe did not say that. He said: "That is quite impossible. The repellent, loathsome, and terrifying qualities which it would have to contain are not in the style of our times. It would have to be music like *Don Juan*. Mozart would have had to compose *Faust*."

An unexpected and alienating answer. Apparently Goethe thought that music would be able to widen the fundamental divergence between the search for knowledge and the inadequacy of the seeker, and thus portray a human problem. As Kierkegaard says, Don Juan is not someone who creates himself by thought, but someone who can only reveal himself musically, since the erotic principle by which he lives evades his consciousness or its conscious verbal expression. Faust, on the other hand, lives by the superiority of his consciousness and reveals himself primarily in monologues. We can hardly imagine that this fundamental difference escaped Goethe. And we wouldn't want to think that he imagined Faust's great monologue, for example, as an all too grand tenor aria. More likely, he sensed an affinity between Don Juan and Mephisto; but this, too, would be superficial.

However that may be, we find Goethe's statement instructive, in that forty-two years after the première of *Don Giovanni*, thirty-eight years after Mozart's death, the dramatist Goethe did not consider Mozart's opera to be a work of the past, ineffectual because its expressive potential, linked to a more formal time, could no longer do justice to a new, previously unformulated subject. On the contrary, he attributed expressive qualities that he missed in the music of his own time (i.e., Beethoven and the early Berlioz) to this music alone. Goethe attested neither to the serene Apollonian quality which the Romantics projected onto Mozart a bit later, nor to the "Grecian lightness and grace" which Robert Schumann attributed to the G minor Symphony, nor to Wagner's view of him as the "spirit of light and love," but rather to his apparently outdated ability to express "repellent, loathsome, and terrifying qualities." Certainly Goethe heard the objectively "beautiful" side, but he seems to have heard more, too: besides the expression of subjectively negative qualities, he heard that mastery of the range of feeling which permitted Mozart to dispose his stage figures *ad libitum* and thus to present musical panoramas that give us insight into his characters.

Incidentally, there seems to be a strange lack of distinction in Goethe's statement between music's mixed elements of subjective and objective potentiality. This is probably due to Eckermann's transcription, for music is not to *contain* but *represent* these negative qualities. One is almost reminded of Mozart's own theoretical statements: on September 26, 1781, he wrote to his father from Vienna about the composition of Osmin's F major aria in *Die Entführung*:

For just as a man in such a towering rage oversteps all the bounds of order, moderation and propriety and completely forgets himself, so must the music too forget itself. But as passions, whether violent or not, must never be expressed in such a way as to excite disgust, and as music, even in the most terrible situations, must never offend the ear, but must please the hearer, or in other words must never cease to be *music*, I have gone from F (the key in which the aria is written), not into a remote key, but into a related one, not however, into its nearest relative D minor, but into the more remote A minor.

Music must "forget" itself in the "most terrible situations": here, too, there is a confusion of subject and object. Nevertheless, in passages like these we gain insight into Mozart's inspired disposition of cause and effect and thus better understand his ability to differentiate between the portrayer and what he portrays. True, this view is bound to its time, a short span in Mozart's development. Five years later he no longer worried whether or not he was insulting the contemporary ear. Of course, he no longer made theoretical statements about his intentions, either. By then no one would have understood him anyway.

Unfortunately, the considerable value of Goethe's statement is impaired by its continuation, for he added, "Meyerbeer might be able to do it, but he would not be open to such a project, he is too much involved with the Italian theaters." We shall not examine Meyerbeer's involvement with Italian theaters: analysis of musical styles was not Goethe's strong point, nor is it our own topic. Yet the Mozart-Meyerbeer alternative, which even then no one else would have come up with so easily, reveals Goethe's fundamental lack of musical sensitivity. Creative geniuses are not necessarily also appreciative geniuses.

We cannot conceive of music appropriate to *Faust,* especially not by Mozart. For us the forty years between *Don Giovanni* and *Faust* marked a powerful change in style. Today Berlioz still seems to be the fitting, indeed the only composer for purely scenically dramatic music. But Goethe wouldn't have him, especially since his friend and musical adviser Zelter didn't think much of him. Goethe's judgment (if we can call it that) indicates that he attributed to Mozart a deeper and wider significance than did later generations, until far into our own century. They heard the magic, the seemingly effortless agility that appears to make light of all tragedy, and yet contains it in the tenderly reminiscent gesture of reconciliation. But they did not notice the enormous range of those other qualities, the analyzable and interpretable ones, and the quality we think of as the mystery of supreme artistic achievement. If we could analyze this quality, the absolute meaning of the artwork would be diminished. Analysis would have to be as artistically valuable as its object, making it accessible. Mozart's interpreters can only paraphrase the value of his work, but no one arrives at the core, the essence that arouses emotions. Once again, we understand quite clearly that this all sounds vague and unscholarly. Yet even the most earnest scholars have allowed themselves to be led astray into interpretations of this very inexplicable element, thinking they found justification for their metaphysical excursions in Mozart the man. The riddle of Mozart is precisely that "the man" refuses to be a key for solving it. In death, as in life, he conceals himself behind his work. The urge to explain the inexplicable must remain unfulfilled; we leave the sphere of knowledge and enter into an area of speculation where we no longer test theses but only try to intuit backward into the past. Here there is no common language: even the terminology of the unknowable varies with each man's degree of consciousness.

We think of Beethoven as a struggling titan. Mistrustful and sublime at the same time, he looks out at us from his portraits as if he had sat for posterity. No one has yet matched him. He has always seemed the prototype of the artist, sovereignly defiant, answering an uncomprehending world with formally eruptive (if not chaotic) works of unremitting affirmation; affirmation, that is, of the universal order, not of the social structure. Unconsciously, he sought out misunderstanding, in order to oppose it methodically with his own morality. Beethoven wanted "to help suffering mankind" (to change society, as some claim today, with a grain of truth), and his ethical intention is not the least reason for his greatness. Mozart had no such intention. By the time he discovered that his latent rebellion had any definable object, that the "genius of obedience" was suffering from this obedience, by the time he had some slight understanding of "society" in its present meaning, he had already withdrawn from it and it had denied him. That was his final ruin.

In trying to define Mozart, posterity has always proceeded selectively, in a strange and limiting way, and often with distressing insecurity. Posterity saw and sees him still in his phases as child prodigy and as a man who died young. The intervening stages point either toward the beginning or the end: carefree, childlike spontaneity is recorded until the Paris journey in 1777, and in 1778, when he "lost" his mother, there is already resignation to fate and foreboding of death. Each "darkening into the minor" (*Molleintrübung*: we will consider this concept later) caught the critics' ear until *Die Zauberflöte*, when, it is said, the childlike cheerful element is heard again in a wonderful and heartening way; the ballast, the "earthly weight" is cast off; only divine simplicity remains. The context of *Die Zauberflöte*, its purposeful design for popular success, the concessions to the audience—none of this has a place in their kind of interpretation. Listening to the opera, we are to become childlike ourselves through its "pure and purifying" effect (Joachim Kaiser).

Everything came easily to Wolfgang (says posterity): within this darling of the muses (though not of society) all inspiration was effortlessly transformed. The point is generally demonstrated by reference to his allegedly typical, enchanting melodies, whose easy flow hints at apparently deeper levels but at the same time seems to renounce plumbing their depths. This mistaken view says: Let us abide in serenity, for life is hard enough. But we would assert that precisely in terms of this apparently most Mozartean element, his contemporaries (Boccherini, for example, or, earlier, Johann Christian Bach, not to mention lesser composers) are more Mozartean than Mozart. Because of the purposeful contrast of tonalities, an essential, recurring technique of Mozart's, we must never isolate melodic ideas from their contexts. He who does so goes astray, hearing the single phrase chosen for transformation (which sometimes reflects no more than the style of the age) but not the sublime and inimitable Mozartean qualities of the transformation itself. Misjudgment is due, in fact, not least to such singling out of elements and the different way they are then heard. Anthologies for piano, for example, prejudice students' early contact with the great composers by these limitations. One of the most widespread and popular methods of falsification is to confuse the approachable with the typical. For then the typical appears to be only what is understandable, easy, playable, and, therefore, playful. Mozart, "the Spirit of Rococo." Even in quotation marks we hardly dare cite this cliché, which generations have read, to their deep deception: "Mozart's greatness is not based on his superiority to his many mediocre contemporaries from the second half of the eighteenth century, but on the wonderful ability of his music to achieve ever-new significance and a new, transformed presence."[17]

If, for instance, in the D minor String Quartet, K. 421/417b (June 1783), we take the D major trio out of the frame of the minuet in the minor, and so detach it from the precisely calculated tension relationship of the larger context, we have an example of exactly that misrepresentation. Above the *pizzicato* of the three accompanying instruments is the voice of the first violin, dallying gracefully as if it were playing the dance of those Nymphenburg porcelain figures that still symbolize Mozart's music on so many record covers. The contrast with the strong dynamic accents and with the chromatic shifts of the framing minuet is lost. What in context has the effect of a cruel joke, music in quotation marks (as if Mozart wanted to parody the popular style in the middle of a movement that he felt his contemporaries could not value properly), appears now to be exemplary, music-box rococo. Here too, then, one may condense what one wishes out of Mozart: here it is condensed out of the "gloomy" Mozart, or at least his dominating will to the minor. "The whole quartet is a gripping testimony to the much-misunderstood pessimism of Mozart, who, in strong contrast to Beethoven, is unable to escape the dark forces in the human heart," says Abert.[18] Again, it seems that Beethoven, the teacher of optimism, arrived too late. This quotation is another example of a method of interpretation which consistently sees in the choice of key and musical gesture the inner state and, in this case, even the world view of the composer. Such foolish simplifications appear, incidentally, in most biographies. An optimistic or pessimistic frame of mind is confused with a psychological disposition to manic or depressive states—as if the philosopher's gloomy vision of the future were determined by his momentary emotional depression.

There have been repeated attempts to construct developmental patterns of the tragic on the basis of Mozart's movements in the minor. Thus, the minuet from the D minor Quartet, with its gloomy tonic key, has been seen as an anticipation of the minuet in the "great" G minor Symphony, K. 550 (July 25, 1788), a trail that begins with the minuet from the "little" G minor Symphony, K. 183/173dB (October 5, 1773) and includes, naturally, the minuet of the G minor

Quintet, K. 516 (May 16, 1787) as a last stop before the great conclusion. It is not our business to test or criticize the historical justification for these comparisons. They clearly imply, however, a system of values which measures greatness by degree of perfection and gives each work a relative value. Surely Mozart's development as a musician cannot be reduced to his increasing facility. Rather, like every great artist, he develops by gradually sounding the depths of his potential world, and conquering it, according to an inner law. This is especially true of Mozart, in that all his experience found its way exclusively into his work, not into the development of his personality, or into a maturation process, or verbally expressed wisdom, or a world view. Like no other, Mozart demonstrates that perfection is not a matter of the wisdom of sedate old age. This is true in large part because he was dependent on specific occasions and social configurations for his commissions and thus produced certain genres in series. The great woodwind serenades (and who could deny the perfection of the woodwind scores?) are works of the "middle" Mozart, written in 1781. All his violin concerti were written between spring and winter 1775. Nearly all the great piano concerti fall between 1783 and 1785, a short period of unlimited creative power and external brilliance which doubtless supported and gave life to his creativity.

Naturally, with increasing maturity he liberated himself from the various schemata that genres impose. It took a while, for example, before he could finally free himself from the stiffness (which we today find hard to enjoy) of *opera seria*, whose rigid rules the sixteen-year-old was still following strictly in *Lucio Silla*, K. 135. But in 1780, eight years later, he wrote the unsurpassed masterpiece of the genre, *Idomeneo*, a work of perfection from the twenty-four-year-old, full of strength, and an inexhaustible freshness of a sort that only sporadically illuminates *La Clemenza di Tito*, a work composed eleven years later (1791). Here, among passages that seem like condensed riches from the earlier operas, stale routine dominates. With some things, then, his way led from "almost, but not yet," through perfection to "no longer." And so we do not do justice to Mozart if we try to hear each piece as part of a pattern of development, heading toward the future, the "nearly" and "not quite yet." The cliché about the "triad of the three great symphonies," the last three, is almost didactically aimed at making the earlier ones seem less significant, although at least three of them (the "Haffner," K. 385 [July 1782]; the "Linz," K. 425 [November 1783]; and the "Prague," K. 504 [December 6, 1786]) are, in their own ways, self-sufficient and comparable to the three "great" ones, the "crown of his symphonic production." We will do better as listeners to take each separate symphony out of chronological context and let them affect us as evidence of an emotional and creative condition, as works that follow their own law and their own necessity.

The "music lover" has found, usually to his dismay, that Mozart the man was "all too human" in his life and its external expression. He misses in him the grand gesture, the "Beethovenesque" will that precedes and points to the creative work, the statement of a life design, the indication of a nuclear idea. It is probably no longer worth taking issue with such a view, especially since we should realize that this stubborn phantom of the "all too human" exists only for those (though they are in the majority) who have never asked themselves if their own secret inner life agrees with what they want other people's assessment of them to be. Yet this censorious description has endured in Mozart literature to this day, and has sometimes brought forth dubious fruit. Thus, Arthur Schurig wrote:

No one will reproach Mozart for his artistic and human one-sidedness [which means, of course, that the author does precisely that]. But let us remember that, above all else, Europeans love universality in their heroic geniuses, and that we Germans honor our adored Goethe as the highest example of such a universal great man. So we are disappointed to recognize that Mozart was the total antithesis of the many-sided Goethe. If Richard Wagner lies below Mozart as a pure musician and is equal to him as an artist, he undoubtedly rises above him as a human being. And the sum of the two, the artist and the man, makes the Master of Bayreuth superior to Mozart. The power with which the creator of *Tristan und Isolde* asserted himself is phenomenal. He who is unable to admire it has absolutely no understanding of the genius's struggle with the world. Such people do not even understand the great Napoleon.[19]

We admit it is possible that we really don't understand the great Napoleon. Besides, to try to understand him within the context of this study seems rather irrelevant. But as far as the "Master of Bayreuth" is concerned, we must note with astonishment that the writer in this strange assessment values self-assertion as an absolute human virtue, one that must be on the credit side of the genius's ledger, even if this self-assertion is not central to his profession—though it is, of course, in Napoleon's case. In reality, artistic and human integrity stand squarely in the way of self-assertion. Of course, we can no longer take this kind of speculative view seriously today. It carries a biographical system *ad absurdum*: the assigning of grades as a critical method.

The separation of the man and the musician—any separation of the genius as himself and as the creator of his work —is the result of an understandable helplessness, but it is, nevertheless, unrealistic and absurd, counteracting any attempt at insight with the insinuation that one side is more understandable than the other. If scholars are embarrassed by the Mozart who was given to unrestrained expressions, who would suddenly break out into coprolalia and other obscenities, if they turn away in confusion or shame from that side of him to which they have no key, it is primarily because their image of the genius was inherited from Romanticism, which made little distinction between truth and poetry in its psychology. The scatological contents of the Bäsle letters were kept secret as long as possible. Now that they have been published, they elicit, primarily, apologia. "They don't speak against Mozart," exclaims one researcher to anyone who feels they might. "He is playacting."[20] Critics are obliged to clean the picture of everything they consider filthy; the extramusical statements of the musical genius must either fall into the realm of aesthetics or touch on an ethical borderland. Is Mozart really playacting? In his extramusical statements he was reflecting whatever stage of his experience he had reached; it determined not only his moods but his opinions as well. He can never be pinned down. He didn't know his own soul, nor was he interested in surveying it. Therefore, he never displayed it, except for a few gloomy moments, mainly in later life.

Attempts to keep Mozart's image clean are older than the image itself, extending back into his lifetime. The publishers Herr Breitkopf and Herr Härtel alternated in trying to clean up the dirty texts of canons by bowdlerizing them, with the natural result that one can hear the original words reverberating rhythmically underneath their substitutions. We lose a certain amount of information, too, for it is precisely these and other occasional pieces that often verify those points of contact between his everyday life and his work; they are usually insignificant occasions, elaborations on coincidental configurations and, accordingly, prosaic made-to-order pieces. They reject any hint of pathos; in fact, they sometimes work against it so categorically one would think they were expressly intended to embarrass posterity. Generally they come, says the apologetic commentator, from "an unbuttoned mood of the maestro," usually a good mood. In contrast to Mozart's "great works," whose origins lie in darkness, these pieces sometimes throw light on a consciously experienced moment of his outer life, a banal moment, in accordance with the secondary importance of his conscious life. He himself probably attached little importance to them; he did not enter them in the catalogue of his compositions. Thus, for example, the so-called Bandl-Terzett, K. 441 (1783?) illustrates a not particularly comic event in the style of a *Singspiel* ensemble. Its musical quality far surpasses that of the text. Characteristically, Mozart consistently failed at every attempt to transfer his silliness, often forced as it was, into music. Wherever his words lack the appropriate tone, his music corrects them. In these *opuscula* growing out of a good-natured, mindless, or vulgar mood, the spirit and elegance of the musical thought usually softens the intended shock of the theme. This is especially true of those canons whose texts deal with—so to speak—fecally immanent imperatives, like "O du eselhafter Martin" (Oh, Martin, you jackass), K. 560 (1788) (given by Herr Breitkopf as "Are you yawning, lazy fellow" in order to divert the phrase "Aufs-Maul-scheissen" [Shit on the mouth] into other channels), or "Leck mir den Arsch fein recht schön sauber" (Lick my arse until it's nice and clean), K. 233/382d (1782?), in Härtel's version "Nichts labt mich mehr" (Nothing comforts me more), or Breitkopf's bowdlerization "Lasst froh uns sein" (Let's be happy) for "Leck mich im Arsch," K. 231/382c (1782), a command that Mozart could not have afforded to give his contemporaries except in the most careless moments of his life, even if, as we gather from some written statements, it is a fair representation of his evolving attitude to life. Here, too, the music does not reproduce the unsublimated text. The slightest touch of vulgarity is alien to Mozart's music, even where the words seem to dictate it; here he has composed against his own text. We wonder if the seeming evidence about even ignoble things deceives us, too.

In other words, Mozart *always* composed against his own texts—against the text of his letters, his notes; against appearances, his bearing, his behavior. Or vice versa: his true language, music, is fed from sources unknown to us; it lives from a suggestive power which rises so far above the object of its suggestion that it evades us. Its creator remains unapproachable.

It seems symptomatic that his external features, too, have never been convincingly represented. Of the portraits by contemporary painters and engravers (lesser professionals and relatively able dilettantes), none bears enough resemblance to another to indicate what lies beneath the surface through one essential factor, beyond the physiognomy in the foreground. The sequence of Beethoven's likenesses enables us to attest to the heightening of his idealization: gradually, with his increasing prestige, the thick-set, crude-featured, plebeian face with the bulbous nose becomes the proud, lofty-browed antagonist; then, it is true, this disintegrates into the life mask, which, because it does not lie, is usually kept secret. His most impressive portrait is probably the one by Ferdinand Waldmüller, who was also the most talented artist to paint him. If we discount the apocrypha, the counterfeits and the copies, we have no idealization of Mozart, except one painterly euphemism, probably unintentional, which is most often chosen by biographers to illustrate their hero: the portrait his brother-in-law Joseph Lange painted in 1782 or 1783 and, strangely, left unfinished. Lange, as we shall see, far surpassed his painted portrayal of Mozart with his verbal one, which has endured beyond his time. He probably would not knowingly have permitted himself any corrections to the truth. Even in its external typical features, the portrait is like none of the other representations—except perhaps in the protruding eyeballs, which appear even more strongly in later likenesses, especially the engraving by Dora Stock (1789). Her work is satisfactory, although all these profiles appear strangely lifeless, like commemorative coins.

Also common to the authentic portraits is the large, fleshy nose with its strongly marked nostrils and the heavy upper lip. But from none of these portraits can we infer any kind of transcending essence—only the outer forms indicate that they represent the same man. Nor do we ever find an imagined *grandezza*, let alone a hint of immortality. Of course, Mozart did not belong to those circles in which the great or merely fashionable portraitists went hunting for models, and he probably would have made a sorry model—he was certainly not handsome. We find that in Mozart's time, unlike earlier periods, even Austrian princes and aristocratic patrons hardly ever found portraitists who reproduced them in a way befitting their temporary fame and position. Johann Christian Bach was, however, painted in London by Gainsborough, and Haydn was painted there by John Hoppner (1791)—it is his only well-painted portrait. The one member of Mozart's immediate circle who found an important portraitist was Karl Ludwig Giesecke. He was painted by Sir Henry Raeburn, though not when he was employed in the Schikaneder troupe, pasting together the libretto of *Die Zauberflöte*, but much later, as an eminent scientist, professor of mineralogy at the Royal Dublin Society.

Some contemporaries who lived into the nineteenth century report that Barbara Krafft's 1819 oil portrait is the one most like Mozart. Painted nearly thirty years after his death, it made considerable demands on the memory of those who praised it. To us, too, it seems a success in its combination of painstaking integrity and artistic ability, an artifact that draws the sum of physiognomic characteristics from portraits of that time, according to the laws of probability. It does not attempt an interpretation but relies on the painting's own sensibility, which follows a definable concept. Mozart's glance is intended for no one, and comes from eyes that see no one, whose expression cannot be fixed, full of meaning and reticent at the same time—although he probably never would have posed in such relaxed dignity. Let's leave it at that.

Copies of the death mask have been lost. Perhaps Constanze or Nissen destroyed them. The existing one is inauthentic. It is as if even Mozart's physical shape was determined to evade representation, a symbolic warning to all his interpreters, and a general one to all who try to interpret the genius "as a man."

    In the following digression we will talk about "genius." The concept originated in the eighteenth century and has become a questionable one. Indeed, we cannot call any of our contemporaries by this term. Not only do we lack the necessary distance from the individual, but we also cannot adequately define the concept in terms of works that are created as we look on. We are dependent on models. What is "genius"? What distinguishes it from "talent"? Human geneticists say that transcendent intellectual achievement will be measurable by degree in the foreseeable future. We need hardly conceal our doubts about this prognosis (some things have demanded our attention in recent years only by virtue of their measurability) any more than about the even bolder prophecy that men will soon be able actively to cultivate such achievement.

But let us retain the concept. The reader knows who is meant: the rare executor of enduring high achievement, independent of social conditions, uncomprehended by sociology and anthropology, recognized but apparently insufficiently comprehended by psychology; the executor of works that have contributed to our own formation and without which we cannot conceive of our own existence. I speak of the creative genius of the past.

What do we know of his inner mechanisms? Only one thing is certain: depression or psychic suffering does not diminish his productivity, unlike other creative people, but increases it qualitatively and quantitatively. Otherwise we know little, or even less than little, even untruths, since we are so often led astray by biographies of the inner life of the would-be genius, who is his own topic for reflection, and reveals and articulates himself externally. Self-reflection, for the genius, is not a general subject; but for the would-be genius, it is not only subject matter but an instrument. He plays the role of a genius and demands tribute as such, calculating all the while how to integrate unproductiveness into his thematic program. He offers us his soul in a begging bowl, in order to make us at least into guilty witnesses, if not the actual cause of his suffering. ("He who weeps now anywhere in the world, /without cause weeps in the world, /weeps over me." Rilke: *"Ernste Stunde"*) The would-be genius always needs society as a partner. Under the pretext of not being able to communicate with anyone, he communicates with society, and expects it to be humbly silent, admiring his greatness. He is effective in part by reproaching us for our inadequate understanding and insufficient willingness to be sacrificed ourselves; he celebrates his wounds.

We realize that the boundaries between the genius and the would-be genius are not always distinct. Objects of a qualitative gradation, the two sometimes can be differentiated only by individual responses. I must therefore leave it to the reader to set his own receptive criteria and to assess who is to be deemed merely admirable in creative achievement and who should be considered a "mystery of transcendent achievement."[21] The would-be genius betrays himself most often in verbal form, for only in words can he formulate his great pretension, a pretension that reveals his inauthenticity.

From time to time, then, the would-be genius has the same effect as the genius: posterity, still uncertain in its judgments, becomes a grateful customer for all the marks of his suffering, as he describes them. It registers them with smug satisfaction, as if it would have provided better living conditions for its hero than his contemporaries did, not realizing that in the case of the would-be genius, misunderstanding is actually a prerequisite for his creative impulse, as well as a sustaining theme.* Posterity moves with a shudder through the ruins of

* Here is a typical complaint about lack of appreciation: "The question is whether the difference between the contemporary world and my own feelings and thoughts is really as great as it seems to me, or is it an antithesis that many artists today must experience. And do I perhaps have

what it sees as his heroic struggle, and thinking his personality can be a key to his work, it makes it into a doll which it clothes in the garments of that work. And lo! the clothes fit! Biographers have made them to measure; the further removed in time, the freer their designs and decorations.

The clothes will not fit the true genius from eras before the French Revolution, before psychological discoveries were made, or were even possible. Neither Haydn nor Mozart can be reconstructed satisfactorily; in some earlier cases we do not even possess the doll, and must try laboriously, groping in the dark, to figure out with dates and facts "how it must have been." Surely they did not deliberately obscure the traces of their lives; they probably just never made reflective statements about themselves outside their work. The true genius is not helpfully communicative, which is not to say that he could not be sociable, sometimes to excess. But this sociability is autistic; in reality, he lacks the key to verbal communication of his inner motivations, except within his art. He does not see himself as the center of suffering in the middle of the world, as does the would-be genius (Rilke: "He who dies now anywhere in the world, /without cause dies in the world, /looks at me."), because he perceives the world only in fragments, with subjective alterations. From his point of view, he is neither approachable nor unapproachable, neither modest nor immodest, for he lacks a partner to whom he might reveal these qualities. He does not create in the palaces of patrons; his creations are not produced according to carefully regulated plans or a sense of decorum. They are completed under pressure. (Gesualdo created in his own palaces, but who can say what impassioned pressure he was under!) He does not seek self-knowledge, gives no account of himself, neglects and consumes himself (unless his constitution and his success during his lifetime permit him to live under other conditions). He

---

more fellow sufferers than I know of or believe? But why is it so extraordinarily painful?" Wilhelm Furtwängler, *Vermächtnis* (Wiesbaden, 1956), p. 23.

burns up, but does not defy the burning; rather, he ignores it. He does not see himself in relation to the world. He doesn't see himself at all.

Beethoven saw himself. He seems to be an exception, but is not, for he saw himself incorrectly. Without much contact from the beginning, he gradually lost all contact. It only seems as if he communicated with the world around him, for it was a synthetic world of his own imagining (usually negative), from out of which he directed his glance at an ideal world. Thus, the existing world had to appear false and deceitful to him. Indeed, we see him today as the only great musical genius before Richard Wagner who tried to subordinate his will to universal ethical demands. The demands remained unfulfilled. The prototype of the great sufferer is not Mozart but Beethoven. Throughout his life he had a heavier load to bear.

Mozart never projected himself into the world around him. He did not know the exhortation "You others!" let alone the exclamation "Oh, you men!" which opens Beethoven's Heiligenstadt Testament and means simply: "I am more than you, it is true, but I would have liked to be one of you." Mozart thought until late in his life that he did belong to the world around him, that he was one among others, though, to be sure, one more able than the others. He would never have tried consciously to tell these others anything about his world, as Beethoven did, and Goethe, who quite possibly never really ate his bread with tears (as his poem suggests he did). If Mozart ever ate his bread with tears, he never considered whether it tasted good or not—he put up with it. He took advantage of the world around him when it seemed to promise him something or had something to communicate. He plunged into it when it promised him distraction; he was receptive to the praise of the few true experts he knew. He was not very sensitive to censure, since he despised or ignored those who censured. At first, he reacted with irritation when he was underestimated; later he became deadened to that, too. He hated servitude and loved freedom, which, when he grew acquainted with it, became his downfall. His reaction to success was not a deep satisfaction with the successful work. We do not know if Mozart ever felt about a work: "Here I have said what I wanted to say." We know of no single case where he might have gone even further to say: "Here I fulfilled my task in the best way possible and it has been acknowledged." We also do not know how he reacted to failures or to the insight that his work was too difficult for the public. We have no evidence of his dismay or even his surprise when the publisher Hoffmeister asked to withdraw from a contract for three piano quartets because the first (G minor, K. 478, 1785) appeared to be "too difficult" and therefore unmarketable. He gave the next one (E-flat, K. 493, 1786) to the publisher Artaria, who apparently thought that it was marketable. The third was never written.

Nothing would have been more alien to him than the idea that society owed him anything more than recognition and respect for his ability, and a job as court musician. Until late (too late) in his life, he did not know who he was. His isolation was the deepest and the most discreet—until the last months of his life, at least, he was not aware of it. Although he sensed it a few years before his death, he repressed the suspicion. Whenever possible he made light of it. He was not used to paying attention to himself, as the would-be genius does (Rilke: "I am an island, and alone") , administering his conscious suffering like an immense estate, and taking good care of it at all times. Unlike Goethe's Tasso, no god gave him the gift of describing his suffering. Therefore, he never grew silent in his torment, which he probably experienced as something other than torment (but what?) and he spoke of other things. But what?

Mozart's external reality was bound by more or less preordained conventions, whose theoretical foundations he would hardly have thought of undermining. He did not see himself as an underprivileged child and ultimately a victim of the *ancien régime*. Only when the system began to close in on him did he grow rebellious, but he was never able to objectify or generalize this one-man rebellion. He lacked connections to like-minded or like-hearted people, and he did not look for them. True, a revolutionary spirit crops up now and then, a flash of scorn for those high-born people for whom he was too lowly—but all this was merely his reaction to personal experience. We have no evidence of any contact or even ac- quaintance with others who were seething inside, and who gave vent to their rebelliousness. We cannot make him into a *Homo politicus*. He read Beaumarchais and probably agreed with his doctrines, but he took no notice of the Revolution; no direct incitement could come to him from so great a distance, and thus no excitement, either. His agreement with general revolutionary movements of the time was intuitive; the *Zeit- geist* spoke to him without touching his consciousness, as though through a veil, and filtered by his instinct for applica- bility. He applied it, then, in *Figaro* and by no means inno- cently. We do not know whether he reckoned with the consequences. They came, in any event, since Vienna dropped him; but we have no reason to think he ever regarded this estrangement as anything other than a worsening of his ma- terial circumstances. Here too, as so often, his discretion confounds us. There is no statement about his growing isola- tion, but rather, like the true fatalist he was, he accepted the given. The concept "resignation to fate" would be too strong; even more so "pious submission." He wrote to Bullinger (July 3, 1778), about the death of his mother, that "God had so ordained it," but it sounds halfhearted, as always when he speaks about God's will. What he means is, "It had to be that way." This is a flourish which says nothing really, but which describes his innermost reaction more exactly than any other formulation.

He did have, especially when his father was alive, a definite conception of himself; he thought he knew how he had to see himself—as industrious, goal-oriented, obedient, and devoted. For a long time he saw himself as wanting improvement (or at least he acted as if he did). But later in Vienna he forgot these conceptions. He escaped his own line of sight. Industry and devotion, if we want to call it that, were forced to function automatically, until he grew satiated with his own virtues. His rare reflective observations are moderate and controlled only in that their theme is moderation and control. Although he demanded moderation from others, especially from his wife, Constanze, he himself was immoderate, not only (necessarily, but only intermittently) in his creative output, but also in the rhythm of his life. He did not exactly despise routine, he simply did not have any. Only when necessary, because of teaching or rehearsals, did his day have a schedule. But in the long run he could not deal with one, and he did not try to see the sense of it. He did not plan vacations or rest periods: they came about, but he was not at rest during them. He composed at the billiard table and while bowling, and probably also at much more prosaic functions. Friends report that he was always working inside, and that is just what we might expect.

Posthumous fame or eternal significance was not one of Mozart's preoccupations—he was too bound up with his work and his daily life. He was not familiar with the concept "posterity." His father, Leopold, thought further ahead in this regard, and it sometimes astounds us just how far ahead he did think. Until the great disappointment and estrangement, until resignation set in, most of his thoughts and plans concerned his son; he was remarkably capable of communicating his plans and constructing visions of the future, always pedantic, but clever, vivid, often correct, even if we cannot believe he really thought the plans would influence his son. Of course, we must not forget that Leopold, born in 1719, was thirty-seven years older than his son. So he was not only an unusually old father but he also belonged to a different age, though one that knew no more about "artistic dispositions" than his son's. This follows convincingly from the literature of the time, which is unconcerned with psychology: after a profound admonition, he who is admonished begins a new life. "Die Weisheitslehre dieser Knaben/sei ewig mir ins Herz gegraben" (May the wise teaching of these boys/be ever engraved in my heart), sings Tamino, confusing teaching with admonition. At that time it seemed easy enough to collect qualities like "steadfastness," "tolerance," and "discretion." Of course, these were virtues that Wolfgang possessed in great measure.

Nevertheless, in one of his recurrent moments of despair about his son's relationship to the world, Leopold Mozart sketches a graphic picture of alternatives. We find it again during the Romantic period, and it has endured as a popular view of the artist's fate. On February 12, 1778, he wrote from Salzburg to the twenty-two-year-old Wolfgang, in Paris:

> It now depends solely on your good sense and your way of life whether you die as an ordinary musician, utterly forgotten by the world, or as a famous Kapellmeister, of whom posterity will read,—whether, captured by some woman you die bedded on straw in an attic, full of starving children, or whether, after a Christian life spent in contentment, honor, and renown, you leave this world with your family well provided for and your name respected by all.

If we substitute "live" for "die," the alternatives are in fact presented accurately: the needy children, the end on a bed of straw—an affecting picture. However, it was destined to miss its point with the addressee, for nothing and no one, not even his father, could have diverted him from the aforementioned "woman" if she herself had not rejected him: Aloysia Weber, sixteen at the time, a promising singer whom Mozart made into a great artist. But Leopold erred primarily in thinking that his son was given a choice between splendor and misery: to weigh things rationally was not in Wolfgang's power. From the beginning the signs pointed to self-destruction. Of course, that was something his father could not guess: he had his eye on Wolfgang's career, the greatest possible exploitation of what he saw as his son's extraordinary abilities. But he overlooked his genius, his inner compulsions, and his intractable will.

We would not be so interested in Leopold Mozart's life if he had not been in control of Wolfgang's until a late stage. Although his father's influence declined in the third decade of Mozart's life, the son remained obedient, or at least resolved to be so. Objectively speaking, Mozart had always obeyed unwillingly, although he himself was not aware of it. The split occurred on May 9, 1781, when Wolfgang resigned from the service of the Archbishop Colloredo; it became apparent and irreparable when he married Constanze Weber on August 4, 1782. After this, the two men were estranged, although they were more or less successful at making light of the new relationship; it is amazing what convention, habit, and Wolfgang's courtesy were able to bridge. It is doubtful that the full extent of their estrangement ever penetrated Wolfgang's consciousness; it may simply have affected him as a discomfort he could not define. Leopold spoke of it later with caustic, often dismissive references in his letters to his daughter, Nannerl; he refers to the son only as "your brother." Nannerl, too, saw Constanze as far below the family's station; in this she was in agreement with her father. She probably did not notice that her brother was a good deal happier with his Constanze, for a few years at least, than she was with her Baron Berchtold zu Sonnenburg. And it probably would not have changed her attitude if she had.

It is hard for us to judge Leopold Mozart today. Not because that air of solitary greatness surrounded him, too—on the contrary: he was neither great nor did he have an instinct for greatness. Although he did evaluate others according to their ability, especially colleagues, he also measured their success and self-assertiveness; throughout his life he could never help speculating how he might detract from their successes to benefit his son. We don't mean to reproach him for this; till the end of his life, in spite of their estrangement, he showed an unabating interest in Wolfgang's compositions, his working methods, his musical and dramatic ideas, and their outcome. For Wolfgang, too, this topic was a saving way out of a strained relationship: reports on his work, notes on rehearsals, and now and then a request for his father's opinion.

It is hard to understand Leopold, primarily because it is almost impossible to assess the motives for his remarks in his precise and abundant verbal documents. To what degree was the writing of this educated, ambitious, basically honest court employee based on his world view, his individuality as expressed in his relationship to the world around him, and how much was it due to his servile nature? How much was convention and how much hypocrisy? What part piety and what part cant? Whatever great qualities he had, he remained fundamentally a lackey, with a strong inclination to submissive accommodation, if not obsequiousness, which sometimes degenerated into intrigue; he could also assume the tone of a Don Basilio. One of his favorite pieces of advice to his son was to "ingratiate" himself, either with the Elector in Mannheim (by first of all courting the children's governess) (letter of December 8, 1777) or with the Countess Baumgarten in Munich (November 20, 1780), or with colleagues who could be useful: "In Mannheim you did well to win the good graces of Herr [Cannabich]" (letter of February 12, 1778). In order to get what he wanted, he adapted his behavior and manner of speaking, without considering that his son might think differently of the methods he took for granted. Of course, he wanted his son to employ his gifts to the best of his ability, to become the embodiment of a *Homo faber*; but mainly he wanted him to compose in the required style. On December 11, 1780, he wrote to him in Munich:

> I advise you when composing to consider not only the musical, but also the *un-musical public*. You must remember that to every *ten real connoisseurs* there are *100 ignoramuses*. So do not neglect the so-called *popular* style, which tickles *long ears*.

We cannot judge how Wolfgang received this exhortation, whether he took it to heart in *Idomeneo*. In any event, Leopold must have feared that his son might make enemies of the public and his fellow musicians. On December 25 he wrote:

> Do your best to keep the whole orchestra in good humor; flatter them, and by praising them, keep them all well-disposed toward you. For I know your style of composition . . .

Leopold always feared what for him was the worst: refusal to satisfy the higher-ups. He had good reason to be afraid.

It is hard for us today to reconstruct the typical mentality of a royal subject during the last days of the *ancien régime*. And not only was Leopold Mozart the prototypical royal subject (the more so since he was in continual contact with princes, first as an employee, later as a man dependent on their favor); he also never expected anything different from his life. In a certain sense, Leopold Mozart is the unusual case of a man who, despite his insignificance in the social hierarchy, knew how to structure his fate according to precise principles. He lived consistent with the pursuit of one goal, which, naturally, he thought he was cheated out of. He was open to aesthetics, receptive to art, although he did not discriminate so much as register it cumulatively (Michelangelo in Rome, "the most beautiful paintings of Rubens" in Brussels); still, he was good at depicting life as he saw it, and, despite some petit bourgeois narrow-mindedness, he was superior to most of his contemporaries of the same rank, a fact he did not attempt to hide. His judgments were overbearing, though often tempered by humor. His humor ranged from vulgarity to parodies of his own weaknesses, especially his pomposity. He threatened Jakob Lotter, the Augsburg printer of his *Violinschule*, that he would get in touch with his wife and advise her to deny her husband his "nightly fiddle practice" until the new edition was printed. Apparently Herr Lotter did not object to this, for Leopold returned often, in the style of a rondo, to these suggestive remarks.

"*Ita clarissimus Dominus Doctor Leopoldus Mozartus,*" he

wrote in a letter to his son in Munich (December 4, 1780), in which for fifty lines he gave him dietetic advice for "catarrh," detailed to the point of absurdity; his self-parody here does not mean that he did not consider himself an unerring adviser on medical matters—in fact, he could not resist giving advice post mortem, too; it seems tragicomic, if not macabre, that, anticipating the news of his wife's death, he sends instructions to his son in Paris (July 13, 1778):

> If this misfortune has befallen you, ask Herr Baron Grimm to let you bring all your mother's effects to him to keep, so that you may not have so many things to look after; or else lock up everything carefully, for since for whole days at a time you are not at home, people might easily break into your room and rob you. God grant that all my precaution is unnecessary; but here you will recognize your father. My dear wife! my dear son! As she fell ill a few days after the bloodletting, she must have been suffering since June 16 or 17. Surely you waited too long. She hoped to cure herself by resting in bed—by dieting—by treating herself. I know how it is. One hopes and postpones from day to day. But, my dear Wolfgang, you must send immediately for a doctor when purging someone with a fever to decide whether one should treat the fever or let it be, since cooling treatments result in more purging. And if one begins elimination at the wrong time, the *materia peccans* burns up. Almighty God! We are in Thy hands.

Leopold's inner conflict was due not least to the tension between his position and his ambition. And yet he never really seems to have complained about his position as deputy Kapellmeister. Probably he would have failed in the higher position: his other interests were too diverse. He longed for enlightenment; he was a keen observer who followed all scientific discoveries with an alert and careful eye; he owned the newest measuring instruments, a microscope, a "solar microscope." He was, along with everything else, a potential scientist.

In spite of his acclaimed, "splendid" *Violinschule*, we would not have heard of him had he not been Wolfgang's father, his teacher, mentor, adviser, and (self-appointed, but honest and devoted) friend. He dedicated his life to making his son into an important musician in the best way he knew. His decision to renounce his own ambitions may have been due, in part, to his insight that he himself was too mediocre to rise very far above his station. But the fact that he remained deputy Kapell-meister all his life was probably not because of his own limita-tions but because there was no vacancy for him at the Arch-bishop's court; to his sorrow, and to Wolfgang's growing fury, the Italians were preferred to the Germans. So the father transferred his ambition to the son. Leopold's devotion is understandable, even self-evident. From his point of view, he made sizable sacrifices for his child. True, he did not make it easy, with his obligatory lessons, especially on the extended Italian journeys from 1769 to 1773. His son sometimes had to work on his assignments until his eyes closed; but that makes no difference to Leopold's righteous and self-righteous view that he sacrificed himself for his son. Whether we like him or not, it is senseless to be emotional about him and take sides, as people usually do. His strange obstinacy, the brazen conviction that he was doing and had done the right thing, is his strong point, too. We cannot begrudge him the satisfaction he took, personally and before God, in wanting the best for his son and devoting himself to that goal. To be sure, Wolf-gang had to hear about it often enough in the critical periods, especially in Paris; his father wrote hundreds of pages of vain exhortations to him. He must have spent whole nights writing, for at this time he still thought his warnings could be effective and that he could rouse his son from his alleged lethargy. Thus, he wrote on July 20, 1778:

> For I think you should consider me your best friend rather than your father; since I have proven a hundred times over *that I was more concerned for your good fortune and plea-sure than for my own* . . .

If we strike the word "pleasure" (*Vergnügen*), which in the eighteenth century had a different meaning, it cannot be denied that the father was right from his own point of view. We cannot refuse him our sympathy. On February 12, 1778, he wrote to Mozart in Paris:

> Consider whether I have not always treated you kindly, served you as a servant his master; even provided you with all possible entertainment and helped you to enjoy all honorable and seemly pleasures, often at great inconvenience to myself!

We hear in this a desperate impotence, and a lack of insight into the uselessness of appealing to his son's reason; it is questionable whether Wolfgang followed his father's injunction to think about it. "Our future depends on your abundant good sense, if you will only hearken to it," his father had written him just a week before (February 5, 1778), with more hope than conviction; but unfortunately, he never understood that good sense was the last thing Wolfgang would ever pay attention to.

Leopold Mozart will always seem an ambivalent figure to posterity. Certainly he was a pragmatist: if he kept his son in touch with the latest tendencies in music, it was to give him greater breadth, rather than depth—it was important to keep abreast of the fashions. He could not bring him up to be a "great musician"; the concept "great" was hardly part of a mind of that time and world. But perhaps he went too far in cultivating every potential of the child prodigy. He saw it as his duty to represent his son as a miracle to people, especially princes, and if the truth be told, to God, too. That meant performing in the courts of Europe like a faultless little machine, a human machine, true, but one that had to function reliably even under adverse conditions; everything had to be perfect, even the visual effect, which was to astonish and move the disbelieving audience. Like Thomas Mann's prodigy Bibi

Saccellaphylaccas, Wolfgang tolerated all this training, probably gladly. He knew no other life and demanded no other. Throughout his life he retained a taste for certain externals, for gorgeous dress, pretty buttons, shoe buckles, laces and trimmings, in retrospective longing for the prodigy he had been, in dissatisfaction with the homeliness of the man he had become. His gratification of this taste probably contributed in great measure to his later financial ruin. In a certain sense he always longed to be back in those days in England when he was still a prodigy, successful and secure in the protection of his father. But the father of his memory became more and more an imaginary ideal, no longer the domineering authority figure who had demanded results and passed them off as his own sacrifices.

Leopold was always aware that he had to take advantage of his children's youth, for all too soon they would be musicians like any other, Wolfgang probably a superior one, but the childlike brilliance, and thus the miracle, would be gone forever. So he wrote to Lorenz Hagenauer on May 11, 1768, from Vienna:

> Or should I perhaps sit down in Salzburg with the empty hope of some better fortune, let Wolfgang grow up, and allow myself and my children to be made fools of until I reach the age which prevents me from traveling and until he attains the age and physical appearance which no longer attract admiration for his merits?

However one takes this passage, it does not show Leopold in a particularly good light. True, we find no such comments later, when the son really had outgrown his day as a prodigy; Leopold made his peace with the change and his ambition was channeled into the more reasonable wish to find a place for his son at a prince's court and, especially, to preserve him from overly extravagant adventures, like his journey with the family of the failed musician and copyist Fridolin Weber, as companion and impresario to the latter's talented second daughter, Aloysia. Wolfgang never mentioned the third daughter,

Constanze, in his letters from Mannheim. Apparently she did not interest him, although at the age of fifteen she was no longer a child by the standards of the time. At least Leopold was spared that misgiving.

The father would probably have been happier if Wolfgang had achieved renown in Salzburg: it would have brought glory to Salzburg, and he would have had his son under his wing, to be his support, not least a material support, in his old age. But he was all too eagerly authoritarian in his manipulations, too carefully observant, reacting in a flash to any symptom of his son's possible independence. For he thought Wolfgang's plans were terrible, confused, naïve; and he was not entirely wrong. We can hardly expect a man like Leopold to have understood that his son was condemned to a tragic fate, no matter how hard he tried to overcome it. We can well understand his vehement protestations against a tie with the Weber family; they didn't match his idea of respectability, and here, too, he may have been right. The dominant motive for all his behavior was the fear, soon justified, that Wolfgang would slip away from him. Leopold Mozart knew his son well enough to recognize or guess the truth underneath the conventional, often tortured style of his letters. After years of experience with him, it didn't require too much penetration. When Wolfgang wrote to him on February 4, 1778, from Mannheim, that he wanted to give up the plan of going to Paris with the flutist Johann Wendling and the oboist Friedrich Ramm, because, although they were good fellows, the former had "no religion" and the latter was a "libertine," the father was probably able to figure out that neither lack of religion nor libertinism were sufficient reasons to drop a promising plan. Something else must be behind it; there was, namely, Mozart's love for Aloysia. Leopold Mozart was clever. But he wasn't clever enough to keep before his eyes the realization that his son would slip away from him sooner or later, that after years of obedience and extreme consideration a resistance would mount in him and he would no longer care about questions of fairness. No one at that time would have had a psychological insight of this kind, and Leopold never learned from experience. He must have died feeling that his son had been unfair to him and had repaid him with ingratitude.

When we look back, it seems even less understandable that Leopold Mozart, unable to accompany his son to Mannheim and Paris because of his duties in Salzburg, had enough trust in Wolfgang's ability to succeed to let him travel without strict supervision on a trip of many months' duration, meant to conclude with the engagement in Paris, but extended to nearly one and a half years because of various delays, which grew more and more intentional toward the end. Leopold must have known that his wife, who accompanied Mozart, didn't have sufficient judgment to counter her son's adventurous plans with solid arguments. Indeed, she never was able to, and we can see her on this journey only as her son's victim, more devoted servant than guardian.

We know no more about Mozart's relationship to his mother than what we have read in biographies about their close family life. We would not want to question it, but the two women, the mother and Nannerl, probably had a rather passive share in it, were more participants than initiators. Mozart's mother is said to have been a beautiful bride, although we wouldn't know it from her strange portrait, the famous but inferior picture of the performing Mozart family painted in 1780–81 in Salzburg by Johann Nepomuk della Croce. She could not be included among the musicians (besides, she was already dead at the time); instead, her portrait hangs in an oval frame on the wall, an almost comic way out of the artist's dilemma. She looks down at her family, rather ill-tempered, which she wasn't in real life. She probably did not play an instrument; perhaps she was not musical. She was definitely a good wife; at least nothing is known to the contrary. We see her as warmhearted, cheerful, insignificant. She had neither the sophistication of her husband nor his utilitarian gifts—and she never needed them, for Leopold was not only her lord and

master but also her devoted protector. With her homely gruff-
ness, her social graces were probably limited, although she
came from a respectable family: she was the daughter of the
prefect of St. Gilgen, Wolfgang Nikolaus Pertl, who occupied
the same post that Nannerl's husband was later given, although the latter was of the nobility. She seems nevertheless to
have had no education; even allowing for the times and her
origins, her spelling (in the original) and style were rather
unrefined:

> . . . I hope that you and Nannerl are well. And what is my
> Bimperl doing? I have not heard anything of her for a long
> time; I am sorry from my heart that the Chief Purveyor's
> wife died so suddenly. Fräulein Tonerl's mouth will prob-
> ably water. (To her husband, October 31, 1777, from
> Mannheim.)

She was also comfortable with scatological language, and
for as long as she was still disposed to joke with her son on her
long journey, she made generous use of the appropriate vocabulary:

> Addio, ben mio. Keep well, my love. Into your mouth your
> arse you'll shove. I wish you good night, my dear, but first
> shit in your bed and make it burst. It is long after one
> o'clock already. Now you can go on rhyming yourself. (To
> her husband, September 26, 1777, from Munich.)

This is about the level of humor of the then fifty-six-year-old
Anna Maria Mozart. And on this level she got along with her
son. The two must have talked a lot about digestive functions
on their long journey; this was perhaps the only theme they
had in common. Characteristically, the only extant letter of
the son to his mother, except for conventional greetings from
his early Italian journeys, is a poem that he sent to her in
Mannheim on January 31, 1778, from Worms, in which he
tells her everything he has to say in reference to anal functions. Written in an apparently good mood, on the way back
from Kirchheimbolanden, where he had made a detour with
Aloysia and her father to perform before the Princess Caro-

line of Nassau-Weilburg, the letter does not supply any information ("Well, now we've been over a week away/And we've
been shitting every day"); but it does give vague plans for the
future ("The Concerto for Paris I'll keep, 'tis more fitting. / I'll
scribble it there someday when I'm shitting"). In any event,
the letter doesn't betray much of that moral sobriety his father
was so urgently trying to exact from him. It is the only testimony to his communication with his mother on this journey;
he does mention a conversation with her in one of the letters
to Bäsle (November 5, 1777), but only because of a fart.

We find it hard to understand Leopold Mozart's decision to have his wife accompany his son on his travels. Did he
really believe that her presence could be a substitute for his
authority, that he could keep the reins in his hands from
Salzburg and direct the pair's plans from there? He must
have credited her with abilities that she apparently did not
possess. We do not know if she herself thought she had authority. It is hard to imagine that she did not understand her
inadequacy soon enough. She had nothing with which to
counter her son's obstinate unworldliness, nothing that would
bring him to his senses—and she must have been aware of it
earlier. Thus, she was forced to set out unhappily to travel
with her son, irresolutely ready to follow him into ruin. She
died away from home, after months of frustrating passivity,
fulfilling the task she saw as her maternal duty (i.e., the care of
his physical well-being) only halfheartedly and imperfectly.
She may or may not have guessed that she had little to offer
him intellectually. She probably didn't think in those terms.

Mozart didn't bother too much about his mother on this
trip, for which oversight his father sometimes reproached him
bitterly. She had to spend weeks in cheap, shabby rooms, in
gloomy and probably not very sanitary quarters, dirty and
inadequately heated in winter. She seems to have put up with
it. This kind of acceptance is one of those riddles posed by the
unprivileged people under absolutist rule. We don't know

what she did all day long: homesickness is no occupation. In letters to her husband she was upright, and tried loyally to glorify Wolfgang's either insignificant or dubious successes. From time to time she added a short postscript to his reports, when he had gone out to give lessons, to dine with a patron, or to spend long social evenings in the family circle of the Kapellmeister Johann Christian Cannabich. When she was alone and could be certain that the letter would be sent before Wolfgang came home, she expressed her worries, but with restraint, ever an incredible and unfathomable model of devotion. We can be certain that she counted the days until the homecoming she was not destined to experience—though it was hard to count them, for their plans were vague and the projected travel dates kept changing. She had to bow to her husband's dictates on the one hand and her son's willfulness on the other. She was a burden to him, although he would not have admitted it to himself. He did not knowingly let her sense it, as she did not let him sense that she would rather have been at home. We cannot judge whether her presence kept him from going astray or prevented any illicit conquests. If she earns our admiration, it is primarily for her mute or muted patience during the long weeks of her quiet martyrdom, suffered of her own volition (insofar as she had volition). A woman used to submission, she was, like her son, fatalistic. Even those who did not actively believe in Him were in the habit of saying "God willing."

And then she died in Paris. Her death has been called a "fateful blow" (Einstein) for Wolfgang and the journey a "fateful journey" (Hanns Dennerlein); the year, like the year 1787, when his father died, a "fateful year" (Abert). As if we needed these external signposts to mark out the path of his life! As we shall see, such an idea is out of the question. To be sure, Mozart often provoked fate in a critical way, but we cannot speak of blows of fate in the sense of sudden crushing caesuras in life. His existential situation, more than his human ties, must have determined his mental outlook, and his situation worsened not in specific stages, but gradually. There may well have been moments when the vision of his hopeless condition towered before him, apparently insurmountable, but he pushed away the old sorrows and the new until his death.

Despite the sentimentalists' reading, neither his mother's death nor his father's was a decisive blow of fate for Mozart, for here in Paris he became an adult (if we can apply that term of development to him), and as an adult he did not have any deep ties to others, except, later on, to his wife, Constanze. In Mozart's case we cannot even speak of that object loss which is usually one of the inner events the genius suffers. For after his childhood, that is, after the onset of puberty, which in a sense he never got beyond, we cannot say with certainty that he ever had any objects to lose. Thus, his father, in his often despairing letters to Paris, reminded him pointedly (and in vain) of his many demonstrations of love during Mozart's childhood, which to Leopold represented a pledge and a promise that this love would endure forever. But the son would no longer respond; he was that child no longer, just as Leopold was no longer that father. And if Mozart later assured his father and sister from Paris, after his mother's death, that he wanted to be an active support to them—"Remember that you have a son, a brother, who is doing his utmost to make you happy" (July 9, 1778)—it was his kind of psychic ruggedness, rising up for the moment and diffused again in a moment. Here, too, he lapses into his artificial style, governed by precise forms. He touches on unpleasant things only reluctantly and very rarely: he would rather pass over them with a leap and a bound, as he does in this letter concerning his mother's death: "Let us therefore say a devout Paternoster for her soul and turn our thoughts to other matters, for all things have their appropriate time." In other words, enough! Object loss? Hardly. After his childhood, his mother had ceased to be a love object—incidentally, we have no protestations of love from

Wolfgang to her as we have to his father. In the score of his life, his mother's voice did not figure.

On the day of his mother's death, July 3, 1778, Mozart, now twenty-two, wrote from Paris to his father: "Now I have a piece of news for you which you may have heard already, namely that that godless arch-rascal Voltaire has pegged out like a dog, like a beast! That is his reward!" If Mozart had been asked, "Reward for what?" he probably wouldn't have had an answer. One wonders what Voltaire meant to Mozart. The Archbishop Hieronymus Colloredo, his Salzburg employer, who was theoretically a partisan of the Enlightenment (although it does not appear to have made much practical difference in his behavior) owned a bust of the "rascal." That he could afford this partiality seems to show that once in a while "Catholic" was still understood in the Greek sense. On the other hand, the bust was draped in a cloth. If Mozart, who hated the Archbishop, had seen it, this alone would have been cause enough to hate Voltaire, Mozart being neither a man of considered judgments nor a partisan of the Enlightenment, at least not at this time. His somewhat halfhearted protector in Paris, the German journalist Baron Melchior Grimm, was also a disciple of Voltaire's, but we would not want to attribute Mozart's justifiably ambivalent feelings about this patron to the latter's connection with Voltaire. It is more likely that at this time, in particular, Mozart wanted to say what his strict and therefore constricting father Leopold wanted to hear, for although Leopold, too, was in his way a partisan of the Enlightenment, his understanding did not stretch to the recognition of a figure like Voltaire. Incidentally, he already knew of the death, and had mentioned it almost as callously a few days earlier (letter of June 29, 1778).

Wolfgang wanted to do right by his father; now and then during this period there were things he tried to make up for (although he probably did not know guilt feelings in our

sense). One such was his apathy about the concessions his father demanded from him, which by Leopold's calculations
were to have led to success in Paris. But mainly he wanted to
prepare his father for certain future plans that required his
approval. Even in euphoric moments, Wolfgang knew that his
father would probably not give his approval, and he did indeed refuse it for Mozart's marriage to Aloysia Weber and a
resulting connection with that not very respectable family.
At this time the connection was not yet accomplished, but was
at hand in the form of a rather extravagant and naïve project:
a trip with the Weber family to Italy, to perform in musical
centers there, with Wolfgang in the role of performer and
promoter. An adventurous idea, but not thought through,
naturally, like nearly all Mozart's schemes.

However one regards this passage—and there are not many
ways to interpret it—it is an example of those numerous statements of Mozart's which are still called blemishes or, in a
schoolmasterish tone of voice, "blots" in books about Mozart,
accompanied by regrets that they cannot be entirely ignored
(how one would like to!). Even Einstein feels this passage is
a "flaw in his letters," and finds in general much about Mozart
the man "alienating" or "regrettable." Since we do not imagine Mozart had two souls, like Faust, but either many or only
one mighty one, a quasi-pluralistic one, we find nothing to
regret about him; but everything estranges. We are forgetting
our sense of proportion if we censure him, bemoan his fallibility, as if geniuses were also obliged to set the norm in all areas
of life, and daily life, too, which was an area alien to him. It
cannot be emphasized too often: we are all beneficiaries of a
seemingly rich documentation, and fall greedily upon that
abundance of clues to Mozart which we lack about other great
men, before and during his time. Where the darkness surrounding the latter abets crude biographical fiction, the light
that seems to surround Mozart's circumstances, which we confuse with light around his psyche, provokes an excessive fever
of interpretation. With it comes a doubtful appraisal, the

mythmaking which goes back and forth between "man and music" and tries to use everything, up to and including his choice of keys, as evidence.

The tone of such a passage in his letters should be neither excused nor glossed over. We have to deny ourselves that kind of comment, positive or negative. The letter runs through a wide range of topics. He begins with the mother's serious illness; then, like an omen, he conjures up the will of God, who might wish to take her to Him. Next he turns to the performance of a new symphony, K. 297/300a, the "Paris," in D major, whose success in concert at the Swiss Hall of the Tuileries he celebrated—after (attention, Leopold Mozart!) saying a rosary—with a good sherbet in a café, and so on. What the letter does not mention is that his mother had already been dead three hours at the time of writing.

To be sure, immediately afterward he wrote a famous letter to a family friend, the Abbé Bullinger:

Paris, le 3 juillet, 1778

Most Beloved Friend!
For you alone.

Mourn with me, my friend! This has been the saddest day of my life—I am writing this at two o'clock in the morning. I have to tell you that my mother, my dear mother, is no more! God has called her to Himself. It was His will to take her, that I saw clearly—so I resigned myself to His will. He gave her to me, so He was able to take her away from me. Only think of all my anxiety, the fears and sorrows I have had to endure for the last fortnight. She was quite unconscious at the time of her death—her life flickered out like a candle. Three days before her death she made her confession, partook of the Sacrament and received extreme unction. During the last three days, however, she was constantly delirious, and today at twenty-one minutes past five o'clock the death agony began and she lost all sensation and consciousness. I pressed her hand and spoke to her—but she did not see me, she did not hear me and all feeling was gone. She lay thus until she expired five hours later at twenty-one minutes past ten. No one was present but myself, Herr Haina (a kind friend whom my father knows) and the nurse. It is quite impossible for me to describe today the whole course of her illness, but I am firmly convinced that she was bound to die and that God had so ordained it. All I ask of you at present is to act the part of a true friend, by preparing my poor father very gently for this sad news. I have written to him by this post, but only to say that she is seriously ill; and now I shall wait for his answer and be guided by it. May God give him strength and courage! O my friend! Not only am I now comforted, but I have been comforted for some time. By the mercy of God I have borne it all with fortitude and composure. When her illness became dangerous, I prayed to God for two things only—a happy death for her, and strength and courage for myself; and God in His goodness heard my prayer and gave me those two blessings in the richest measure. I beg you, therefore, most beloved friend, watch over my father for me and try to give him courage so that, when he hears the worst, he may not take it too hardly. I commend my sister to you also with all my heart. Go to them both at once, I implore you—but do not tell them yet that she is dead—just prepare them for it. Do what you think best—use every means to comfort them—but so act that my mind may be relieved—and that I may not have to dread another blow. Watch over my dear father and my dear sister for me. Send me a reply at once, I entreat you. Adieu. I remain your most obedient and grateful servant

Wolfgang Amadè Mozart

This letter is supposed to be a "devastating document," "the most glorious monument to a child's love," which "engraves" the image of his mother "indelibly in the hearts of later generations" (Paumgartner). To us it seems rather that Mozart's emotion is kept within the limits of baroque convention. We sense that some librettist of an *opera seria* had a part in its writing: the expression of the tragic content is based on models. "Mourn with me, my friend. This has been the saddest day of my life." This opening exclamation reminds us of a letter he wrote to Constanze thirteen years later (June 11, 1791): "Crie avec moi contre mon mauvais sort!"—but there he was writing about a canceled concert. The letter to Bullinger also turns quickly to the invocation of higher powers. At this time especially, Mozart was all too happy to make use of them. "I am firmly convinced that she was bound to die and that God had so ordained it," he writes with an unconvincing, fatalistic gesture, which, however, by no means indicates cold-bloodedness. Rather it shows an inadequate contact with the superficial necessities of life. When dealing with them he always fled into the realm of the artificial and declamatory.

Looking at this letter in the original, we have before us a calligraphic jewel, so beautiful one would think it had been intended for future admiring generations as an exemplary document of its special kind.* Although we can see in most of Mozart's manuscripts this special kind of mastery, we can also gather from some of the letters of 1781 (which we would be more correct in calling a "fateful year," since it was when he finally broke with the Archbishop) how much his handwriting could reflect his inner turmoil when he really was devastated. The letter of May 9, 1781, to his father, beginning with the angry outburst "I am still seething with rage!" dem-

---

* Annette Kolb sees in the letter "exquisite characters, drowned in grief." She, too, finds in Mozart's reaction to this "fateful blow" an occasion for poetry: "But who can say what surprises the earth of his soul had in store for an artist like Mozart, what seeds would shoot up in consequence of any experience?" And she finds an answer: "The lighthearted, epicurean Mozart, given to jest, is here the realist, the professional, the expert. No one measured with so much fine feeling that gaping abyss into which the good Frau Mozart was pulled, far from the shores where she felt so at home, where Salzburg lay under the vault of the sky, and where there reigned discussion about the day's events, the love one bore one's family, about throwing darts, where words went flying back and forth, and where there was laughter in the company of friends and conversation about the price of butter." Annette Kolb, *Mozart* (Erlenbach-Zurich and Stuttgart, 5th edition, 1970), pp. 105, 106. One sees there are no limits to the realm of interpretation.

onstrates this rage: it abandons all restraint. The writing is chaotic and uncontrolled, a hand that "Beethoven carried to the height of perfection."

A few days later Mozart told his father about the death. Again, we are surprised at Leopold's intelligence, revealed in the letter from this unusual man (July 13, 1778) : "Your mother has passed away! You try too earnestly to console me. No one does that so zealously if he is not driven to do so by the loss of all human hope or by the event itself." There follows a nice slip: "I am now going to lunch, but I will have an appetite." He left out the word "not."

A few weeks later, at his father's request, Mozart described the course of the illness. After asking permission to be brief, since he had other things to do, he filled twelve pages, going into the minutest details of the three-week-long illness, with cruel precision, as if he had set out to describe the medical history *ad absurdum*. Everything is narrated, all the complaints, symptoms, and pains, with the help of the date, the time of day, and the exact hour; doctor's visits, bloodletting, dose and type of administered medications, reaction to them, elimination, everything. (To be sure, none of this reveals what the illness was.) Since it is extremely improbable that Mozart kept a diary, we can confirm that his phenomenal memory was by no means confined to music, being exercised here on the most unlikely topic. Or is this, too, one of those parodies of the banal which he indulged in during moments of delight in the absurd? More of them later.

Voltaire did not die like a dog, though that might have been the version current in bigoted Paris circles. He died, at least to all appearances, a repentant sinner, in the lap of the Church. We will never know whether this return was a last diabolical brainstorm or a true confession. On the other hand, Mozart himself, if he did not die like a dog, died in circum-

stances that make us almost suspect Voltaire of a posthumous
revenge for the slander.

The artistic yield of the Paris months is slight: we do
not actually know whether his dissatisfaction, his dashed
hopes, are to blame, but we think not, for he often composed
under more malevolent stars; under difficult conditions he
was always able to escape to his work. Perhaps the hunt for
commissions or "vacancies" took too much out of him; moreover, it is less the quantity than the quality of the Paris compositions which leaves us so dissatisfied, spoiled as we are by
his great works. Mozart surely was trying to write according to
the "Parisian taste," but we are surprised that he could be
untrue to himself to such a degree. Whether elegant or elegiac,
never before or after did he stylize his light occasional pieces
so much or "toss them off" without questioning the fashion.
True, even in the insignificant occasional pieces we find that
unmistakable passage (here not even a "little phrase," but
only a tiny figure), as, for example, in the G minor of the
middle section of a B-flat gavotte from the ballet music to *Les
petits riens*, K. Anh. 10/299b (early summer 1778); or suddenly,
in the otherwise rather slight piano variations on "Ah, vous
dirai-je, Maman," K. 265/300e (written around the same
time), in the middle of an unending C major an indispensable, precipitous C minor variation, which rips open a
panorama in which we recognize him, the profound Mozart of
the minor, lurking in the background. In Paris he is also
capable of applying his "meaningful" G minor elegantly and
with purposeful ease, as in the variations on the melody (magical in itself) "Hélas, j'ai perdu mon amant" for violin and
piano, K. 360/374b, dated 1781 in the Köchel catalogue. We
find this date highly unlikely, since Mozart did not find inspiration in such pastoral gallantry after his stay in Paris.
Here, in any case, the G minor makes a charming little elegy;
not so much varied as embellished in new ways, it seems to be

the lament of an abandoned girl, who will, however, find consolation soon enough.

The symphony that was so important to him, whose success he celebrated with a reportedly large helping of sherbet, K. 297/300a ("Paris"), is an ironic work, composed for a public he did not credit with too much understanding. His main purpose was to please, and he did please. He had to meet the demand and did it in good measure: he offered a choice of two andantes. He himself had no preference; they were simply two products, the second of which (the weaker, incidentally) "suited." It was all right with Mozart; everything in Paris which could serve to postpone his return to Salzburg was all right with him.

But these interpolations in the minor, these miscellaneous pieces, are still not indicative of the "fundamental" Mozart. Two important works in the minor from the Paris period, however, are different. They are the E minor Sonata for piano and violin, K. 304/300c and the A minor Sonata for piano, K. 310/300d, probably written one after the other, during June and July 1778. People have, of course, tried to explain the "tragic" mood of these two works, especially the latter, by referring to the "fateful blows" of this year—his mother's death, the forlorn time in Paris, the professional dead end, and so forth. Abert speaks of "the valiantly resolved soul's resistance to something inexorable,"[22] as if our appreciation of the music needed programmatic support, an explanation other than that of Mozart's depressive phases and impulses, whether or not they are dependent on external events. These phases inevitably set in motion creative currents in the unconscious which are communicated to us as emotional stimuli. Einstein actually says: "The key of A minor—and sometimes A major as well, 'in a special light'—is [sic!] for Mozart the key of despair."[23] We wonder what the "special light" might mean and what it illuminates. On the other hand, Werner Lüthy holds A minor to be Mozart's "key of grief,"[24] though for most other critics that would be G minor, insofar as it is not the "key of destiny" (Einstein). It is hard to find one's way in this labyrinth of sensibilities. Actually, it seems to us that this kind of assertion draws life only from the omission of whatever contradicts it. If we examine Mozart's A minor, we see, precisely in this instance, that he used it (along with other keys, but always purposefully) for expressing the grotesque or foreign, for the "*alla turca*," first in the finale of the ballet *Le Gelosie del Serraglio*, K. Anh. 109/135a (Milan, December 1772), then in the finale of the A major Violin Concerto, K. 219 (December 20, 1775); in the allegretto of the A major Piano Sonata, K. 331/300i (summer 1778); at the same time as the A minor Sonata, and in other "*alla turca*" episodes. Mozart always used the minor when expressing deliberately exotic elements, clearly recognizable by their rhythm, beginning with the "*alla turca*" episode in G minor in the early G major Symphony, K. 74 (Milan, 1770).

Thus, summary assertions about the significance of keys can be based only on the interpreter's receptive feeling; at best, it is only coincidentally related to the composer's intention. We learned this lesson especially in connection with the A minor Rondo for piano, K. 511, composed during work on *Don Giovanni* (March 11, 1787). In our opinion, it has been overloaded emotionally. We, too, automatically prick up our ears at Mozart's use of the minor, but we do not necessarily switch over immediately to "tragedy," "destiny," or the "daemonic." Rather, to us that very A minor Rondo seems to be Mozart's "*valse triste*," whose chromatically ascending crescendo evokes a strange, evanescent melancholy. It is unique because of a certain salon quality, rare in Mozart, as in the F major episode, which sounds like Chopin. We do not mean to suggest that our remarks about this piece are definitive, but only to give an example of the variety of its effects, which can never be considered universal.

"*Que s'est-il donc passé?*"—What in the world happened? asks Saint-Foix[25] of the A minor Sonata, apparently unable to continue seeing, as he would have preferred, an organic development in Mozart. This fundamental question is the best demonstration of what biographical misunderstanding consists of: the view that something has to happen, that an experience has to be had, which affects the artist so deeply and precisely, which hits the mark so truly, that it destroys his firmly established method and leads the work in a new direction, into a new dimension, as a result of which the artist is no longer the same. There is no better evidence of posterity's anomalous relationship with artists, portrayed at these "turning points," than this question typical of biographers. We are urged to visualize "Wolfgang Amadeus" as he hurries through the streets of Paris, overcome by a sudden deep sorrow, arriving home and throwing himself at his work, to write down the music in profound agitation, probably in a chaotic frame of mind (the manuscript contradicts this view, by the way). Or he throws himself at the piano and plays the sonata through, swaying his head fervently at the *rubati*. And now we are supposed to wonder, if by this time it has not turned into a leading question, what the cause of this sorrow is? The answers have in fact been suggested: in this case, the death of his mother and of the family friend, the organist Anton Adlgasser in Salzburg, heartache about Aloysia, and even, according to Hanns Dennerlein, the death of the Elector Max Joseph in Munich.

What really happened? The question is actually quite easy to answer. Mozart had penetrated new territory; a latent aspect of his ability, a natural expansion of his potential, had revealed itself, as it was bound to sooner or later. Actually, it is arbitrary to ask this question in regard to the A minor Sonata; there must have been earlier stages, and therefore earlier works about which it might just as well have been asked—the E-flat Piano Concerto, K. 271 ("Jeunehomme"), for example, written in January 1777, i.e., one and a half years earlier. What had happened *there* to result in the C minor andantino, this profound recitative in dialogue; who is speaking to whom? The answer is that Mozart is speaking to himself in his untranslatable language. For "music has at least as definite a meaning as words, although it cannot be translated into words" (Mendelssohn). Einstein contends that Mozart never surpassed this concerto. I myself would say that he did, but one cannot argue about value judgments on the very highest level, only about whether this "level" exists. And if we reach further back, what had happened in Salzburg in October 1773, when, not yet eighteen, Mozart wrote the so-called little G minor Symphony, K.183/173dB? Here, in this very first symphony in the minor, there are already flashes of the late Mozart, the profoundly alien Mozart, in the surging power of the allegro con brio, with its seventh leaps and its syncopations. Obscure references in letters from Italy to his sister in the years previous to this have led biographers to conclude that it stemmed from a first, passionate love. We know nothing about it.

If we really want to keep playing this game of proofs (it leads nowhere) we can reach even further back, for example to the E-flat Symphony, K.184/161a, of the same year (March 30, 1773). Almost (but not quite) still in the form of an Italian overture, the symphony has a C minor andante in which something does seem "to happen," namely the development of a thoroughly conventional beginning into a new wealth of polyphony, suddenly betraying unexpected emotions. But what kind of emotion? Certainly these early symphonies are in general more restrained, less "passionate," than the A minor Sonata. Merely by virtue of their genre they would be less direct than a work for piano solo. We automatically assume that sonatas are played through at once, perhaps even before they are written down, and thus reflect the eruptive character of something just conceived. But that, too, is simply not true of Mozart, who usually kept his compositions in his head, complete in all their voices. So we cannot measure the degree of his spontaneity.

I have actually tried to find traces of spontaneous emotion in Mozart's autographs. The puzzling, enigmatic Adagio for piano in B minor, K. 540, written on March 19, 1788 (between the Prague and Vienna premières of *Don Giovanni* and shortly before the E-flat Symphony, K. 543), seemed to me especially suitable. Mozart's only other movement in B minor is the adagio of the Flute Quartet, K. 285 (December 25, 1777), a piece with melodic charm but otherwise insignificant. (Although Pedrillo's Romanze in *Die Entführung* is in B minor, it never maintains this key to the end of a musical phrase.) The fact that Mozart attributed some importance to his choice of key in this adagio is proven by his writing the key, "*H mol,*" into his thematic catalogue, something he had never done before. I thought this work did have an emotional content; it seemed to be the musical transposition of an inner process which could not be related in words because it had not taken place in an extramusical reality.* But here, as everywhere, the manuscript shows that the act of writing out the music was a purely technical one, the product of perhaps no more than half an hour of intense but relaxed concentration, in which clarity and legibility were of greatest importance. A wonderfully straight and lively configuration of notes, without even the tiniest correction, this, like the letters, is a masterpiece of calligraphy. And here, too, nothing is betrayed.

The turning point in Mozart's life during this "fateful year" of 1778 was definitely not the loss of his mother, nor of anyone else, but rather that for the first time in his life he was

---

* "Everyone who knows and loves the work agrees that in it the spirit of music has taken on form and sonority in one sublimely significant moment. One may try to get at it with analyses, but, however thoughtful they may be, one realizes at the end of all efforts that the true mystery begins only after them." Wilhelm Mohr, "Über Mozarts Adagio in H moll (K. 540)" in *Acta Mozartiana*, 9th series, 1962, vol. 4, p. 67.

alone, independent. It was a new, welcome state, but one not to be trusted, for father Leopold still ruled—though at least from afar. At first the son did not feel quite at home in his new state, but soon, and with growing confidence, he accepted it and acted on it. He suddenly felt what freedom could mean, what it might be like if he had no father. This feeling of freedom was responsible for his again taking up the plan of traveling with the Weber family, of presenting Aloysia and building her into a star with him as her accompanist, and more, of course. It was probably a bad plan, but we can't be certain. Perhaps he would have succeeded, though not with Aloysia. She would probably have left him at the first opportunity, to make her own fortune. But he was not about to weigh such considerations; he visualized a future of freedom, an illusion his father disabused him of roundly. Leopold Mozart, increasingly embittered by the meager results of this expensive journey, which had forced him into debt, tried to tighten the reins, and finally ordered his son to return to Salzburg. From his point of view, the decision was justified, for the trip had been a fiasco from the beginning. At least father and son agreed on that point, though it pained the father more than the son.

Mozart was not familiar with the concept of "artistic conscience," not even when the thing it describes had long since begun to live in his unconscious, not even when it ruled him so completely that it was the only impulse that kept him alive. But that was not until ten years later; it was a long time before Mozart sensed that his mission in this world was not to satisfy his employers and adapt to their demands. It may be that he never really learned. But in the end he had understood his mission well enough to lose these employers. He took his chances, and as we know, punishment followed after. Not that he would have felt it beneath his dignity to produce German dances and minuets by the gross (his feelings of dignity lay in other areas), but he did it reluctantly; his time was too important to him, for it was running out. He had to produce these dances until the very end of his life; toward the end he even had to increase his production. In Paris, at least, he did not regard it as a compromise to compose in bulk, to copy or imitate, when necessary, all the current styles, as long as it was useful to do so. In order not to have to return to Salzburg he was ready to make use of any opportunity to give the Parisians what they wanted; but he was not given the chance. It was not exactly that he was undesirable; he was simply not needed. He was offered the post of organist at Versailles, but he refused it, for he felt something better would turn up. Nothing did. Besides, he had never been very interested in the organ, and the post as organist that he eventually took in Salzburg was truly a last resort: an instrument he didn't much like in a city he liked even less. He probably regretted his decision about Versailles.

It was also in Paris that Mozart first came to understand that something about the ruling class was not as it should be. At least, he was no longer prepared to accept them. He no longer took everything as it came, as his father did and demanded that he do. He probably didn't think in terms of "social justice" at this point; he did not see himself as typical but rather as a disadvantaged partner of this ruling class, making use of his right to protest if it did not accord him the rank he deserved. As the child of a different era, he had pride, unlike his father. Indeed, his pride grew at times into overbearance, intractability. But he would never have thought of objectifying it or deducing from it a general rule for social behavior. For not only did he lack like-minded peers equal to what he rightly thought was his own artistic stature, but also, no theory existed which might have reached his circles. He alone governed his social sensibility, his feeling for justice. "The best and truest of all friends are the poor. The wealthy do not know what friendship means" (to Bullinger, August 7, 1778).

And so his passive rebellion began in Paris. Mozart was no flatterer and no sycophant like his father, and in Paris he learned how the aristocracy worked. The humiliations they inflicted on him outraged him; they outrage us still today. They read like contributions to a source book on the reasons for the French Revolution. A letter of May 1, 1778, to his father, describing his visit to the Duchesse de Chabot, gives a picture of the insults he had to tolerate:

M. Grimm gave me a letter to her, so I drove there. The main object of this letter was to recommend me to the Duchesse de Bourbon (who was in a convent the last time I was here), to introduce me to her again and to recall me to her mind. Well, a week went by without any news. However, as she had asked me to call on her after a week had elapsed, I kept my word and went. I had to wait for half an hour in a large ice-cold, unheated room, which hadn't even a fireplace. At last the Duchesse de Chabot appeared. She was very polite and asked me to make the best of the clavier in the room, as none of her own were in good condition. Would I perhaps try it? I said that I should be delighted to play something, but that it was impossible at the moment, as my fingers were numb with cold; and I asked her to have me taken at least to a room where there was a fire. "Oh oui, Monsieur, vous avez raison," was all the reply I got. She then sat down and began to draw and continued to do so for a whole hour, having as company some gentlemen, who all sat in a circle round a big table, while I had the honor to wait. The windows and doors were open and not only my hands but my whole body and my feet were frozen and my head began to ache. There was altum silentium and I did not know what to do for cold, headache and boredom. I kept on thinking: "If it were not for M. Grimm, I would leave this house at once." At last, to cut my story short, I played on that miserable, wretched pianoforte. But what vexed me most of all was that Madame and all her gentlemen never interrupted their drawing for a moment, but went on intently, so that I had to play to the chairs, tables and walls. Under these detestable conditions I lost my patience. I therefore began to play the Fischer varia-

tions and after playing half of them I stood up. Whereupon
I received a shower of éloges. Upon which I said the only
thing I had to say, which was that I could not do myself
justice on that clavier; and that I should very much like to
fix some other day to play, when a better instrument would
be available. But, as the Duchess would not hear of my
going, I had to wait for another half hour, until her husband
came in. He sat down beside me and listened with the greatest attention and I—I forgot the cold and my headache and
in spite of the wretched clavier, I played—as I play when I
am in good spirits. Give me the best clavier in Europe with
an audience who understand nothing, or don't want to
understand and who do not feel with me in what I am
playing, and I shall cease to feel any pleasure. I told Grimm
all about it afterward. You say that I ought to pay a good
many calls in order to make new acquaintances and revive
the old ones. That, however, is out of the question. The
distances are too great for walking—or the roads too muddy
—for really the mud in Paris is beyond all description. To
take a carriage—means that you have the honor of spending
four to five livres a day and all for nothing. People pay
plenty of compliments, it is true, but there it ends. They
arrange for me to come on such and such a day, I play and
hear them exclaim: "Oh, c'est un prodige, c'est inconcevable,
c'est étonnant!", and then it is—Adieu. At first I spent a
lot of money driving about—often to no purpose, as the
people were not at home. Those who do not live in Paris
cannot imagine how annoying this is. Besides, Paris is
greatly changed; the French are not nearly as polite as they
were fifteen years ago; their manners now border on rudeness and they are detestably self-conceited.

We do not know whether the Duchess paid Mozart or simply
dismissed him with compliments. Often all he received was a
present, the most valuable of which were probably gold
watches. Over the years he accumulated so many of them that
he thought of draping himself with them during presentations
so that gracious givers might hold their present back and
reach, after all, for a filled purse. He became increasingly
angry in Paris, and soon he no longer paid visits to the people

his father wished him to visit: he simply did not want to. Finally, he visited only his friends and comrades. His time was too dear for endless walks on the "filthy" streets. Paris at this time was far dirtier than other cities; sanitary conditions were also less than perfect. Pedestrians used house entranceways as latrines; indeed, everyone used them for the relief of all bodily needs, great and small. Excrement, collected in pits underneath the houses, was carried off and used as manure, a business in the hands of concessionaires. In certain quarters the stench must have been unbearable, and one wonders if, given these conditions, Mozart still used the "little outhouse" with as much gusto as he apparently (and demonstrably) did otherwise.

Most of all he suffered from wounds to his pride and honor as a musician. For twenty-four two-hour lessons in composition which he gave the daughter of the Duc de Guines, he was dismissed with three louis d'or, which he refused. We do not know how much he finally received. Greatly annoyed, he reported the event to his father, not least in order to teach him that one could hardly count on success, given such conditions, such niggardly humans as partners.

The relevant passages in his letters to his father also throw light on the influence of Mozart's moods on his portrayal of objective circumstances. In the beginning, perhaps in euphoric moments of confidence that some success was possible in Paris, the young lady still had "a great deal of talent and genius, and in particular an incomparable memory" (letter of May 14, 1778); Mozart was always quick to use the word "incomparable" in his letters. But when, two months later, his euphoria had abated and he experienced instead an ever more hostile reality, the pupil became "not only thoroughly stupid, but also thoroughly lazy" (letter of July 9, 1778). At first her harp playing was "magnifique" and her stingy father played the flute "incomparably." For them Mozart wrote the Concerto in C, K. 299/297c, for flute and harp, two instruments he did not care for; and in accordance with his increasingly open antipathy to both the musicians and their instruments, the Concerto became one of his insignificant works of this period.

Neither in Munich, Mannheim, nor Paris did any court or administrative body attempt to retain Mozart. They only detained him, and that finally stopped, too. So the trip failed because of the princes' lack of interest; there was simply no opening available; inferior men ruled the scene, men who knew better how to assert themselves. We can only guess how much Mozart's own halfheartedness, his insufficient energy, his unconscious defensiveness, and his overt unwillingness to deal with human inadequacies contributed to his failure. Certainly he was as much unable to put himself in the proper light as others were unable to recognize him for the man he was. Unimpressed by any courtly splendor, he was too indolent to cloak himself in the aura of the great artist, much as it would have helped him. Yet he was just as unable to arrange things from a practical viewpoint, however great his wish for more money (money would have meant freedom). He would have liked to exploit his advantages, but was incapable of it. And he also lacked the style of a serene *grand seigneur*, like the "Ritter von Gluck," who had been able to indulge himself by appearing at rehearsals in nightcap and nightshirt, to let aristocratic admirers dress him there. Imagine Mozart carrying on like that! A man like Gluck could afford caprices and whims; he wore his papal order as if it were a secular title. This "plebeian genius" (Romain Rolland) grew into his role, as, incidentally, did Beethoven, who knew very well that the Viennese would take "van" as a noble title and prudently did nothing to correct them.

Mozart was, of course, concerned with his outer appearance, and spent sizable sums on it; these expenses figure in the balance of his ruin, too. Muzio Clementi, who met him in 1781 at the beginning of his brilliant period in Vienna, took him "for an imperial chamberlain because of his elegant dress," a portrayal which differs from our image of him. But contemporary opinions do not agree, even about his appearance; everything seems to aim at confusing his image. "Small, quick, active, with weak eyes, an unimpressive figure," Ludwig Tieck thought, though he met him, it is true, in a half-darkened Berlin theater in 1789, when his brilliant period was long since over.

It would be nice to know how much Mozart's appearance betrayed the out-and-out eccentric, or what impression he gave away from the piano, when he was listening, or fell silent, or spoke, or moved abruptly. To his royal public he was certainly a feast for the ears, but not for the eyes. He was not the kind that nobles drew into their circle as one of their own, but rather the kind they slapped on the back. Nor the kind women looked at twice. He did receive, especially in Mannheim, support and friendship from some musicians—instrumentalists and Kapellmeisters—who were more firmly established, but he squandered the friendship of inferior colleagues (and all of them were inferior, really) because of his complete lack of diplomacy, the open and not always innocent display of his superiority. After all, he composed better than they, played better than they—why should he hide it? But one can imagine the feelings of a composer like Giovanni Giuseppe Cambini, for example, whose composition Mozart played from memory in Cambini's presence before other colleagues (April 1778), only to follow it with variations on it in his own manner, as if demonstrating how he would have written it. Cambini did call out, "Questa è una gran Testa!" but what else could he say? "But I am convinced that he did not enjoy it," Mozart wrote to his father (May 1, 1778) and was probably right. No one enjoyed such things, and so Mozart accumulated enemies.

On September 26, 1778, Mozart left Paris with the firm intention not only of delaying the journey home as long as possible but also of taking every opportunity to stop on the way, for a concert or a commission. He arrived in Mannheim on November 6. Six weeks, then, for the Paris–Mannheim stretch: well may we ask what he was doing on the way, how he diverted himself. Eight days in Nancy, where he was happy (there was no place where he was not happier than in Salzburg); more than two weeks in Strasbourg, where he gave three sparsely attended concerts. Two companions on the endless coach journeys are mentioned—an honest German businessman and a dubious comrade about whom we learn only that he had "the French disease," i.e., venereal disease; Mozart had nothing more to say of him. On December 25, 1778, he arrived in Munich. His key experience here was probably his disappointment about his reunion with Aloysia Weber, who had been engaged in Munich as a singer, thanks, not least, to what she had learned from him. She must have let him know unmistakably that there was no question of her marrying him. This "rebuff," the "coldhearted rejection by the newly established prima donna," has been portrayed in every biography as a sign of the inferior character of a coquette. However, we have no evidence that Aloysia ever saw anything more in Mozart than an instructor, albeit an extraordinary one, whose good will and devotion could be exploited. He would have been a burden as a potential lover, even earlier in Mannheim, if his protestations had ever overstepped the bounds of submissiveness. She surely saw all too clearly that he admired her, that she could wrap him around her little finger; but there is no evidence that she tried to do so. She resolutely made use of his admiration in her own interest; but it is not likely that she ever gave him hope of being more than her teacher. He himself, however, never had sufficient sensitivity to assess correctly how people responded to him. Approachability and inaccessibility were qualities that Mozart did not register in his relationships; in the realm of human contact he was always a helpless foreigner. This explains his tie to Constanze, whom he later substituted for her sister Aloysia, and about whose feelings toward Mozart nothing is known. What we read about them is the critic's positive or negative wishful thinking.

A digression: In 1829 Vincent and Mary Novello, a married couple from London, set out on a "pilgrimage to Mozart." Vincent, of Italian origin, was an organist, composer, conductor, and co-founder of the London Philharmonic Society and the publishing house Novello, Ewer, and Company. Mary, of half-German descent, was first and foremost a wife, a "middle-class lady," who called her husband "Vin" and whose favorite word was "delicious." To us they seem the epitome of a cultured bourgeois couple, eager, honest, honorable, solid, more ready than able to understand. The ostensible purpose of the trip was to deliver a gift of £80, which had been collected in London "by enthusiastic admirers of the delightful compositions of Mozart." It was for his surviving sister, the former Nannerl, the widowed Baroness Berchtold zu Sonnenburg, nearly blind and living in poverty. (For Beethoven, whose circumstances they probably underestimated, the admirers had collected £100 a few years earlier.) The real reason for the journey, however, was for Vincent Novello to gather material for a biography of Mozart. He was not equal to the task, but then neither were the first three Mozart biographers, who were nevertheless undaunted by their inadequacy. Novello, on the other hand, never did write his book—for this we are grateful. He was not only too tactful to pump surviving contemporaries but he also refused to listen to reports that disparaged the ideal image of the admired man and the people close to him. He regarded such unwarranted reports, which threatened to destroy his romantic view, as presumptuous. But since both Novellos, independently, kept diaries,[26] we have at least partial portraits of our protagonist filtered through two different informants.

The former Nannerl, now seventy-eight years old, accepted the gift with thanks, but could not give any useful information. The fact that she had hardly known her brother would not have stopped her from conjuring up their shared past, but she was simply too feeble to express herself coherently. Besides, she was probably aware that her sister-in-law, who was also still living in Salzburg (though they did not see each other), had triumphed after Mozart's death and that she was no match for Constanze. Constanze knew how to play her role as informant and hostess to the hilt, and she could afford to do so. At least it speaks well of the two ladies that they seem to have avoided making gibes at each other (something Vincent Novello would have nipped in the bud, in any case).

We will come back to Constanze's statements and to the reports of other survivors. But first, Aloysia.

In the summer of 1829 Aloysia Lange, née Weber, visits Mary Novello in her hotel room in Vienna.[27] Vincent, industrious as ever, has gone out to improve himself intellectually, probably by listening to some unfamiliar Mass. Aloysia, the once celebrated singer, now an old lady of sixty-seven (she will live another ten years), gives Mary the impression of a broken woman lamenting her fate, not without tears. Her revelations must have been a bit embarrassing to the ears of an English-woman accustomed to tact and discretion. Aloysia complains that despite her age she still has to give singing lessons, since her husband, who lives apart from her, does not give her enough money. This is quite possible: Joseph Lange, who was now seventy-eight, lived mostly in the country and may have tried to keep the unhappy memories of his career far from him. But Mary is not much interested in this present misery; her interest is Mozart; she asks about him and Aloysia responds gladly. In reality, Mozart loved her until the end of his life. Mary: Why then did she refuse him in Mannheim and later in Munich? Aloysia: She just was not able to love him. Very plausible. She did not recognize him for what he was. Less plausible, but not out of the question. Her sister was always a little jealous of her. Improbable, but possible—her sister was inclined to jealousy. Mozart was probably better off with Constanze. That is most likely correct. At least, according to Mary, Aloysia spoke of Mozart with much love and with regret. She accused the Viennese of having brought about his ruin. Correct.

This heart-to-heart between the two women seems to us a

worthy moment in Mozart's afterlife, this evocation in a Viennese hotel room on a summer afternoon, thirty-eight years after his death, fifty years after the disappointment of his one-sided love affair. On the one hand, it may seem regrettable that Vincent wasn't present; he would perhaps have sketched a different aspect of her report, for the diary entries of the couple complement and balance each other. On the other hand, Aloysia might not have talked so freely in the presence of a man. Strangely enough, Vincent records no regret that he missed the conversation; he probably thought it was all too personal, none of his business. Neither of the Novellos ever mention Aloysia, Mozart's great love, again.

We learn various things about Aloysia from the notes of her husband, the actor and painter Joseph Lange,[28] whom we will discuss extensively later. She was a prima donna, not only because of her rank in musical life, but also because it was in her nature. Her musical intelligence was outstanding; her piano playing, too, was extraordinary. She had a sure artistic sense and the emotional disposition of a true artist, doubting herself deeply and therefore prey to severe depressions that interfered with her work. For years she suffered from psychosomatic stomach cramps. As she grew older she became melancholy and sickly. She had six children (we know their birth and death dates). Mysteriously, her own brilliance faded with Mozart's death; there is something almost poetic in this fact. Once the original Viennese Donna Anna, a celebrated Constanze in *Die Entführung* on tours to Berlin and Hamburg, she later appeared in charity concerts; she separated from her husband and faded away.

Aloysia was sixteen when Mozart met her in Mannheim. She must have understood that she owed the new direction in her life to his stimulating teaching, but there was no question in her mind of his ever being a lover or husband.

Probably he was not attractive enough physically. That he never recovered from her refusal until the end of his life is at least open to doubt: he was relatively quick to get over human disappointments, and we do not know if they ever really touched him deeply at all. His version of the affair (a later report, to be sure) is different from hers, though not necessarily correct. Three years after their rupture (letter of December 15, 1781), his former goddess seems to him "a false, malicious person and a coquette." Although we consider this assertion untrue, we do understand the purpose of his intentional misrepresentation: by portraying her as a vixen, he was trying to make his father see Constanze, her sister, in a better light. But his father, skeptical to begin with, was in this case also thoroughly forewarned, and Wolfgang's tactic failed.

Loyalty is not one of the qualities we can attribute to geniuses in general or to Mozart in particular, but even if we could, it would not have been a strong point of Mozart's character. On the contrary, disloyalty confronts us here and there, a tiny, hidden "dissonance." But we should not judge it. It is just the all too apparent purposefulness of Mozart's malicious *sorties* that disarms us, if we are indeed forearmed. On April 4, 1787, Mozart writes his father, assuring him (with a bad conscience?) that he had written him an extensive letter but that it never reached his father's hands because of the "stupidity of Madame Storace." "Stupidity" may have struck his father as appropriate, but in reality Mozart found "Madame Storace" anything but stupid: on the contrary, he was in love with her. A parallel instance, then: the beloved is again denounced to the father. Not exactly a nice habit, but not serious.

Nancy (more precisely Anna Selina) Storace, half English, half Italian, enchanting in her portrait, called by Mozart an outstanding singer, was the first Susanna in *Figaro*. He probably found her "incomparable," although to judge by the music he wrote for her, he did not credit her with a range like Aloysia's. As he had done for Aloysia eight years before, he wrote one of his great concert scenas for her, the recitative "Ch'io mi scordi di te" followed by the E-flat major aria "Non temer, amato bene," K. 505 (December 26, 1786). It recalls *Figaro* somewhat, but is more like *opera seria*, colder and distanced. Certainly Mozart did not intend it to be cold, for it was his homage to the twenty-one-year-old girl. In his thematic catalogue he made the significant entry: "For Mlle. Storace and me." In this case "for me" means that the orchestral accompaniment is supplemented by a piano *obbligato* that he himself played at the première, probably in February 1787. It was a rather heavy and not altogether successful combination, attributable to his wish to be near his beloved singer as long as possible, for she was soon to leave Vienna. She died in 1817, and probably possessed some letters from Mozart, which she prudently destroyed.

These two loves, the one, for Aloysia, well documented, the other a secret, define the upper range of Mozart's capacity for love. Here his erotic impulse, probably sublimated, includes the essential element of reverence for the women's artistry. No doubt Mozart idealized these relationships to a certain extent, admiring these women doubly (beloved plus artist). In Aloysia's case, but not Nancy's, his idealization resulted in almost embarrassingly submissive behavior, which is unlikely to have achieved its intended effect on his beloved. The letter he sent from Paris to Aloysia in Mannheim on July 30, 1778, reveals this worshipful pose:

Paris, July 30th, 1778

Dearest Friend!

Please forgive me for not sending you this time the variations I have composed on the aria which you sent me. But I have thought it so necessary to reply as quickly as possible to your father's letter that I have not had time to copy them and therefore cannot let you have them. But you shall certainly have them in my next letter. I am hoping that my sonatas will be engraved very soon—and I shall send in the same parcel the "Popoli di Tessaglia," which is already half finished. If you are as pleased with it as I am, I shall be delighted. Meanwhile until I have the pleasure of hearing from you whether you really like this scena—for, since I have composed it for you alone,—I desire no other praise than yours—I can only say that of all my compositions of this kind—this scena is the best I have ever composed. I shall be delighted if you will set to work as hard as you can at my Andromeda scena "Ah, lo previdi," for I assure you that it will suit you admirably—and that you will do yourself great credit with it. I advise you to watch the expression marks—to think carefully of the meaning and the force of the words—to put yourself in all seriousness into Andromeda's situation and position!—and to imagine that you really are that very person. With your beautiful voice and your fine method of producing it you will undoubtedly soon become an excellent singer, if you continue to work in this way. The greater part of the next letter which I shall have the honor of sending you will consist of a short explanation of the manner in which I should like you to sing and act this scene. At the same time I urge you to work at it for a little by yourself—and then you will see the difference—which will be a very useful lesson for you—although indeed I am quite sure that there won't be very much to correct or alter—and that you will sing my passages in the way I desire—for you know by experience how I like my compositions to be sung. —In the aria "Non so d'onde viene," which you learnt by yourself, I found nothing to criticize or correct—you sang it to me with the interpretation, with the method and the expression which I desired. So I have reason to have every confidence in your ability and knowledge. In short, you are capable—most capable—so that all that I ask you (and this I do beg you most earnestly to do) is to be so good as to reread my letters now and then and to follow my advice—resting assured and convinced that my sole object when I say and when I used to say all these things, is and always will be, to do as much for you as I possibly can.

Dearest friend! I hope that you are in excellent health—

I beg you to take great care of it—for good health is the best thing in the world. Thank God, I am very well, as far as my health is concerned, because I watch it. But my mind is not at rest—nor will it be until I have heard (and what a comfort that will be) that your merits have received their just reward. But my condition and my situation will be the happiest on that day when I shall have the infinite pleasure of serving you again and embracing you with all my heart. This too is all that I can long for and desire, and my only consolation and my sole comfort lie in this hope and desire. Please write to me very often. You have no idea how much pleasure your letters afford me. Please write to me whenever you have been to see Herr Marchand—and tell me something about your study of stage acting—to which I urge you most warmly to apply yourself. Basta, you know that everything that concerns you interests me very greatly. By the way, I have a thousand compliments to deliver from a gentleman—who is the only friend I care about here, and of whom I am very fond, because he is a great friend of your family and had the good fortune and the pleasure of carrying you about in his arms and kissing you hundreds of times when you were still a tiny child. He is Herr Kymli—painter to the Elector. For this friendship I have to thank Raaff who is now my intimate friend, and therefore yours and also the friend of the whole Weber family, knowing, as he does, that he could not be my friend, unless he were yours also. Herr Kymli, who has a great regard for you all, is never tired of talking about you, and I—I never stop talking about you. Hence my sole pleasure is to converse with him; and he, who is a true friend of your whole household and who has heard from Herr Raaff that the greatest kindness he can render me is to talk about you, is forever doing so. Addio, for the present, dearest friend! I am very anxious to get a letter from you. So please do not keep me waiting and do not make me suffer too long. In the hope of having news from you very soon, I kiss your hands, I embrace you with all my heart, and am, and ever shall be, your true and sincere friend

W. A. Mozart

Please embrace your dear mother and all your sisters for me.

This letter is not only literally written in a different language (Italian) but it also speaks a language of its own, that of the distant hopeful admirer. Aside from its instructions, it is conventional and clumsy. Its careful diction of sensibility, and its sentimentality, also make it a letter typical of its time. The essential thing, namely, that the writer is under the spell of the recipient, is not mentioned, but only hinted at. But the fair creature knew that anyway. Her "calculating coldness" has become a cliché of all superficial biographies, a unique and important motif in the score of the "eternal feminine."*

The rupture with Aloysia in Munich took place between the eighth and the thirteenth of January 1779, the last days of the journey that had failed, but also the last days of freedom. Finally, on January 13, Mozart, with a heavy heart, left for Salzburg in the company of his cousin Maria Thekla, or "Bäsle" ("Little Cousin"), whom he had asked to come to Munich.

On January 8 he had finished the Recitative and Aria "Popoli di Tessaglia," K. 316/300b, mentioned in his letter to Aloysia, which he had begun in Paris. At the time he probably still hoped to present it to her in honor of their engagement, again forgetting to think his plans through. For after she had refused him he would not have been in the frame of mind to finish it, even though, as we stated, he was very quick to recover from such "blows." He must have designed the work expressly for Aloysia's type of voice and ability; to judge by this concert aria, she must have had phenomenal volume, as other opinions confirm. Consisting of the recitative "Popoli di Tessaglia" in C minor and the aria "Io non chiedo, eterni Dei" in C major, the scena is a tour de force for a high dramatic soprano; its pathos and declamatory brilliance leave us strangely cold today. It is a virtuoso piece for solo oboe and

* "We see her as a deceptive will-o'-the-wisp. Beautiful as sin, seductive as perdition, blessed by her great art, she pulls the wool over the eyes of the innocent, chaste youth who pleads for her love, pleads in vain, and yet later on receives the love of all mankind." Carola Belmonte, *Die Frauen im Leben Mozarts* (Augsburg and Berlin, 1905), p. 50.

bassoon, too, but primarily for a voice that must know no strain, a prima donna's voice, moving in *concertante* rather than *cantabile* runs, and reaching up in the *stretta* to G above high C. If Aloysia could sing that without sounding comical, she must have had an advantage over other singers even to this day. Of course, today we can hardly judge what was comical then. Strangely (or perhaps significantly) the music of these grand scenes for his sweethearts is totally lacking in any sensuality. It has the splendid, sublime formality of *opera seria*, but no touch of the erotic. Cherubino is still a long way off.

As he writes, Mozart himself felt this scena was the best thing he had ever composed in this genre. We might note that he had not written very *much* in this genre yet. Nevertheless, we feel the concert aria "Ah, lo previdi," K. 272 (August 1777), for example, is more successful in its spareness and restraint, and quite a bit more profound, perhaps because it was written not for his beloved but for the concert singer Josepha Duschek, who was two years older than Mozart and no longer a desirable young girl. Thus, no personal feeling was involved; he could reserve that for the material itself (the tale of Andromeda) and objectify it. Objective distance had from the beginning suited him better. He was always master of the fiction of opera: emotions, but not his own. This aria, too, he gave to Aloysia to sing, and the passage referring to it in his letter ("I advise you to watch the expression marks—to think carefully of the meaning and the force of the words—to put yourself in all seriousness into Andromeda's situation and position!—and to imagine that you really are that very person") bears witness to his deep artistic understanding and his ability to communicate it to others. Suddenly we seem to see a totally different Mozart, the critical and clever judge, a combination of creator and interpreter who, when it is a matter of what really motivates him, drops all jests and banality and silliness. True, at the time of this letter he was still motivated by his love for the singer, but in these lines she is in the background. The thing itself, its correctness and verity, is what counts.

We are always surprised by Mozart's critical objectivity and judiciousness. On November 22, 1777, he wrote to his father from Mannheim:

> At six o'clock today the gala concert took place. I had the pleasure of hearing Herr Fränzl (who is married to a sister of Mme Cannabich) play a concerto on the violin. I like his playing very much. You know that I am no great lover of difficulties. He plays difficult things, but his hearers are not aware that they are difficult; they think that they could at once do the same themselves. That is real playing. He has too a most beautiful, round tone. He never misses a note, you can hear everything. It is all clear-cut. He has a beautiful staccato, played with a single bow, up or down; and I have never heard anyone play a double trill as he does. In a word, in my opinion he is no wizard, but a very sound fiddler.

Here, too, we have the balanced Mozart, who never goes too far with excessive enthusiasm, except where personal relations play a role; then players must be either "incomparable" or "thoroughly stupid." In presenting the facts here, he maintains his sense of proportion and critical equilibrium.

His relations with Aloysia and Nancy occupy one end of his erotic scale. We cannot avoid assigning Constanze to a less lofty position; in her case, fixation and dependency play a part. At the time of his love for Aloysia, and perhaps not only then, there was also someone at the opposite end of the scale, his cousin Bäsle.

He first met Bäsle in 1777 in Augsburg, the second stop on his Paris journey. She was the daughter of Leopold's brother, Franz Alois Mozart, owner and operator of a printing press. A frivolous, lovable girl, she was two years younger than her cousin Wolfgang. We have a portrait of her, a rather dilettantish drawing by an unknown artist, in which her head is out of proportion to her body. She looks robust and pert, decked out stylishly with shawl and bonnet "in the French style." That was the way Cousin Wolfgang, who ordered her portrait from Mannheim, wanted it, probably as a visual aid to his memory of lively hours spent together. But one never knows whether such a superficial portrait actually aids the recipient's memory or just his imagination. In this case, the corners of her mouth would be an anatomical rarity; and the flower held in the girl's hand could hardly be the bloom of chastity. Of her later years we know only a few dates. Her apparently free mode of life resulted in at least one illegitimate child (it has been claimed that a clergyman was the father, but diligent Bäsle scholars have erased this slur on the clergy), and she died as the "life companion" to a postmaster, "advanced in years," on January 25, 1841, in Bayreuth.

Bäsle herself left virtually no records. From the ceremoniously long-winded and downright crude lines to her uncle Leopold on October 16, 1777, we gather that verbal expression was not her strong point. "It is impossable to expres how joyfuly I feel upon the fortunit arrival of my so very dear cousin as well as of his mother . . ." etc. Of course, the letters to her cousin, unfortunately lost, were probably a lot less ceremonious.

From Augsburg, Mozart wrote to his father on October 17, 1777:

> On the morning of this day, the 17th, I write and declare that our little cousin is beautiful, intelligent, charming, clever and gay; and that is because she has mixed with people a great deal, and has also spent some time in Munich. Indeed we two get on extremely well, for, like myself, she is a bit of a scamp. We both laugh at everyone and have great fun.

Mozart was nearly twenty-two at the time. He had written his E-flat Piano Concerto, K. 271, and his great Divertimento in B-flat, K. 287/271H, a few months before. It cannot be denied that in this light his letter seems exceedingly infantile, like the

letter of a sixteen-year-old. But we have by now become accustomed to this incongruity in him. We cannot assume that
the two young people entertained themselves solely by mocking
others; Mozart's later letters to Bäsle are rather clear on this
point. Thus, he writes shortly after their farewell on November 5, 1777, from Mannheim, asking her to deliver his "compliments" to two women, mutual acquaintances:

> And say that I beg the youngest one, Fräulein Josepha, to
> forgive me, why not?— Why should I not beg her to forgive
> me? Strange! Why should I not? Say that she must forgive
> me for not having yet sent her the sonata I promised her and
> that I shall send it as soon as possible. Why not?— What?—
> Why not?— Why should I not send it?— Why should I not
> dispatch it?— Why not?— Strange! I don't know why I
> shouldn't— Well then—you will do me this favor.— Why
> not?— Why should you not do it?— Why not?— Strange! I
> shall do the same for you, when you want me to. Why not?
> Why should I not do it for you? Strange! Why not!—I can't
> think why not?
>
> Do not forget also to send my compliments to the papa
> and mama of the two young ladies, for it is a gross fault to
> forget must shall will have one's duty to father and mother.

The sense of this letter becomes clearer if we substitute for
the word "send" (*schicken*) another that rhymes with it
(*ficken*—"fuck"). For that reason, the writer corrects himself
sanctimoniously and substitutes a synonym for *schicken*
(*übersenden*); but only to release a torrent of verbs to correct
the lapse of forgetting father and mother, thus setting up the
false piety again. In any event, the question "Why not?" must
have occurred to the cousins often enough at the beginning of
their relationship, until they came to see that there was no
reason why they should not "do it." Wolfgang is clearer in a
later letter. "A propos, since I left Augsburg, I have not taken
off my trousers, except at night before going to bed . . ."
(December 3, 1777). A kind of confession of faithfulness.

The legend of Wolferl, the little lad from Salzburg, created in the early nineteenth century and forcibly upheld in order to keep Mozart's life as close as possible to the Sunday-school version, is based on passages like some we have cited. It goes hand in hand with the "chaste youth" legend; the two imply and further each other. But the trouble is that the first is a simplification and the second an extenuation of the true facts—an extenuation, let it be noted, only if we choose to accept the standards of those champions of Mozart's "purity" who would like to deny their hero, even at the age of twenty-two, the right to sexual intercourse. It is hard to understand why, unless it is because they object to illegitimacy. In the nineteenth century people believed they had to credit the "great masters" with all the qualities they took for virtues, especially abstinence in every sense (they were even reluctant to grant drinkers their wine), in order to make them into moral examples. For that reason, they simply denied them any trait the middle class would consider a vice. For biographies had not only to be edifying, they also had to encourage emulation of the great—as if the "simple mortal" might raise himself to the level of geniuses by upholding their standards and living up to their imagined virtues. Thus, the genius became the victim of his chroniclers' fantasy, and of their lack of it, and especially of their categorical definitions of what ought to have been. Anton Schindler destroyed two-thirds of Beethoven's conversation notebooks, with the result that their contents will always be the subject of vague speculation, and an opportunity for fantasy. And thus he achieved precisely the outcome he wished to prevent.

On August 28, 1799, Constanze Mozart wrote to the publishers Breitkopf and Härtel, who were planning a life of Mozart: ". . . the letters to his cousin are tasteless, of course, but very humorous and deserve mention, although they should not be printed in their entirety." And she added, "I hope you will not print anything without letting me read it first." At least she acknowledged that the Bäsle letters were worth mentioning, which is to her credit. But here already we encounter that right of the widow, which has since become a well-established tradition. Constanze may also have destroyed a number of Mozart's letters, and especially letters from her enemy Leopold Mozart to his son. Her second husband, Georg Nicolaus Nissen, rendered many passages in the letters illegible—but not illegible enough: most of them were deciphered anyway. Nissen's successors have done everything possible to force posterity to accept as fact their wishful notion of the eternal boy-man, a mixture of lucid Apollonian, innocent child of nature, and radiant darling of the muses.

In the twentieth century people claim to be enlightened, and smile condescendingly at the narrow views, the prudish discretion, of their naïve predecessors. With excuses and regrets for the dark places of the artist's psyche, which they cannot do anything about, they admit that in addition to everything else Mozart was "human." In· this connection "human" always means the opposite of higher things and has a negative value. We are always asked not to hold it against the hero for having this side, too. Stefan Zweig, who owned the originals of most of the Bäsle letters, sent a copy of them to Freud in 1931,[29] with an accompanying letter:

> I hope that you, as one who understands the heights and depths, will find the enclosed private printing, which I am making available only to a *narrow* circle, not entirely irrelevant: these nine letters of the 21-year-old Mozart, of which I publish *one* here in its entirety, throw a psychologically very remarkable light on his erotic nature, which, more so than that of any other important man, has elements of infantilism and coprophilia. It would actually be an interesting study for one of your pupils, for all the letters revolve consistently around the same theme.

This characterization of Mozart is without doubt correct, even if the secretiveness in handling the letters amuses us today. Even Stefan Zweig felt that predispositions of this kind should not be everybody's business, and that biographies must of necessity omit certain things. He followed this precept in his own biographical works. Although it is entirely incorrect to say that all the letters revolve around the same theme, eight of the nine letters do contain a scatological element. This theme also runs like a sporadically recurring melody throughout the score of his extramusical life. But Zweig is wrong when he calls coprophilia a part of Mozart's erotic nature. The two predispositions are totally separate; it is just that they coincide in his relationship to Bäsle, who belonged to the "low zone" of his erotic attachments.

Bäsle was presumably Mozart's first love. Biographers usually refrain from more precise definitions and intentionally obscure the affair, making light of it. Einstein calls it "teasing," Schurig a "proper little love affair!" (even here, it seems, a genius must conform to the rules); Paumgartner finds that Mozart didn't scrimp "with his cousinly friendship"; Erich Schenk contends that the attachment was a "charming, playful relationship."[30] "A quite harmless, gay flirtation that developed between the two young people," writes Abert. Like most others, he is embarrassed by the affair and is forced to use an airy vocabulary to dismiss it. Yet others (I won't take the trouble to name them) speak of the "high-spirited Mozart," the "clownish Mozart," the "coarsely comic joker," who is engaging on the one hand in an "amorous dalliance" and on the other in "foolish pranks." The reader can make his own choice.

Regarding this relationship, one could argue that a man of genius has a right to demand our discretion, since his genius is revealed only in his works. But this argument has become irrelevant: we know that we must examine a great *oeuvre* under the aspect of all the elements of its creator's life, even when, as in this case, they do not ultimately reveal it. An attempt can fail only if it is made; we learn from the failure.

Besides, it is too late now to doubt our right to investigate his life and even to ferret out bedroom secrets. The secrets are already public property. They are adulterated victims of the inaccuracy of popular authors, those awful simplifiers, who begin by repressing their own fallibilities and end, necessarily, by censoring their hero's, insofar as they do not actually reprove him for that which is also latent in themselves. Under these conditions, making all the material available can serve to defend the subject, even where it seems to reveal something "negative." As in the case of Beethoven, we are suspicious of the "purity" zealots. Their standards of purity are modeled on their own ego, as they themselves perceive it; the sinister depth of this ego is hidden from them, and manifests itself as a perverse moral stance at the wrong time. Their version of what a man like Mozart was like need not concern us.

The question of the true relationship between Mozart and his Bäsle would concern us a lot less (at some point, all men and women have to confront the facts of nature, and someone then has to play the role of partner—in this case it happened to be Maria Anna Thekla) if it had not stimulated an aspect of his productivity that is by no means insignificant. It is part of Mozart, integral to him. In these letters to Bäsle (though not exclusively in them) a certain side of Mozart's character is revealed especially clearly, indeed insistently. And in truth the letters, especially if read superficially, give a picture of a peculiar infantilism, and not just because they often revel in descriptions of the processes and functions of the lower body, although that is the main reason they were so long unpublished. A selection transcribed into High German, abridged and therefore bowdlerized, was the only one considered suitable for middle-class bookshelves. Granted, the letters are not always appetizing, especially if we put ourselves in the situations they suggest. Furthermore, in the eighteenth century and earlier, the bodily functions and their organs were called not by their Latin names but by their vulgar ones.

And the Mozart family, especially, was particularly drawn to fecal comedy, with the possible exception of Nannerl, who, with a colorlessness that was almost intense, seems not to have permitted herself even this kind of self-expression.

But fecal parlance apparently fires Mozart's verbal fantasy with unbounded joy at the prospect of possible variations on this theme. His imagination grows immediately beyond the purely abstract; but his onomatopoetic variations return again and again to this linguistic treasure trove. The chain of associations seems to work like a rondo. Kindled by anality, it always returns to it, at least in the letters to Bäsle, where associations usually remain below the belt, ostensibly at least. On February 28, 1778, Mozart writes to her:

Perhaps you think or are even convinced that I am dead? That I have pegged out? Or hopped a twig? Not at all. Don't believe it, I implore you. For believing and shitting are two very different things! Now how could I be writing such a beautiful hand if I were dead? How could that be possible? I shan't apologize for my very long silence, for you would never believe me. Yet what is true is true. I have had so many things to do that I had time indeed to think of my little cousin, but not to write, you see. So I just had to let things be. But now I have the honor to inquire how you are and whether you perspire? Whether your stomach is still in good order? Whether indeed you have no disorder? Whether you still can like me at all? Whether with chalk you often scrawl? Whether now and then you have me in mind? Whether to hang yourself you sometimes feel inclined? Whether you have been wild? With this poor foolish child? Whether to make peace with me you'll be so kind? If not, I swear I'll let off one behind! Ah, you're laughing! Victoria! Our arses shall be the symbol of our peacemaking! I knew that you wouldn't be able to resist me much longer. Why, of course, I'm sure of success, even if today I should make a mess, though to Paris I go in a fortnight or less. So if you want to send a reply to me from that town of Augsburg yonder, you see, then write at once, the sooner the better, so that I may be sure to receive your letter, or else if I'm gone

I'll have the bad luck, instead of a letter to get some muck. Muck!—Muck!— Ah, muck! Oh, sweet word! Muck! chuck! That too is fine. Muck, chuck!—muck!—suck—oh, charmante! muck, suck! That's what I like! Muck, chuck and suck! Chuck muck and suck muck!

Now for something else. When the carnival was on, did you have some good fun? One can have far more fun at this time in Augsburg than here. How I wish I were with you so that we could run about together. Mama and I send our greetings to your father and mother and to you, little cousin, and we trust all three of you are well and in good spirits. Praise and thanks be to God, we are in good health. Don't believe it. All the better, better the all. A propos, how are you getting on with your French? May I soon send you a whole letter in French? You would like one from Paris, would you not? Do tell me whether you still have that Spuni Cuni business?

"Spuni Cuni" are among the secret words that recur in these letters. Unfortunately, we can no longer determine their meaning. From the context they might be erotically suggestive; it remains a profitable object of speculation. The *toccata* of this letter virtually reproduces the act of composition itself, associative garlands of short note values. In between are recitative-like exclamations: "Oh, sweet word!" (probably Mozart had been reading a libretto with the exclamation "*O dolce parola*").

Infantilism, without doubt. He never entirely outgrew it; we still find similar passages in his last letters. But it is more than that. Mozart's verbal fantasy is ignited not least by convention and the forms of its articulation. His extraordinarily developed comic sense, which later sometimes took on daemonic dimensions, responded directly to these external stimuli, to rituals and requisites, to situations created by the banality of daily life. This sort of thing set a mechanism within him in motion, a kind of compulsion to vary any theme, like those impassioned spoonerists who, to the agony of those present not sharing their urge, continually succumb to their need to twist words. A combination of words, a metaphor, however insipid and tasteless, in writing or said aloud, suddenly takes on a new aspect in the glaring light of the absurd, becomes ludicrous, like a doll that one stares at without blinking, and opens up undreamed-of possibilities for variation.

For example, in accordance with custom, Mozart, in his letters to his father, greets all his Salzburg acquaintances with perfunctory and dreary regularity. But gradually he becomes aware of the absurdity of this custom. He proclaims its absurdity in the letter of October 25, 1777, and closes, still in comic irritation:

> Well, addio. I again kiss Papa's hands and embrace my sister and send greetings to all my good friends; and now off to the closet run I, where perchance shit muck shall I, and ever the same fool am I.
>
> Wolfgang et Amadeus Mozarty
> Augsburg, Octobery 25th,
> seventeen hundred and seventy seveny.

Here, as so often, he anticipates the charge of foolishness before it is made. Significantly, it is only in letters like these that he calls himself "Amadeus." Shortly thereafter (November 26, 1777) the much-abused custom of greeting absolutely everyone is parodied more pointedly and radically in the postscript to his mother's letter to his father. He has grown sick of the custom; in a state of desperate fatigue, which is transformed into a fierce delight in absurdity, he composes a list of friends, acquaintances, patrons and fictional characters, whipping it into a *stretta* of suppressed fury:

> If I could find some more room, I would send 100,000 compliments from us 2, I mean, from us two, to all our good friends: particularly to the A's:—the Adlgassers, Andretters and Arco (Count); B's:—Herren Bullinger, Barisani and Berantzky; C's:—Czernin (Count), Cusetti and the three organ pumpers [*Calcanten*]; D's:—Herren Daser, Deibl and Dommeseer; E's:—Mlle Barbara Eberlin, Herr Estlinger and all the asses [*Esln*] in Salzburg; F's:—Firmian (Count and Countess and their little molly-coddle), young Franz and the Freihof of St. Peter's; G's:—Mlle, Mme and the two

MM. Gilowsky and the Councillor too; also Herren Grétry and Gablerbrey; H's:—the Haydns, Hagenauers, Theresa Höllbrey: J's:—Joli (Miss Sallerl), Herr Janitsch the fiddler and Hagenauer's Jakob; K's:—Herr and Frau von Küsinger, Count and Countess Kühnburg and Herr Kassel; L's:— Baron Lehrbach, Count and Countess Lützow, Count and Countess Lodron; M's:—Herren Meisner, Medlhammer and Moserbrey; N's:—Nannerl, our court ninny, Father Florian, and all night watchmen; O's:—Count Oxenstirn, Herr Overseer and all the oxen in Salzburg: P's:—the Prexes, Count Prank, the Lord High Cook, and Count Perusa; Q's:— Herren Quilibet, Quodlibet and all quacks; R's—Father Florian Reichsigel, the Robinigs and Maestro Rust; S's:— Herren Suscipe, Seiffert and all the sows in Salzburg; T's:— Herr Tanzberger, our butcher, Theresa and all trumpeters; U's:—the towns of Ulm and Utrecht and all the clocks [*Uhren*] in Salzburg, especially if you put an H in at the beginning; W's:—the Weisers, Hans the Wurstmaker and Woferl; X's:—Xantippe, Xerxes and all whose names begin with an X; Y's:—Herr Ypsilon, Herr Ybrig and all whose names begin with a Y; and, lastly, Z's:—Herr Zabuesnig, Herr Zonca and Herr Zezi at the castle. Addio. If I had room I would write something more, at least my compliments to my good friends. But it is impossible, for I don't know where I could work them in. I can't write anything sensible today, as I am rails off the quite. Papa be annoyed not must. I that just like today feel. I help it cannot. Warefell. I gish you nood wight. Sound sleeply. Next time I'll sensible more writely.

But of course this comic despair, too, is only an escape. For his father, indignant at his son's aimlessness, had been pressuring him again and again in every letter to report on his plans and prospects. Thus, this letter, in its painstaking detail, its alphabetical debauch, also bears witness to a kind of repression. Since there was no occasion for optimism about his professional life, he put thoughts of the future from him in favor of his game-playing mechanisms, and at that time still with temporary success. His father was perplexed—but then his son always perplexed him.

The word "humor" is much abused. Its meaning changes not only with each possessor of this so-called quality but also with the intellectual capacity of the person using the word. Among the supremely gifted (who do not have an exclusive right to humor, much as we wish they did—for the standard of tolerability sinks rapidly on lower levels), a humorous bent does not spring from the wish to contribute to merry-making or to see the world happy. On the contrary, it comes from the urge to emphasize the weight of daily living, the "business of life" (Cesare Pavese) by setting up levity as a counterpoint to its gravity, by emphasizing the absurd, by fiercely underlining what is grotesque, paradoxical, unjust. To be sure, the process is usually unconscious, as is the fear of revealing oneself by being serious. Unconscious, too, is the reluctance to communicate, to have to generalize one's private reality and therefore be exposed to the misunderstanding of others, who are not worthy of communication. So humor becomes a handy means of self-protection and is consciously used in that way. It serves as a cloak to make the wearer unrecognizable. Assuming the garments of another, lesser person, the cloaked figure can withdraw from intercourse and allow the illusory disguised figure to enter the ranks of the jokers and fools. The highly talented are also convinced that it is best for all concerned to drown out the "earnestness of life" with fun, if not silliness; or at least to prevent any mutuality of perception between the ego and the despised Other. The charge of insufficient dignity or, in Mozart's case, childish behavior is taken gladly into the bargain; it is proof of the world's misunderstanding, the impossibility of communicating in conventional language, and it justifies the joker's mode of behavior.

And yet it is rare to find humor in those whose genius is not verbal: from Beethoven to Gustav Mahler there extends an exemplary line of great men who seem never to have laughed; their minds were allied exclusively with poetic minds of similar bent. It was oppressive elitist solemnity that linked Schoenberg with Stefan George; the absence of laughter is probably also the only thing that the latter had in common with Rilke.

Mozart was different; his sense of humor was boundless and unbounded, though not sublime. The haughty, witty retort was not his style; he lacked not only the education for it but also the desire and ability to adapt to the mentality of his partner. We know of no authenticated clever rejoinder from him, and all evidence of his ready wit belongs in the realm of legend. But otherwise he mastered the range of humor from low almost to high; he adapted it to the occasion. Already as a youth he had a spontaneous, exuberant inventiveness. On August 14, 1773, he wrote from Vienna to his sister, adding a postscript to a letter from his father to his mother:

> Weather permitting. [His father had probably just said these words, and they "were in the air."]
> I hope, my queen, that you are enjoying the highest degree of health and that now and then or rather, sometimes, or, better still, occasionally, or, even better still, qualche volta, as the Italians say, you will sacrifice for my benefit some of your important and intimate thoughts, which ever proceed from that very fine and clear reasoning power, which in addition to your beauty, and although from a woman, and particularly from one of such tender years, almost nothing of the kind is ever expected, you possess, O queen, so abundantly as to put men and even graybeards to shame. There now, you have a well-turned sentence. Farewell.
>
> Wolfgang Mozart

These chains of association also dominate the Bäsle letters in part, but there they are directed to lapidary functions or to intimate insinuations. Only much later, toward the end of his life, does he add a sophisticated self-deprecation. In between lies the level of the truly banal, which he parodied in more articulate moments. Even when a situation called for seriousness, this recurrent banality, which we find rather disconcerting, was one of his anchors to the everyday world. There is also, from time to time, a kind of tavern humor which (let's admit it) embarrasses us. Thus on October 2, 1782, he wrote to the Baroness Waldstätten, patron and friend of the first Viennese years, accomplice to his marriage plans and their realization:

> I can say with truth that I am a very happy and a very unhappy man—unhappy since the night when I saw your Ladyship at the ball with your hair so beautifully dressed—for —gone is my peace of mind! Nothing but sighs and groans! During the rest of the time I spent at the ball I did not dance—I skipped. Supper was already ordered, but I did not eat—I gobbled. During the night instead of slumbering softly and sweetly—I slept like a dormouse and snored like a bear and (without undue presumption) I should almost be prepared to wager that your Ladyship had the same experience *à proportion!* You smile! you blush! Ah, yes—I am indeed happy. My fortune is made! But alas! Who taps me on the shoulder? Who peeps into my letter? Alas, alas, alas! My wife! Well, well, in the name of Heaven, I have taken her and must keep her! What is to be done?

The Baroness, a lighthearted lady, living apart from her husband, and of no very good reputation (a matter of indifference to her), probably took these confessions as they were intended: perhaps she even found the letter funny. Incidentally, Mozart borrowed money from her shortly thereafter: perhaps she was his first creditor.

The Bäsle letters are unique in their own way. If Mozart had been merely a talented man, he would have been considered doubly gifted. But with a genius, this kind of speculative classification is superfluous. The concept of a double-genius would be senseless, since part of the essence of genius is the possession of other latent or potential capabilities. They usually never come to the fore, since they are overshadowed by a great ruling one (except with the Renaissance man, who did not yet experience the difference in disciplines as an inner law). The artistic genius who produces something good, perhaps even great, in an area other than his own is the exception. William Blake was master (if you will) of two disciplines that complement each other and perhaps even share a visionary intensity, although he was not a good enough draftsman to express it in his drawing. Goethe was a bungler as a draftsman and as a scientist a dreamer, albeit one with inspired intuitions. Mozart's musical genius shines out in his words as well, when he manipulates them like musical associations; thus, their information retreats into the background in favor of conjured-up images. His active verbal fantasy comes to dominate, triggered by the slightest excuse. His compulsive delight and ease in association are capable not only of producing euphony and rhythm with disparate and seemingly arbitrary combinations of sound but also of keeping the connotations always in mind. In writing he yields himself up to the flow of words, going far beyond the comprehensible, reveling on, intoxicated by the sounds and the continually changing meanings they suggest. In this intoxication the inhibitions of convention and bourgeois taste fall by the wayside. On November 13, 1777, Mozart wrote to Bäsle from Mannheim:

> Now do send her a sensible letter for once. You can make jokes in it all the same. But tell her that you have received all your letters which she forwarded, so that she may no longer worry and fret.
>
> Ma très chère nièce! cousine! fille! mère, soeur et épouse!
>
> Bless my soul, a thousand curses, Croatians, damnations, devils, witches, sorcerers, hell's battalions to all eternity, by all the elements, air, water, earth and fire, Europe, Asia, Africa and America, Jesuits, Augustinians, Benedictines, Capuchins, Minorites, Franciscans, Dominicans, Carthusians and Brothers of the Holy Cross, Canons regular and irregular, all slackers, knaves, cowards, sluggards and toadies higgledy-piggledy, asses, buffaloes, oxen, fools, nitwits and dunces! What sort of behavior is that, my dears—four smart soldiers and three bandoliers? . . . Such a parcel to get, but

no portrait as yet! I was all eagerness—in fact, I was quite sure—for you yourself had written the other day that I was to have it soon, very, very soon. Perhaps you doubt that I shall keep my word? Surely you do not doubt me? Well, anyhow, I implore you to send me yours—the sooner, the better. And I trust that you will have it done, as I urged you, in French costume.

How do I like Mannheim? As well as I could like any place without my little cousin. Forgive my wretched writing, but the pen is already worn to a shred, and I've been shitting, so 'tis said, nigh twenty-two years through the same old hole, which is not yet frayed one whit, though I've used it daily to shit, and each time the muck with my teeth I've bit.

On the other hand, I hope that, however that may be, you have received all my letters, that is, one from Hohenaltheim and two from Mannheim; and this one, however that may be, is my third letter from Mannheim, but the fourth in all, however that may be. Now I must close, however that may be, for I am not yet dressed and we are lunching this very moment, so that after that we may shit again, however that may be. Do go on loving me, as I love you, then we shall never cease loving one another, though the lion hovers round the walls, though doubt's hard victory has not been weighed and the tyrant's frenzy has crept to decay; yet Codrus, the wise philosopher, often eats soot instead of porridge, and the Romans, the props of my arse, have always been and ever will be—half-castes. Adieu. J'espère que vous aurez déjà pris quelque lection dans la langue française, et je ne doute point que—écoutez—que vous saurez bientôt mieux le français que moi; car il y a certainement deux ans que je n'ai pas écrit un mot dans cette langue. Adieu cependant. Je vous baise vos mains, votre visage, vos genoux, et votre—enfin, tout ce que vous me permettez de baiser. Je suis de tout mon coeur

votre très affectionné neveu et cousin
Wolfgang Amadè Mozart

An elemental outburst. And at the same time an artificial text, totally under control, with no useful information for today's reader, but with great powers of suggestion. The introductory self-admonition is due most certainly to a conversation with his mother, who sat in the room as he wrote. At work on some handicraft, perhaps, or idle, but hardly disapproving. He does not follow his own admonition; it is only an introduction, after which the curtain rises. The performance begins with bombastic levity; a cavalcade roars onto the battlefield, a procession of dignitaries and indignitaries, the jester cavorting behind them, and all this only to curse the more strongly that his Bäsle had not sent him the apparently promised portrait (it came later). There follow the inevitable fecal jokes, after that the list of the letters he has written which, as always, he remembers exactly; this flows into the evocation of their love affair as a parodied drama; we are in *opera seria*, but also in a tragedy popular at the time, whose characters he degrades into props for his arse; thus, it continues, like a recitative, toward the fermata of the final cadence, the (puzzling) word "half-castes." The last section, resembling a française, is a *stretta* to end the composition. In it he cautiously conveys his suggestive, and therefore essential, message, only to break off before the intended climax: "Je vous baise vos mains, votre visage, vos genoux et votre—" The completion is found perhaps in a much later letter to Constanze (May 19, 1789) in which he evokes her "lovable, kissable little arse."

Whether this letter gave Bäsle as much pleasure as it gives us can no longer be ascertained. Its explosive spirit cannot have been entirely alien to Maria Anna Thekla, even if she did not thoroughly understand the dramatic apparatus he conjured up.

She was probably a simple creature, who earns our respect in areas other than the intellectual, for after this exchange of letters she enters Mozart's life once more. At the end of his lamentably unsuccessful journey, he calls her to Munich (December 23, 1778), where, as he writes, she may perhaps be given "a great part to play." The kind of part is not completely clear; the only certain thing is that it was not the role Bäsle was hoping for. At best it can only have been the *"terza*

persona" at his projected betrothal to Aloysia, although we
don't know what she would have done there—acted as a kind
of bridesmaid? Be that as it may, the plan says nothing for
Mozart's delicacy but confirms, rather, his unfamiliarity with
human interactions. Bäsle did in fact come to Munich, but
the engagement did not take place. So Wolfgang consoled
himself with her in his bitter disappointment over the journey's
crowning failure. She had to bear with him, and accompany
him on his delayed return to Salzburg, the hated city, back to
his strict and embittered father, and back into the Archbishop's service: the return of a beaten man. It was not a
particularly easy role for his cousin, who would doubtless have
preferred marrying him to keeping him amused for a few
weeks. It speaks well of her character that she resigned herself
to the role of friend (although it is probable that their relationship during the short time in Salzburg was not entirely
platonic). It may be that her emotional life was not particularly deep, as has been asserted (and is always asserted, whenever the configuration of Mozart's relationships offers the
chance to detract from his partner's importance). We at least
can remember her with the appreciation she deserves. Though
he was far beyond her, though she hardly can have guessed at
his greatness, it probably meant a good deal to her cousin that
she stood by him in moments of deep dejection and gave him
what she had to give; otherwise he would not have had her
come to Munich. To us at least it is important that she inspired him to write documents of unique value, demonstrating
a facet of his personality which never appeared again with
such intensity.

It is because of Aloysia and Bäsle, these two opposite
ends of the scale, that some people have asserted that Mozart
led a double life. Double lives, however, are lived consciously;
they are always the active fulfillment of a double morality.
But the behavior of geniuses, and indeed of artists in general,
is determined and ordered by their work. Certainly there are

instances when a man's life runs in profound counterpoint to the creation of his *oeuvre*, but these depths are usually kept quiet and the evidence destroyed. As for morality, in Mozart's case it cannot be denied that his erotic life was played out on various levels of consciousness, expressed, if at all, in extremely different ways. Sometimes, if it was not Mozart we were talking about, we would have to assume that his was a rather philistine, bachelor-dinner morality, especially at the time when Aloysia, the goddess, still hovers like a vision in the future, while Bäsle, the sex object, is treated significantly more brusquely. This intimacy, these premarital "little sins," would naturally have to be kept hidden from the sublime Aloysia. After the wedding everything would be different. One could, of course, argue that the milieu of Bäsle's home, headed by her father, an upright citizen and honorable craftsman, was significantly more respectable than that of Fridolin Weber, the copyist and prompter, and also, as the father of four daughters, a ruined man.

The Bäsle letters reflect unsentimental pleasure in common memories and perhaps the hope of reliving them, or at least of finding a substitute for them. The letter to Aloysia breathes the timorous hope of the admirer who expects to be rejected, but it also expresses what was probably justifiable admiration for her art. At the same time, he also knew the two Cannabich women, who kept him busy, each in her own way. Cannabich, some of whose compositions, incidentally, are still worth listening to, was the Kapellmeister of the famous Mannheim orchestra. His wife Elisabeth, who apparently consoled Wolfgang after his sad return from Paris, was at this time about forty years old and in the last months of her sixth pregnancy. At the time of his nearly daily visits to this household, her social style seems so coarse that we would be inclined to doubt his reports about her, even if his intentions had been laudable (they were not). Rather loose language must have been typical of this circle of serious if by no means outstanding musicians; as Mozart wrote to his father (November 14, 1777), there was much talk "of muck, shitting and arse-licking"; he probably would not have partaken so "godlessly" if the "ring-leader, known under the name of Lisel (Elisabetha Cannabich) had not egged [him] on and incited [him]." Wolfgang wrote this to his father with his usual undiplomatic frankness. His father of course reacted sharply, not because of the activities described in the letter, but because it revealed a lack of seriousness and an obvious waste of time.

While "Elisabetha" apparently possessed certain Bäsle-like traits, her oldest child, thirteen-year-old Rose, inclined more toward Aloysia's end of the scale, although, of course, she lacked her "*grandezza*" and probably also her deportment. She was Mozart's piano student, and he portrayed her in music (she is unique in this regard). He calls her (December 6, 1777) "a very pretty and charming girl" (to this extent he swings to the other end of the scale) who is "very intelligent and steady for her age; . . . she is serious, does not say much, but when she does speak, she is pleasant and amiable." This virtuous listing of her virtuous qualities makes us almost uneasy, as if there were something wrong. But since, as we know, Aloysia occupied first place in his heart, it is probably a matter of a parallel inclination. We can conclude from it that Wolfgang also responded to steadiness and seriousness, or at least to what he thought were symptoms of these qualities. In the twenty-two-year-old's letters, cut to measure for his father, we see a tinge of the hypocrite, the evidence of a feigned taste for virtue.

Our distance in time enables us, in contrast to his contemporaries, to see synchronisms in Mozart's life: all these relationships were going on simultaneously, although the affair with Bäsle was conducted only by letter at this point. So there is, undoubtedly, a priggish quality to these documents; but it is only simulated, and therefore somewhat double-edged: at this time, and in general, Mozart was concerned to present himself to his father as sober, to compensate for his lapses. Naturally Leopold didn't buy it, and with good reason.

Rose Cannabich, then (of all people), he portrayed musically in the Sonata in C, K. 309/284b (November 1777), written for teaching purposes and therefore a portrait to be played by its subject. According to Abert, the girl must have been "rather a rogue," to judge by this sonata. This opinion seems incomprehensible to us, even if we were to regard the whole sonata as her likeness (which is not the case), for it is written in what Leopold Mozart called "the rather artificial Mannheim style." But, as Mozart explained to the violinist Christian Danner, it was only the andante that he modeled on her, and he felt that that was successful: "like the andante, so the girl." And in fact this image of the girl seems to agree with the one he gave his father: serious, modest, steady, well-behaved, rather boring. It seems this pupil did not inspire him all that much, and one might ask whether the restraint, the simplicity of musical thought (unusual even in the Mozart of that time), exhausting itself in the elaboration of an already simple theme, might not be intended as gently ironic. But that is improbable, for the movement has all the character of a reverie, sentimental to the point of being elegiac; most of its liveliness comes from an excess of dynamic markings which the musical content does not justify. Mozart's over-emphasis on the contrasts between *forte* and *piano* would indicate a strange (and unique) overestimation of the material that the markings are meant to serve. "Pretty" would be the right word for these mannered figurations—Leopold may have been right in considering them artificial. But Rose Cannabich really was very pretty, as we learn from the painter Wilhelm von Kobell, who spoke enthusiastically about her appearance.

As far as we know, this middle movement of a sonata is the only one of Mozart's compositions intended as the portrait of a real person. We would have liked more such portraits. Not that they would tell us anything about their models, but they might have illuminated one facet of their creator's subjective vision and proved that now and again he did take cognizance of another human being.

For Mozart was an imperfect connoisseur of people—on the surface. Of course, he never tried to know them; his need for personal contact did not extend so far. It was his father's habit, not his, to assess people for their potential usefulness (it probably would have helped Mozart had he done more of that). Pragmatic thinking was alien to him. But he was by no means totally free of feelings of envy; he was ultimately no superman in his reactions to his fellows. Besides, his kind of life at times forced emotions on him that his reason would perhaps have rejected. Just as a mathematical genius sometimes fails at simple addition, being at home in loftier regions of thought, so Mozart was incompetent in his judgments of people, for he perceived them mainly in terms of the qualities that fitted in with his pattern of thinking. Thus, throughout his life he was prepared to overlook weaknesses in anyone who was close to him artistically or who promised some kind of enrichment. He must have incorporated some traits of people he knew in the psychological conceptions of his operatic characters—it cannot be otherwise. To a certain degree he used traits of the singers for whom he wrote the roles. But he certainly wasn't conscious of his choice of models. The grand dimensions of the characters in his great operas indicate that some talent for characterization must have lain inherent in him, ready to be awakened by one or another singer. Luigi Bassi, from Pesaro, who was twenty-two when he created the role of Don Giovanni, is said to have been an outstanding actor, but it is unlikely that he was the decisive inspiration for the role. Mozart did not classify his fellow men according to their artistry, character, or appearance. Mozart's relationship to a singer or student was determined by the latter's development under his aegis, i.e., by his role in Mozart's consciousness; the rest did not concern him. Certainly, the process of building an operatic character was conscious, but he probably would not have had an answer if asked where the musical idea for a figure like Osmin or Basilio came from. He just invented them. And his invention was always of inferior quality when he had no human original as a model; when he sought in vain within himself and heard no inner echo; and when humanity had to be presented not as an individual quality but as a principle—Sarastro, for example.

Superficially, then, Mozart's conscious judgments of people (which he probably would not have called judgments) are usually wide of the mark or self-contradictory. But because he usually has a definite reason for his judgments, and because they are therefore so often aimed at one particular end, they never make claims to general validity. Still, there are places in the letters where his unbelievably precise observations would seem to refute our statement. On closer examination, however, we notice that they are less evidence of an understanding of human nature than of a superior stage instinct, with exact descriptions of scenes and their possible effect on an audience. At the beginning of his trip, on October 11, 1777, Mozart writes a postscript from Munich to his father:

> A certain Court Councillor, Effele by name, who is one of the best Court Councillors here, sends his most humble greetings to Papa. He could have been Chancellor long ago, but for one thing—his love of the bottle. When I first saw him at Albert's, I thought, and so did Mama, "Goodness me, what a superlative idiot!" Just picture him, a very tall fellow, strongly built, rather corpulent, with a perfectly absurd face. When he crosses the room to go to another table, he places both hands on his stomach, bends over them and hoists his belly aloft, nods his head and then draws back his right foot with great rapidity. And he performs the same trick afresh for every person in turn.

This "Effele" was a certain Andreas Felix Oefele. The cultivated secretary of Duke Clemens Franz of Bavaria, he was already seventy at the time, and the victim of a stroke,[31] which Mozart of course did not know. Otherwise he would have criticized the man's physiological eccentricities, such as slurping beverages, less harshly. Well known for his sharp opinions, Mozart was also touched and softened by physical or pecuniary misfortune. During this stay in Munich, a rather pathetic reunion took place with the gifted composer Joseph Mysliweczek, whom Mozart had known in Bologna and who, after a dissipated and prodigal life, was wasting away in Munich, disfigured by syphilis. The meeting moved Mozart to tears.

On December 27, 1777, Mozart wrote from Mannheim to his father:

> I have now added Herr Wieland to the list of my acquaintances. But he doesn't know as much about me as I know about him, for he has never heard any of my compositions. I had imagined him to be quite different from what I found him. He strikes you as slightly affected in his speech. He has a rather childish voice: he keeps on quizzing you over his glasses; he indulges in a sort of pedantic rudeness, mingled occasionally with a stupid condescension. But I am not surprised that he permits himself such behavior here, even though he may be quite different in Weimar and elsewhere, for people stare at him as if he had dropped from Heaven. Everyone seems embarrassed in his presence, no one says a word or moves an inch; all listen intently to every word he utters; and it's a pity they often have to wait so long, for he has a defect of speech that makes him speak very slowly and he can't say half a dozen words without stopping. Apart from that, he is what we all know him to be, a most gifted fellow. He has a frightfully ugly face, covered with pockmarks, and he has a rather long nose. In height he is, I should say, a little taller than Papa.

So much for the poet Wieland. The observation is clear and complete: the pedantic rudeness, the stupid condescension (all conceivable), and yet, let us be fair, a most gifted fellow, nothing against his mind. Fairness rules the description; it is unclouded by any emotion. After this portrayal we hardly need any imagination of our own to picture him; we can even hear the little speech defect, which Mozart then gave to his Curzio in *Figaro* (though Michael Kelly, the first singer of the role, claimed this idea for himself).

Nowhere is the lack of human insight revealed more clearly than during his great journey, in those letters from Mannheim and Paris; they show that Mozart assessed his own father incorrectly. In the letters he is always under the delusion that he appears credible to his father. Apparently he never learned from experience that this was not the case; that, on the contrary, his father was never taken in by any of the plans, which were probably stupid, or by the assurances of circumspection or of good sense. Naïve is hardly the right word for the way in which Wolfgang tells his father about his extravagant plans at exactly the wrong moment, just when gravity and determination are expected of him. It is virtually incomprehensible that he could have mentioned the plan of an Italian journey with the Weber family (February 4, 1778) without trepidation; unimaginable that he hoped his father would catch fire at this idea and help with letters of reference (as Wolfgang wished) to pave the way in Italy for the traveling family and their protector, Wolfgang Amadè Mozart. Only from the angry and despairing reaction of his father did Wolfgang gather that once again he had done everything wrong, whereupon he immediately tried to strike a different tone. But he was no more successful with a righteous tone; Leopold saw through him and was annoyed. When Leopold remonstrated with him about the vulgar diversions in the Cannabich home, he sent in a contradictory report shortly afterward; Leopold certainly knew what to make of it: "At six I go to Cannabich's and give Mlle Rosa her lesson. I stay there to supper, after which we talk or occasionally they gamble. If it is the latter, I always take a book out of my pocket and read—." Good try, Wolfgang, but it won't do. Which book was it, actually? And how did "Lisel" react to such behavior? Certainly Leopold Mozart would also have liked to know why, under these circumstances, Wolfgang did not prefer to go home and keep his mother company, bored as she was in her shabby quarters, consumed by longing for Salzburg.

This leads us back once again to that letter of July 3, 1778, after the death of his mother, the letter about the success of his symphony, about Voltaire's dying like a dog. Here we see the two divergent tendencies united in a narrow space. After enjoying the sherbet, he "said the rosary, as I had vowed" (good boy, Wolfgang) "and went home—for I always am happiest at home" (even in Paris, in the dark apartment?) "and always will be" (hear that, Leopold?), "or else in the company of some good, true, honest German who, if he is a bachelor, lives alone like a good Christian, or, if married, loves his wife and brings up his children properly." Here Mozart seems to be writing not only for Leopold but for a child's schoolbook. He executes his proofs of virtue with method, if not with consistency: he forgets himself too often to be consistent or else he lays it on too thick. Leopold's first thought must have been, "Something is wrong here." He probably did not suspect the thing that was already wrong, that his wife lay dead in the next room; his suspicion was aimed at a different target. But Mozart had not broached the subject yet; it appears first, significantly, as an obscure suggestion: after the invocation "Well, God will make all things right!" (that popular formula for repressing everything unpleasant) there follows the cryptic sentence: "I have a project in my mind for which I daily pray to Him. If it is His divine will, it will succeed, and if not, then I am content also." We do not believe this last claim; he himself did not believe it. He is talking of course about the marriage he planned to Aloysia Weber, and preparing his father for it, although the latter was not to be softened by appeals to God. The fact that later it was not even Aloysia but Constanze did not make things better. On the contrary, if it could not be helped, Leopold would probably have preferred an illustrious singer to her lusterless sister.

As far as we can determine, Mozart employed this purposeful hypocrisy only in letters to his father; the most he did in other cases was to flatter his correspondents for his own convenience. True, he was not always entirely honest with his wife later on, and he must have kept some of his earnings and escapades from her. To others he was open; as far as his positions permitted, he even told his grand employers to their faces just what he had on his mind, without considering the consequences, which quickly followed. As must be expected, legend and anecdote have proliferated in this area. We will save ourselves the trouble of quoting them here.

Such nonsensical assurances of virtue pervade the entire correspondence between Mozart and his father. They reach their absurd climax in the letter from Vienna of July 25, 1781, in which he wrote: "God has not given me my talent that I might attach it to a wife and waste my youth in idleness"; a year later he was a married man. Under the circumstances we cannot assume that his father was surprised. Three months before (May 1781), at the latest, with the break from the Archbishop, his surprise had given way to a new and upsetting knowledge of his son. Now he was forced to revise his relationship to him. In Leopold's letters to his daughter he sometimes speaks of Wolfgang in a tone of dismissive disapproval. But perhaps we are reading him incorrectly. Leopold was not in the habit of glossing over unhappy facts. Doubtless he was deeply hurt, and for the rest of his life felt that his ungrateful son's self-reliance was foolish. There is something moving, in the beginning, about Wolfgang's assurances of loyalty to him, about his efforts to retain his father's favor; the attempt, magnanimous in itself, to activate what was left of paternal kindness. But soon it becomes a strain; he does it grudgingly. The ambivalence of their relationship, always latent, turns into virtual love-hate after 1778, and in 1781 it comes to the surface and remains there until the father's death. After that Leopold is rooted out of his son's memory. Mozart certainly knew how much he had to thank him for, but this knowledge became a burden, first in Paris, and later in Salzburg and Vienna. Gradually, he must have realized how his father had also sinned against him, by educating him to be dependent. In his letters from Paris, Wolfgang first reveals a covert emotion,

usually unconsciously, but sometimes with open if cautious
irritation; in Vienna, however, the emotion becomes explicit,
if still couched in extenuating language; for Mozart never
wanted to hurt his aging father. At least, that is how we imagine it. His letters seldom show with absolute certainty what he
wanted and what he didn't.

Mozart had not wanted to return to Salzburg, this
much is certain, either to the narrowness of the city (though
others extolled its "cosmopolitanism") or to the Archbishop's
service, or, despite his assurances to the contrary, to his father's
house. During his last two years in Salzburg he was driven by
the desire to break away, to show the world what he was
capable of. Above all, he was longing to write operas. He was
dissatisfied, and so bored that he let his boredom grow into a
kind of pleasure, to be borne stoically. He felt condemned to
the enjoyment of a distressingly easy comfort, suffering under
conditions and necessities that other members of Mozart's circle found quite bearable, and even pleasant. For service to the
Archbishop was only moderately demanding—anything but
slave labor. This we learn from the diaries of various friends
and his sister, Nannerl; when Mozart was in the right mood
and had nothing else to do, he himself kept up her journal,
describing the vegetative life in a humorous (or often ill-
humored) way, sometimes with parodistic intent, in pointed
contrast to the dry, unemotional entries of his sister, whose
voice he assumed.

In the following passages from August 13 to 21, 1780, he is
of course himself the so-called brother.

The 12th: at half past eight, church. Then to Lodron and
Mayr. Afternoon Katherl at our house. And Fiala. Thunder-
storms and heavy rain.

The 13th: at 10 o'clock to the cathedral for the 10:00
Mass. Then to Surgeon-Katherl's. Herr Wirtenstädter contributed the target. Barber-Katherl won. Played Tarot cards

with the Tarot cards. At 7 o'clock took a walk in the Mirabell gardens just the way, in the Mirabell gardens, one takes
a walk, as one takes it, took, as one takes. Rainy, but no
rain. Little by little . . . the skies clear!

The 14th: at 8 o'clock, Mass. Then to Hagenauer, Mayr,
and the Chief Purveyor. Afternoon to Lodron. At 3 o'clock,
in the cathedral. At 5 o'clock, Feigele came with my brother.
At six o'clock, a walk. Nice weather. Rain at 9 o'clock.

The 15th: at 9 o'clock to the cathedral. At 11 o'clock to
Hagenauer. Ate there, as Papa and my brother dined at
Andretter's. Dessert up at the Maiden. At half past five
Hansel accompanied me home. At 7 o'clock took a walk
with my papa in the Mirabell gardens. Fine weather. Thun-
derstorms in the afternoon, and rain.

The 16th: at half past six to church #) . To Mayrs', but
home right away since nothing was happening since they
were not at home but at the Lazarette chapel. Afterward to
the daughter of the Chief Purveyor, not by his present wife,
the third, nor by the next-to-last, the second, but rather by
his first wife. Afternoon at Lodron's +).

#) You didn't add that Wirtenstädter was there on fur-
lough.

+) You didn't add that B. Frauenhofer was there on
furlough. After supper went to the *Finalmusik* at the court
and at the College Chapel. Rain, then clearing. And rain
again.

The 17th: at 9 o'clock to church. At Lodrons' and Mayrs'.
Afternoon at Katherl Gylofsky's ×). My brother came with
Schachtner. Afterward, Papa came too. Rain.

×) With Katherl at the home of Mlle the Saint, who picks
her nose with her big toe.

The 18th: at 6 o'clock at Frau von Mayr's. Then with her
and her daughter to the Lazarette chapel. Heard Mass there.
At half past nine home. To the Chief Purveyor. Afternoon
at Lodron's. 7 o'clock took a walk. Fine weather. Turning in
the evening. Rain.

The 19th: While shitting, my humble self, a jackass, a
pair of breeches, again a jackass and finally a nose, in
church. Stayed home, a pipe up my arse, pipe to my arse

a bit. Afternoon Katherl at our house. And Herr Foxtail, too, whose arse I dutifully licked; O delicious arse!— Dr. Barisani came, too. Rain all day.

The 20th: 10 o'clock Mass. The foxtail of a jackass whom I wore out and the jackass who licked me contributed the target like a jackass. My brother won. Then played Tarot cards. Dreadful weather. Nothing but pour, pour, pour etc.

The 21st: at half past six to Mass. At Mayr's and the sawbones'. Afternoon at Aquatrono. Mlle Brown-bassoon at our house. Amused ourselves here. Rain, but gradually clearing or cleaning in the evening or erring.

The 22nd: at 8 o'clock to market near the Church of the Trinity. At Lodron's and Mayr's. The Abbate Varesco at our house in the afternoon. At half past five went out and polished off a chicken. Fine weather.

The 23rd: arose at 6 o'clock and to Mass at 4 o'clock. At quarter past five to Hagenauer. At 11 o'clock to the Chief Purveyor. Afternoon to Lodron. At half past seven Katherl at our house. At 7 o'clock took a walk in the Mirabell gardens. Fine weather. Aren't I a scamp? Or a foxtail, jackass and scissor-legs?

The 42nd: at half past 8, to Gylofsky. To the cathedral. At 10 o'clock to Lodron. At 3 o'clock we three went to watch bowling at the Stieglbräu. At half past five a walk. Fine weather. Birds of a feather.

The 52nd: at the Augustiner. At I to church 7 o'clock went. To Chiefmayr and the Purveyor.

Lodron at our house in the afternoonish. We went to Fiala's. At 3 o'clock all six of us went walking, welking, wulking, wolking, wilking. It day a fine was.

The 62nd: apud the contessine de Lodron. Alle dieci e demi I was in the templo. Afterward at Mayrs'. Post prandium signorina Catherine chez us. We habemus joués Tarot cards. At sept heure we took a walk in the horto aulico. We had the most pulchras tempestas imaginable.

The 72nd: at 10 o'clock in the cathedral. Heard the 10:00 and 10:30 Masses. Afterward paid a call on the Robinigs. Fiala contributed the target, I won. Played Tarot cards. At quarter past six Count Thurn at our house. At 7 o'clock took a walk with Papa and Bimperl. Fine weather. A bit of rain in the afternoon. But then fine again. A party and music in Mirabell today. At 10 o'clock Pinsker and two violists played a *Nachtmusik* for us.

The 82nd: a half to niney, blow one out behindy in church. At quarter past niney, blow one out behindy at Mayrs'. The Chief Purveyor. Afternoon to Lodron's. Young Weyrother at our house. At half past five took a walk in the Dietrichsruhe gardens. Fine weather.

But during these last years in Salzburg Mozart's day was naturally not confined to playing with Tarot cards, throwing darts, or going for walks. He was an organist, which meant not only service but productivity. And it is amazing how little he did produce, after the promising beginning, the imperial flourish of the great C major Mass, K. 317, "Coronation" (March 23, 1779), a *maestoso* that quickly fades. His determination to play the role of a church musician seems to have died away all too soon; it introduces a relatively unproductive period, even in his secular music. Only the unique Sinfonia Concertante for violin, viola, and orchestra in E-flat, K. 364/320d (summer 1779), stands out as a radiant example of musical liberation. Further attempts in this genre remained fragmentary.

Fragments, too, are his sacred compositions of this period: seven bars of a Magnificat, K. 321a, thirty-seven bars of a Kyrie, K. Anh. 15/323, twenty-six bars of a Gloria, K Anh. 20/323a, and other beginnings, testimony to his apathy in between secular occasional pieces, divertimenti, marches, and serenades.

This is the time of the church sonatas, unburdened and unimportant pieces which have nothing to do with the Church except that the organ has a part in them. Mozart must have been only too happy to observe the obligatory brevity of the form. Only when he had the prospect of composing an opera under favorable conditions (*Idomeneo* in Munich) did he once again reach a high point in sacred music: the *Vesperae solennes de confessore*, K. 339, composed in 1780, shortly before leaving for Munich, in happy anticipation of the coming opportunities for self-development. It is an ambitious and elaborate work, in which he consciously utilizes all his instrumental and polyphonic resources, which, already great, were of necessity muted in Salzburg. The richly scored choruses and the ambitious orchestral apparatus, including trumpets, trombones, and timpani, reflect both his wish to expand his potential and, in large measure, the fulfillment of that wish. In this sacred work, as in parts of the Coronation Mass, his contrapuntal art is still displayed with open pride. Later, in the C minor Mass, he uses counterpoint with a good deal more restraint, and thus with more mastery. While still in Mannheim, Mozart had much to say about "sacred style," but later he no longer worried about "stylistic purity." What is "purity"? What is a "sacred style"? Did Palestrina or Orlando di Lasso write in it? Or is it not rather a matter of the style of the time in question, during which many composers, including Palestrina, of course enjoyed side leaps into the secular, or even dance steps, but in which serious music *was* sacred music; a time when all painting had to portray biblical events? The discovery of mythological subjects came later, and changed neither palette nor brushstroke.

The solo numbers of the C minor Mass, K. 427/417a (summer 1782–May 1783), especially the soprano parts, differ only slightly in expressive form and content (Mozart would have used the French word *expression*) from certain passages of the great concert or opera arias. The "Agnus Dei" of the Coronation Mass anticipates the Countess's "Dove sono" in *Figaro*. The "Kyrie" turns into Fiordiligi's aria "Come scoglio," transposed into B-flat. Mozart did not use such coloratura cadenzas, usually only decorative, elsewhere in his Da Ponte operas (except in Donna Anna's outburst in "Non mi dir" [No. 25] in *Don Giovanni*, an aria which Berlioz condemned). There are reverberations in the unfinished "Et in-

carnatus est" from the C minor Mass, an aria in the Italian
style which Mozart might just as well (or badly) have put into
the mouth of one of his secular female characters, if it wasn't
so much weaker than the ones he wrote for the Countess Almaviva or Pamina. Abert is right to wonder whether Mozart,
if he had completed the work, would not have become aware
of this break in style, a throwback to the "worst Neapoli-
tanism."[32] Einstein, on the other hand, finds this piece "over-
whelmingly sweetened and naïve,"[33] a strange opinion, even if
we substitute "sweet" for "sweetened."

How might this Mass have sounded, given the inadequate conditions of the première (if it really took place) on
October 26, 1783, in St. Peter's in Salzburg? The first soprano
part was sung by Constanze Mozart, about whose skills of interpretation little bad is known, but absolutely nothing good,
either. We also learn nothing about this Salzburg debut
through the eyes and probably overly critical ears of the biased
father and sister. The Mass was a fragment; Mozart patched
the missing movements together with sections from earlier
works, we no longer know which ones. He did it with the same
insouciance as when later he removed the liturgical founda-
tion from the entire work, to replace it with a secular one for
the cantata *Davidde penitente*, K. 469 (March 1785). This was
a piece commissioned by the pension fund for musicians'
widows (at least there was *something* of that sort by then!),
which probably did not pay enough to warrant an original
composition. Da Ponte is said to have written the text, but we
don't think so. Not only does it consist in part of doleful
recapitulations, which would not have been Da Ponte's style,
but it also has all the weak points of an interpolation after the
fact: long-drawn-out syllables extending through several bars,
resulting in the false emphasis that always occurs when Mozart
is not paying attention to the text. In this case, since the music
came first, Da Ponte wouldn't have been paying attention to
the music. He probably did not need this kind of work at the

time, since commissions for libretti were piling up. But whoever the poet for *Davidde* was, Mozart accepted him. He certainly had his reasons, and almost as certainly these reasons had less to do with artistic necessity than with practical considerations. We doubt that the two performances in the Burgtheater subsequently justified these practical considerations; it certainly wouldn't have been the only time that his calculations had proven wrong.

It was operas that Mozart wanted to write, as his Masses conclusively show. It is the only "professional" desire he expressed repeatedly, and with growing emphasis.

We know less about the extent of his inner involvement in the creation of great works in other genres. Only about the six quartets dedicated to his great inspiration Haydn, and conscious products of his art, formed not least out of a certain creative ambition, do we perhaps know more than about his opera work, especially the late operas. In fact, not until the Da Ponte operas do we sense that truly great air of a universal creator consciously exploiting his full potential. With *Idomeneo*, it is true, we already sense the composer's happiness at the dawning realization of his creative powers, but only with the Da Ponte operas do we also have his satisfaction in finally having found the long-sought-after material and the author appropriate for it. If these three operas have never been surpassed, it is not only because Mozart was "at the peak of his creativity" when he wrote them but also because (as we all can hear) the material was more fulfilling than any he worked with before or after.

Even *Idomeneo* and *Die Entführung* are already more than mere masterpieces of their kind; even they break out of the bounds of the *opera seria* and *Singspiel* genres. But the revolutionary Mozart is the Mozart of his last eight years. It did not occur to the Salzburg Mozart or to the Mozart of the Italian journeys, still under his father's supervision, to step beyond the conventions of the various genres. Besides, he still had not had enough experience to change an unchangeable pattern, i.e., to open up the form.

The *Singspiel* is governed by the monstrous convention of closed numbers between spoken dialogue. In performing the dialogue, the singer must move outside his own métier, and his persuasive powers as a speaker are usually rather feeble. Since the text is poetically unsatisfying (always the case), the public is asked to make a leap of good faith. Although the texts of *opera seria* have no greater literary value, they at least are filtered or covered up entirely by the stylization of the *secco* recitative. Neither in *opera seria* nor in *opera buffa* do we hear the text as independent poetry, and only in an ideal setting (for example, *Don Giovanni*) do we hear it as the verbal definition of events whose drama takes place primarily in the music.

Sarastro's spoken tirades, his pontificating style, do not always make it easy for us to take him seriously, as, for example, in the phrase "Pamina, das sanfte, tugendhafte Mädchen, haben die Götter dem holden Jünglinge bestimmt, dies ist der Grundstein, warum ich sie der stolzen Mutter entriss" (The gods destined Pamina, the gentle, virtuous maiden, for the noble youth Tamino; this is the reason I rescued her from her proud mother). He has actually only just learned for a fact that there is such a "noble youth." Of course, the *Zauberflöte* text is overloaded with a seemingly pellucid morality, and so is perhaps not the best example of the *Singspiel*. Mozart's first work in this genre is almost more typical, the light little piece with three marionette figures, *Bastien und Bastienne*, K. 50/46b, composed by the twelve-year-old in late summer 1768 in Vienna, and probably performed in an appropriate setting in the garden theater of Dr. Mesmer, though this is not certain. Written with obvious joy in vocal contrasts (for a long time afterward, in *opera seria*, he had to do without a bass voice) and joy in the possibility of evoking a pastoral quality with his instrumentation (the horns show his relative success), the piece strikes us as fresher and significantly more natural than the stilted *opere serie* written when he was sixteen, more or less under duress and always under pressure. Even the jump *in medias res*, the short *intrada* in G major, is convincing in its transparency and its melodic imagination. Beethoven, no less, made use of it for the beginning of the "Eroica"; Abert thinks this is a coincidence, and we would not want to exclude the possibility, for it is unlikely that Beethoven had studied the score of *Bastien*. In Colas's mysterious questioning of the magic book, to the text "Diggi, Daggi, schurry, murry" (No. 10), C minor stands for the exotic foreign quality of a good-naturedly rustic and totally undemonic magician, a merry use of the minor. In any event, this little work has a narrative directness that cannot be called merely precocious. This, too, is the work of a child genius.

We are loath to apply the term "precocious" to Mozart. Used precisely, it refers to those who mature before others, but not to those very talented individuals who keep their edge on others throughout life. "Maturity" is not necessarily a qualitative concept; it denotes the end of a natural stage of development. But in Mozart's case this stage was anything but natural, since the brilliant child was systematically encouraged to produce what a less sensitive audience would consider "mature." If he did not appear personally as a performer, the visual effect of a prodigy was lost, but the public wanted its enjoyment nonetheless, without considering the age of the provider. It wanted to hear an opera the way an opera ought to be. It was not always easy for the child or the adolescent Mozart to satisfy his public. At times he had to work very hard to be taken seriously even by his singers.

His first *opera buffa*, *La finta semplice*, K. 51/46a, written before *Bastien und Bastienne*, between April and July 1768 in Vienna, is the work of an extraordinary child. His experience,

musical and emotional, is not yet great enough for a masterpiece that would meet his later standards. But the opera shows
us that even at the age of twelve, Mozart had studied the
genre carefully and acquired its expressive techniques: he was
not least a genius at imitation. But there is more to the opera
than mere technique; Rosina's aria "Amoretti" (No. 12) in
E major (rare in Mozart), with its sighing figures, does evoke
an emotional state (certainly not his own). We cannot judge,
of course, whether little Mozart had encountered such a state
in "real life" or in the operatic form itself. In this case his
knowledge of the musical material surpassed his perception of
the reality it was to portray. For *"perception* is definitely not
one of the inborn attributes of creativity."[34] But the opera's
quality is not exhausted in this one aria. There is far more in
the work than the more or less innocent attempt to imitate.
We also have an early manifestation of the dramatist trying
systematically to expand the outer limits of his kingdom.

It has been called disgusting that in *La finta semplice* a twelve-
year-old dealt with degrees of adult love bordering on the
lascivious. But such criteria emerged only later, after the discovery of "childhood," when the nineteenth century's moral
judgments gained ground. In Mozart's time no one would have
thought to call his theme objectionable or unsuitable for a
child; erotic immaturity was not one of the concepts of the
time—we have plenty of evidence of that. Besides, these marionettes are not all that grownup; they are concoctions of one of
those "poets of the theater," watered-down Goldoni, and not
even the best Goldoni. Actually, it was the twelve-year-old who
made them into adults, if adults with one especially salient
side, that of tenacious and exclusive lovers. Deeper human
panoramas are opened up only later; the apotheoses of the
great ensembles are not yet in evidence.

In the realm of *opera seria*, too, Mozart's early works
interest us primarily as specimens of the genre, not solely because of the quality of the music, but because of the kind of

demands this genre makes on the music. The rigid form of *opera seria* is nearly as hard to enjoy as its unvarying subject matter. Compared to the ponderous loves of *opera seria*, the light infatuations of *opera buffa* seem positively true to life. Even when we do evaluate this or that number positively, it is more because it has kept its promise rather than because of any absolute merit. Yet even in those operas there are erratic signs of the "inimitable Mozart" hitting on one of his great themes for the first time, especially in *Lucio Silla*, K. 135, begun in Salzburg, completed in Milan in 1772, a work of the sixteen-year-old. The *terzetto* in B-flat, "Quell' orgoglioso sdegno" (No. 18), which closes the second act, is a nearly successful attempt at an ensemble of individual vocal lines. But here (and hereafter) it is the *recitativi accompagnati*, in particular, that denote the true Mozart. In them he was able to be more expansive than in the long arias, with their inherent constraints, for the *accompagnati* are governed by no strict form. No boundaries limit the rhythmically loose accompaniment; nothing is repeated; everything furthers the drama; destiny does its work, the merriment or gloom of the situation sound out *ad libitum*. Mozart's early *recitativi accompagnati* still show no individual emotional landscapes (for in *opera seria* there are only collective souls, the noble and the lowly, and those who alternate between them in torment, choosing ultimately—and always in time— to be noble). But they do present an objective treatment of the dramatic situation and the subjective moods of the people involved—love, hatred, agitation, or tender resignation—and beyond everything else is the luminous atmospheric background. In the *accompagnati* to *Lucio Silla* Mozart is already exercising his power over figures of his own creation and making the most of his achievements. An example is the splendid allegretto for strings, accompanying the essentially hollow words of Silla in the first act: "Mi piace? . . ." (before his D major aria, No. 5); even better is Cecilio's C major andante "Morte, morte fatal . . ." (before the Chorus, No. 6). As always, Mozart knew exactly what he had to do with "morte"—this cue never failed to be an inspiration.

We know nothing about the young Mozart's attitude to his libretti. As an incipient theatrical pragmatist, as the executor of commissions, he did not quibble about their quality. He accepted the accepted form. Changes requested by a singer were carried out. We do not know whether he was satisfied with the finished works. Perhaps it depended on their success. We find the typical *opera seria* rather painful: an indiscriminate gilding of ancient mythology or history with fictive portrayals of goodness and kindness, created so that the ruling-class audience might attribute these qualities symbolically to itself; an offering of a kind of aesthetic Byzantinism, whose forms were nearly always the same. The chief supplier was Metastasio, but others were also involved in the undertaking —"court poets," "poets of the theater," whose products Metastasio polished to a high shine. Sometimes the opposite occurred and a libretto of Metastasio had to be adapted to a particular situation: say, a prima donna or a castrato had to have special treatment; then a lesser poet was called into the act. Only one thing did not exist: collaboration between poet and composer. Usually the composer was given the text along with his commission, even if it had been used for decades by all kinds of other composers. Some favorite libretti had been set twenty different times.

The language of these texts is dead and artificial; it created its own vocabulary, and a unique verbal style, rich in extended tirades, exclamations, and apostrophes. It seems designed expressly to take the place of the action; since nothing on stage ever furthers the plot, we must usually content ourselves with messengers' reports or other descriptions of offstage events. The little that does happen is reserved for the recitatives; the arias and the few ensembles are solely for commentary, either on the singer's state of mind or the general situation. The arias tend to be endless; because they had to put the singer's qualities in the best possible light, they are full of relentless phrase or word repetitions. For example, Cinna's

B-flat aria in *Lucio Silla*, "Vieni ov'amor . . ." (No. 1), has 281 bars of music for 8 dreary lines of text (the Catalogue Aria in *Don Giovanni* has 172 bars of music for 30 lines).

In *Lucio Silla*, the longest arias with the most extravagant coloratura were given to the famous singer Anna de Amicis in the role of Giunia. Today we can hardly believe that people listened to these arias with pleasure or even patience; we begin to lose heart as soon as the motor of the *ostinato* slows down and heads toward the *fermata*, the springboard for the coloratura's acrobatics. (Incidentally, I usually feel the same way in concertos when the cadenza is about to begin.) Giunia's E-flat aria "Dalla sponda tenebrosa" (No. 4) is made for a voice used totally as an instrument, required to blare out like a trumpet in the coloratura passages. It is a coldly comic bravura number. But Mozart must have felt differently about it: even six years later, in 1778, he had Aloysia Weber sing this aria. The castrato Rauzzini, probably an outstanding singer with an enormous range (Nancy Storace's coach, incidentally), sang the role of Cecilio, whose minuet-like A major aria (No. 21) would match many a later bravura number if it did not suffer from a miserable text: "Pupille amati, non lagrimate," are the words; *opera seria* is full of commands to various parts of the body not to reproduce the character's inner feelings so that he will not betray himself to the outside world, which he then proceeds to do at great length. Even though we might enjoy certain recitatives with their surprise effects (e.g., Cecilio's sudden outburst from the *secco* "Ah, corri" into the great *accompagnato* with its lightning-like figures in the strings), we are always led back into the barren wastes of long strophic arias. Sometimes we even have the feeling that Mozart himself was fed up with these texts; the "tempo grazioso" of the G major aria "Se il labbro timido" (No. 10) is sung by Celia in a gay staccato, as if she would rather be Despina in *Così*: but it is her task to distribute 24 words over 135 bars, so she sometimes distributes the accents of the syllables rather arbitrarily: "ma nel lasciarti, oh Dio!" turns into "manel lasciarti odio." Sometimes these invocations make us wonder which god they can have been directed at: Zeus or Eros or, in anticipation, the God of Christianity.

It also strikes us as odd that apparently little value was placed on contrasting voices. The six characters in *Lucio Silla* range from soprano to tenor. Even the "third man," Aufidio, the eternal confidant, who, in accordance with the rules, is given the function of the loyal adviser, sings not in a comforting, humane bass but is another tenor. True, he is given only one aria, about military matters ("Guerrier," No. 8, suggesting Figaro's "Non più andrai" in theme and key [C major]). But *Figaro* is still a long way off—the distance from an aria of high quality in relation to the *opera seria* of the time (surpassed only by Gluck) to the absolute quality of the inimitable.

After *Lucio Silla*, Mozart returned to *opera buffa*, at first only as an interlude, with *La finta giardiniera*, K. 196, a mighty step from the first *"finta,"* no longer so *"semplice."* It was written in 1774–75 for Munich and had its première there on January 13, 1775. Unfortunately, a part of the original Italian text has been lost; we have to refer to the German libretto, especially for the recitatives. Mozart approved of it on the whole (perhaps he even worked on the translation), although it certainly would not have satisfied him a few years later. Whether it satisfied him at the time, or whether he just put up with it because he wanted to write operas, we do not know. The operas of the later Mozart, from *Idomeneo* on, always convey the impression of an absolutely conscious creative power, as if Mozart had asked himself how much of human affairs and feelings, actions and longings, he could bring to the material at hand, which was bound to be meager compared to his own artistic dimensions. He increasingly ignored the prescribed external standards. For this reason we tend, when listening to the early operas, to speculate how Mozart might have composed this or that text five or ten years later, assuming he would not simply have discarded it. For example, what would he have done to Belfiore's C major aria

(No. 8), an "Andante maestoso"—"Hier vom Osten bis zum Westen" ("From the East to the West") is the German title, while the Italian "Da scirocco a tramontana" opens up an entirely different dimension by referring to wind directions—in which a satirically monumental catalogue of forefathers is reeled off? Instead of writing a *buffo* aria, as others had done, he would have composed the entire list, which includes Marcus Aurelius and Alexander the Great. We would have recognized them all, clothed by their shabby descendant in pompous garments. At least we would have recognized them as we do the female types, which (twelve years later, of course) Leporello spreads out before poor Donna Elvira in his Catalogue Aria. But if Mozart did not exploit the thematic range here, in comparison with his later standards, he composed beyond it in other places. Ramiro's aria "Va pure ad altri in braccio . . ." ("If you too forsake me") (No. 26) plunges suddenly to a mysterious depth. Composed in C minor (the minor portion of this opera is significantly larger than in later operas, especially—once again—in the *accompagnati*) in the *seria* style, but conventional no longer, it is bold and strangely pure at the same time. One of the *accompagnati* is a unique specimen, the like of which Mozart never composed again: the adagio of the recognition scene "Dove mai son!" ("Where can I be?") (No. 27), which takes place in "a beautiful, pleasant garden." Above the strings and oboes, a hunting motive sounds in the horns, indicating rusticity; a pastoral ambiance is created. This is one of the rare times when Mozart composed "nature," a tamed, rococo kind of nature (a garden, not a forest). The recitative of the two people who diffidently come to know each other (though not in the biblical sense) generates different variations of the same musical motive. The variations finally "evaporate" in a *ritardando*, suggesting a sleepwalking quality, a midsummer night's dream.

Thus, the individual elements of this opera are multivalent. The third finale (No. 28) could be part of a sacred work, at the end reminiscent of the Requiem. Not that something sacred was intended: Mozart made no distinction between a joyous Gloria and an ensemble of joyful operatic characters, peacefully united.

Il Rè pastore, K. 208, the next opera after the *Giardi- niera*, is Mozart's last before the giant step to his unmatched *Idomeneo*. We find it utterly dull; it was commissioned as part of his "service" for April 23, 1775, on the occasion of the Arch- duke Maximilian's state visit to Salzburg, and was written for a Salzburg company which Mozart did not or would not credit with much ability. The only guest artist was the castrato Tom- maso Consoli, from Munich, who sang the *primo uomo* role of Aminta. With its libretto from off the rack of Metastasio's shop, the opera shows clearly that it was time for Mozart to break out of this form, with its endless succession of weari- somely rhetorical recitative dialogues, always culminating in exclamations like "Oh, Dio," "Oh, numi," "Stelle," etc., and interrupted by declamatory arias during which the action, which never makes much headway in any case, comes to a com- plete standstill. When, for example, Tamiri in her A major aria "Se tu di me fai dono" (No. 11) asks the same question, "Perchè son'io crudel?" fully eighteen times, so that her be- loved Agenore's accusation seems crushed under a vocal tread- mill, we no longer need to hear the answer. It was not in the composer's power to alter or enliven this form; quite literally, his task was only to "set to music." And here that is all he did.

Not much from these *opere serie*—from *Ascanio in Alba*, K. 111, written in 1771 by the fifteen-year-old in Milan, to *Il Rè pastore*—has survived into our own time. Of the latter only the brilliant "rondeaux" in E-flat, "L'amerò" (No. 10), sur- vives, perhaps because of its violin *obbligato*, which requires a concertmaster to play it with an illustrious guest singer, no longer, of course, a castrato. Mozart, too, must have liked this particular aria; for a long time afterward he had his singer friends perform it at various concerts. For us, all these *stanzas* and *strettas* are museum pieces, brought out now and again to keep our view of the *oeuvre* complete, to display not only the

great works but also the promising beginnings among otherwise only historically interesting compositions.

The reader has probably noticed, and will continue to
notice, that some of Mozart's important works are not treated
in this study. Since I have neither the competence nor the
inclination to write musical analyses of his works, I shall necessarily devote more space to those that offer a starting point
for conclusions about the figure of Mozart himself. Although
the early operas are not really helpful, it seemed necessary to
mention them, not only because of the jewels that shine out
from them intermittently, but also because they provide an
introduction and set a standard for measuring Mozart's development in the late operas, and particularly the increasing in-
vestment of his own, somewhat more identifiable feelings in his
work. Of course, we can conclude no more about Mozart's
emotional experience from his operas than from his other
works, including the sacred ones. But the range of his opera
characters' emotional experiences throws light on Mozart's
mastery of an applied psychology that has no need of words.
He probably would not have known the words; but if he did
not have the experiences in depth, he must at least have had a
passing acquaintance with them.

The fifteen- and sixteen-year-old Mozart had his commissions to fulfill and would hardly have been in a position to take issue with the quality of his libretti. At this time
he probably didn't consider them inferior; after all, even
adult composers were satisfied with them. The texts were not
chosen but parceled out; only the great Gluck could afford to
mold his librettist Calzabigi (who, to be sure, was slightly
superior to the others) according to his wishes. Mozart tried to
do this with Varesco when writing *Idomeneo*, but he could not
get more out of him than was there in the first place. The
stylized figurines and artificial "staged" situations were the

only things at Mozart's disposal. He had to infuse them with whatever objectified feeling he could bring to them; they had to kindle his imagination. He did what he could, and sometimes, suddenly, he could do a lot: Giunia's great scene among the tombs in *Lucio Silla* (set not in the radiant E major of a moonlit night but in the solemn gloom of E-flat), with its truly eerie harmonic power, surpasses all the conventional operatic scenes Mozart had written before. Already the music is not simply following the action but directing it, and revealing its theatrical rationale. This was the unconscious principle of Mozart's writing in all his later operas. The scene was not well received at the première. Anna de Amicis was not in good voice, very likely from jealousy of the *"primo uomo,"* the castrato Rauzzini, whose entrance the Archduchess applauded (this after the royal couple had kept the performers and the public waiting three hours for their arrival). One must assume that, at a time when the significance of a stage work could not be separated from the occasion of its première, the composer's confidence about his own absolute quality would be severely impaired, if not destroyed entirely, by such goings-on.

With Goethe's remark to Eckermann, we established that more than forty years after its première, *Don Giovanni* was still able directly to arouse emotion as a tragicomedy of human behavior. Today this emotion would be filtered through the prerequisite for accepting the art form "opera": the tacit agreement between its creator (as the representative of the genre) and the public (who must accept the demands he makes on them). What are the demands? A theatrical fiction, whose logic is arbitrary and at times absurd, is to become an image of reality by means of its music. We are asked to identify, outside the realm of words, with representatives of various moral ideas, and to integrate them, as presented, into our reality.

The inadequacies of number-operas no longer elicit in us the discontent that led to music drama. We no longer believe that "old" is synonymous with "old-fashioned." Though if we distinguish strictly between respect and enjoyment, between historical greatness and enduring relevance, Mozart has to be the only true representative of the genre, especially in his three Da Ponte operas. Without actually bursting it, he filled the framework of *opera buffa* with human beings, so intensely, and with such a combination of passion and serene distance, that no one else has ever equaled it.

We wonder if the classical opera seems further removed in time, further removed from life than the classical drama, because the performers sing rather than speak. Doesn't the spoken theater sometimes make greater demands? It expresses a reality in which we recognize nothing except the sound of the language, while music at least never claims to reproduce reality. Even Schiller, in his theoretical writing, welcomed in opera the possibility of doing away with the spoken theater's "servile mimicry," as he called it.

It seems to us, then, that the difference in our acceptance is based simply on the quality of the work. For a truly inspired work carries us beyond any thematic improbability or formal impurity. When Goethe's *Götz von Berlichingen* ends with the words *"Edler Mann! Wehe dem Jahrhundert, das dich von sich stiess"* ("Noble man, woe betide the century that rejected you") and *"Wehe der Nachkommenschaft, die dich verkennt"* ("Woe betide the future generations who misjudge you"), this emotional appeal brings into play an extradramatic element which offends the inner rule of dramatic plausibility; the invocation of posterity is out of keeping with the drama, and in this case incomprehensible as well. Even if prophecy were an effective dramatic technique, we could refute this particular one with the fact that no one has ever taken the trouble to misjudge Götz, and in addition, no one has ever cursed the century he lived in. But when, in Shakespeare's *Richard III*, Lady Anne spits with hatred into the face of her husband's murderer and then, a few minutes later, declares herself ready to marry this murderer, we are witnessing an absurdity of plot which does no damage to the monumental dramatic structure.

For her change of mind takes place in a language whose persuasive eloquence not only bridges over any psychological improbability but also transforms it into metaphorical reality. In it, the semantics and music of language are united in the same way that opera, ideally, transforms emotion into musical tones.

The greater an opera is—the more the music illuminates and clarifies its subject matter—the easier it is for us to accept the genre, and the more willingly we submit to its fundamental principle and to the operas that represent it. On the one hand, opera seems to suggest analogies to our unconscious lives (unnamable and undefinable); on the other hand, its evocative power removes us from life into wish fulfillment. When music awakens our latent sensibilities, we feel good, celebrating, in our devotion to the artifact, one destination of our flight from so-called daily life. My mother once told me of overhearing an elderly lady at a performance of *Tristan* who turned to her companion after the curtain had fallen on Isolde's "Liebestod" and said, her face covered with tears: "Yes, that's the way life is!" There is no objective truth to the lady's statement, for we know that life is *not* that way; but she had identified herself as the ideal, indeed the quintessential audience. She had found confirmation for her deeply rooted wish fulfillment, for her identification with the archetype of the lover and beloved, and thereby testified to the success of the creator's aim. His music had triumphed; the verbal material had become overpowering in its musical setting, in the wordless language that reveals the inner life of the one who speaks it. So we must wonder whether the creator's inner life is also revealed in these musical tones, and to what degree.

Wagner's characters are not free. Like the figures of Greek tragedy, they simultaneously suffer their individual destinies and carry them out, unable to escape them, accompanied persistently by their motives. They are ruled not by gods only but also by *dei ex machina*, love and death potions, and magic. They totter under the heavy burden of their mythos, which predetermines their actions, but which they do not perceive. Wagner's particular kind of greatness lies not least in his transcendent identification with his heroes, culminating, perhaps, in *Tristan*, but beginning with *Der fliegende Holländer*.

The powerful and truly unique effectiveness of *Tristan*, in both libretto and score, is due to its sometimes stifling emphasis on passion; a permanent apotheosis holds us prisoner. Every character bears a mythic weight that sets us free to empathize. In our own identification with his protagonists, we sense their creator's deep emotional involvement in his work. But we experience Mozartean opera (especially the three Da Ponte operas) differently. Of course Mozart, like Wagner, rules over the action, breathing life into his creations, identifying with them in their actions and reactions; but he holds himself remote from us by maintaining an imperturbable objective distance. He never passes judgment on a protagonist, not even when most of the other characters have nothing but judging on their minds (as in *Don Giovanni*). Free of value judgments, beyond all morality, he presents both positive and negative attributes (if we can speak of positive attributes at all, for nearly all the characters' qualities are revealed in relationship to the negative hero, Don Giovanni, who controls them). Mozart is astoundingly and perplexingly fair in apportioning his lavish empathy among the strong characters as well as the weak, the despairing as well as the triumphant, the evil as well as the good—though the last get short shrift in this opera. No character is given the opportunity to be actively good, for when mischief is the rule, each man keeps his own counsel. *Don Giovanni* is not about love—unlike *Tristan*, which is about nothing else.

Wagner once said: "Nothing is more characteristic of Mozart's career as an opera composer than the careless indiscriminateness with which he went to work: he thought so little about opera's fundamental aesthetic scruple that he engaged in setting any libretto offered him with the greatest impartiality."[35] It might be noted that the quality of this language conveys its intended meaning imperfectly. At least we can hardly agree that opera is based on an aesthetic "scruple." We would also call the "greatest impartiality" an untruth if it had been Wagner's intention to detract from Mozart's posthumous fame, which it was not.* In any case, the statement is a strange one. The truth is that the aesthetic element was the decisive and predominant factor in all Mozart's operas from *Idomeneo* on. His few, but unequivocally clear, theoretical remarks reveal that his operas had to be based on a precise concept, though it was not an ethical theme, as Wagner (and Beethoven) would have wished, but rather an exclusively musical idea, which the text had to satisfy—the text, that is, and not the subject matter. For the latter was already a given, as soon as Mozart had decided on a libretto. It would not have occurred to him to meddle with the personalities of his characters, but he did intervene in the manner of their presentation. Mozart never composed messages or declarations unless they were part of a character (the servant Figaro, for example), except in *Die Zauberflöte*, whose music is significantly weakest when the breath of a depersonalized ethical law wafts over the proceedings. Nor did he take advantage of his opera figures to lay bare his soul. No superimposed will makes them act in his own image; rather, a superimposed mind allows itself to be guided by them, gets to know them deeply, and effects their thorough and overpowering expression.

---

* To be sure, Wagner qualifies his admiration for Mozart by saying that "in none of his absolute music, not even his instrumental works, is his art developed so broadly and richly as in his operas."

It seems that nineteenth-century critics were unable to apply any standard to a work of art from the past other than the criteria they themselves considered valid at the time, as if the conditions of creation had never changed. Wagner had no taste for *buffo* plots; he was allergic to anything he took for frivolity. Like Beethoven, he was closed to all art that was not the testimony of an extremely personal involvement; his many nasty swipes at his contemporary Offenbach make this clear. Nor did critics of the nineteenth century wish to acknowledge the realities of a different epoch, the external constraints on the artists of the eighteenth century. Both Wagner and Beethoven despised the libretto of *Così*, and even reproached Mozart for ever having touched it. It seemed to them the height of "indiscriminateness." We find such a misjudgment incomprehensible, if for no other reason than the evidence of Mozart's dramaturgical results.

A mitigating factor is that Wagner did not know Mozart's infrequent theoretical remarks. If he had known them, he probably would have taken Mozart to task for pragmatic thinking, for adapting himself to what was "needed" and to what promised to please. And, in fact, the historical thinking of Romantics falters when it is a question of material necessity. They do not like to see their predecessors "in service."

On May 7, 1783, Mozart wrote to his father:

Well, the Italian opera buffa has started again here and is very popular. The buffo is particularly good—his name is Benucci. I have looked through at least a hundred libretti and more, but I have hardly found a single one with which I am satisfied; that is to say, so many alterations would have to be made here and there, that even if a poet would undertake to make them, it would be easier for him to write a completely new text—which indeed it is always best to do. Our poet here is now a certain Abbate Da Ponte. He has an enormous amount to do in revising pieces for the theater and he has to write per obbligo an entirely new libretto for

Salieri, which will take him two months. He has promised after that to write a new libretto for me. But who knows whether he will be able to keep his word—or will want to? For, as you are aware, these Italian gentlemen are very civil to your face. Enough, we know them! If he is in league with Salieri, I shall never get anything out of him. But indeed I should dearly love to show what I can do in an Italian opera! So I have been thinking that unless Varesco is still very much annoyed with us about the Munich opera, he might write me a new libretto for seven characters. Basta! You will know best if this can be arranged. In the meantime he could jot down a few ideas, and when I come to Salzburg we could then work them out together. The most essential thing is that on the whole the story should be really *comic*; and, if possible, he ought to introduce *two equally good female parts*, one of these to be *seria*, the other *mezzo carattere*, but both parts equal *in importance and excellence*. The third female *character*, however, may be entirely buffa, and so may all the male ones, if necessary. If you think that something can be got out of Varesco, please discuss it with him soon. But you must not tell him that I am coming to Salzburg in July, or he will do no work; for I should very much like to have some of it while I am still in Vienna. Tell him too that his share will certainly amount to 400 or 500 gulden, for the custom here is that the poet gets the takings of the third performance.

Perhaps this letter would only have convinced Richard Wagner all the more of Mozart's questionable artistic motivations. But it would have forced him to revise his judgment of "indiscriminateness." Mozart knew exactly what he wanted and needed; but he started with the form, not the content.

This letter also attests to the fact that four years before *Don Giovanni* and six before *Così fan tutte*, Mozart wished to write an opera exactly like them in structure and arrangement of roles, a wish so strong that he intended to make do with a lesser librettist, the Abbate Varesco, the poet of *Idomeneo*. He apparently expected a great deal from the contrasting effects of this distribution of roles. Of course, this letter also proves that the choice of material was not of first importance; who the figures are, how they are anchored in myth or tradition, is less important than what they can offer on the stage, how they can unfold there—in short, their theatrical effectiveness. The fictive realm they come from is unimportant. None of them has a prior advantage; all that matters is what they are meant to be and what they will become. The characters will not appear wrapped in the garments of their history but will take shape only in the hand of their creator. It is he who makes their history. Thus, Don Giovanni had no predetermined meaning for Mozart, as he has come to have for us; without Mozart, without the proportions and dimensions he brought to the figure, Don Giovanni would scarcely be the archetype he is now, with a history so well explored.

For *Don Giovanni*, more than all Mozart's other operas, and probably more than all other operas generally, is a "character piece," dealing with one single figure whose fate is enacted. Others contribute to his destiny, but do not reveal the facets of their own souls, which either have nothing to do with the hero or else are not illuminated by him. One could almost say they do not even possess other facets. In *Figaro*, on the other hand, it is the "situation" that is the determining factor, a "pre-revolutionary" configuration, though Mozart did not see it that way, even if he understood it subconsciously. In *Così*, too, it is the situation. None of the figures (figurines) plays the main role; the piece is borne by abstractions, by claims and proofs, however false.

Mozart must have read several hundred libretti in the course of his life and discarded nearly as many. He probably would have been happy to set one or another of them, but he lacked the commission. And when he did get it and had found a plausible libretto, he was still a long way (despite Wagner's belief) from accepting the text as it stood, except in the early *opere serie*.

It is improbable that he had an active part in writing the

libretto of *Die Zauberflöte*. Nothing speaks for it and much does against, as we shall see. But his part in the realization of the Da Ponte operas is obvious from the start. We can see it in the divergence between libretti and scores, and in letters to his father we have proof of his intervention in the texts of *Idomeneo* and *Die Entführung*. Reports on his work had been a main topic of his correspondence with Leopold Mozart from the beginning; he continued to report long after their estrangement. After his Paris journey, Mozart usually wrote at great length about his compositions, and with *Idomeneo* the topic of opera and the problems it presented was added. He presented his musical and dramatic concepts with great clarity and intelligence, giving assessments, not always benign, of the musicians he used, either willingly or reluctantly, in performances. The letters also throw light on Mozart's rapid development into a pragmatist and tactician; he would go along with a misplaced bravura aria as a *conditio sine qua non* for a prima donna if he considered her "incomparable," or he would cut a singer's number if he did not like him.

On November 8, 1780, Mozart wrote to his father from Munich and asked him to tell the Abbate Varesco (a Salzburg court chaplain and a rather sorry librettist) about the changes he wanted to make in *Idomeneo*:

I have just one request to make of the Abbate. Ilia's aria in Act II, Scene 2, should be altered slightly to suit what I require. "Se il padre perdei, in te lo ritrovo"; this verse could not be better. But now comes what has always seemed unnatural to me—I mean, in an aria—and that is, a spoken aside. In a dialogue all these things are quite natural, for a few words can be spoken aside hurriedly; but in an aria where the words have to be repeated, it has a bad effect, and even if this were not the case, I should prefer an uninterrupted aria. The beginning may stand, if it suits him, for the poem is charming and, as it is absolutely natural and flowing and therefore as I have not got to contend with difficulties arising from the words, I can go on composing quite easily; for we have agreed to introduce here an aria andantino with obbligatos for four wind instruments, that is, a flute, oboe, horn and bassoon. I beg you therefore to let me have the text as soon as possible.

And on November 13:

The second duet is to be omitted altogether—and indeed with more profit than loss to the opera. For, when you read through the scene, you will see that it obviously becomes limp and cold by the addition of an aria or a duet, and very gênant for the other actors who must stand by doing nothing; and, besides, the noble struggle between Ilia and Idamante would be too long and thus lose its whole force.

Since the "second duet" was omitted, we cannot judge whether the scene in question would have turned out "limp and cold." We simply observe with what sharpness of disposition, what dramaturgic sureness, how clearly and decisively Mozart expressed himself when it was a matter of his work.

In fact, no scene in *Idomeneo* turned out limp or cold. The store of creative power in the young and wholly awakened Mozart, the wealth of invention, have made this work the absolute crown of *opera seria*, if one can still call it that. For it is more: the formal latitude of the *recitativi accompagnati*, expanded by Mozart into high drama and treated with the greatest freedom of expressive techniques and musical devices, as never before accomplished and matched afterward only in *Così fan tutte*, clearly anticipates music drama. True, even here we have to hear a few arias as concessions to the vanity of the singers; Mozart himself heard them that way at the time. At that point his goal was still the perfection of what was desired, the quality of the product, so to speak, though he may well have realized for the first time, during this very opera, that he not only had produced perfectly what was desired but had also dared to go far beyond it. But at this point we cannot be sure how aware he was of the new elements, or how fond he still was of the conventional. He considered Idomeneo's bravura aria "Fuor del mar" (No. 12) one of his best pieces, although this "storm at sea imagery" (Abert) leaves us relatively cold; nowadays it is hard for us to tolerate tenor coloratura. We have to remember that the man who sang the part, Anton Raaff, was sixty-seven years old and already at the end of his brilliant career. But next to this kind of showpiece, which both singers and public desired, there are arias of unique perfection and proportion, especially Ilia's second aria "Se il padre perdei" (No. 11), which contains a two-bar figure in E-flat that recurs in the andante of the G minor symphony (bars 4–6) and in the portrait aria of *Die Zauberflöte* (bars 7–9), like a kind of abstract monogram, but without thematic connotations.

The E-flat quartet, "Andrò" (No. 21), is Mozart's first true ensemble number. Musically it is up to all the later ones, although the text still did not permit him to individualize the four different characters. Had he had a suitable text, at this point he would already have mastered the disposition of the four voices and the art of letting each develop to carry out its own destiny. For during these stimulating months in Munich, on holiday from Salzburg, a period of deep satisfaction, his dramaturgical ability took a giant step forward, his mastery grew wider: the theater there must have had a significant influence on him.

In *Idomeneo* we have a work whose creation coincided with its rehearsal period, an ideal situation in a way. We imagine that Mozart wrote the score and then rehearsed it with the singers (only the two women he knew from Mannheim really satisfied him: Dorothea Wendling [Ilia] and her sister-in-law Elisabeth Wendling [Elettra]). He then tried out rearrangements of the text. Where dramatic continuity did not permit them, he asked for changes from his librettist, Varesco, in precisely detailed letters that his father relayed. Varesco was reluctant to revise: he thought of himself as a great poet. But Mozart knew the vain Abbate was anything but that, and responded to his refusals by simply cutting, as, for example, when the castrato del Prato (Idamante), whose

abilities Mozart did not esteem very highly, did not understand his part. Mozart certainly had some small, though creative setbacks here. But, in return, he was happy with the
orchestra. They were former Mannheim musicians whom he
knew and admired. It is tempting to assume that the orchestral richness of this opera, the voluptuous instrumentation of a
kind he was never able to use again, grew out of heartening
moments during the rehearsals, when he saw just how much he
could ask of these musicians. Then he indulged himself, yet
never by using the instrumental potential wastefully. The
orchestral sound of *Idomeneo* is never thick, but always of the
greatest, most delicate transparency.

The period of *Idomeneo*, from late fall 1780 to spring
1781, was, in fact, one of the happiest of his life. Constanze
reported this to the Novellos and we have no reason to doubt
her; even if Constanze was not a reliable source, she would
hardly have invented a happy time in her husband's life which
did not include her. Mozart must have told her about it. Here,
too, coincidental information taxes our imagination heavily:
can we, for example, imagine a conversation between Mozart
and Constanze during which he says to her: "During that time
in Munich, rehearsing *Idomeneo*, I was really happy then!"?
We cannot. We cannot get close to a Mozart who reminisces,
either. This memory in particular must have been meaningful
to him. In a woman-to-woman conversation, Constanze told
Mary Novello of a strange incident:[36] One evening during the
visit to Salzburg in summer 1783, when she and Mozart were
singing the quartet "Andrò" with two other people (who
might they have been?), Mozart grew so upset that he burst
into tears and bolted out of the room. Constanze followed
him, and took quite a while to comfort him. This story, too,
is certainly no fiction. We would like to know what she had to
comfort him about, and again we curse the Novellos' restraint;
if Mary had asked a short, surprised question, we would know

more. Of course, Mozart may not have divulged the reason for his outburst to his wife, but it seems improbable that she had neither a guess nor a theory. This is the only evidence of such an outburst, and characteristically, the way we learn of it is puzzling. The quartet deals with death, but we doubt that his emotion was stirred by this theme. More likely, he was moved by a memory of certain events from that earlier time, and probably not by a disappointment but by a moment of happiness, which the present or the intuited future could not match.

Mozart knew quite well how to instruct his librettists in dramaturgy, as his concept for *Die Entführung*, written in a letter to his father on September 26, 1781, demonstrates:

> Now comes the rub! The first act was finished more than three weeks ago, as was also one aria in Act II and the drunken duet (*per i signori viennesi*) which consists entirely of *my Turkish tattoo*. But I cannot compose any more, because the whole story is being altered—and, to tell the truth, at my own request. At the beginning of Act III there is a charming quintet or rather finale, but I should prefer to have it at the end of Act II. In order to make this practicable, great changes must be made, in fact an entirely new plot must be introduced—and Stephanie is up to the eyes in other work. So we must have a little patience. Everyone abuses Stephanie. It may be that in my case he is only very friendly to my face. But after all he is arranging the libretto for me—and, what is more, as I want it—exactly—and, by Heaven, I do not ask anything more of him.

Gottlieb Stephanie (the younger), actor and author, adapted for Mozart the comedy *Belmonte und Constanze*, by the businessman and writer Christoph Friedrich Bretzner. When Bretzner heard of Mozart's composition, he protested publicly:

> A certain individual, *Mozart* by name, in Vienna has had the audacity to misuse my drama *Belmonte und Constanze*

for an opera text. I herewith protest most solemnly against this infringement of my rights and reserve the right to take the matter further.

Christoph Friedrich Bretzner,
Author of *Das Räuschgen*

This solemn protest against an individual by the name of Mozart deserves to be remembered. But let it be said in Herr Bretzner's favor that he later changed his opinion about this man and in 1794 even translated *Così fan tutte* into German.

Mozart's report on his work for *Die Entführung* is the last such report we have. We assume that he also wrote extensively to his father about the creation of *Figaro*. His father observed the work on it when he visited his son in Vienna in 1785, during the great period of the piano concerti. Leopold, tremendously pleased, described to his daughter how splendidly they were performed.

Mozart wrote the last piano concerto of this series a few weeks before finishing the score of *Figaro*, and performed it, a month before the première of the opera, at a subscription concert in the Burgtheater on April 7, 1786. This date can be considered the end of his great Viennese period, for henceforth the virtuoso Mozart lost ground and was soon forgotten. We do not know how he responded to this decline. At first, work on *Figaro* still loomed before him, and his trips to Prague and his successes there also diverted him; but gradually it must have dawned on him that he was no longer needed, as Count Arco had prophesied.

All Mozart critics have always called special attention to the minor-key character of the C minor Piano Concerto, K. 491 (March 24, 1786), as if Mozart had wanted to get one more exhaustive minor work off his chest before the nearly continuous major of *Figaro* (anticipated, perhaps, by the "malicious humor" [Abert] of the allegretto movement). In the first movement in particular, the minor is considered downright relentless. Abert speaks of a "titanic defiance" and naturally, therefore, of a "nearly Beethovenesque effect." I, too, hear in this movement a gloomy agitation, but strangely enough I hear in it (even aside from the E-flat major passages) a major mood, violent and energetic, to be sure, but not "tragic" (Einstein and everyone else). I do not find the initial presentations of the minor key in Mozart's absolute music so ostentatiously intentional: in the syncopations of the D minor Concerto, which seem to creep forward; in the controlled attack of the first violin above the *ostinato* of the second violin and the viola (without the second viola or cello) of the G minor Quintet; or in the hurried character of the high strings, almost flitting by, above the briefest anticipation of the low strings' accompaniment in the G minor Symphony. I claim no more, it should be emphasized, prove nothing more by this way of hearing than that there is a fundamental variety of possible responses.

Mozart's works in the minor are so rare that when we do suddenly come upon them we prick up our ears and search for a particular motivation: why here, precisely? Let it be understood that we seek, not an occasion, not an external cause, but the determining factor within the sequence of his works. Of course, we seek in vain. Is it really a decision for "the tragic"? Since we have no definition for a musical equivalent of what we call in words "the tragic," the question cannot be answered.

We cannot use the operas to prove the moods that were intended; what is compelling is the mode chosen. Don Giovanni's descent into hell, transposed into D major, would be a grandly heroic scene, and while we can conceive of it in some other minor key, the D was certainly of determining importance for Mozart. Why? We do not know. To deduce a system, let alone an aesthetic, from his use and distribution of keys, as is still done, is misguided. D minor cannot apply exclusively to the frightful ruin of an incorrigible "dissolute," for the Requiem, K. 626, Mozart's last opus, in which his greatest and final existential experience becomes one with his work (we wouldn't want to assert this definitively, but there are good reasons to assume as much), is in the same key as *Don Giovanni*; in fact, probably the last bars he ever wrote, the "Lacrymosa," are in the same key as the final downfall of his great reprobate. Except for the theme of death, they have nothing obvious in common; on the contrary, heaven and hell are both in the same key. Of course, the great D minor works of absolute music, the string quartet, K. 421/417b (June 17, 1783), and the piano concerto, K. 466 (February 10, 1785), offer no help either. Quite the contrary. Whoever looks to the choice of key for a clue to the expression of emotional experiences in Mozart's life should be on his guard: in the first example, D minor is connected not with death but with birth, with Constanze's first confinement during the composition of the quartet. (No one could have predicted, despite all parents' resignation at the time to the rule of infant mortality, that the child, Raimund Leopold, would die two months later.) Abert calls D minor Mozart's "key of fate" (for Einstein, it is G minor). Let us offer Abert one indisputable interpretation of his view: both birth and death are destiny.

Incidentally, Constanze told the Novellos more about the circumstances of this composition: not only was she having labor pains (in the same room? in the next room?), but her husband even (cold-bloodedly?) composed her cries into the music. To this Ludwig Finscher says: "The idea of degrading Mozart's music into a clinical graph is unusually stupid, even for the school of vulgar romantic-heroic historical writing."[37] The spirit of this assertion is so correct that we are reluctant to contradict its content. But we must: first, there are no limits to the stupidity of "vulgar romantic-heroic historical writing," although the scholar may ignore it. Second, it would have been so farfetched for Constanze to invent her story that we believe it. Not even a Constanze could make up something like that. The statement changes neither the way she wanted to be seen nor the way she really saw herself. It neither increases nor decreases her importance. Why, then, should this particular detail of memory have stuck so strongly? Constanze even sang the labor-pains passage to the Novellos. Unfortunately, Vincent did not take it down. But we are probably right in assuming that it was the sudden *forte* of the two octave leaps and the following minor tenth (bars 31–32 of the andante), a brief uproar that quiets down, in a syncopated passage, to *piano*. These are figures that otherwise do not occur in Mozart.

The meaning that we, as listeners, might attribute to a key does not permit us to reason *a posteriori* about the composer's intentions in using it, except for Mozart's realization of sound images in connection with certain instruments. Let us stay with D minor. Not only is it my favorite key in Mozart (I take the liberty of this kind of subjective preference), but it has been less interpreted and less prejudged than G minor or E-flat major, for example. The only contemporary statement about it I have been able to dig up is by the composer Grétry: he found D minor melancholy. But we must take into account that there was still no standard concert pitch and that, normally, pitch was somewhat different from our own, perhaps more than a half tone lower, and that the D minor of the time would sound to us like a rather low C-sharp minor.

Aloys Greither sees D minor as Mozart's "daemonic, gloomy key, the key of a metaphysical shudder."[38] Certainly, why not that, too? We take issue only with the objective validity of such (typical) apodictic statements. Not only do they pose a recurrent question: "Whose metaphysical shudder? Ours or Mozart's?", but we also feel that this shudder is influenced by the subject matter of *Don Giovanni* on the one hand and of the Requiem on the other. Would the metaphysical element hold true for the String Quartet, or for the Piano Concerto, despite the predominantly "gloomy" content of these works?

Mozart even composed "An die Hoffnung" ("To Hope") in D minor, one of three poems he set to music, K. 390/340c (1780), from a best seller of the day, *Sophiens Reise von Memel nach Sachsen* (*Sophie's Journey from Memel to Saxony*), by Johann Timotheus Hermes, a long-winded, today almost intolerable narrative in five volumes, which Mozart read (to the end?) in his last months in Salzburg. He made a strophic song out of the poem, 15 bars, "mässig, gehend" (andante moderato), but with a restrained *espressivo*; without too great an emotional participation, it seems to us, perhaps the result of a little creative pause while reading. Admittedly, the poem deals with loss of hope more than with hope, but there is nothing metaphysical about it. His next D minor work is metaphysical, written soon after, during his happy months in Munich, the time of *Idomeneo* and the great Serenade for 13 winds in B-flat, K. 361/370a, the "Gran Partita." Having escaped his unbeloved Salzburg, in a great flowering, in the wish to prove himself or perhaps even establish himself once and for all, he wrote between these two above-mentioned works the Kyrie in D minor, K. 341/368a, that short, brilliant piece of sacred music. For many it is the convincing index of his faith, before which one of his interpreters, Einstein, would even "like to fall to his knees." We are no less enthusiastic about this grandiose work, even if our admiration would perhaps take a different form. "Daemonic gloom"? We don't hear it that way. "A metaphysical shudder"? Perhaps; or is it joy in the growing ability to evoke such a shudder, and, in addition, satisfaction with the musicians at his disposal, who offered him the possibility of enormous development? We know that Mozart made do with inferior performance conditions, but we also know that a "splendid" orchestra inspired him, that he was happy to revel in what was "incomparable," and he happened to revel in D minor. Let us keep to Werner Lüthy's observation about characteristic keys: "like A minor, D minor also includes a whole range of feelings within its domain."[39] No doubt. This statement is true as indubitably as, for example, the observation that people can differ about almost everything in life.

Leopold Mozart, who was anything but an enthusiast, writes in his *Violinschule* in 1756 that a composition transposed from F major to G major "has a completely different effect on the listener's ear." He is right again, our cool, clever Leopold. For he doesn't say that this transposition evokes the *same* response in everyone, and he prudently guards against bringing up his own feelings by way of example.

Nevertheless, let us play out this little game to the end. Mozart did not write that much in D minor. Passages that utilize D minor as a parallel key to F major, or as a variant of the tonic D major, cannot be used as examples, although there are sometimes incomparably delightful contrasts as a result. In the thirteen-year-old's D major Serenade, K. 100/62a (a so-called *Finalmusik*, which is not a dirge but a divertimento to celebrate the semester's end, in this case that of the Salzburg Gymnasium), the trio of the third minuet is in D minor. But what here is still a prescribed piece, a rococo dalliance, appears later in weightier form in the important D major Serenade, K. 250/248b (July 1776), the "Haffner Serenade," in the D minor trio of the "menuetto galante." In this magical *sempre piano* of the strings, with its remote, elegant melancholy, its languishing, sighing motive, we have an objective example, a typical manifestation of rococo, indicating its spirit like a detail from a painting by Watteau; no metaphysical shudder, but rather its contrapuntal opposite, in an immanent world. I am speaking here about one subjective reading, an interpretation that other passages do not offer me, as for example in the D major Quartet, K. 499 (August 19, 1786), where the D minor trio seems to be totally conventional; here the contrast is in the tempo and dynamics, a sudden nervous flitting in the middle of the weighty *forte* of the minuet. There remains only the Fantasia for piano, K. 397/385g (Vienna, 1782), an independent piece in D minor, a pithy fragment. It seems to us to be among the works Mozart dreamed up daily at the piano but did not usually write down, just as he never wrote this one down entirely. Perhaps he was interrupted and did not want to go back to it later; it was not important enough. And yet, in these pieces in particular, we hear the loose structures of Mozart the improviser, who played for himself for hours and carried many listeners away with his extemporaneous ideas. We have read reports about them from surviving contemporaries: "Incomparable!"

It is often hard to resist the assumption that Mozart experimented with keys to test out on himself the extremes of expressive possibilities. Thus, for example, in the fifth of the string quartets dedicated to his friend Haydn, K. 464 (January 10, 1785), the key of A major, which is so often a radiant key in his work, is peculiarly "alienated," in a strange, introspective manner we cannot explain; almost generalized, as if the key were standing for another, indefinable, key. But, of course, everyone will find his own example in this area of differentiated responses, too. The key of A major "means a charming, lyrical style for Mozart" (Hans Engel). One can find as much evidence for this kind of assertion as for its opposite.

Einstein called the six quartets dedicated to Haydn "music made out of music"—not bad! "Filtered" art, he says, putting the adjective in quotes. Even if we don't understand that entirely, we will let it stand. "Music made out of music"—that sounds incomparably clearer than "music from out of a full heart"; it reflects our interpretive defeat so much better than any attempt to translate the untranslatable. We would do well to take up this formulation and consider all of Mozart's absolute music "music made out of music," as an exercise to counteract our automatic response to works that the critics have made all too familiar.

If we hear Mozart's keys as conscious choices, not as the spontaneous expression of the composer's momentary frame of mind, we by no means imply that we are not also experiencing the minor keys as "gloomy," or "tragic," or sometimes even "despairing." Our feeling is not limited to the minor itself, but overflows and spreads, often intensified, into a major key within the minor, especially E-flat major within G minor. Neither the adagio of the String Quintet, K. 516 nor the andante of the K. 550 Symphony sounds as if it is in a major key; the "gloomy character" is not broken but underlined. These contrasting movements do not change the listener's mood; rather, there is a consistency to them, which sustains our tension as we await the new beginning of the "poignant" minor. Only the E-flat andante of the early G minor Symphony, K. 183/173dB (October 5, 1773), seems to interrupt the mood of the entire work, to tell us something in a different spirit. But what? Mozart used these contrasts as a stylistic technique most artistically and adroitly, sometimes with positively insidious intent: the tragic-sounding minor cavatina preceding the last movement of the Quintet, K. 516, grows to a restrained pathos, only to break out, after a *fermata* and a truly ominous pause, into a G major rondo. The frightening triviality of the main theme of the rondo seems to be intensified in the secondary themes, reaching a bleak gaiety. A despairing major? How would Mozart have responded to this view? Would he have grinned and said, "That's it, don't you think?" or would he have stared at us without understanding and said, "I don't know what you mean"?

No one has ever satisfactorily explained the different emotional effects of the two modes. No one will deny that, different as night and day, major and minor awaken the most opposite feelings; indeed, no other artistic discipline commands a contrast even remotely similar to this polarity, as clear-cut as turning a switch on and off. Why (to reduce the question to its simplest form) does the minor third make us sadder than the major third? Why is soft (*molle*) sadder than hard (*duro*)? There have been explanations which speak to our minds, but not to our direct sensations when we experience this fundamental difference.

Naturally, within the radius of objective reception, there are subjective differences. Although there is scarcely a listener who hears the minor as "positive" and "affirming" in contrast to the major, there are surely also those who sometimes hear Mozart's major as "negative" and "negating." The B-flat Piano Concerto, K. 595 (January 5, 1791), and especially the C major String Quintet, K. 515 (April 19, 1787), will not strike any of us as cheerful or happy; the overpowering statement of these two works is not about joy. But everyone will explain his reaction differently; we can neither comprehend nor measure perceptions of feeling. To state it with appropriate precision: this or that listener may experience this or that piece of music as more or less happy or sad. Of course, many subjective responses agree that certain pieces are negative, for example, the B minor Adagio for piano, K. 540, or the Masonic Funeral Music, K. 477/479a, which no one could hear as a manifestation of *joie de vivre*. But within this totality of feeling there will be divergent emotional reactions; they will have a much smaller range with the minor keys than with the major. Even where interpreters agree about the "tragic" content of a piece, the degree will vary, and with it the descriptive attributes applied. Of course, we can never prove that the composer felt the way we do.

Hardly any serious student of Mozart can have avoided playing this game of key speculation, for it is fruitful and open to all; everyone can play and, by sharing his experience, can consider himself a winner. There would be losers only if some witness were found to swear that Mozart wrote the andante of the G minor Symphony, for example, in high spirits, in a great creative moment, feeling himself capable, in a truly imperious way, of mediating for the listener the experience of a tragic feeling. Only then would our interpretive fever be quelled. Let us remember what Mozart himself wrote to Anton Stoll on July 12, 1791:

Stoll, my dear, . . .
You've been swilling some beer!
The minor, I hear,
Is what tickles your ear!

Let us take as an example the Serenade in C minor for
eight winds, K. 388/384a, written in 1782 for Prince Liechten-
stein. We, like all previous commentators, find this grandiose
work infused with a strange gloom. The minuet, especially,
because of the tension between its courtly dance character and
its key, seems fiercely daemonic. Both Abert and Einstein have
asked how it is possible that such an outburst of negative
feeling could have pleased a prince, and his dinner guests, in
the way they expected and demanded of its genre, a *"Nacht-
Musique."* Thus Abert writes about the recurrent seventh
motive of the main theme in the first movement: "Here is the
devastating outcome of this soul's struggle, which already anticipates the later Mozart: to resign oneself and endure the
struggle until the very end."[40] Such an interpretation seems
farfetched to us, and the assumption of both scholars, that
Mozart's society experienced this piece of music in the same
way we do, strikes us as unhistorical. It may be tempting to try
to twist music into a manifestation of emotional depths borne
with self-control, but such an approach ignores the ways of the
unconscious. The interpretation is not that easy. As for the
response of his contemporaries, even if we assume that a good
share of the Prince's dinner guests strongly felt the tensions of
the major-minor polarity, it does not mean that they necessarily experienced the range of feelings in any context other
than the enjoyment of a demonstration of melodic and harmonic richness and variability of "expression." A serenade had
to comply with a certain form, but it did not have to renounce
all emotional depth; the "sentiment" evoked was the listener's
business. Shallowness was beyond Mozart. In this case he consciously composed, if you will, a companion piece to the Serenade in E-flat, K. 375 (October 1781), a negative to the posi-

tive. The piece had to be ready within forty-eight hours; he didn't have much time. We do not exclude the possibility that he was angrily fulfilling his obligation, and, assuming their misunderstanding of his music, deliberately darkening the atmosphere of his patrons' evening, but that is unlikely. For it would also imply that he was aware of the gloomy character of the music, which is not the case: a letter to his father (July 27, 1782) reveals that he had to compose it for winds, because the Prince had no strings in his *Kapelle*. Otherwise, he writes, he would gladly have sent the piece to Salzburg, where, he thinks, it could well have been used for the celebration in the Haffner household of young Sigmund's elevation to the nobility. True, Mozart did not love Salzburg, but it is not likely that he wanted to avenge himself on his native city by writing gloomy music for a tribute to one of its most prominent citizens. He was probably unsure himself about the emotional content of this piece. He did not remember the act of creation; copying was an automatic process, during which he was already detaching himself from the work. So perhaps the listener is hearing in this piece a preconscious content that has bypassed its composer; it would not be the only time.

Presumably because money was scarce, Mozart interrupted the composition of *Don Giovanni* in spring 1787 to work up a few "publishable items," composing the string quintets in C major and G minor, K. 515 and 516. Since chamber music was normally published in sets of three, he needed another piece, and with probably neither the time nor the desire to write it, he abruptly arranged the Serenade for winds into a String Quintet, K. 406/516b, to the detriment of the work, which is written so clearly for the wind timbres. Although it was not common for two of a set of three works to be in the minor, he either did not care or, more likely, did not even notice this disproportion. In the end, the quintets did not turn into "publishable items," either, but instead could not be "disposed of": they were "too difficult"!

No one any longer asserts that music is an "absolute world of tones and sonorities." But neither can anyone explain the paradox that it is, on the one hand, transitory in its performance, but also "something eternal" in its continuity, a treasure store that is immediate to us only when it is presented again and again. Be that as it may, today we have to think of music as an important medium of information. But the information, the partnership between the informant and the informed, escapes both analysis and calculation, because it conveys no semantic meaning. It cannot be translated into words, but exists and functions parallel to them, as a supplementary and yet full-fledged means of expression. This is true, of course, only for absolute music, that is, music without extramusical content. It comes to us as a stimulus; as such it mobilizes feelings that are reserved exclusively for it and is assimilated according to the receptivity of the listener. We exchange our feelings, compare our associations, and from the result conclude something *a posteriori* about the possible "situation" (*Befindlichkeit*) (Heidegger's "translation" of the word "mood" [*Stimmung*], which seems useful to me here) of the creator. Our pleasure consists in identifying with the creator, in feeling after him what he might or "must" have felt during the creative act; at the same time, we know that it will remain a mystery and would not want it any other way. The act of listening is not our only gratification. There is also the simultaneous attempt at interpretation, for ourselves and others, the attempt to translate the untranslatable; the perception and reproduction of a piece of information which is executed in an extralingual discipline, setting our feelings in motion on an extralinguistic plane. The counterargument, that the true composer would be able to set an emotional state, communicated verbally, into music in his subjective style, is not valid, for a verbal communication is already a program, which music can transcribe, more or less evocatively: program music. When the conscious motivation of a creator is anything other than the intention to bring tones and sonorities into a certain order, by following an inner dictate according to an unconscious law and a conscious thought process, a different discipline is called into play. Music is replaceable when it expresses something that need not be expressed exclusively in music: it becomes either the object of a descriptive success or a failure. Mozart's music is not that kind, for he was "not a painterly composer" (Schopenhauer).

The Köchel catalogue* lists 626 works. It will always remain provisional in that it does not contain what is lost, it justly questions what has been rediscovered, and from edition to edition it jockeys what is dubious from the main catalogue to the appendix and back again. In addition, it is synthetic, for it is not the composer's own catalogue of works. Mozart did not note down his fragments and did not start keeping a catalogue until very late, with the E-flat Piano Concerto, K. 449. Dated February 9 ("Hornung"), 1784, it was composed for Barbara Ployer, one of his most gifted students. Mozart started his catalogue at the time of his great successes as a composer and virtuoso, because of his sudden, heartening understanding of his own importance; he entered only what he thought was up to his standard. He did not record arrangements, like that of the Woodwind Serenade, K. 388/384a, into a String Quintet, K. 406/516b. Four years after writing the C minor Fugue for two pianos, K. 426, in December 1783 (before he began his

* Ludwig von Köchel, *Chronologisch-thematisches Verzeichnis sämtlicher Tonwerke Wolfgang Amadé Mozarts* (*Chronological Thematic Catalogue of the Collected Compositions of Wolfgang Amadé Mozart*). The Köchel catalogue's chronology was decisively altered by the scholarly work of Alfred Einstein, who edited the third edition between 1936 and 1946. The German Democratic Republic edition has retained Einstein's numeration. In the West German edition (seventh unrevised edition, Wiesbaden, 1965), some changes were made by the editors, Franz Giegling, Alexander Weinmann, and Gerd Sievers. Where it is applicable, this book provides the latest, chronologically most accurate number after a slash, giving first the obsolete number still most often found in standard works and on concert programs and phonograph records. Cited dates conform to the seventh edition, indicating either the day the manuscript was completed or Mozart's entry of it into his own thematic catalogue.

catalogue), he added an adagio to precede it and arranged the piece for string quartet, K. 546 (June 26, 1788). Mozart recorded: "A short Adagio for two violins, viola, and bass, for a fugue I wrote a long time ago for two pianos." This was his idea of order. He also made no entries for miscellaneous pieces he thought unimportant. The Köchel catalogue, on the other hand, is a scholarly work, giving a number for every discarded sketch, every beginning, even if it is only three bars long; it includes what was abandoned, attempted, lost.

The musicologist Leo Schrade writes: "If one divides the entire output (according to quantity only) into groups of 100 compositions, it is remarkably apparent that Mozart wrote approximately the same amount in every four-year period. This is an astounding regularity, a continual productivity which I believe is due not only to his ever-ready creative power, but also to the artistic discipline of the composer."[41] The invention of this "four-year-plan" strikes us as arbitrary. Furthermore, "creative power" cannot be measured by opus numbers. When Schrade writes that his tabulations "may resemble loathsome statistics," he is wrong only because they do not *resemble* them—that is what they *are* (if one can call statistics loathsome and not merely irrelevant). Actually, Mozart's creativity reached a high point both qualitatively and quantitatively in the four years from the beginning of 1784 to the end of 1787. In this period he wrote twelve (more than half) of his piano concerti; a horn concerto; a symphony; five quintets for various combinations of instruments, among them the E-flat, K. 452 (March 30, 1784) for piano, oboe, clarinet, horn, and bassoon, which he himself, at least at the time of composition, held to be the best work he ever wrote. And it is indeed unique, in its melodic development and in the mastery of the wind instrumentation integral to it. Each instrument is presented in its deepest individuality; each performs like a virtuoso soloist and at the same time in a *cantabile* fashion, sometimes playing only one figuration, and then passing it on to the next instrument, which picks it up in a version appropriate to it. It is as if the woodwind sound were dictating the melodic lines.

Also written during this four-year period were five string quartets, two piano quartets, three trios, five sonatas, *Figaro, Don Giovanni*, the short opera *Der Schauspieldirektor* (K. 486, February 3, 1786) , various Masonic pieces, nearly all his lieder, plus—we are still talking about the same four years!—several important miscellaneous works like *Ein musikalischer Spass*, K. 522, *Eine kleine Nachtmusik*, K. 525, the A minor Rondo for piano, K. 511, and, of course, many numbers to be inserted into the operas of other composers. In addition, there were rehearsals for the two great operas, his repeated appearances as pianist and accompanist in Vienna during the first year of this period, as conductor in Prague during the last, and his activity as a teacher. Never before, and certainly never after, did Mozart have as many pupils as in these four years; not only did he give them private instruction, he also composed for them. For his composition students (Thomas Attwood, Barbara Ployer) he planned assignment notebooks, for his piano students he composed pieces that were primarily pedagogical, but also independent compositions, sporadic supporting voices in the score of his "productivity," such as the Five Variations for Piano Four Hands on an Andante in G major, K. 501 (November 4, 1786). Generally thought of as a "piece in *style galant*," it contains systematic exercises for looseness and facility for each of the four hands. A classroom exercise, but not in the literal sense; for the five variations (among them a descending chromatic one in the minor) are dictated by a musical rationale, both charming and "right" in a stunning way, 155 bars of music perfect for teaching, use, and enjoyment.

A kind of hectic contentment, if not euphoria, characterizes the beginning of this period; sometimes Mozart positively reveled in being overburdened. At first he wrote down only the violin part of the B-flat Sonata for violin and piano, K. 454 (April 21, 1784), for the Italian violinist Regina Strinasacchi. There was no time to write down the piano part; at the concert he played it by heart from sketchy cues. But we are safe in assuming (this sonata is proof of it) that such feats did not impede his creative power, but, on the contrary, gave it wings. He was needed and he wanted to be needed. At this time, in 1784, he still liked to think of himself as a successful man; here and there we see him as he saw himself from the outside, for example, in letters to his father which relate his day's activities, slightly edited, of course: at six o'clock his hairdresser wakes him; at seven he is dressed (a whole hour for his toilette, almost a levee); work until ten o'clock, then teaching. Afternoons were given over to Viennese society: there were preparations for concerts and public appearances, or participation in private performances at the homes of various princes or patrons, especially, since 1782, in the home of Gottfried van Swieten, where for years Mozart had to appear (aside from evening concerts) every Sunday at twelve noon. He appeared gladly, for Bach, Handel, and Graun were sung and played, and probably also the oldest composers then known, like Buxtehude (at this time music history did not extend any further back into the past). We do not know how roles were distributed at these musicales; we do know that musicians like Salieri, Starzer, and Teiber took part in them, as did several others whose names and stature are no longer known.

Van Swieten was a pedant. Erudite but sterile, he expected the same thing from his musicians' collegium: erudition, which he tried to convey, and sterility, in that he offered none of his performers the opportunity to demonstrate his abilities as a composer. Still, he was one of the few Viennese who did not want to hear "something new all the time"; he preferred to have old music played in new arrangements. He considered Bach and Handel the eternal masters; later he included Haydn. Mozart, while still a living contemporary, never reached this status. We do not know if van Swieten, who outlived him by twelve years, honored the deceased with performances of his works. At any rate, he was the one who acquaintd Mozart with the music of Johann Sebastian Bach. Mozart took Bach's music home, studied it, and, urged on for some reason by Constanze, wrote his own series of fugues, which we think of as a torso, incomplete. We will return to this.

If we accept the division into four-year periods, these overabundant years from 1784 to 1788 are important, not only because of the portion of his "life's work" outlined above, but also for an additional, more mysterious reason. This was a time of experimentation and discovery, of testing instrumental combinations outside the influence of the familiar or the desired norms, without consideration for the necessities of production or for the audience he served in his public performances. In these years his many-tracked musical life acquired a more intimate side: private pleasure. Around 1783 he met the clarinetist Anton Paul Stadler, an insignificant composer, but a highly ranked virtuoso and an apparently passionate experimenter in the area of the clarinet family, which at that time included the basset clarinet and the basset horn. The latter strikes us as almost archaic today, and has a rather lugubrious sound. Mozart had already acquainted himself with the clarinet in Munich, but not until Stadler gave it life did it attain the meaning for him that it retained until the end. Not only did he write the Quintet, K. 581, and the Concerto, K. 622, for Stadler, but he also added clarinet parts to the G minor Symphony, K. 550, for Stadler and his brother Johann (to its detriment, as some think: the conductor Felix Weingartner thought that the "indescribably chaste delight" of the symphony was lost by this enlargement). Mozart wrote clarinet and basset horn *obbligati* to some arias in *Tito* for Stadler, for he took him along on his last journey to Prague. He must have found Stadler a pleasant traveling companion, a "good fellow." And he has entered the Mozart literature as a jolly sort. His thoughtlessness and unreliability, now notorious, obviously didn't bother Mozart; only posthumously were they chalked up to his "dark side." It is possible that duets with him were not confined to music; perhaps they played billiards or bowled together, and it is entirely possible that Mozart did indeed compose the E-flat Trio for clarinet, viola, and piano, K. 498 (August 5, 1786), the "Kegelstatt" trio, while bowling. It certainly is not the only one of his works whose magic belies its place of composition. The story goes that it was written for his pupil Franziska von Jacquin. Quite possibly he remembered an assignment or a promise while bowling, and undisturbed by the noise of the falling pins and the players, he conceived a poetic, luminous piece for Franziska (piano), Stadler (clarinet), and himself (viola).

The basset horn occurs for the first time in Mozart in the B-flat Woodwind Serenade, K. 361/370a (spring 1781), and soon thereafter in *Die Entführung*, where it is used exclusively to accompany the unhappy Constanze in her G minor aria "Traurigkeit" ("Sadness") (No. 10). It is also used to portray sadness in the Masonic Funeral Music, K. 477/479a (November 10, 1785), in which, for the first time in Mozart, the instrument takes on an "official" function. But "unofficially," for his private pleasure, he had already dealt intensively with its strange sounds and possibilities. Indeed, it seems as though he reveled in combining certain woodwind timbres during many an hour of his private musical life from 1783 to 1785; this in his hectic period, during stolen days, so to speak, and especially on the nights when Stadler brought along a couple of friends to rehearse the five Woodwind Divertimenti, K. Anh. 229/439b, probably in various combinations. Instruments were exchanged (clarinet or basset horn, basset horn or bassoon?) until the players probably agreed on three basset horns. These were likely experiments for no particular reason other than joy in the inexhaustible game itself, always with different players, always in different combinations. Toward the end of 1785, these games resulted in the five mysterious Woodwind Pieces in B-flat and F: brief, sometimes fragmentary sketches, among them twenty-seven bars for two basset horns and bassoon, K. 410/484d, like something in shorthand, perhaps composed in a few happy minutes. The complete 106-bar Adagio, K. 411/484a, for two clarinets and three basset horns, is a wonderful short bonus, like a sudden profound inspiration among the projects on his official schedule, such as, at just this time, a Masonic work for three-part male chorus with organ, K. 483, to the text "Zerfliesset heut', geliebte Brüder" ("Bid farewell, beloved brothers": one cannot help wishing in this case that the brothers had taken this imperative to heart) and *Der Schauspieldirektor*, K. 486, which is merrier, since here, at least, Mozart was in one of his elements.

It may well be that these hours of experimentation were among the happiest of his life. Happy, too, were those evenings when Mozart brought along three of his wind-player friends to Jacquin's home to perform with them his Notturni, K. 436–439, 346/439a, in which three basset horns accompany two sopranos and a bass—an almost random, "whimsical" instrumentation and yet, in a strange way, successful. These were settings of texts in the Metastasian manner (lovely ones, incidentally), ensembles of "light music," *Hausmusik* designed for a happy circle of participants, tender and intimate; flowing melodies full of half quotations, reverberations, reminiscences and anticipations of things to come, hidden pearls he probably forgot soon after. Köchel lists them as "presumably 1783," but that seems unlikely. His friend Gottfried von Jacquin was hardly sixteen years old then (and no prodigy like Mozart); besides, his friendship with the Jacquin family is documented only after 1785. At any rate, these *opuscula*, too, and the casual evenings when they were performed, fall into the four-year period in question, enriching not only us but Mozart, too. These were surely his happiest years.

It is hard to explain today why the Da Ponte operas had so little success in Vienna, how it is possible that they left the Viennese rather cold. We forget that Mozart was no more than one among many, and among them not the most popular.

Even if the operas were full of daring innovations, bursting out of the frame of the familiar, how is it that the Viennese did not at least recognize that their abundant "popular" material was better than that of other operas? Why is it that Mozart became almost a folk hero in Prague? Were people there really more advanced in music appreciation? That must have been the case. But, more importantly, in Prague that class of the arrogant *arbitres spectaculorum* à la Zinzendorf, who held expertise to be a privilege of the nobility, was weaker than in Vienna.

It is tempting to think of Prague as the collective discoverer of Mozart. To Mozart's astonishment and delight, people were whistling *Figaro* on the streets, *Don Giovanni* was a monumental success, and if *Tito* failed, it was because it was written less for Prague than for the high society that had assembled there for the coronation of the Emperor Leopold as King of Bohemia. After they left, the opera was better received, although it could have been called "old-fashioned," even then, and its libretto must have been incomprehensible to a general audience. Obviously the success of the other operas had not been lessened by the foreign idiom in which they were written: their music made them comprehensible.

Mozart's luster in Vienna was based primarily on his piano playing, on the growing prestige of the pianist, and only secondarily on his role as the *"compositeur,"* who also wrote the things he played so splendidly. But by 1785 the Viennese were tired of his concerts; they demanded "something new"; Count Arco would have said, "I told you so, Mozart."

The première of *Le Nozze di Figaro*, K. 492, on May 1, 1786, though splendidly staged, caused no change in his fortunes. Not a failure, but certainly no success. One of the many new shows that, like the others, would not last long, it was greeted with indifference. Mozart was not lucky enough to be taken seriously as an opera composer in his chosen homeland. It does not speak well for the musical knowledge of the "educated circles," musicians themselves, that they were unable to separate the material of a stage work from its form, the words from the music, the message from its treatment: "what" and "how" were tossed into the same pot. *Figaro*'s reception at its Italian première before the Archduke at Monza in fall 1787 is an example of how the opera "product" was treated: after two acts the Archduke had had enough of Mozart's music and ordered the two remaining acts performed with the music of one Angelo Tarchi, who had also set the same libretto. We do not know if he judged Tarchi the better composer: he probably would have preferred seeing the play without music, for of course he wanted to know how the events turned out. He presumably would not have been pleased by the ending. Mozart was not present; he probably knew nothing about these proceedings. But they wouldn't have surprised him: neither composer nor librettist had any rights to a work as long as it was paid for, and arbitrary interference was common everywhere.

So people in Vienna grew lethargic toward the little composer Mozart; he was no longer a good source of excitement. *Figaro* was to be the beginning of his ruin. The upper classes, used to seeing themselves as characters in *opera seria*, glorified in everlasting kindness and sovereignty, did not feel offended exactly, but they didn't much like it: the reaction began more with sneers than with indignation. In *Die Entführung* there had still been a lord and lady who got into dire straits: Belmonte and Constanze, from the best families, had for some inexplicable reason strayed into the Orient, were shipwrecked, as happens in those parts, and an even greater lord, a ruler (a Turk, it is true, but a high-class Turk), had the opportunity of expending his generosity on them. The social class was kept more or less intact. Of course, it was assisted by servants, but the servants, Blondchen and Pedrillo (diminutive even in their names), were faithful and devoted; rebelliousness was beyond them. In *Figaro*, on the other hand, the game went against the ruler—only a count, of course, but still one with the power to command, who had ruled long and freely over his subjects until his inferiors thwarted him. Their spokesman, the Count's opponent, is a servant, and he ends up the victor. The Viennese aristocracy did not like that; they responded negatively to this servant, who expresses his confidence in such radiant C major. Perhaps they grew uneasy at the diabolical *secco* "Bravo, signor padrone!" and even more so at the following *cavatina*, "Se vuol ballare, signor contino" (No. 3); perhaps they all felt like *signori contini*, annoyed by the subliminal anger being expressed (like Masetto's "Signor, sì!" in *Don Giovanni*) in a malicious, feigned submissiveness. Figaro, the valet, a former barber, who ruins an amorous adventure of a man of their own kind, who not only deprives the Count of his prey but turns this open victory into a principle the world will never be free of again—this Figaro was not someone they could identify with. There were more agreeable characters, pleasanter topics, more tractable composers.

Following its model, the nobility, the bourgeoisie soon began to avoid Mozart, too. At first this developed slowly. Looking back now, we see it as a kind of party game; the game begins with the players' passive participation, silence, a pointed averting of the eyes, and ends with the ejection of the undesirable person. The subscription lists to Mozart's concerts gradually shrank, until in 1789 only one name was on the list: Gottfried van Swieten, patron to the last, though it did not cost him much to remain one. Where were they, then, Countess Thun, Baron Wetzlar, the Baroness Waldstätten, that friend of carefree days? They were still alive and would long remain so. Jacquin, too, was still alive, but not for long. Where were Mozart's pupils Barbara Ployer and Therese von Trattner? They all were absent, as were commissions for compositions, except for the unending assignments for dance music. After 1790 Mozart was not merely overlooked but snubbed. Joseph Weigl and Salieri were performed, "his" singers—Caterina Cavalieri, Vincenzo Calvesi, his sister-in-law Aloysia—were singing, his friends the Stadler brothers were playing, everything continued in more or less its usual way. Only Mozart was no longer called upon, not for any party, any celebration; while everywhere in Europe, in capital cities and in the provinces, his operas were performed and earned large profits for the promoters, he, as was the custom in the business, received nothing. The certificate he gave his pupil Joseph Eybler on May 30, 1790, wasn't worth anything in Vienna: Eybler intended to try his luck elsewhere, in places where Mozart was appreciated. But in the end Eybler stayed in Vienna, succeeded Salieri as Court Kapellmeister, and was later raised to the nobility. Haydn received an honorary doctorate at Oxford University and became a member of the Royal Swedish Academy, honorary member of the Felix Meritis Society in Amsterdam, member of the Institut de France in Paris, honorary citizen of the city of Vienna, honorary member of the Philharmonic Society in St. Petersburg; Mozart, the prodigy of yesteryear, showered with honors as a youth, the star of the concert halls only a few years earlier, lost ground.

This downward turn is not of course totally explained by the negative reception of *Figaro*. Nor does Joseph Lange's assertion that Mozart was the victim of envy and intrigues suffice, although there is a grain of truth to it. Lesser colleagues (Leopold Kozeluch, Peter von Winter, and others) certainly did their best to force him out, but they could not eliminate him entirely. He was slandered, Constanze later testified. Quite possibly, but what was the nature of these slanders? Another, more recent verdict claims he offended society's code of honor because of his gambling debts.[42] But who, other than his comrades, would have sat down with Mozart at the gaming table? The gentleman and his servant? Besides, the Vienna of Joseph II cannot be compared to that of Schnitzler. It does seem certain that one of the reasons for his growing isolation was his own failure to meet society's expectations. Mozart, too, knew *Figaro* was no fairy tale. His theme yielded a model for his own behavior; an unconscious drive, probably long latent, came to the surface and tempted him to stop living according to the rules imposed on him from outside. He began "to let himself go."

Around 1790, Vienna had temporarily abandoned Mozart;

it seemed to be waiting until this unpleasant and ultimately asocial character, uncomfortable and potentially rebellious, had transformed himself by his death into a great man, still unapproachable, but in a positive sense. After his death, the process reversed itself. *Die Zauberflöte*, attuned, with the help of the experienced Schikaneder, to the taste of a Viennese audience, did not miss its mark. Mozart's popularity began to climb; it spread at first through the rest of Europe, where the name Mozart was already respected, and finally reached those who had left him in the lurch during his lifetime.

The choice of *Figaro* was his, not Da Ponte's. That in itself reveals a potential rebelliousness, for Beaumarchais's play had long been banned in Vienna. Mozart probably read it in translation and was well aware that the subject was a sensitive one, which is not to say that it was his intention to write a revolutionary opera. Mozart is not giving out moral grades here, either. The choice of key neither prejudges nor betrays anything, and it is unique to this opera that representatives of opposing principles (Count, Countess, and Figaro) all express themselves in C major as soon as it is a question of their emotions, the Countess even when we would expect her to sing in C minor or G minor, as in her "Dove sono" (No. 19), when she nostalgically laments her sad fate.

Actually Count Almaviva is the only nobleman in this play, for even Countess Rosina, as we learn from *The Barber of Seville*, is the former ward of Dr. Bartolo, comes most certainly from a bourgeois family, and could as easily have married Figaro, after he proves to be Bartolo's illegitimate son. To be sure, she does not act like a ward in this opera: she has attained a kind of nobility, which her noble spouse lacks. Her emotional nature is not tarnished by the fact that she harbors certain secret desires. Almaviva's desires, on the other hand, are not secret; he is a petty monarch, a spoiled tyrant. Usually in a bad mood, and unwilling to give up his rights, he is Mozart's most unsympathetic character, including even Osmin and Monostatos, who cannot be called to account for trying to make the best of their slavery. There is only one moment when the Count has the chance to reveal himself, at the beginning of the third act: "L'onore . . . dove diamin l'ha posto umano errore!" ("Honor . . . what has it come to because of human frailty!"). Unfortunately, this text is set as a recitative: at precisely the moment when the Contessa's name is mentioned, the music swings from the minor back to the major, but we would like to have heard this thought in an aria, with full instrumental interpretation. His brief moments of regret are not to be trusted; when, in the finale of the last act, he asks the Countess to forgive him for having been too frenzied, wanting to make everything all right after his spree, his leap of a sixth at "Contessa, perdono," and the following seventh at "perdono, perdono!" can hardly mean a true change of character. The prognosis for the rest of their marriage would be very bad if the Countess really wanted to remain the angel of purity she has consciously made herself out to be. After Susanna has eluded him, he will hook someone else; but it is doubtful that the Countess will go on expressing her death wish, as she does in the *cavatina* "Porgi, amor" (No. 10) (not in G minor, as one might expect, but in E-flat major). In Beaumarchais these doubts are cleared up: in the third part of the trilogy, she bears a child to her godson Cherubino, a development we already see coming at this point—and it serves the Count right, too. It is obvious that Cherubino, breathless, bedazzled, and dazzling, to whom even the hardheaded Susanna nearly falls victim, this "youthful Don Giovanni" (Kierkegaard), this half-child, sent off willfully and unwillingly to be an officer, will not stay long with Barbarina, the gardener's daughter (a marriage, incidentally, that we feel to be a misalliance, for we know her father, Antonio, only as a half-drunken, devious toady and spoilsport). But Barbarina, too, has hidden resources: she will find comfort soon enough. If she has resisted the approaches of the Count, whose skirt-chasing not even the tenderest youth can forestall, she betrays a precociousness that astonishes even Figaro. "E così, tenerella,

il mestiero già sai di far tutto sì ben quel che tu fai?" he says
to her ("For your tender years you know your business amaz-
ingly well!"). Her magical little F minor *cavatina* "L'ho per-
duta" (No. 23), the only minor aria in the opera, with its
subtle accompaniment of muted strings alone, deals only with
a lost ornament pin, but it could just as well be about her lost
innocence. We wonder what the first singer of this role, the
twelve-year-old Nannina Gottlieb, may have thought about it.
Who knows, perhaps she, too, was a little minx. She later joined
Schikaneder's troupe and created the role of Pamina (though
that would not necessarily have restored her own virtue).

Susanna rules over the opera, omnipresent. A truly brilliant character, she projects reason more than feeling. She is
an unerring planner, smarter and more calculating than her
fiancé. Potential victim to her master, she dupes him and lures
him, calmly and cunningly, into the trap. But she never deceives us about her true intentions; breathtaking in her rationality, she replies to the shadowy A minor of the Count
with her clear C major during their third act duet "Crudcl!
perchè finora . . . !" (No. 16). Later she will rule over her
husband; there is something astonishingly sturdy in everything
about her; her inclination to tenderness comes rather late,
and, if we read it correctly, is a little unmotivated, like the
stirrings of a tardy conscience. Its magic, however, is overwhelming: not only do the glorious melodic lines of her F
major aria, "Dèh, vieni . . ." (No. 27), reproduce her subjective feeling (less, perhaps, her immediate reaction to the noc-
turnal events she has engineered than the beginning of a new
dimension to her emotional life), but the harmonies also indicate the unique atmosphere of the situation. This "garden
aria" is also a textual jewel within the outstanding libretto,
perhaps Da Ponte's greatest achievement.

It is not entirely clear whether Susanna is just coolly using
words and music to test her fiancé or whether they actually
reflect her dream of fulfillment in their future union. We

confront here the question that will concern us with *Così fan tutte:* does Mozart want to differentiate between true feeling and its counterfeit? Perhaps in this case Mozart is being Mozart, enabling a character he admires to express her wishful ideas. He was fond, not only of this character of his own invention, but also, as a secret ingredient, of Nancy Storace, who created the role. And perhaps this aria, more than the concert aria mentioned earlier, "Ch'io mi scordi di te," K. 505, reveals his personal involvement, part real, part fantasy, with this singer. He rewrote the aria several times; it appears in the opera in its third or fourth version. Did Nancy want it that way? In this case he did bring his own feeling into the opera, and identified with Susanna's beloved, Figaro—both with his love and with his joy in rebellion. Of course, Susanna is quite cool toward her beloved, and shortly before the seemingly happy ending she treats him to a box on the ears; but from *Die Entführung* to *Don Giovanni,* a box on the ears seems to be a cure-all in Mozart, ever a resounding confirmation of fidelity.

In Vienna at this time, Nancy Storace had become the rival of Aloysia Lange, whose star was already on the wane. Nancy was obviously favored by the court; her yearly salary was nearly six times what Mozart earned there in 1791 for his year's contract for forty-seven dances. She must have had unique charisma and her own special vocal magic. As we have noted, Mozart apparently did not trust her vocal range. Her brother, Stephen Storace, Mozart's friend (but not, as has been claimed, his pupil), did trust it: in his *Gli Equivoci* (December 1786), which was premièred in Vienna a few months after *Figaro,* and is an attractive opera, though derivative of Mozart, the leading female role, which demanded an upper range greater than Susanna's, was given to his sister.

The first cast of *Figaro* was, quite simply, outstanding, reports Michael Kelly, the first Basilio and Don Curzio, perhaps attributing a share in this brilliance to himself. It is probable that Mozart wrote Basilio's aria "In quegli anni" (No. 25), which is not very well motivated either textually or dramatically, for Kelly, whom he esteemed personally; it is a miniature monodrama embodying the story of the ass's skin, which protects the wearer not only from inclement weather but also from lion attacks, because it looks so contemptible. At the point in the aria when the skin is first used effectively, the music, with clear comic intent, modulates from B-flat to G minor. The loyal Kelly, full of seemly respect for the esteemed composer, has described the *Figaro* rehearsals:

> All the original performers had the advantage of the instruction of the composer, who transfused into their minds his inspired meaning. I shall never forget his little animated countenance, when lighted up with the glowing rays of genius;—it is as impossible to describe it, as it would be to paint sunbeams.[43]

A satisfying, credible report, though written in 1826, forty years after the première, and thus a glance into the past. Kelly was the only member of the cast still alive, but he does not seem to have glorified the facts for that reason; on the contrary, we think they must have been just as he describes them. Da Ponte would have been the only other witness still alive; he was residing in America, where he lived for another twelve years.

The reception of the opera at its Viennese première was lukewarm to cool: the people it described were sitting right there. Count Zinzendorf, a conscientious chronicler, lacking all wit (who passed his time entering in his diary banal goings-on and the goings-on he made banal, usually concerning the weather), wrote on the evening of the première: *"a 7ʰ du soir à l'opeta le Nozze di Figaro, la poesie de la Ponte, la musique de Mozhardt. Louise dans notre loge, l'opera m'ennuya . . ."* A frosty observation. We cannot conclude from this terse entry whether the opera bored him because his fellow nobleman Almaviva's domestics got on his nerves or because he was with the aforementioned Louise. But then, everything bored him.

Mozart conducted the second performance, too, at which five arias had to be encored; the third performance was conducted by Joseph Weigl, Haydn's godson, then twenty-two years old, who was soon to be a more successful opera composer in Vienna than Mozart ever was; there were seven encores. This time Zinzendorf wrote in his diary: *"La musique de Mozart singuliere des mains sans téte . . ."* One wonders why he went to hear it again. We do not know if Mozart ever addressed himself to the effect of his music. After he entered the facts, including the cast, in his thematic catalogue on April 29, 1786, two days before the postponed première, he did not mention *Figaro* again until January 1787, when he was confronted with its overwhelming success in Prague.

With the E-flat Piano Quartet, K. 493 (June 3, 1786), a sister work to that in G minor, K. 478 (October 16, 1785), Mozart returned to his daily routine, as dictated by financial exigencies. But he was no longer able to earn money by writing chamber music. The Viennese public could make nothing of these two unique works, the outcome of his newly won, almost serene introversion (for example, the A-flat larghetto of the second). They preferred hearing Kozeluch and Ignaz Pleyel. Mozart's publishers urged him to write something easier, pieces that could also "hold their own when performed with average skill." Mozart voluntarily withdrew the two works, but his willingness to provide what the public wanted was gone for good. He served himself and his pupils, or those of them who were left. Around this time only Franziska von Jacquin was still his piano student for certain. For her he wrote a Rondo in F for piano, K. 494 (June 10, 1786); but perhaps it was really for himself, written in a half hour when he had nothing else to do. Possibly he remembered the great period of his piano concerti, for in addition to its strict rondo form, the work contains an imposing written-out cadenza.

As we have indicated, various disparate works of great range, some of the highest quality, occur in the period between *Figaro* and *Don Giovanni*, particularly at the beginning of 1787. Possibly *Figaro*'s success in Prague in December 1786 encouraged Mozart, for the last time, not to let himself be deterred in any way.

It is worth pointing out Mozart's diverse activities during these months. What we can prove is incomplete; possibly his field of activity was greater than we know. The visit of the young Beethoven is generally thought to be a biographical high point; if it really took place, it would have been in spring 1787. The idea of this meeting is very attractive, but we do well to doubt that it ever came to pass; the two would have taken silent cognizance of each other. The fact that Mozart never bothered to write about it proves nothing, but that Beethoven, too, Mozart's admirer, never mentioned meeting the creator of works he later speaks of so frequently relegates the episode to the realm of anecdote.

We are accustomed to seeing Mozart's work excluded from his extramusical communications. He scarcely ever wasted a word to outsiders about what really moved him. Especially while he wrote his greatest works, his verbal statements not only are confined to prosaic routine but are also interspersed with an (often forced) silliness, which will astonish only those who think a genius must maintain and demonstrate in every statement and action the highest level of the spirit that singles him out from all others. Actually, it is more characteristic of the *would-be* genius to be continually expressing his awareness of his own importance.

All the stranger, then, is the famous letter to his father of April 4, 1787:

This very moment I have received a piece of news which greatly distresses me, the more so as I gathered from your last letter that, thank God, you were very well indeed. But now I hear that you are really ill. I need hardly tell you how greatly I am longing to receive some reassuring news from yourself. And I still expect it; although I have now made a habit of being prepared in all affairs of life for the worst. As death, when we come to consider it closely, is the true goal of our existence, I have formed during the last few years such close relations with this best and truest friend of mankind, that his image is not only no longer terrifying to me, but is indeed very soothing and consoling! And I thank my God for graciously granting me the opportunity (you know what I mean) of learning that death is the *key* which unlocks the door to our true happiness. I never lie down at night without reflecting that—young as I am—I may not live to see another day. Yet no one of all my acquaintances could say that in company I am morose or disgruntled. For this blessing I daily thank my Creator and wish with all my heart that each one of my fellow creatures could enjoy it. In the letter which Madame Storace took away with her, I expressed my views to you on this point, in connection with the sad death of my dearest and most beloved friend, Count von Hatzfeld. He was just thirty-one, my own age. I do not feel sorry for him, but I pity most sincerely both myself and all who knew him as well as I did. I hope and trust that while I am writing this, you are feeling better. But if, contrary to all expectation, you are not recovering, I implore you by . . . not to hide it from me, but to tell me the whole truth or get someone to write it to me, so that as quickly as is humanly possible I may come to your arms. I entreat you by all that is sacred—to both of us. Nevertheless I trust that I shall soon have a reassuring letter from you; and cherishing this pleasant hope, I and my wife and our little Carl kiss your hands a thousand times and I am ever

your most obedient son
W. A. Mozart

At the time of this letter Leopold Mozart was, in fact, already fatally ill. Wolfgang's observations seem to suggest that he at least suspected as much, but they do not reveal it unambiguously, and they sound like an evasion. Furthermore, they are not his own thoughts, but are the faithful paraphrase of a work published in 1767 by the popular philosopher Moses

Mendelssohn, *Phädon, Oder Über die Unsterblichkeit der Seele (Phaedon, or On the Immortality of the Soul)*. Mozart owned a copy, and must have read Mendelssohn's first book, too, unless his father, or a better-read friend, like van Swieten or his educated brother-in-law Joseph Lange, who had met Mendelssohn, called his attention to these meditations. For we can hardly imagine that Mozart was a great reader, except as a purposeful seeker of scores and libretti.

Let us table the question of how honest was his intention to be in his father's arms "as quickly as is humanly possible" if matters were "serious." Such a statement stems more from self-deception, a more or less routine idea of piety, than from a real impulse on his part. Or, more likely, this is another instance of his well-known repression: everything will turn out all right, God willing.

In all the Mozart literature no one has challenged this letter's apparent proof of the great discovery, the longed-for sign of the deepest "pervading inwardness." The search for the causes of emotional upheaval here comes to an end. This was the starting point for the theory of a Mozart conscious of his fate, half in love with easeful death; yet it is almost undignified, this exhibition of "irrefutable" proof that "Wolfgang Amadeus" was not just a carefree, thoughtless joker during his life. The presence of death in his emotional life, so the argument goes, is proven here conclusively. But is it really?

To do justice to this letter we must look ahead. One of Mozart's later letters deals with death; it is in Italian, written when death was already near. There is some well-founded doubt about its authenticity, especially because it evinces an attitude toward death different from the first letter. In September 1791, Mozart supposedly wrote to Da Ponte:

My dear Sir, I should like to take your advice, but how can I? My spirit is broken and I cannot divert my eyes from the vision of that stranger. I see him continually before me;

he entreats and urges me, and impatiently asks for my work. I continue to compose because that fatigues me less than resting. Anyhow, I have nothing more to fear. I know well, from what I am experiencing, that my hour is near, that I am on the point of death: I shall die without having known any of the delights my talent would have brought me. And yet life is so full of beauty, and in the beginning my career showed auspicious prospects! Alas! one cannot alter one's own destiny. Nobody on earth is master of his fate, and I must be resigned; it will be as Providence decrees. For myself I must complete my funeral hymn and I would not like to leave my work unfinished.

Much speaks for this letter's authenticity. Not the mention of a funeral hymn, namely the Requiem, nor the mysterious stranger who brought him the commission, and whose vision pursues him (on the contrary, that would speak more for a romantic falsification), but the employment of those well-known clichés in the face of death, typical of Mozart, especially after his mother's death: the irrevocability of fate, the need to comply. In a certain sense, then, this letter is the opposite of the one to his father: death is portrayed, not as man's dearest friend, but rather as his mild enemy. Of course, one speaks differently when comforting a dying man and when one is beginning to experience death oneself.

Also speaking for the letter's authenticity is its stilted, artificial style, the language of opera libretti, typical of Mozart's Italian. Thus, the counterfeiter, if not a librettist himself, would have been able to imitate this language, though it is clear he was not an Italian. But why the Italian language? The imaginary recipient could have been someone other than Da Ponte. Perhaps the forger chose him because it was known that he had asked Mozart to travel with him to England. The letter does sound like a reply, as if the writer, compelled by the inevitability of fate, was refusing some request. The sentence: "I continue to compose because that fatigues me less than resting" is very persuasive. Here a psychologically insightful observer has, perhaps for the first time, stated a behavioral truth common to all creative men: the escape into creativity. Was it Mozart himself in one isolated moment of self-analytical reflection?

The original of this letter has been lost. No biographer knew it. If it is a forgery, it is a gem of inspired identification with the composer. So we do not take it amiss, whoever its author was. It shows us Mozart before his death, not only as one often imagines him, but as one would wish him. The tone of quiet resignation is un-Mozartean, of course, and the hint of a euphoric transfiguration is wishful thinking. Nevertheless, the letter does have the air of sovereignty we have noted elsewhere, the dignity of a man who knew no self-pity or sentimentality. In contrast to other counterfeits, which are usually designed to denigrate, dishonor, or slander their object, this document would be an anonymous tribute and a hint to posterity. To be honest, it is regrettable that its authenticity is in doubt. We try not to paint idealized portraits, but cannot help it if something in us keeps painting them.

The free appropriation of the thoughts and words of literary minds, or of people who were thought to be such, was not a way out for Mozart alone; rather, it accorded with the expressive style of the period. While the letter to Da Ponte might be considered a profound personal statement if it was authentic, the letter to his father of 1787, which we held to be apocryphal until its rediscovery in 1978, is an appropriation of this kind. The core of the letter seems totally atypical, both in its reflections and in its wording. Until late in his life, if not at the very end, Mozart cared about his external appearance and spent large sums of money on it, but as far as we know, he no longer tried in the last years to see his inner life as others saw it, or to imagine how descriptions of his emotional state would affect the world (and this, perhaps, did him harm). To find the "key . . . to our true happiness" was as alien to his way of thinking as all other contemplation of the meaning of life. He understood more and more that his own life had an objective meaning, but he never spoke about it.

Can we, within the framework of our general helplessness in interpreting his soul, imagine Mozart writing this letter? Doesn't it seem as if he were stepping out of himself for a moment to appear briefly, in a last, guilty act of love for his father, as that son he no longer was to his father? Presumably he did not even consider that his father might have recognized the ideas from his own reading, though it may have been Leopold himself who suggested that his son read Mendelssohn. Above all, he did not consider that his embittered father would read the assurances about his daily thanks to the Creator with the skepticism they deserve. As far as we know, he never answered his son.

Most biographers consider this the crowning verbal revelation of spiritual achievement on Mozart's part. We see it as the fervent wish that his father remember him kindly in his last moments. That wish surely does honor to the author of the letter and to its honored recipient.

Death as the "true goal of our existence" (Horace: *"mors ultima linea rerum est,"* mistranslated) was for Mozart surely no more than a figure of speech. If we read him correctly, he was one of those who accept death as their inevitable destiny, without wasting any words about it. From this point of view, it seems as if the letter were written to suit the wishful thinking of biographers; for it is virtually their approved, collective method to contemplate death by using the example of great men; it is a means to promote their own repression of this *"ultima linea."* Men who cannot come to terms with death try to use the composure of their heroes to hold themselves together. They cling to models of identification. But men who can look at the *"linea"* with composure do not discuss it. Mozart was one of these.

Mozart's talent did not lie in the verbal expression of his inner feelings. Except for his sudden, short outbursts in the last letters to Constanze, dictated by grief (but always under control), we can reduce such statements to a few patterns, almost basic forms; here, too, he had his stage sets and his stage grammar and rarely went beyond them. He lived in a "prepsychological" age, when people were increasingly sensitive to the psyche, but when it still had no formulated science. A doctrine was even further off. Expression of the life of the psyche, if necessary at all, was confined, for better or for worse, to what poets had written about it. Or vice versa; whoever found adequate and comprehensible language for it was called a poet. In the best of cases these poets were Goethe (*Werther* was popular; Mozart had read it) and Shakespeare, though in inadequate, somewhat inaccurate translations. Wieland, Klopstock, and Gellert were widely read philosophers, like Mendelssohn. In the worst of cases, though, there were minor and now forgotten dramatists, and numerous court poets, i.e., librettists, Metastasio heading the list. Their diction set the style for the class to which the Mozarts belonged. Whoever chose to write about his own emotions entrusted them to these men, to their vocabulary, their syntax, rhetoric, and powers of evocation. In fact, it seems as if certain norms and rules of *opera seria* characters were operating in the behavior of the audience, as if personal behavior had to be adapted to certain predetermined models, some of them so grand that the real content they expressed in no way justified them.

Thus, in his verbal statements the musical innovator Mozart was only too happy to use ready-made phraseology and its corresponding theatricality. During the act of writing, he identified with a character who was not himself, as the discriminating recipient of his letters could discern. At any rate, the correspondence between father and son had already tapered off around this time. The solitary Leopold Mozart's everyday remarks were now directed to his daughter, who had been living for three years in St. Gilgen, as the wife of the prefect Johann Baptist von Berchtold zu Sonnenburg.

She had had many admirers, but Leopold had found none of them acceptable. He ruled over his daughter, too, until her marriage; he may, in fact, have destroyed her hopes for happiness by rejecting a man who did not suit him, the Salzburg Minister of War, Herr d'Yppold, whom Nannerl may have loved and whom Wolfgang liked as well. So Leopold was responsible for the rather sorry marriage of convenience to the elderly Herr von Berchtold, twice a widower, whom she married in 1784. Berchtold paid 500 gulden to her as a *"Morgengabe"* (bridegroom's gift) *"in praemium virginitatis,"* and we may assume that he could be sure of *"virginitas."* He was a stingy pedant; otherwise nothing bad is known about him, but then nothing good is, either.

Leopold's letters to his daughter have to do in part with household affairs; he sent her codfish, chocolate, limes, etc. His intimate remarks about his son strike us as peculiarly cool. We would not want to insinuate that the lonely man was smug or took delight in his son's misfortune, but "I told him so!" does seem to be a recurrent undertone. Yet we have to be careful with such interpretations. Leopold Mozart was a master of laconic description; he knew how to regulate the emotional content of his letters precisely. One is inclined to load the correspondence between father and son with an emotional content it neither has nor should have. When communicating matter-of-fact news, both writers seem to be deliberately holding back any commentary, so that the other can fill in the details himself. Indeed, we are sometimes tempted to add the exclamation "Just imagine!" or "Can you believe that!" to their reports.

Nevertheless, the father's remarks about his son in his letters to his daughter do not sound affectionate. When Wolfgang told him of the birth of his third child, Johann Thomas Leopold (October 18, 1786), Leopold wrote on October 27 to Nannerl, "You will read in your brother's letter, which I en-

close, that your little Leopold now has a comrade in Vienna."
We don't know if he ever extended his congratulations. "Little Leopold" was Nannerl's son, whom the solitary grand-
father had taken to live with him as a companion. He tried to
keep this arrangement secret from Wolfgang, for when Wolfgang and Constanze were planning a trip to England he had
refused to keep their son; the journey was never made. Of
course, his refusal was aimed more at Constanze than at Wolfgang. If his son resented it, he did not let his father know it.
Wolfgang overlooked nearly everything in everyone, and especially in his father. He innocently sent the two Storaces and
Michael Kelly, who passed through Salzburg on their return
from England, to visit his father. The father received them
dourly and described the visit to Nannerl as a nuisance; his
special scorn was directed at the (apparently voluminous)
luggage of Nancy Storace. And shortly before his death he
wrote to his daughter (May 11, 1787): "Your brother is now
living in the Landstrasse No. 224. He does not say why he has
moved. Not a word. But unfortunately, I can guess the reason."

Obviously Mozart had been reluctant to tell his father of
the move from their spacious, elegant apartment in the
Schulerstrasse to a more modest one (April 23, 1787). For it
symbolized the beginning of social decline and of material
misfortune. That is what Leopold guessed, as he had guessed
other things. He knew how Wolfgang responded to life's vicis-
situdes; he could read very well between the lines of his letters.
His insight into his son's mentality is often exceptionally
sharp. And we cannot demand from him comparable insight
into himself: what father of such a son would have done better?

The move of the Mozart family (Wolfgang, Constanze,
Carl, housemaid, starling) was certainly due to straitened circumstances. The fact that Mozart felt he had to interrupt
work on *Don Giovanni* speaks for that, too; he had to have
something for immediate sale; there is no other explanation

for the composition of the two String Quintets in C major and G minor, K. 515 and K. 516, for who would have commissioned them? At this time he could no longer expect commissions from Viennese circles. Not until the end of 1787 did he receive the usual commission from the court for regular deliveries of dances, for which he received an imperial chamber composer's salary of 800 gulden a year.

It is hard for us to think of these two quintets as dictated by material need; but then, many of Mozart's great works were written under shabby circumstances, though they never betray it, let alone the fact that no one could use them and that he sometimes received nothing for them.

These two quintets again raise the question of whether Mozart forgot the occasion for his works or whether he himself did not perceive the "gloomy" profundity of some of them. The C major work seems to us like a partial demonstration of what Mozart was capable of producing in this key: the quintet shows one side, *Figaro* the other. To be sure, immediately after the opening of the quintet, there is a shift to C minor, as if a final judgment were still pending. But he decides on a major *sui generis*.

Digression: I say "shift" because I do not like to use the musicological term *"Molleintrübung"* ("darkening into the minor"). To me it is indicative of the inadmissible value judgments of music analysis. Why "darken"? The day is not conceivable without the night, but which twelve hours are intrinsically better? We return here to a topic already touched upon, for it is a primary reason for this study: when Abert speaks of the finale of the early G minor symphony, K. 183/173dB, as a "confession" which "knows not the liberating spirit of a Haydn finale, let alone one by Beethoven," calling the work "pessimistic," "written in a dark hour,"[44] he is succumbing (not for the first time, as we have seen) to a confusion of subject and object. If one thought the error through to its logical conclusion, one would have to conclude that

Goethe harbored suicidal intentions because he wrote *Werther*. And yet Abert was one of the truly great experts on musical grammar. He writes, for example, that "E-flat major in the older Neapolitans was the key of dark, solemn pathos, used when calling upon deities and in ghost scenes."[45] Was he reluctant to acknowledge that Mozart, however carefully, did adopt some musical conventions? Has his experience of the "content" at times blurred his perception of the "form"?

The G minor Quintet puts us into the same mood as its companion in the major, though it is governed by a more energetic impulse; it is "more eloquent," especially the agitating and agitated E-flat major Adagio, which the overly appreciative Einstein calls "the prayer of a lonely man . . . what goes on here can perhaps be compared only to the scene in the Garden of Gethsemane. The chalice with its bitter draught must be emptied, and the disciples are sleeping."[46] Here we do best to put our faith in the word "perhaps."

It is no surprise that these two quintets, in particular, have suffered an excess of emotional interpretation, especially the G minor. And indeed it does speak a language that inspires us to share in an inexplicable process. Alternating between urgency and remoteness, it affects us (there can hardly be an exception) as profoundly tragic. Ultimately we cannot deny that our receptive potential is reacting not to an abstract progression of notes but to promptings from the rich supply of a magician. He offers us experiences, suggests associations with moments we have lived through, traumas of the past evading extramusical comprehension. And if we don't happen to think of "Gethsemane" when listening to the G minor Quintet, if we feel Abert's views about "cutting pain," "sobbing sadness," or "a fatalistic plunge" are misguided, we still cannot deny that we, too, are moved. Why else should we need music but for its ability to satisfy our longing for emotional experience, without our having to undergo the deep tumult at its root. In the end we always experience Mozart's music (like Beethoven's) as the catharsis resulting from one man's sublimation of his personal crisis.

Mozart's hope of marketing these quintets was disappointed. In April (during work on *Don Giovanni*) he offered them on a subscription basis, "beautifully and correctly copied," through his lodge brother and friend (and probably already his creditor) Michael Puchberg. The works would be available beginning in July. But in vain; no one subscribed. On June 25, 1788, Mozart extended the subscription period until 1789, and this too was in vain. Vienna preferred lesser minds: Kozeluch, Dittersdorf, Eberl, Gyrowetz, and the rest. No one wanted anything to do with emotionally turbulent music. On April 23, 1787, the Viennese correspondent for Cramer's *Magazin der Musik* (Hamburg) reported that Mozart had gone astray: "A pity that his deliberate, truly admirable attempt to renew his creativity has taken him too far and profits neither heart nor soul . . . his new quartets . . . are too highly seasoned—what palate can endure them for long?" The same journal confirms in 1789 "that he has a pronounced inclination for the difficult and the unusual," which can hardly be denied.

We do not know whether, at the time of the quintets' rejection, Mozart had already spent the honorarium of 100 ducats from the Prague commission for *Don Giovanni* or if he had not yet received it. In any event, he must have needed some immediate income. For this reason he wrote a few lieder for his "dearest, most beloved friend," Gottfried von Jacquin, who probably paid him for them at once, only to publish at least two of them later under his own name. But Mozart did not hold this against him. There was no copyright then; both giver and receiver were liberal in their disposition of the intellectual property of the other. Mozart, who sometimes gave away smaller compositions the way an author today gives out autographs, was not very particular about it; in fact, he seems to have forgotten some of his larger works as soon as they were copied. Thus, for example, he was "quite surprised" at the quality of the D major Symphony, K. 385, "Haffner," written for Salzburg, when his father returned the manuscript to him in 1783, one year after its performance. He wrote then: "It must surely produce a good effect" (February 15, 1783). We can assure him that it does.

People also used to be more liberal with quotations and borrowings. Many helped themselves to parts of the Divertimento in E-flat for winds, K. 252/240a. Franz Gruber used the andante of the first movement for his Christmas carol "Silent night, holy night . . ." and the presto assai must have inspired the rondo of Beethoven's C major Piano Concerto. Mozart, too, certainly borrowed from others. But in every case it may be only a strange coincidence, like the sudden and astonishing anticipation of *Tristan* in the chromaticism of the andante con moto in A-flat of the E-flat String Quartet, K. 428/421b.

At the end of May 1787 Mozart wrote to Gottfried von Jacquin:

Vienna, May 29th, 1787

Dearest Friend!

Please tell Herr Exner to come at nine o'clock tomorrow morning to bleed my wife.

I send you herewith your Amynt and the sacred song. Please be so good as to give the sonata to your sister with my compliments and tell her to tackle it at once, for it is rather difficult. Adieu. Your true friend

Mozart

I inform you that on returning home today I received the sad news of my most beloved father's death. You can imagine the state I am in.

Possibly Herr von Jacquin could imagine Mozart's state; we cannot. We cannot see him writing such a letter, cannot understand what is hidden beneath this reserve, if anything at all is hidden. Perhaps his father's death appears solely as the postscript to a series of everyday news because he had not yet assimilated its full impact; at any rate, it is not enough to interrupt the banalities. First we have Herr Exner, probably a kind of barber-surgeon who was to bleed the ailing Constanze (we always shudder at the thought of all that spilled blood); then Mozart confirms that he sent off two lieder, "Amynt" and the sacred song. They have not been identified; probably Jacquin had sent them to him for his appraisal, for he was a composer himself. The sonata for Jacquin's sister with the exhortation to tackle it at once—all of this before the sad news—is the C major Sonata for piano, four hands, K. 521, written on May 29 (one day after his father's death); its andante in F major already points to *Don Giovanni*, breathing the magic of the wavering coquette Zerlina, containing a quotation from her aria "Vedrai, carino" (No. 19) and even the motive "E naturale." This movement, too, offers us the minor outburst so typical of Mozart, the sudden yet predictable change of mood as a stylistic technique. This sonata provides a good opportunity for setting up a vertical scale of comparative values. Abert finds it "less important," Einstein "splendid," Paumgartner "a gem." The Zerlina movement, according to the Frenchman Saint-Foix, is "like a lied," i.e., German; the German Abert finds it "like a rondo, French." Dennerlein calls it a "stately song." No one thinks of Zerlina, and yet this is the only affinity that can be proven—although, of course, we attach no particular meaning to the proof. Mozart did not consciously husband his storehouse of ideas. When, for example, at the words "donne vedete" in Cherubino's B-flat arietta (No. 11) in *Figaro*, he reaches back fourteen years, to an old idea from the allegro of the D major Sonata for piano, four hands, K. 381/123a (1772), it may be a distinct *déjà vu* for us, but for him there was certainly no connection, conscious or unconscious.

A few days after the letter to Jacquin, on June 2, 1787, Mozart wrote to his sister:

Dearest Sister!

You can easily imagine how grieved I was by the sad news of the sudden death of our most dear father, since the loss is the same for both of us. As I am unable to leave Vienna at this time, and would do so primarily for the pleasure of embracing you, and since it would hardly be worth the trouble as regards the estate of our dear departed father, I must confess that I too agree with you about a public sale. But I will await an inventory first, to decide on the selection. If however, as Herr von d'Yppold writes, a *dispositio paterna inter liberos* exists, I will have to read this *dispositio* before I can make further decisions. Thus I will wait for an exact copy of it and will tell you my opinion at once, as soon as I have looked it over. Please give the enclosed letter to our dear, good friend Herr von d'Yppold. Since in the past he has so often shown himself to be a friend of our family, I hope he will also be so good as to represent me in these concerns. Farewell, dearest sister! I am forever your

faithful brother
W. A. Mozart

P.S. My wife sends greetings to you and your husband, as do I.

The emotional content of this letter is confined to the first sentence. But even this seems artificial, rather forced, especially since the death was not all that sudden. The letter to his father of April 4 means that Mozart must have been prepared. The rest of the writing is extremely matter-of-fact and terse, the instructions rather blunt. He names a family friend, the same Herr d'Yppold whom Nannerl would have liked to marry, as his representative in the business of the inheritance; it was probably a legal requirement. Whether in addition he did not trust his brother-in-law's and sister's honesty, we do not know. We cannot believe his regret at being unable to embrace his sister. This was one of his stage formulae, one of the fillers he dispensed *ad libitum*. He seemed to use them with a particular lack of conviction when his mind was on other things; and when was his mind not on things other than superficial communication with his so-called fellow man? Where is there ever even a hint from the mature Mozart that the personality of any other individual had affected him or that anyone's psychological makeup had impressed him? We can gather how remote was his desire to embrace his sister from the simple fact that he never tried to see her afterward, although a visit in connection with his journey to Frankfurt would have been easy to arrange. It is not known whether he ever did see his brother-in-law face to face. They certainly would not have had anything in common.

Two days after the letter to his sister, Mozart's starling died in its cage in his study. Mozart dedicated a detailed elegy to it:

> *A little fool lies here*
> *Whom I held dear—*
> *A starling in the prime*
> *Of his brief time,*
> *Whose doom it was to drain*
> *Death's bitter pain.*
> *Thinking of this, my heart*
> *Is riven apart.*
> *Oh, reader! Shed a tear,*
> *You also, here.*
> *He was not naughty, quite,*
> *But gay and bright,*
> *And under all his brag*
> *A foolish wag.*
> *This no one can gainsay*
> *And I will lay*
> *That he is now on high,*
> *And from the sky,*
> *Praises me without pay*

In his friendly way.
Yet unaware that death
Has choked his breath,
And thoughtless of the one
Whose rime is thus well done.

June the 4th, 1787   Mozart.[47]

Reading this poem (if we can call it that), we cannot help thinking of a more worthy object for tears. But we do not wish to speculate about the difference in Mozart's relationship to these two dissimilar victims of death (father and starling). He can hardly have been thinking of the coincidence, either—or was he? Nor is it probable that he wanted to distance himself forcibly from the thought of his father's death by singing about a substitute object. Mozart simply liked to have a bird nearby; he kept the starling's successor, a canary, in his room until only a few hours before his death. The starling had had its role in his life. On May 27, 1784, he had bought it for 34 kreuzer; it lived with him for three years and, if we can believe Mozart's notes (ornithology by no means rules out the possibility), the bird could sing the first five bars of the variations theme in the finale of the G major Piano Concerto, K. 453.

The quality of this eulogy reveals that Mozart was not a poet, but we find this doggerel important both for its own sake and as evidence. The months we have just dealt with raise the question of the mysterious synchrony of his inner life, of that score in which *Don Giovanni* and various lesser works, the death of his father and that of his bird, the quintets and the inheritance each had its own part, however divergent in importance and quality.

Ein musikalischer Spass (A Musical Joke), K. 522, dated June 14, 1787—now the sequence becomes almost macabre—was the first work Mozart copied out after the news of his father's death. Its other title, *Dorfmusikanten-Sextett*, may

have been the idea of his embarrassed chroniclers, who wanted
to salvage a crumb of piety in light of the death. But Mozart
did not give it this title, and it doesn't completely suit the
work. In the last analysis, its malicious will to triviality is by
no means totally comic. Nor is bad performance the object
of this truly grandiose parody (Mozart wouldn't have concerned himself with that), but rather incompetent composing.
The wonderfully feigned lack of imagination is aimed at inferior quality, and does not attempt grotesque humor. In fact,
Mozart's target was a synthesis of his colleagues. The fashionable composers of the time, his uninspiring pupils, all are
victims of this merciless "joke"; but their "intellects" are
parodied and thus transformed into intellect. The synthetic
composer taken to task is probably a general representative of
the non-Mozart and non-Haydn music of the time—second-
rate, superficial, stubbornly and enduringly devoid of any
significant idea. "Seldom in music has one mind exerted itself
so much to seem so mindless," says Abert in his detailed interpretation of this work.[48] The interpretation is a masterpiece
of musical analysis, proving that interpretations gain authenticity when the *conscious* motivation of the music is clearly to
challenge other music, when the interpreter can then have no
reason to look into the creator's inner life; then science becomes gay. Of course, Abert does not investigate the mysterious origins of the work; no one has, for the solution to this
riddle might not fit into the ideal biographical picture.

The autograph manuscript was completed two weeks after
the news of his father's death. But since Mozart carried his
compositions around in his head for days before setting them
down on paper, the idea must have existed earlier. Naturally
we cannot say whether the inspiration for a musical joke after
his father's death was a coincidence or not. It does seem certain that the death of Leopold Mozart, for years such a dominant figure in his son's life, must have released some unconscious response, and it also seems probable that it was a feeling
of liberation. Can this have been conscious? Might he have
expressed it? It is possible that *Ein musikalischer Spass* was self-

therapy, either to conquer his grief or else to laugh off his guilt feelings at his lack of sympathy. We cannot plumb the depths and shallows of Mozart's inner motivations. What occurred to Mozart when his father died? Apparently the ludicrous incompetence of his colleagues and pupils. Absurd, but not unthinkable. It is more probable, however, that nothing conscious occurred to him at all on his father's death, but all the more occurred to him for *Don Giovanni*, instead.

He must have been following some inner need when writing the *Spass*, for he cannot have had a commission for it. Time pressure stimulated him, a behavioral response he had in common with many artists. It is improbable that the *Spass* was ever performed during Mozart's time. It was simply something for his own enjoyment.

Two days after writing this joke, on June 16, Mozart was again forced to deal briefly with the rapidly fading memory of his father. In this case, too, he wrote to reinforce his claim to a portion of the inheritance:

Vienna, June 16th, 1787

Dearest, most beloved Sister!
I was not at all surprised, as I could easily guess the reason, that you yourself did not inform me of the sad death of our most dear father, which to me was quite unexpected. May God take him to Himself! Rest assured, my dear, that if you desire a kind brother to love and protect you, you will find one in me on every occasion. My dearest, most beloved sister! If you were still unprovided for, all this would be quite unnecessary, for, as I have already said and thought a thousand times, I should leave everything to you with the greatest delight. But as the property would really be of no use to you, while, on the contrary, it would be a considerable help to me, I think it my duty to consider my wife and child.

A cool letter. Probably he wrote in haste. Again the death is described as unexpected, as if Mozart had never doubted that his father had been hale and hearty to the end. But the logic of this first sentence is also peculiar in another way: he was not surprised by his sister's silence because he could easily guess the reason. These words are deeply untruthful; he did not take the matter to heart (or mind). The rhetorical passages that follow do not change anything, either, these protestations of brotherly love laid on with a trowel. On the contrary, they are used to introduce the real purpose of his letter, the indication that he is not about to renounce any part of the estate due him, or at least that he wants equivalent value. Possibly Constanze had a hand in writing this; that is how it seemed to those who could not bear such a materialistic hero.

With Mozart's agreement the estate was auctioned off. His brother-in-law offered him 1,000 gulden. It was probably a fair offer.

On August 1, Mozart wrote to his sister:

Vienna, August 1st, 1787

Dearest, most beloved Sister!

At the moment I am simply replying to your letters, so I am writing very little and in great haste, as I really have far too much to do. As both your husband, my dear brother-in-law, whom I ask you to kiss a thousand times for me, and I are particularly anxious to wind up the whole business as soon as possible, I am accepting his offer, on the understanding, however, that the thousand gulden shall be paid to me not in Imperial but in Viennese currency and, moreover, as a bill of exchange. Next postday I shall send your husband the draft of an agreement or rather of a contract between us. Then the two original documents will follow, one signed by me, the other to be signed by him. I shall send you as soon as possible some new compositions of mine for the clavier. Please do not forget about my *scores*. A thousand farewells to you. I must close. My wife and our Carl send a thousand greetings to you and your husband, and I am ever your brother who loves you sincerely,

W. A. Mozart

The Landstrasse, August 1st, 1787.

If Mozart had been asked if he really loved his sister sincerely, he probably would have been taken aback. He did not realize that he had not loved her for a long time, that she had become a matter of indifference to him, just as he did not realize that he had already forgotten the reason behind this correspondence, their father. As far as we know, his son never mentions him again. He promises to send his sister new "compositions . . . for the clavier," asks her in return for his "scores," the originals of his works in his father's estate. But above all, tucked away among the assurances of 1,000 kisses and 1,000 greetings is the matter of 1,000 gulden, and in the currency most advantageous to him: 1,000 Viennese gulden were equal to 1,200 Salzburg gulden. These calculations have already turned the emotional content of the letter into an impatient exercise by rote, an exercise which includes, as convention dictates, his wife's respects and those of his three-year-old son, Carl.

He is in haste, he writes. He always wrote that at the beginning of letters he did not want to write; we know that trick. He had a lot to do. When didn't he? But one never knows what Mozart *had* to do and what he himself decided to do. Was he thinking about a musical joke, or did he have to come up with his bundle of minuets for the court, easy enough to do, after all? Possibly he was referring to *Eine kleine Nachtmusik*, K. 525, G major, which was completed ten days later (August 10, 1787). This may have been a commissioned work, written in haste, for, as far as we know, he never wrote these easygoing serenades without a commission. They were usually for some celebration in an aristocratic household. Perhaps one of these aristocrats had thought of Mozart, and he was able to earn a few gulden. Today, he would be able to make a living from only three or four of these serenades: *Eine kleine Nachtmusik* is his most popular work. But even if we hear it on every street corner, its high quality is undisputed, an occasional piece from a light but happy pen.

Too much to do: most of his lieder were also composed during these months of work on *Don Giovanni*. Perhaps the commission from Jacquin had whetted his appetite. The series of lieder is uneven in quality; it includes both important and totally worthless songs, and a parody, "Die Alte," K. 517 (May 18, 1787), in which an old woman complains about the "younger generation" in a mock-tearful E minor: "Zu meiner Zeit, zu meiner Zeit, bestand noch Recht und Billigkeit" ("In my day, in my day, people still had morals"), she avows, accompanied on the keyboard by an antiquated continuo bass, and singing "somewhat through the nose." Hagedorn's original text is about a man, *Der Alte*, not a woman. Who can have changed the title? The old Leopold Mozart was still alive, but he was dying. Again a strange coincidence? This lied at just this time? Written down two days after the G minor Quintet, it seems like a satyr play to the tragedy. Liberation after an expenditure of grief?

Thus, Mozart's significant lieder were written during work on *Don Giovanni*, during the complications of the inheritance, the move to new quarters, the quintets (the C major was written on Schulerstrasse, the G minor on Landstrasse), the incipient financial worries, the *Nachtmusik*, the *Spass. Das Lied der Trennung*, K. 519 (May 23, 1787), in F minor, was set to a macabre text of one Klamer Eberhard Karl Schmidt, war and land minister in Halberstadt, a friend of the poet Gleim and obviously a precursor of black Romanticism, if a lesser one:

> *Die Engel Gottes weinen …*
> *Dies Denkmal, unter Küssen*
> *auf meinen Mund gebissen,*
> *das richte mich und dich!*
> *Dies Denkmal auf dem Munde,*
> *komm' ich zur Geisterstunde,*
> *mich warnend anzuzeigen,*
> *vergisst Luisa mich.*

(The angels of God are weeping . . ./This remembrance,
bitten/among kisses upon my lips/shall guide us!/With
this remembrance upon my lips/I shall appear at the
witching hour/to warn her/if Luisa forget me.)

Mozart's music to this text anticipates Schubert, as it does in
the next lied, in C minor, where a Luise figures: "Als Luise die
Briefe ihres ungetreuen Liebhabers verbrannte" ("On Luise's
Burning the Letters of Her Faithless Lover"), K. 520 (May
26, 1787, words by Gabriele von Baumberg, who had had an
unfaithful lover). In these lieder, especially the marvelous
"Abendempfindung" in F major, K. 523 (June 24, 1787, words
by Joachim Heinrich Campe), Mozart's music goes far beyond
the weak poetry of the texts. He had broken new, quite unexpected ground, anticipating the dramatic expression of Romantic feeling, a heightened, often feverish passion. He
certainly did not search for these poems, but found them
in the assorted almanacs that circulated at the time, or in
already extant song collections (one of them was called *Die
singende Muse an der Pleisse* [*The Singing Muse on the
Banks of the Pleisse*]), texts already used by various composers.
Mozart was no more exacting in his choice than were his lesser
colleagues. If we examine the kind of thing he set to music, we
conclude that he was insensitive to pure poetry. True, after
fifty-eight measures he did abandon a "Bardic Lay on Gibral-
tar," K. Anh. 25/386d (December 1782), which begins, "O
Calpe! dir donnert's am Fusse" (O Calpe, thy foot is thunder-
ing). Although he thought it "sublime and beautiful," it was
too "exaggerated and pompous."

His last work before completing *Don Giovanni*, probably the last interruption of that task, was the Sonata for
piano and violin in A major, K. 526 (August 24, 1787). As
little is known about its composition as about its first performance. A commissioned work? For whom, then? It seems to us

like a breathing spell, an introverted action before the grand
spectacle of *Don Giovanni*, anticipating nothing of the opera
despite the similarity in key. On the contrary, it seems to
lead radically away from it; even the shift to D minor in the D
major andante is a D minor different from *Don Giovanni*'s.
Did Mozart write the sonata for himself? With *Don Giovanni*
still a long way from completion, a trip to Prague in the offing,
finances unsettled? There are plenty of reasons for assuming
that an accumulation of work stimulated him to even greater
production, that he welcomed the burden of additional tasks.
But perhaps it happened differently. Perhaps some violinist
approached him, needing a good piece for his concert the
following Thursday, and said, "Say, Mozart, couldn't you . . .?"
And Mozart could. The fact that this glorious work is one of
his most important sonatas does not necessarily mean that it
was not composed in a few hours, as a favor.

On September 3, 1787, not long before Mozart's departure for Prague, his friend and personal physician, Sigmund
Barisani, one of three chief doctors at the General Hospital in
Vienna, died, aged only twenty-nine. In the spring he had
written a poem in Mozart's *Stammbuch* (a cross between a
poetry album and a guest book). Mozart now wrote below
it:

> Today, 3 September of this same year, I was so unfortunate
> as quite unexpectedly to lose by death this noble man,
> dearest, best of friends and preserver of my life.—He is at
> rest!—but I, we, all that knew him well—we shall *never*
> be at rest again—until we have the felicity of seeing him
> again—in a better world—and *never more to part*.—Mozart.

We are already used to Mozart's stylistic extravagance from
his letters. Here again we have the same "thought," which
would speak for the authenticity of the last letter to his father,
referring to the death of Count Hatzfeld. We have seen sufficient examples of this flowery language, like the phrase about

his dearestmostbelovedfriend. If we wanted to test these al-most automatic formulas for their objective truth and honesty, we would have to inquire how many "dearest, most beloved friends" Mozart had then, anyway. In reality he had none, at least not after Hatzfeld's death, and even in that case we know nothing about the intensity of their friendship. It does not surprise us that this death was "unexpected"; every death was unexpected, since he never thought of anyone else's well-being, except Constanze's. Nevertheless, even if the epithet "preserver of my life" probably comes from his treasure chest of routine superlatives, the entry does honor to the deceased. Let us remember that Mozart never dedicated such a eulogy to his father, to whom he owed much more. We may assume, in any case, that he was not all that preoccupied with specula-tions about that "better world," where he hoped to join his friends, "never more to part." We would hazard the guess that during the time of *Don Giovanni*, there was no one close to him anymore, except, as he thought, Constanze.

Who was Da Ponte? To do him justice, we should try to forget what Mozart biographers have said of him, which is hard to do. He is always described as a "scintillating person-ality," a phrase that includes a touch of disapproval, of "look-ing askance." Still, it is the most favorable thing said about him, and because it is so ambiguous, its truth cannot be chal-lenged. Usually, though, he comes off worse: he was "without character" (Erich Valentin), "without scruples" (Schurig), an opportunist and adventurer. Hardened by love affairs, he had an eye always and above all to his own advantage, espe-cially where his share in Mozart's fame is concerned. And somewhere, covertly but unmistakably, anti-Semitic feeling usually crops up, first in the implication that his reasons for converting were purely utilitarian. Actually it was the Bishop of Ceneda, Monsignore Da Ponte, who suggested that the nine-year-old be baptized, but there was never an opportunity until his father, the leather merchant Geremia Conegliano, was

widowed and decided to marry a Catholic.[49] In 1763 Conegliano and his three sons from his first marriage were baptized,
among them the fourteen-year-old Emanuele, whom the
bishop destined for the priesthood; as was the custom, he gave
him his own name, Lorenzo Da Ponte, and paid all the costs of
his education and room and board. Lorenzo must have been a
promising young fellow.

He was ordained on March 27, 1773, but he never performed the offices of the priesthood, and would scarcely have
been suited to it. But he must have been particularly suited to
pedagogy: his classes in various seminaries in the Veneto were
unusually successful; obviously he knew how to stimulate his
pupils and help them understand the subjects he himself was
interested in: classical Latin, Italian and French literature. He
became a disciple of the Enlightenment, an admirer of Rousseau, and, along the way, a ladies' man, engaging in several
love affairs. It is not totally clear which side of this double life
was responsible for his ultimate flight, a liaison with a high-
ranking Venetian lady who had a child by him or the public
debate he and his pupils held at the seminary in Treviso in
1776, challenging the prevailing social structure by asking
whether civilization, through Church and state, had made
mankind any happier. He first took cover in Venice at the
home of his paramour (or one of them), went on to Gorizia,
and, when it got too hot for him there, to Dresden, where the
court poet of Saxony, Caterino Mazzolà, who later adapted
the libretto of *La Clemenza di Tito*, broke him into his new
vocation. In 1782 Da Ponte came to Vienna with a letter of
introduction to Salieri; he was ultimately engaged as a librettist, *"poeta dei teatri imperiali,"* and remained there for ten
years. He met Mozart at the home of his "fellow member of
the tribe" (as Abert puts it!), Baron Wetzlar; Mozart reported
the acquaintance several times, though only obliquely, to his
father, and expressed the hope that a collaboration might result. We know nothing else about this important artistic relationship. Da Ponte's own memoirs,[50] though worth reading,

are unreliable and colored by a strong desire for self-glorification.

Thus Da Ponte was in his late thirties when he wrote the three libretti for Mozart, and had behind him not only various libretti for other composers but also several professions and periods of changing fortune. When Leopold II cut down on musical activity in Vienna in 1790 as a result of the Turkish War, Da Ponte was one of the first to be sacrificed. He went to Trieste, fell in love with a young Englishwoman named Nancy Grahl or Krahl, went with her to Paris and then to London, where he remained for thirteen years and wrote a few libretti for second-rate composers. In 1805 he emigrated with Nancy to America, undergoing yet another metamorphosis; he worked in New York mainly as a language teacher and even for a time as a professor at Columbia College. They had four children, and when one of them died, Da Ponte was inconsolable for a year; the former adventurer had become a model husband and devoted father. He died in 1838, at the age of eighty-nine.

We have sketched this brief outline to indicate the uneven nature of this life, certainly not "immaculate" in its beginnings but always controlled, confident, and ultimately undaunted, a life that outlasted its high point by fifty years; the life of a man who bore declining fortunes and recurring twists of fate with rare resignation and confidence. Unlike numerous adventurer types of his time, his life (especially after its early turning point) was not a struggle to assert himself in the role of a great man but simply to survive and maintain himself. In old age, in America, we see him as an ordinary man in a community of ordinary people, among the earliest Italian immigrants. He tolerated his decline with composure, and it is not surprising that he tried to build up his glorious past in his memoirs. We should not hold it against him if he exaggerated his little victories and successes. Mozart's splendor shines upon him, too, the composer's best (or, rather, his only good) librettist.

When did Mozart and Da Ponte meet, how did they talk to each other? Did they argue, or agree at once? Did the "Teuton" like the "Latin"? We know nothing about it. All we have are a few corrections to the libretti in the scores, slight changes in the texts or stage directions, which make it seem doubtful that the composer consulted the librettist; otherwise nothing. We would give a lot for notes, however brief, of a conversation during which Mozart perhaps insisted on a change, suggested a cut, or, in consideration of this or that singer, an addition to display the voice more fully. Nor is anything authentic known about his own opinion of the three Da Ponte operas. Forty years after the première of *Don Giovanni*, Constanze stated that he esteemed this opera above all his other works: that would not surprise us. And yet, we cannot imagine Mozart saying, "That *Don Giovanni* really was the best thing I ever wrote."

We find Mozart forever silent, eloquent only in his diversionary tactics, communicative only in his works, which, by his design, have nothing to say about their creator. He built for us edifice after edifice, apparently never looking back. Now and then he was confronted with some work from his past, the performance of an opera in Frankfurt or Schwetzingen, or when an earlier manuscript came into his hands. Then he would be surprised by its quality. Certainly he did express his satisfaction with this or that work, but the Viennese Mozart never uses enthusiastic superlatives, either for himself or for others. What did he think, for example, of Gluck? His admiration for Haydn is documented, but which work, which movement, which turn of phrase or idea moved him? Which of his own works was he really proud of, which sonata movement or aria did he like to perform for others? Even after the completion of his greatest works, he never had the feeling of having "given something to the world." He did not rest on his laurels, but kept on writing, obeying the exigency of the moment. In his own thematic catalogue, all are equal, at least in a formal sense; both works that last the length of an evening and lesser ones. He kept no record of their reception. Naturally he expressed his joy at the fact that everyone sang or whistled *Figaro* in the streets of Prague; not even the most sublime genius is indifferent to such popularity. But what conclusions could or should he have drawn from it?

After the great success of *Don Giovanni* he returned to his daily schedule by composing a few lieder. The first was entitled "Des kleinen Friedrichs Geburtstag," K. 529 (November 6, 1787); it deals with a "tender, young lad" who goes to school and church like a well-behaved boy, doing only good, and who is finally blessed by God. No wit, and no musical wit, either; a strophic song, very boring, in F major. After the great libertine is punished, the good little boy is blessed: it seems like a joke. Was it? We do, in fact, sometimes have the feeling that Mozart was trying to obliterate the traces of his creative processes, thus asking us to accept his great and unique achievements as riddles, solved and then forgotten. We are to waste no time thinking about the degree of his involvement with them, just as he wasted no time thinking about his future fame.

Of course, we cannot restrain ourselves: the attempt to track down the creative genius, to catch even the slightest glimpse of him, is in itself a satisfying occupation. The failure of our attempt is reckoned into our guessing game: there can be no winners.

Don Giovanni brings us no closer to Mozart, either. We must be content with the little and scattered information the score gives us about the work process and the relationship of the creator to his creations. For they are his, not Da Ponte's. Da Ponte delivered the optimal framework, a textual proposal poetically brilliant in places, nearly perfect dramatically, witty in the secco recitatives; if some individual behavior is crude in a *buffo* way, the text is rich in open-ended passages that gave

the composer the freedom to continually adjust his distance
from the material. He had the possibility of remaining de-
scriptively "close-up" or of distancing himself almost con-
trapuntally, to evoke other levels, where words lose their direct
function. Because he took advantage of both possibilities, Mozart added a new dimension to the genre.

When Leporello, in his Catalogue Aria, finds the appropriate musical motive for the types of women his master allegedly
prefers, the *"gentilezza"* of the brunette, the *"costanza"* of the
raven-haired (it is surprising that his master should value
constancy, which can be of no use to him), we detect a parodistic intent in the diatonically descending scale, but it is balanced by the chromatically ascending *"dolcezza"* of the
blonde. Who is doing the parodying? We seem to have here
observations about genetic characteristics that go beyond the
powers of discernment of Leporello, the descriptive voyeur.
Not only is each alleged feminine attribute set to music, but
Leporello, too, is revealed in all his rigid views on the erotic
tastes of the ruling class. We can assume that his master was
somewhat more exact in his typological knowledge. In general,
Leporello never defines himself, but is put together by his
experiences (usually passive ones, by necessity). In the Mozart
literature he has usually been portrayed as a crafty but servile
coward and as the helpless tool of his master's willfulness; his
name can be derived from *"lepre,"* the hare, or from *"lepore,"*
from the merry humor he shows in the Catalogue Aria, and
not only there. (The aria is an act of twofold loyalty, by the
way, for he advises poor Donna Elvira, who naturally is not
about to listen, to desist from following his master, for her
own good, while trying at the same time to get rid of her for
his master's sake.) There is nothing of the "sly scorn of this
fellow" (Abert), nor are we by any means dealing with a dolt.
Never at a loss for a retort, this is a man of feeling and reason;
he is right in trying to take the blindfold from the pitiable
lady's eyes, very earnest in emphasizing, throughout the tonic
octave, the words "Voi sapete quel che fà," which he hammers
at her in his truly exhausting D major tirade: "You know

yourself, my lady, the things he does." Here is spirit and rationality; here Mozart sticks to the text; he himself becomes Leporello.

Leporello is abused, and yet indispensable, and we cannot help feeling that he is, in his way, trying to educate his master by continually threatening to quit. For ultimately he shows himself to be the epitome of loyalty at Don Giovanni's downfall, when he pleads with him to save himself, to repent for his soul's salvation (at which point he, too, is finally permitted a D minor passage). The *buffo* "oibò," which he first cries out anxiously, turns finally into "Sì! Sì!"—i.e., "Repent!" Like is obviously not repaying like in this case; we learn to appreciate Leporello (if we have not always done so). And what do we appreciate about him? An embodiment of Mozart. Such a character would never have attained this stature if he did not contain in himself the chameleon nature of his creator.

Of course, we must wonder whether Leporello would go on supporting villainy of this kind after such a finale. But that is only a secondary question within the great complex of questions about the psychological truths in Mozart's operas. Are the two brides in *Così fan tutte* going to be happy with their fine cavaliers after each woman has fallen in love with the other's admirer, and while the men are disguised in the most grotesque costumes to boot? Do these configurations ask almost too much of us? Do we put up with them only for the sake of the music? Or is it that the music makes the psychological element plausible?

Let us look for a point of orientation in the other characters, first in Don Giovanni himself. He is not Mozart's creation, of course: Mozart got him from Da Ponte, who got him from Bertàti, who got him from Tirso de Molina, who got him from legend. A negative, problematic hero, and yet compelling and forceful, the unique Don Juan Tenorio, who killed the commandant of Ulloa after seducing his daughter, haunts Spanish dramatic literature. Only through Mozart, however,

has he become an archetype, the proverbial example, a cliché
for the womanizing hero. That, however, is a misinterpreta-
tion.

Only through Mozart is he conceivable; when we conjure up
the image, we mean this particular Don Giovanni. He is never
connected with words, as is Hamlet, that archetype who reflects on being or non-being, who opens up a world of ideas
which goes far beyond his own persona, a world in which
various others were later to founder. Don Juan does not reflect; he is not given to thinking, but rather to living out his
own existence, one determined by thoughtlessness. We cannot
conceive of him in words, just as he would never try to conceive of himself in words. If he comes to our mind, it is not as
one who thinks or formulates, as the one who pronounces the
words "Deh vieni a consolar il pianto mio!" (let alone "Oh,
ease my pain and let us be happy"). Rather, we think of him
solely in his musical manifestation, in his insistent D minor
passage, "No! No! No! No!" the final refusal before his downfall, or in the strangely seductive A major "Là ci darem la
mano," which he uses to bedazzle Zerlina. We don't even have
a visual figure before our eyes when we conjure him up (Kierkegaard, before the advent of phonograph records, preferred
hearing the opera from the lobby, but we, who have records,
are presented with his picture, complete with goatee, lace col-
lar, and tights *ad nauseam* on the covers of record albums). We
feel his breathtaking presence, but we learn only the tiniest bit
about his daily life as a seducer. And a very inauspicious bit it
is, too: everything is going downhill. Dame Fortune has abandoned him, although he isn't aware of it yet. It is the others
who reveal the dreams and nightmares surrounding this character, the almost global activity of this overpowering fiend.

Musically, he is many-tracked; there was much about him to
compose: a lord of a manor, from a good family, probably
lesser nobility, but, nevertheless, not a real gentleman. Ladies'
men are always slightly disreputable or have something of the
parvenu about them. It would have been more proper, for
example, for Don Giovanni to invite the old Commendatore,

even if he was a ghost, to dinner himself, especially since the Don is standing right next to his servant, whom he forces for some incomprehensible reason to deliver the invitation for him. Nor would he talk so much about money in the banquet scene, where he makes it emphatically clear to us and all present that he can afford these culinary treats (as if we had doubted it), only to comment maliciously and all too insistently on the compulsive nibbling of his servant, whom he also makes a point of continually tyrannizing. We wonder if he really does tyrannize him, or if it is only in words, which do not count for much here? In his own attempt at a translation, Mozart indicates that anonymous women are to be present in this scene; perhaps this direction was observed in the productions in Prague and Vienna. But even this very reasonable pantomimic addition does not explain the imperial upswing of the music, the grandiose finale atmosphere, the orchestral display and the radiant D major of this banquet scene to end all banquet scenes. It all seems to stand for something else; destiny lurks in the background. It is as if the great emphasis on this moment symbolizes one last intense indulgence in sensual pleasure before the catastrophe. The hero, consciously at least, is not aware of his doom, but we see it coming, and the composer was probably looking forward to it. In scenes like this one, the text seems no more than a subliminal figured bass beneath the powerful, universalizing musical action.

We must still investigate the degree of Mozart's identification with his most important hero. But first let us turn to Donna Anna. Hers is the greatest secret, a riddle we cannot solve. If we go by her words, she is utterly insufferable, a cross between a crybaby and a fury; feeling about her is so ambivalent that it has stimulated an immense interpretive exegesis, which of course has nothing whatever to do with Mozart. E. T. A. Hoffmann was the first, attributing to her, deep down, an uncontrollable passion for her seducer. And, in fact, she is seen in a permanent, usually exalted state of agitation; she never, under any circumstances, speaks calmly. Hoffmann and later critics were probably responding more to their own intoxication with the music, which set their imaginations in motion. We do the same thing today, though we are compelled to work with psychological categories and search for symptoms in the music. The eloquence of her music drowns out any persuasive power in her language, so that we have to impute to her a motive other than simple grief at the loss of her father—namely, that she has yielded to his murderer, her seducer. I don't think we would find rape credible, even an attempted one. Don Giovanni is not the kind of man to steal what is not freely offered him as the fruit of the only art he has mastered. The motif of daughterly love (never really convincing, not even Cordelia's for her father, King Lear) is also too weak to justify this music; it is only an excuse, the occasion for two splendid arias and for the great, treacherous *accompagnato* "Don Ottavio, son morta!" (No. 10). Here Donna Anna runs through four minor keys with declamatory bravura, out of breath and taking ours away; she seems to be looking for the one key that can express the horrible wonder of it all. Yet everything is whispered, as if she wants to conceal the essential point from Don Ottavio and from herself, too (which indeed she does). For, even though the night in question has just ended, her account of it comes quite late, later, in any case, than our questions about it; but Don Ottavio would probably be afraid to hear the answer. Nor do we ever have one to our satisfaction. Donna Anna's musical posture, introduced by the sudden C minor chord in the brass, supported by the evocative *stringendo* of the strings in rising thirds, seems to betray that she has experienced the great, fateful moment and would like to hold on to it, as she holds on to the sleeve of her seducer, so firmly that he is strangely unable to tear himself loose. Is Donna Anna lying? It is hard to believe that she really could have taken Don Giovanni for her fiancé, Don Ottavio, that night (is it the same night?), especially since it is improbable that Don Ottavio, being who he is, would steal into her bed-chamber. In light of this conflict, Donna Anna's plight becomes a mono-drama of the soul.

Donna Anna leads us a guessing game: rich in guesses, poor in possible solutions. It has to do with the erotic element, which is only hinted at, as if it were illicit. How can a girl hold on to a strong man long enough for her father to arrive to challenge the seducer? Is it that she enjoyed the theft of her innocence and doesn't want to let the thief go? Moreover, her father and her seducer are as good as neighbors, and yet we are supposed to believe that she has not heard of the latter's bad reputation. Of his 1,003 victims in Spain alone, surely a few must have been in this vicinity. And her fiancé, Don Ottavio, hasn't heard anything about it, either?

Don Ottavio is not very exciting himself. It is hard to picture this unimaginative, virtuous young man as the spouse of an imperious and passionate woman. Of course, Bernard Shaw thought he would marry her and that they would have twelve children, but here, as so often, Shaw cannot resist a witticism at the expense of accuracy. There is nothing to indicate a happy marriage or the patter of little feet about the house. On the one hand, Don Ottavio is totally dependent on his fiancée; on the other, his tragedy is precisely that he is no match for her in terms of an inner life. It is improbable that Da Ponte wanted to portray him as ludicrous, but it is hard for us to see him otherwise, hard, in fact, not to laugh at him, "the bridegroom of all bridegrooms" (Adorno). This is especially true of his reply to his adored one's narrative in the minor. It comes breathlessly and, for him, very late. With his exclamation, in the major, "Ohimè! Respiro," he seems to agree to be deluded; after having convinced himself of her virtue, he doesn't want to hear anything more about it, nothing that might call it into question again. And indeed she tells him no more. But something in her is always expressing it; her unconscious is formulated not in words but in music that is not always comprehensible and not always happy, as in "Non mi dir," in the passage "Forse un giorno il cielo ancora sentirà pietà di me." This is a monstrous coloratura passage in which the *a-a-a-a* of "sentirà" extends through 9½ bars, until it reaches the 6–4 chord. Berlioz, otherwise a great admirer of Mozart's, never forgave him for this. He wrote: "Here Donna Anna seems to dry her tears and give herself over suddenly to indecent merry-making"; he thinks even the word "shameful" too weak "for branding this passage. Mozart has committed one of the ugliest, most senseless crimes in the history of art, going against all passion, all feeling, good taste and good reason."[51] A severe judgment, the judgment of a Romantic who did not want to acknowledge circumstances to which Mozart accommodated himself without protest. Presumably Teresa Saporiti wanted to show off her technique, and Aloysia Lange (the Vienna Donna Anna) probably did, too. Nevertheless, we too agree that Mozart has gone off the track in this instance; but it is only one of those tributes rendered to his singers which we have to take into the bargain now and then. We think we know what is driving Donna Anna. Her role provides us with the extreme case of a counterpoint of words and music. In the text she bemoans the death of her father for the length of two acts, and is frustrated in her plans to avenge him. Musically, however, she ranges through totally different worlds. But which?

We do not know. Though we know that our attempts at interpretation are condemned to failure, we try nevertheless to translate things into a psychological rationale; we cannot help trying to categorize the characters' motivations. That is, we construct a logical system which runs parallel to the musical-dramatic event, a system set in motion and kept on its path by our passive fantasy. It is certainly tempting to attribute Donna Anna's emotions more to a love-hate feeling about the hero than to a wearisome grief for her father. We know her father only as a dying man in the dark of night, and after that only as a ghost; but we are continually confronted with the compelling attraction of her seducer, even when he is not on stage.

Thus, our experience of the opera, guided and sometimes heightened intensely by the music, is not exclusively passive; rather, we actively consider possible and actual, potential and probable causes for the characters' behavior. The transcendent quality of the music lies in its evocative ambiguity; if we ask ourselves what this music would be like if Mozart had consciously wanted to portray Donna Anna's passion for Don Giovanni, we conclude that it would be exactly the way it is. Mozart's dramatic music does not indicate motives for the characters' behavior or merely underline it; it does not follow the text, but directs it or leads it to that plane of expression where music is a parable of life itself. Mozart is capable of using onomatopoeia to indicate agitation, a heartbeat, the awe-inspiring moment, or the portrayal of a future situation, like the trumpet triplets in Figaro's aria "Non più andrai." But he never writes program music; rather, he uses certain places in the plot as starting points to rise into that absolute sphere where music stands independently for human passions, becoming a metaphor of the concrete action. Schopenhauer is right: Mozart was no "painterly" composer. (Of course, Schopenhauer includes Rossini in this category, too, and both are contrasted with Beethoven and Haydn: one is never quite content with the remarks of literary geniuses about music.)

No "painterly" composer. Rather, one who constructs his action himself, orienting it around the turning points in the given text. Thus, it is the music that makes the unbelievable believable and the thoroughly improbable truthful. The textually one-dimensional action is set to music; it is self-evident, therefore, that words cannot describe the metamorphosis taking place. It is the music that explains and interprets, excites, soothes, and appeases. Stock characters, prepsychological inventions, take on reality only in the music—that is, in Mozart's music, not in music before it and not for a long time afterward. We can count on the fingers of one hand the composers who were able to universalize the motives and psychic impulses of their characters in music. Of these Mozart was the first.

Thus, until Wagner, we never find efforts equal to the music even in the best libretti; rather, they are occasions for the development of the musical score. As in *Finnegans Wake*, a text of one line would have to represent a score of many staves in order to plumb the depths of music like Mozart's; an interpretation is out of the question. Don Giovanni's malicious and unnecessary remarks about his servant are not sufficient to "justify" their share in the score; Donna Anna's music speaks louder than her words, just as, on a smaller scale, Barbarina's loss of a pin in *Figaro* opens up a delicate spectrum of other losses. Of course, this multidimensionality was not part of Mozart's extramusical thought; he composed what was possible, what each character would be capable of, given his personality. When we listen, we also confirm that all these characters have a metaphysical component. Something indefinable is revealed to us, an element of profound objective truthfulness, derived from the music alone. Mozart distributes, indeed lavishes, his wealth of invention and feeling on the most subordinate characters; even an Antonio in *Figaro* has his share in the riches. But what do we mean by "subordinate"? Some characters are reduced only when they get to the stage, because of bad direction or bad acting: Masetto, for example, the stocky, eternally clumsy peasant lad, whom even Adorno would have us consider "a perfect blockhead." As if Zerlina, for whom Adorno declares his admiration in an incomparable essay,[52] would be obliged to wed that kind of fellow. Nor does the music portray him that way: has no one noticed that the Masetto of the F major aria "Ho capito" (No. 6) is furious in his oppression, a potential rebel, that he is the equal of the Figaro who sings "Se vuol ballare," only more helpless, more powerless, for it is not yet the time for revolution? In Italian "Signor, sì" is an idiom indicating a false, angry submissiveness. Da Ponte knew what was happening, and so did Mozart. Directors should cast Masetto with a tall, slim actor, goodlooking if possible, instead of reaching for the standard "*buffo* blockhead." Only then is his aria done justice. For when he hands over his weapons to the disguised Don Giovanni, with a lack of suspicion which is (admittedly) not very well-considered, it happens in a recitative.

Even in the most intricate ensemble scenes, Mozart succeeds in portraying each situation from the inside and outside simultaneously, both the subjective experience of those taking part and the objective panorama of the action as the audience experiences it. When, in that most grandiose of all finales, at the end of the second act of *Figaro*, the tipsy gardener Antonio reels onto the stage as the orchestra suddenly modulates from C major to F major, as he tries to give vent to his rage over his trampled bed of carnations, not only does Mozart hold five different threads of characterization firmly in his hand, but, beyond this, he suggests, by the whirring eighth notes of the high strings, the increasing confusion of an already delicate situation. The tension grows even greater at the appearance of Marcellina's party of three (*più moto*) and then, in the *prestissimo*, breaks off unresolved at the point of highest intensity: the dissatisfaction of all concerned is turned into our deepest satisfaction. Perhaps Brahms was thinking above all of this scene when he said to his friend, the surgeon Billroth, "In my opinion each number in Mozart's *Figaro* is a miracle; it is totally beyond me how anyone could create something so perfect; nothing like it was ever done again, not even by Beethoven."[53]

In the A major trio "Ah taci, ingiusto core" (No. 16), as musical characterization the most wonderful composition in *Don Giovanni*, three positions are made clear, three souls revealed in their deepest profundity. Everything takes place in a nearly restrained andantino, with a minimum of dynamic contrast, from *piano* to the *mezzo forte* of the false assurances, and back to the *pianissimo* with which the scene is whisked away. Four minutes of monstrous action: Donna Elvira, already badly maltreated, is here misused outrageously. With false avowals of love, Don Giovanni lures her into the garden and then changes clothes with Leporello; the servant is to seduce her or at least enjoy himself with her while Don Giovanni seduces her maid. This number, sublimely ironic in one sense, a perfidy in another, betrays (literally) even in the manuscript Mozart's truly diabolical pleasure in portraying the deceptive maneuver. We find corrections, hasty crossings out, emphatic repetitions of dynamic markings, all serving to clarify the meaning to the last detail, and, as a consequence, to outdo the text by making it cynical. Mozart even reveals his malice by changing Da Ponte's stage directions. *"Con affettato dolore,"* "with feigned anguish," Da Ponte instructs the hero to express his contrition over Elvira's mistreatment. But Mozart, getting into the spirit of the role, was obviously not satisfied with that. He wrote into the score: *"Con trasporto e quasi piangendo,"* "with extreme abandonment and nearly sobbing," as if the hero, calling out "M'uccido!" ("I'll kill myself!") three times in the next minute, were about to realize his intention there on the spot. Originally, in fact, the score had it four times, but apparently that was too much for Mozart, for just proportion was his guiding rule.

"Anima di bronzo," Leporello calls his master after this trio. Let us translate it as "soul of iron" or, more freely, "soul of ice." We will examine whether Mozart himself, identifying strongly with his hero, becomes an "anima di bronzo." The examples already cited would almost suggest it. His hero, at any rate, is true to the term, embodying it in its most evil form, but always with a bold, radiant logic. Triumphantly, he demonstrates for us how the negative principle conquers all— until his own end is reached, as wretched as it is unexpected. Characteristically, the very same betrayed Elvira, the same tyrannized servant, and also even the spirit of his victim and nemesis, try to save him from it. He controls them all, an elemental presence holding them together. Even when he is not onstage he is never far away. As his guilt accumulates, as the others begin, if rather halfheartedly and unwillingly, to close in on him, he demonstrates the range of his negative morality, deterred by nothing and no one. His display culminates in the B-flat ario (No. 11) "Finch' han dal vino" (sometimes called the Champagne Aria, as if wild *joie de vivre* always has to be symbolized by champagne). He gaily shouts out his freedom from all moderation and, in the minor modulation at "Ed io fratanto," his daemonic spirit. Thus, a strange and profound objective amorality rules over the entire opera, for the only happy person in it is the evildoer, until a few minutes before his sudden end. Only he laughs; the others have nothing to laugh about. They remain unhappy, even at the resolution of the opera, for when the center is lacking, they no longer have any dramatic function, and therefore no vital function, either. And since everyone knows that morality does not lead to happiness, even the false consolation of the concluding finale does not restore it. "Questo è il fin di chi fà mal," they assure each other. "Such is the end of evildoers." But even this assertion does not lift their spirits, perhaps one reason being that it is not true.

This *scena ultima* of *Don Giovanni* has repeatedly been attacked over the years. Gustav Mahler omitted it in his 1905 production, and Adorno censures Klemperer for not leaving it out of his recording:

> Klemperer retains the last scene, after the descent into hell, out of a neoclassical, intellectual love of convention dating back to Cocteau and, ultimately, Nietzsche, out of a resistance to Wagner's music drama. Meanwhile, the restoration of the topos of a happy ending, just because it would be nice to have one, is no longer satisfactory. The grandeur of the Commendatore-scene transcends and focuses all the play-acting which has gone before; after it, whatever is restored must be a letdown. No appeal to style can govern

a work which, at its height, renders its own principle of stylization impotent. To include the weakness of a finale in the major is no happy return to form: it proves how irrevocably lost the *dixhuitième* style has become because of Mozart. Stage performances should do without the finale; explaining it as ironic only makes its claim to validity more in doubt. Ultimately Mozart himself (if the issue is a dubious fidelity to the text) would have gone along with cutting it. The work must be protected from an intermittent, strained naïveté, which the Commendatore-scene, the last baroque allegory with the power of a primeval image, condemns retroactively to silliness.[54]

Adorno is being hard on Klemperer: to imply that Cocteau was his mentor borders on malice. But beyond that, the whole idea is wrong, especially since the plagal cadence at the end of the penultimate scene has the effect of an interrupted or deceptive cadence, not of a conclusion. Of course, any scene coming after what is probably the greatest scene in all opera will be a letdown, but the idea that a work has to end with its dramatic high point is just as great an aesthetic error as the one Adorno rebukes Klemperer for. The letdown of the final scene reproduces our own disillusionment; it is deliberately calculated. In addition, we would hardly call the *scena ultima* weak; in it the central motifs of the opera are once again presented to us through individual characterizations. Therefore, it is highly debatable whether Mozart "approved" the cut of this scene in the Vienna production, or whether he was accommodating some wish from above or below. It would not have been the only time. Wolfgang Plath and Wolfgang Rehm, the editors of *Don Giovanni* in the *Neue Mozart-Ausgabe*, write:

Strictly speaking, there is only one version of *Don Giovanni* which has an absolute claim to authenticity; that is the opera as it was composed for Prague and performed there on October 29, 1787, with unparalleled success. Likewise, this is the only version which can be called definitive. The so-called "Viennese version," after all we can conclude from the source material unearthed, is anything but clear; rather it is by nature variable, experimental, open-ended.[55]

Right. Strictly speaking, the Viennese adaptation is no "version" at all but something produced *ad hoc*, to which Mozart had to accommodate himself. But this was no isolated instance; surely he often had to do that; we just don't know what the conditions were. What, then, is "authenticity"? To be precise, everything Mozart composed, whether he wanted to or not, whether successful or not, is authentic Mozart.

"Dubious fidelity to the text": Adorno is allergic to it. We are, too. But we understand something entirely different by it and certainly not the performance of a stage work in its proper sequence. Rather, we associate it with the "music-making" of various "collegia" or "camerate" or "consorti," whose endeavor it is to reconstruct the supposed original conditions; with playing "original instruments," if possible by candlelight; with the efforts of purity fanatics who "enter into the spirit" of it all, and for whom the discovery of past performance practices becomes a mania and their re-creation a commandment. We believe that Mozart, always on the lookout for improvements in instrumental technology, and seldom satisfied, would have preferred the concert grand of today to the Walter-Hammerflügel of his own time. We know that no orchestra was big enough for him. On April 11, 1781, he wrote to his father:

> I forgot to tell you the other day that at the concert the symphony went magnifique and had the greatest success. There were forty violins, the wind instruments were all doubled, there were ten violas, ten double basses, eight violoncellos and six bassoons.

That's the way he liked it. When, on April 17, 1791, Salieri conducted a concert with 180 participants at which Mozart's G minor Symphony, in the version with clarinets, was probably included, we do not think that Mozart protested the large orchestral forces.

Mozart's musical thinking eludes us. He puzzles us most in those places where the music is serious, even when the material would seem not to warrant it. Traditionally, critics have always tried to find parodistic content in these numbers, but in vain: we cannot be sure. Even in *Così fan tutte*, happiness and melancholy and their counterfeit become one. As some characters never reveal themselves fully (Is Countess Rosina an angel in her thoughts, too? Is Osmin perhaps a profoundly sad figure?), so Mozart, too, never reveals his own secret, his creative intuition about experiences he never had. As if he himself were the medium, he traces human motivations, puts himself in the emotional states of his characters, their longings, dreams, and turmoil. But he omits the causes: what is Donna Anna really concerned about? What is Fiordiligi feeling? Although all the questions we can pose have already been answered by Mozart, we cannot transpose his answers back into extramusical language. The answers come out of the music; without it they are inexplicable. The psychograph of his characters can be plotted only in musical notes.

Dramatic thinking is easier to follow. Here Mozart looked for literary models in order to correct his librettists when he was not satisfied with them. From Munich, where he was working on *Idomeneo*, he wrote to his father on November 29, 1780:

Tell me, don't you think that the speech of the subterranean voice is too long? Consider it carefully. Picture to yourself the theater, and remember that the voice must be terrifying—must penetrate—that the audience must believe that it really exists. Well, how can this effect be produced if the speech is too long, for in this case the listeners will become more and more convinced that it means nothing. If the speech of the Ghost in Hamlet were not so long, it would be far more effective. It is quite easy to shorten the speech of the subterranean voice and it will gain thereby more than it will lose.

This stage instinct, this apportioning intelligence, is always surprising. Seven years before *Don Giovanni* we have his critique of Shakespeare, which he acted on with supreme results. Not only is the Commendatore's appearance more concise (and naturally more mysterious because of the music), it is above all more consistent. The ghost of Hamlet's father is seen by his son, by Horatio, and by the officers of the watch, but not, strangely enough, by the Queen, whose conscience it should trouble. But the Commendatore's spirit is seen by all concerned, the innocent as well as the murderer. The latter's conscience, it is true, is not troubled, but he *is* destroyed. Granted, Mozart did not invent him, nor did Da Ponte nor his predecessor Bertati, from whom Da Ponte took some lines for this scene verbatim. But the overwhelming presence of this apparition, the brief flash from an immeasurable world beyond, that is uniquely Mozart. Da Ponte, too, had read Shakespeare (in French translation) and understood him. He must have known *Hamlet* extremely well. In the B-flat Quartet "Non ti fidar, o misera" (No. 9), Don Ottavio and Donna Anna comment on the appearance of the unfortunate Donna Elvira: "Cieli! che aspetto nobile! che dolce maestà!" A nice text, which reminds us of Ophelia's words on seeing the apparently demented Hamlet, "O! what a noble mind is here o'erthrown" (III, i). And Don Giovanni's observation of the time of night before the ghost stirs, "Oh ancor non sono due della notte," recalls Horatio's "I think it lacks of twelve . . . then it draws near the season" (I, iv) before the father's ghost appears. This affinity did not escape Mozart's contemporaries. The correspondent of the Frankfurt *Dramaturgische Blätter*, on seeing *Don Giovanni* in 1789, found the music "splendid—only too elaborate here and there" and had to admit "that the scene at the churchyard filled [him] with dread. Mozart seems to have learned the language of ghosts from Shakespeare."

Only as a ghost does the Commendatore become real. We never know exactly what he actually was in life. The German translation of Commendatore, "Komtur," is hardly sufficient, for that would mean that he was no more than a seigneurial administrator of Church lands. Is he the commander of a garrison, or, more probably, governor of a town? In any event, he is a *"vecchio,"* an old man, widowed, father of a marriageable daughter, all the convenient classical nonsense. King Lear's three daughters, Ophelia, Miranda, are all half orphans, born late to their parents, as are Goldoni's various Rosauras and Beatrices, not to mention the full-fledged orphans of classical literature and *opera buffa* who must be adopted by guardians, and those in *opera seria* whose orphanhood is never explained. The only mothers in Mozart are Marcella in *Figaro*, who comes by her child like the Virgin Mary, and the great and primeval mother figure in *Die Zauberflöte*, the Queen of the Night, that powerful representation of archaic matriarchy in the struggle against the world of men.

Yet there is hardly a stage work in the history of the theater whose nonsense we accept as gladly as *Don Giovanni*'s; for example, the apparent unity of time, and its consequence, that everything takes place at night. At night the Commendatore is murdered, buried, and restored as a monument, the *"statua gentillissima."* At night Donna Elvira arrives from Burgos in her traveling garb, laments her misfortune on a street corner to no one in particular, changes clothes, and moves into a house. And the only erotic adventure the hero brings off takes place as if on the periphery, and is reported to his servant (whose lady friend it concerns) in a recitative. We wonder when, in such a crowded period of time, it might have happened.

Interpreters and directors have naturally tried to bring some logic to this series of events, but in vain. This opera, for some reason, loses verisimilitude when dramaturgical order is imposed on it. Through the music's evocative power, the concrete action disintegrates, and with it our sensitivity to time and history; we release ourselves from the bonds of time and forget that in this breathless sequence of events, heightened by the continual scene changes, only one thing is consistent: coincidence. We do not question its probability, at least not until later; while we experience it everything makes sense. Our deep satisfaction lies in the inconceivability of the action, the ambiguity of its motivation, in the recognition of its mystery, not in the solution. We play at solutions, but they do not get at the thing itself.

We know of only one certain reason for Mozart's writing *Don Giovanni*: the commission. In contrast to Vienna, Prague had received *Figaro* enthusiastically. The Prague impresario Bondini thus commissioned Mozart to write an opera for 100 ducats—so Mozart wrote *Don Giovanni* for 100 ducats (exactly 450 gulden). We must realize that an opera was a commercial product. There was no supply of operas to fall back on; a repertoire was not assembled but written to order. Hundreds of operas were composed every year.

Part of the score was written in Vienna, part in Prague, and some numbers probably during the rehearsals, Masetto's, for example. The player of this role was the only member of the cast whom Mozart had never heard (most had already appeared in *Figaro*); thus, he had to see and hear him before knowing what he was capable of. Though anything but a pragmatist in his daily life, Mozart was a theatrical pragmatist who knew how to sacrifice the realization of an ideal image (if indeed he had one) to the conditions of reality. In a certain sense, then, all his roles have come down to us as limited by the stage conditions of the moment. How might *Idomeneo* have sounded if its first singer had been twenty years younger? Giuseppe Lolli must at least have had a certain acting range at his command, for in addition to Masetto, he had to sing the

Commendatore (today, accustomed as we are to vocal categories that were then unknown, we find this hard to imagine), and perhaps that is the reason Mozart waited until the last minute to compose the second finale. His monumental design for the stone guest suggests that he trusted the singer of these two contrary roles with a great deal, and probably demanded a great deal from him. Of course, we must not compare the typical elaborate display accorded this scene today with the conditions of that time. There was no theory of stage direction in our sense of the term; action, gesture, mime were hardly synchronized; everyone did whatever he could; improvisation substituted for rehearsals, people didn't "take it so seriously." Greater demands were made on the audience's powers of imagination, and were probably met: their passive imagination was more basic and naïve than ours is now.

The manuscript of *Don Giovanni* contains deletions and corrections, but never betrays haste, only the swift hand of a man who thinks more quickly in notes than his pen can write. The act of copying, that unavoidable evil and burdensome duty, was, as soon as he decided to do it, automatic. Mozart's memory functioned photographically; while he was writing he held conversations or listened to someone talk. We have ample evidence from Mozart himself about this phenomenal gift: ". . . everything is composed, just not copied out yet . . ." he wrote to his father on December 30, 1780, about his work on *Idomeneo*. No coyness, just matter-of-fact information, written "in haste," as usual, for he had to get on with his task. And to his sister he wrote on April 20, 1782:

> I send you herewith a prelude and a three-part fugue. The reason why I did not reply to your letter at once was that on account of the wearisome labor of writing these small notes, I could not finish the composition any sooner. And, even so, it is awkwardly done, for the prelude ought to come first and the fugue to follow. But I composed the fugue first and wrote it down while I was thinking out the prelude.

He did not write this to his sister to appear a mental gymnast, but only to explain the unusual ordering of the two parts. He was speaking of the Prelude and Fugue in C major, K 394/ 383a (April 1782). He wrote out the Fugue from memory, complete in his head, while composing the Prelude at the same time. Perhaps he already had yet another work in his head while copying that down. Strangely enough, this particular Prelude is a study in complicated pianistic techniques, problems of touch: we see here that he also had the potential capabilities of the hands on his mind.

Thus, despite excessive embellishments, which condemn this anecdote, like most of the others, to the realm of light-hearted legend, we may confidently believe in the tradition that Mozart copied out the overture to *Don Giovanni* in two early-morning hours on the day of the performance. But the hot punch Constanze prepared for him, the jokes and stories with which she was obliged to amuse him are probably invention. He wrote out the piece as his memory dictated; everything had already been composed. The manuscript begins with a smeared ink blot in the region of the horns and bassoons; it contains the usual blotting marks (the ink didn't dry fast enough for him), and a total of three bars of corrections in the clarinet parts, where violent strokes look like exasperated head shaking. It contains the dynamic markings so typical of Mozart, dashing strokes; the *fp* of *fortepiano*, especially, always seems like the stenographic symbol for a movement that sets the whole static, controlled page of the score into swinging waves of motion, bringing it strangely to life. Though the paper is yellowed by time, what is on it looks fresh, as if it had just been written, as if the ink from the pen of the "incomparable" Mozart had not yet dried. The manuscript is legible everywhere, and it surely put no special demands on the copyists, who must have had to collect it, still wet perhaps. There was no time to rehearse the overture, anyway. We cannot guess how it sounded. We are no longer able to appreciate a piece as audiences of those times did; we do not know what was demanded or expected, what conformed to the contemporary sense of beauty or harmony. What is certain is that we would have found any opera performance imperfect and improvised, even though the ensemble was much better then. Performance practices were lax: actors were allowed to follow their interpretive inspiration of the moment, to make jokes. When Mozart himself was at the glockenspiel one evening and made generous use of it during a performance of *Die Zauberflöte*, Schikaneder, playing Papageno, called over to him, "Shut up!" When the orchestra lost the beat and had to start over, certainly no one took it amiss. And in this particular case Mozart himself apparently wasn't taking continuity too seriously.

In his operas, Mozart created characters equal to Shakespeare's in their dramatic presence, unique nature, and individual detail. If they are not nourished out of the depths of their souls' conflict, if music cannot replace words to indicate psychological entanglement, or illustrate the polarity "to be or not to be," Mozart's characters are effective in a different way, which words cannot paraphrase. As soon as their roles are determined, as soon as their themes are stated and their characters indicated, their fates and souls are then fully and exclusively turned into music. Mozart did not have to take them from life; the libretto was enough, despite its often fatal adherence to prescribed forms (though this was relaxed by Da Ponte), to what was successful (at the time) and, not least, its reliance on gradually enfeebled *dei ex machina*. The characters of the three Da Ponte operas are more tangible, and despite some *buffo* excesses, more truthful than those in his other operas, where they serve, rather, to represent principles; more tangible, too, than all other opera characters up to Wagner and Richard Strauss. With Strauss, the characters' presence and vital magic are due in large part to Hofmannsthal's poetry; in terms of the pure art of giving meaning to a character, the Marschallin owes more to the poet than to the composer and Elektra owes more to her first poet than to her second.

Wagner's Hans Sachs grows into a powerful projection of humanity; his milieu does not permit him to reveal his greatness, but he is well aware of the fact and we can trace how far he rises above this milieu both in the libretto and in the music. Wagner's legendary characters, like Mozart's, are profoundly human in their emotions, but their world is not ours (the comparisons cannot be drawn in every respect) and their experience cannot be measured by ours; hardly any of us will identify with Lohengrin. Tristan and Isolde, ruled by love until the end, are superterrestrial, exemplary. They are on a grand scale, and unique; they will never have successors. A Figaro, on the other hand, a Susanna, a Zerlina, a Leporello, and a Despina are neither configurations nor archetypes, let alone personified ideas. They are part of us; whoever knows happiness through art must see in them a part of its cause.

Mozart conceived his characters intuitively and preconsciously. Since, however, it was not life but music that moved him, or rather (there is no other way to put it), since music was his life, his relationship to real people was distanced without his being aware of it. He "received" his concepts of character and worked them out on a preconscious plane. In this creative process he sublimated life in its universality without knowing it: the stage character reveals himself to the audience while bypassing the mediator, the composer. Whatever part of Mozart's human understanding might have emerged and been applied to daily life had already been drained by this process of sublimation. It was a much weaker understanding, paler, duller, and was either applied to external life as a cliché, whether appropriate or not, or worked in trivializing counterpoint to it. Thus, his relationship to others was of secondary importance in his life. Surely he had been an extremely sensitive, affectionate child. The extravagance of his affections, however, was simply a part of his emotional makeup and not bound to particular people. As he grew up, he honored his parents, for he had been taught to honor them, and the Mozarts did have a well-defined and admirably united family life. Nevertheless, despite year-long separations from one or the other parent, he never really missed them. He adored Aloysia Weber, but when she rejected him, he transferred his love for her to her younger sister Constanze, whom he married and with whom he was, in his own way, happy. He had neither the inclination nor the time to analyze other people or his relationship to them, just as in his creative life he was above any extramusical hypothesizing. Mozart came to need company more and more, at times urgently; he needed female singers and pupils for the erotic atmosphere they provided; and as a strange substitute gratification, he needed Constanze, who was growing colder toward him. But it never occurred to him to analyze these needs, even when he was well aware of his subjective feelings. A passage, which we shall return to, from his letter of July 7, 1791, to Constanze is utterly unique: "I can't describe what I have been feeling—a kind of emptiness, which hurts me dreadfully—a kind of longing, which is never satisfied, which never ceases, and which persists, nay rather increases daily." It is the only statement in Mozart's extant letters in which he refers to his inability and, probably, unwillingness to explain his feelings. But he was aware of the feeling itself, the emptiness, the dissatisfaction. This is where Saint-Foix's question would have been a propos: *"Que s'est-il donc passé?"* But here it might also have been easier to answer: he had had enough. Yet we don't hear that in his music. Precisely because we forget the creator in listening to his music (and that is his intention), we are shocked by his few verbal statements of this kind. In his music he freed himself from himself; indeed, he tried not to exist apart from it. And so at times his behavior takes on the character of self-abnegation, described by witnesses who usually misunderstood or misinterpreted it.

Who was really close to him? If we believed the claims of surviving contemporaries, there would be a sizable list. For his death provoked many people to say something about him; during his lifetime his anomalous conduct may have made some of them uneasy. They had been helpless in the face of his eccentric behavior, which in his last years was at times puzzling and unpredictable, and, in his last months, occasionally insufferable. After his death their helplessness mellowed into an affectionate understanding, but unfortunately, they are always imprecise when describing the object of their understanding. The witnesses were primarily concerned to show that they had been close to him. They fought for a place at his side, or at least within the radius of his attention. But still, we must wonder whether anyone at all was close to him during the last years in Vienna, whether he really had a friend who was more to him than merely someone he referred to as such in his letters. Was there someone he really would have hated to lose touch with, whose well-being really concerned him, for whose life he feared, someone who called up feelings in him greater than the conventional ones we find so often in his letters? Probably not; human ties, as we know them, were alien to him. Nor did he need them. The expression of his waning will to live was necessarily directed at the one person who would be hardest hit, as he thought, by its complete eclipse. This was Constanze, the imaginary beloved, at first a replacement for the member of the original cast, the prima donna in life as onstage, Aloysia. Aloysia was a significantly more complex and diverse phenomenon than her sister Constanze, full of pretensions, of course, but also possessed of an artistic conscience that troubled her until the end of her life; for in contrast to Constanze, she was not only capricious but vulnerable as well.

Aloysia was right in thinking Mozart would be better off with Constanze, who played no role in the tragedy of his estrangement from society. It seems improbable that she ever suffered mental torment, and even her physical sufferings seem primarily to be an excuse for her visits to spas. Constanze had a lighthearted, instinctual nature; she granted Mozart (and perhaps not only him) erotic, or at least sexual, satisfaction, but was unable to offer him the happiness a lesser man needs for self-realization. In that regard Mozart was egocentric; his standard, in all matters of human feeling, was the feeling he himself invested, not the response of a partner. He did not perceive the degree of response, or at least he perceived it only when, as in the case of Aloysia, the response was not forthcoming. His isolation was extreme, but it also protected him from wounds to his ego. His hopes for Aloysia, presumably never encouraged by any cooperation on her part, grew, nourished by his own imagination; when confronted with reality, the hopes disappeared. And the same thing probably happened with a few subsequent loves. He misread his own relationship to other human beings, not only when it was a matter of erotic attachment. Thus, he did not realize until very late, at the end of his life, how greatly his fellow men had insulted him. Only then did he suddenly find himself alone; he discovered that his echo as an artist had long since died away. No wonder the discovery destroyed him. His works were far off in the past; he no longer heard them.

Constanze Mozart is the rare case of a key biographical figure who cannot be reconstructed from any autobiographical document whatever, at least not while she was still Constanze Mozart. Even statements by others about her are scarce. We are almost exclusively dependent on letters addressed to her and on the few, usually unfriendly, references of surviving contemporaries. During her eight years as Mozart's wife she left not one single document of her own. The letters to her husband have been lost; either he lost them (he seems to have been extremely careless about looking after things) or they were destroyed by Constanze and Nissen. Why?—we do not know. Perhaps they would have revealed to posterity insufficient evidence of the love and concern she claimed to have felt for her spouse. Nissen asserts in a puzzling, but not completely unbelievable, way that she "cared more for his talent than for his person, and was sorry for him when he was deceived."[56]

Deceived by whom? Perhaps Nissen means Aloysia. In that case, Constanze would have told her second husband that she had had only a surrogate role in her first marriage: not very likely.

We can imagine Constanze as Mozart's wife only in a painfully limited way. And only in 1829 does she emerge as an independent figure, sixty-seven years old and Nissen's widow. The Novellos describe her as a "well-bred lady" whose conversation was "peculiarly attractive." In her "delightful residence," with a lovely garden and a beautiful view, she held open house for everyone who expressed admiration for her first husband, much to her own satisfaction. In her ten years with Nissen in Copenhagen she must have learned something about propriety, if not exactly sophistication.

In Vienna, to the Novellos' surprise, people had little good to say about Constanze. The Novellos could ignore the fact that the loquacious and effusive banker von Henickstein found her a bad singer and actress; after all, Constanze had never expected to equal her exceptional sister Aloysia. But that a distinguished, respectable man like the piano maker Andreas Streicher (Schiller's friend and fellow pupil in his youth, and Beethoven's friend in his declining years) should speak badly of her greatly distressed the honest couple. Their desire for biographical refinement forbade them to pursue this negative direction further, especially since the topic was "a sore one" with Streicher himself. As tactful Britishers, they were probably offended that he even raised the curtain on this shady side. Vincent writes acidly in his notebook: ". . . private affairs and gossip upon matters with which the world at large has nothing to do I have not the least inclination either to learn or to record."[57] Fair enough. However, he was only too eager to take up "private affairs" when they were on the sunny side.

Constanze was not a real singer, and not a musician at all. Still, she could sight-sing and play the piano. She had an ear and taste and her own musical moods. Thus, she fell in love with the Bach fugues her husband brought home from van Swieten's house; suddenly she wanted to hear only fugues, thought them the "most artistic and beautiful" music— indeed, she craved them the way a pregnant woman craves certain foods. Her sense of order seems to have expressed itself exclusively in the enjoyment of strict contrapuntal pieces. It was she who encouraged Mozart to write fugues.

And so Mozart wrote fugue after fugue for Constanze. How- ever, nearly all of them remained fragments. One after another, he wrote a quarter, half, three quarters of a fugue; all of them break off, as if he was reluctant to satisfy Constanze fully. Per- haps her sense of order did not go so far as to require comple- tion. But by and large we do better to look for the cause of their incompleteness in the music itself. The G minor Fugue fragment, K. 401/375e, from spring 1782, which Mozart dis- continued, oddly, only shortly before the end (the last eight bars are in a strange hand, probably Maximilian Stadler's), with its rigid, almost cramped counterpoint, shows an all too narrow dependence on Bach. It must have been hard even for Mozart to tolerate: he seems to have broken down shortly before the coda. Perhaps he wanted to wean Constanze from her predilection. How we would like to hear this fugue played by Mozart himself. He played it alone; others could master it only in a four-hand arrangement. Later on he was able to free himself from this dependence on Bach, with the great Fugue in C minor for two pianos, K. 426 (December 29, 1783), one of his most powerful keyboard works. Here he becomes Bach's equal. In four parts, purely abstract, and of an unparalleled harmonic boldness, it is his crowning work in this genre. It was certainly no longer something written simply for Con- stanze's enjoyment but for some more immediate reason, for himself and a pupil. Therese von Trattner, perhaps? Or Bar- bara Ployer? We do not know. Whatever the case, this work remains exemplary—a victory, as he was well aware.

Wolfgang, psychologically and tactically mistaken in dealings with his clever father, as always, wrote in his letter of December 5, 1781, the following ominous passage:

> You say that I must remember that I have an immortal soul. Not only do I think it, but I firmly believe it. If it were not so, wherein would consist the difference between men and beasts? Just because I both know and most firmly believe this, I have not been able to carry out all your wishes exactly in the way you expected.

Apparently Leopold Mozart, after reading Moses Mendelssohn, had directed his son's attention to his immortal soul. Still, it is a mysterious passage, extremely undiplomatic given the developing situation, along the same general lines as a telegram saying: START GETTING UPSET! LETTER FOLLOWS. The clear-sighted Leopold probably wondered immediately what was afoot. Although, since his son's break with Salzburg, he could no longer count on his tractability, let alone obedience, he was perhaps repressing his intuition of how far in the opposite direction his son had gone. He knew that a new and horrible surprise was in the works, and probably guessed its nature, too. He called upon his son to explain his cryptic remark. And then came the letter of December 15, 1781, in which, after the usual rhetorical introduction, Mozart paints a picture of his fiancée, Constanze, colored by his wish to attain his objective. Unfortunately, therefore, it is not a reliable portrayal; but it does give us some information about the writer and his relation to the girl he portrays:

> Dearest father! You demand an explanation of the words in the closing sentences of my last letter! Oh, how gladly would I have opened my heart to you long ago, but I was deterred by the reproaches you might have made to me for *thinking of such a thing at an unseasonable time*—although indeed thinking can never be unseasonable. Meanwhile I am very anxious to secure here a small but *certain* income, which, together with what chance may provide, will enable me to live here quite comfortably—and then—to marry!

You are horrified at the idea? But I entreat you, dearest, most beloved father, to listen to me. I have been obliged to reveal my intentions to you. You must, therefore, allow me to disclose to you my reasons, which, moreover, are very well founded. The voice of nature speaks as loud in me as in others, louder, perhaps, than in many a big strong lout of a fellow. I simply cannot live as most young men do in these days. In the first place, I have too much religion; in the second place, I have too great a love of my neighbor and too high a feeling of honor to seduce an innocent girl; and, in the third place, I have too much horror and disgust, too much dread and fear of diseases and too much care for my health to fool about with whores. So I can swear that I have never had relations of that sort with any woman. Besides, if such a thing had occurred, I should not have concealed it from you; for, after all, to err is natural enough in a man, and to err *once* would be mere weakness—although indeed I should not undertake to promise that if I had erred once in this way, I should stop short at one slip. However, I stake my life on the truth of what I have told you. I am well aware that this reason (powerful as it is) is not urgent enough. But owing to my disposition, which is more inclined to a peaceful and domesticated existence than to revelry, I who from my youth up have never been accustomed to look after my own belongings, linen, clothes and so forth, cannot think of anything more necessary to me than a wife. I assure you that I am often obliged to spend unnecessarily, simply because I do not pay attention to things. I am absolutely convinced that I should manage better with a wife (on the same income which I have now) than I do by myself. And how many useless expenses would be avoided! True, other expenses would have to be met, but—one knows what they are and can be prepared for them—in short, one leads a well-ordered existence. A bachelor, in my opinion, is only half alive. Such are my views and I cannot help it. I have thought the matter over and reflected sufficiently, and I shall not change my mind. But who is the object of my love? Do not be horrified again, I entreat you. Surely not one of the Webers? Yes, one of the Webers—but not Josefa, nor

Sophie, but Constanze, the middle one. In no other family
have I ever come across such differences of character. The
eldest is a lazy, gross, perfidious woman, and as cunning as
a fox. Mme Lange is a false, malicious person and a coquette.
The youngest—is still too young to be anything in particular—she is just a good-natured, but feather-headed creature!
May God protect her from seduction! But the middle one,
my good, dear Constanze, is the martyr of the family and,
probably for that very reason, is the kindest-hearted, the
cleverest and, in short, the best of them all. She makes herself responsible for the whole household and yet in their
opinion she does nothing right. Oh, my most beloved father,
I could fill whole sheets with descriptions of all the scenes
that I have witnessed in that house. If you want to read
them, I shall do so in my next letter. But before I cease to
plague you with my chatter, I must make you better
acquainted with the character of my dear Constanze. She is
not ugly, but at the same time far from beautiful. Her whole
beauty consists in two little black eyes and a pretty figure.
She has no wit, but she has enough common sense to enable
her to fulfill her duties as a wife and mother. It is a downright lie that she is inclined to be extravagant. On the contrary, she is accustomed to be shabbily dressed, for the little
that her mother has been able to do for her children, she
has done for the two others, but never for Constanze. True,
she would like to be neatly and cleanly dressed, but not
smartly, and most things that a woman needs she is able to
make for herself; and she dresses her own hair every day.
Moreover she understands housekeeping and has the kindest
heart in the world. I love her and she loves me with all her
heart? Tell me whether I could wish myself a better wife?

One thing more I must tell you, which is that when I resigned the Archbishop's service, our love had not yet begun.
It was born of her tender care and attentions when I was
living in their house.

Accordingly, all that I desire is to have a small assured
income (of which, thank God, I have good hopes), and then
I shall never cease entreating you to allow me to save this
poor girl—and to make myself and her—and, if I may say

so, all of us very happy. For you surely are happy when I
am? And you are to enjoy one half of *my fixed income.* My
dearest father, I have opened my heart to you and explained
my remarks.

The wish to marry Constanze was apparently the outcome of
autosuggestion; Constanze and her mother shared in initiat-
ing the maneuver. The mother directed the intrigue systematically, in a truly professional way. She was like a stage
type, the mother-in-law of farce, malicious and petty. Constanze was scarcely less adept in her role: in her social circles,
Mozart passed for a man with a future, a good catch for someone who could act quickly.

Within a few weeks the net was drawn tight; the relationship
of the lodger to the landlady's daughter was already compro-
mised by this time, and could no longer be called entirely innocent. This configuration turns up again later, incidentally:
Nissen was Constanze's lodger before he became her husband.
Soon Mozart's overly developed sense of honor would no longer
permit him to disengage himself from the ties that bind (to
use the phrase in its literal meaning would be going too far).
And so he began to deceive himself, as part of his unconscious
fatalism vis-à-vis the world and its claims. He began to love
Constanze because something in him had decided to do so. It
had to be someone, after all, and she would be the one.

His father never forgave him for this step. Leopold Mozart
had certainly never been one to show greatness, but he did not
even have the dignity to accommodate himself to unalterable
necessity when it went against his will. His own harshness
worked against him. Wolfgang, who did have greatness, who
never had to excuse pettiness because it never affected him,
did not let his father sense his reaction to this injury. But he
must have been distressed by the frosty behavior of his father
and sister when he visited Salzburg with his wife in 1783.
Constanze was given no presents, no appropriate gift, no appropriate kindness. Understandably, she never forgave Leopold and Nannerl as long as she lived, just as Nannerl never

forgave her for marrying her brother. As old ladies in Salzburg they lived near each other for years without ever even seeing one another.

Thus, a certain Constanze Weber has gone down in history. If someone had predicted this at the time of her marriage, no one would have been more surprised than she. Although she lived to experience Mozart's fame, to enjoy the financial benefits (doing her best to augment them), she never had a real understanding of her husband's greatness, not even after his death, when his special prestige became obvious. Then she could at least believe the fact of his greatness.

Thinking of her, we are seized by a kind of lethargy; we would be inclined to confess that nothing in particular occurs to us about her. But, like Leopold, she is an integral part of Mozart's life; she even helped to shape his posthumous fame after his own departure from the scene. Let us try, therefore, as best we can, to reconstruct her image.

She was twenty years old when Wolfgang married her. In her portrait, painted in 1782 by her brother-in-law Lange, she is not beautiful. The area of the lips is strangely askew; it looks almost swollen. The eyes are disproportionately large, quite contrary to Wolfgang's description of them in the letter to his father. True, the portrait is clumsily painted; it makes her seem almost deformed, and although it apparently found favor at the time, we can assume that Constanze did not look much like it. Lange, though not a dilettante, was probably a better actor than painter, and Constanze was probably a good deal more attractive, for in the course of her life she had a sizable number of admirers. In her later portrait, painted by Hans Hansen in 1802, which shows her, aged forty, the future wife of the state counselor Nissen, she projects a certain ladylike, if stiff, dignity. Of course, this picture, too, is no masterpiece.

One sees, at any rate, that Mozart, in his letter to his father, did not attempt to prettify the image of his beloved. We wonder, in fact, if he did not paint her a little too dull, to avoid the impression that he might have been taken in by false glitter. There is a certain finesse in the way he stresses above all the plainness of his bride-to-be, and emphasizes his own cool, objective eye. For he knew well that his father was hardened to all his many euphemistic exaggerations. Whether Leopold took the business about duties as a wife and mother seriously we do not know. We find it exceedingly funny, like all Wolfgang's bourgeois domestic moments. It more likely alarmed Leopold, since he assumed the opposite, and with good reason. As it turned out, Mozart did not wait for his father's consent to marry; it arrived only after the wedding.

In other ways, too, Mozart presents himself in these letters as totally matter-of-fact. The need for patched pockets and laundered linen, as a reason to marry, is nothing compared to the blunt way in which he broaches the topic of his awakening sexual drive. He uses it as an opportunity to assure his father of his virginity, as though he still owed him an accounting; as though, in fact, he was still eager to give such an accounting, so that his father might take everything into consideration and approve his decision. There is no hypocrisy at work here, and no philistinism: while writing, Mozart saw himself as pure, innocent, untouched, the sober husband and future father, modeled in Leopold's image. It did not occur to him that his father would find it hard to see him in the same light. Apparently Mozart never asked himself whether his father had ever approved of any of his decisions, or even taken them seriously. He was as great a stranger to the world of reason as to the sphere of human relations. He was guided solely by the aim of the moment. In this case, he had to handle a ticklish message to his father; objectivity was required, and so he employed what he took for objectivity. He did not consider that his father might see matters differently; he had no "worldly wisdom" at his disposal, and he never put himself in the place of the recipient, either of his letters or of his oral protestations.

All the things he wrote here about Constanze were contrary to the truth. She may have dressed simply and done her own hair, but only because she lacked the means to dress elegantly and have others do her hair. She understood nothing about running a household; at least she repressed any such knowledge as long as Mozart was alive. We do not know if she really patched his pockets and laundered his linen, but it is unlikely; they had a servant girl for that kind of work. And we do not dare judge if she had a "kind heart." The question mark at the end of the statement "and she loves me with all her heart?" would almost seem to be a significant Freudian slip. In his letters Mozart used to call her his *"Weibchen"* (little wife). This term was accurate in more ways than he knew or than its use at the time (that is, as a rhyme, more or less, for *"Täubchen"* [little pigeon], as in *Die Zauberflöte*) would indicate. She was the prototype of the little woman, as far as we can judge from Wolfgang's letters to her. All his protestations, his warnings, his entreaties and assurances and exhortations seem to define her rather clearly, in both positive and negative senses, solely in relation to her "feminine qualities," never on neutral ground. He addresses her reason or judgment only rarely (but then emphatically). Constanze's emotional life was lived on the superficial level of direct sensations, to which she also responded directly. She yielded to her drives, loved pleasure, was totally impressionable and therefore, of course, very adaptable; she "went along with everything." And since Wolfgang, too, inclined to chaotic disorder in his outer life, it was the most natural thing in the world for her to share this disorder and thereby promote it. For this feature, in particular, biographers have reproached her roundly; like all reproaches, theirs are unjust. Although her wastefulness played a part in the family's financial ruin (Wolfgang himself bears the remainder of the blame), it was not greater than Mozart's own immoderation, and certainly not "prodigality." She made up for it, besides, in a different area of conjugal life, at least during their first seven years. The gift for economical management of the household is invariably expressed in other aspects of the matrimonial relationship as well; an excessive concern for the household would have hit Wolfgang, if we judge him correctly, especially hard in one regard. The virtue of domestic orderliness rarely comes unattended, but brings with it other qualities that only Philistines and frigid personalities hold to be virtues. Mozart was neither the one nor the other. And herein lies one explanation for the eight years of their more or less happy married life, despite some faltering: it was rooted in the earth of erotic understanding.

If we read the letters of his journey to Berlin, Leipzig, and Dresden, from April to June 1789, we find, in addition to the diverse factual information, intimate passages that refer to this relationship, wavering between doubt and gratification, a strange mixture of pedantic detail and erotic straightforwardness, often united in one single letter. On May 23, 1789, he reproaches her for not writing more often:

Berlin, May 23rd, 1789

Dearest, most beloved, most precious little Wife!

I was above measure delighted to receive here your dear letter of May 13th, and only this very moment your previous one of the 9th, which had to find its way from Leipzig to Berlin. Well, the first thing I am going to do is to make a list of all the letters which I sent you and then a list of the letters which I have received from you.

I wrote to you on April 8th from the post stage Budwitz
                on April 10th from Prague

             on April 13th⎫
                  and 17th⎭ from Dresden

             on April 22nd (in French) from Leipzig

             on April 28th⎫
             and May 5th⎭ from Potsdam

            on May 9th⎫
              and 16th⎭ from Leipzig

            on May 19th from Berlin

and I am now writing on the 23rd.
    That makes eleven letters.

I received your letter of April 8th on April 15th in Dresden
of April 13th on April 21st in Leipzig
of April 24th on May 8th in Leipzig ⎞ on my
of May 5th on May 14th in Leipzig ⎠ return
of May 13th on May 20th in Berlin
of May 9th on May 22nd in Berlin
That makes six letters.

You see that there is a gap between April 13th and 24th.
So one of your letters must have gone astray and thus I was
without a letter for seventeen days. So if you too had to
spend seventeen days in the same condition, one of my letters
must have been lost.

Here we must imagine Mozart in Berlin, sitting at night in his
probably shabby room at the inn by the Sartory Stucco Works
on the Gendarmenmarkt, taking out Constanze's letters to jot
down his disappointing list. But letters are perhaps not the
only thing he takes out. Later in the same letter he writes:

On Thursday, the 28th, I shall leave for Dresden, where I
shall spend the night. On June 1st I intend to sleep in
Prague, and on the 4th—the 4th—with my darling little
wife. Arrange your dear sweet nest very daintily, for my little
fellow deserves it indeed, he has really behaved himself quite
well and is only longing to possess your sweetest. . . . Just
picture to yourself that rascal; as I write he crawls onto the
table and looks at me questioningly. I, however, box his
ears properly—but the rogue is simply . . . and now the
knave burns only more fiercely and can hardly be restrained.

These lines were crossed out by Nissen, and were made visible
once more (like many other passages) by Ludwig Schiedermair,
using a photographic technique.[58] Only the omissions indicated
by dots could not be deciphered. They were probably crossed
out repeatedly and very heavily. Under the circumstances we
are somewhat surprised at how much Nissen and Constanze
(after mutual agreement?) let stand. In the previous letter, for
example, dated May 19, from Berlin, we read:

. . . for how on earth could you think, or even imagine, that
I had forgotten you? How could I possibly do so? For even

supposing such a thing you will get on the very first night a thorough spanking on your lovable, kissable arse, and this you may count upon.

Even if this sentence does not necessarily throw light on any wild sexual practices, it does amaze us that the aging Constanze and her worthy spouse let the sentence stand as it is. Possibly Nissen remembered this kissability himself, thinking back to the time when Constanze was still his young landlady, though he does not really seem the type.

Be that as it may, Constanze seems to have expressed the fear that Mozart might forget her: obviously a moment of jealousy—not the only one—and a sign of love. On the other hand, it is not clear whether we should take the fact that his "little fellow" had behaved himself "quite well" and not *very* well as a qualification on his part; probably not, for in the letters from this trip, above all, his erotic tie to Constanze seems especially strong and unequivocal. He always carries her portrait with him and appears to celebrate in an extremely suggestive manner the ritual of setting it up and packing it away again. On April 13, 1789, he writes to her:

> . . . if only I had a letter from you! If I were to tell you all the things I do with your dear portrait, I think that you would often laugh. For instance, when I take it out of its case, I say, "Good day, Stanzerl!— Good day, little rascal, pussy-pussy, little turned-up nose, little bagatelle, Schluck and Druck," and when I put it away again, I let it slip in very slowly, saying all the time, "Stu!—Stu!—Stu!" with the peculiar *emphasis* which this word so full of meaning demands, and then just at the last, quickly, "Good night, little mouse, sleep well."

This "Stu—Stu—Stu" recurs often, as do other components of this erotic secret language. Some are almost onomatopoetic in their suggestiveness. They seem to have certain discoverable meanings. The "peculiar *emphasis*" would speak for that.

But, for all the satyr playfulness, "honor" is never forgotten: Mozart returns again and again to Constanze's behavior; it never completely lets him rest, and he apparently never fully trusted her in that regard. Even at a distance some reports seem to have reached him, unless they were merely guesses or fears of his own. On April 16, 1789, he writes to her from Dresden:

> I beg you in your conduct not only to be careful of *your honor and mine*, but also to consider *appearances*. Do not be angry with me for asking this. You ought to love me even more for thus valuing our honor.

We will not hold it against him that here, at least, it was "appearances" that concerned him most. He was trying to salvage his reputation, though it could not have been saved by Constanze's good conduct. But he returns to the theme of honor when he complains repeatedly about her all too free behavior in Baden. Now and then we can even share his distress; for example, when she gives a party in Baden, thinking her husband has concluded a good business deal, while in reality nothing had come of it. And even if something had come of it, it would have been nothing more than a new loan—but it was just that kind of thing that seems not to have bothered Constanze.

We cannot legislate our sympathies for this or that character in the drama, but we have tried, as much as possible, not to take sides or show emotion; we hope that we have learned something from the errors of existing biographies. In Mozart's case they usually present us at the outset with their author's exact position, which he then retains with rigid consistency. Pro-Leopold or anti-Leopold, but especially pro-Constanze or anti-Constanze. She is the pointer on the scale, but more than her own worth she shows the inclination or disinclination of the judges who weigh her. Paumgartner writes, "The fact of Mozart's unshakable attachment to her justifies all Constanze's weaknesses."[59] This seems to us a debatable judgment, of the kind we are trying to oppose with new ways of thinking.

So often unappreciated, criticized as loose and careless, a profitable subject of popular literature and therefore perennially misrepresented, Constanze does not gain her own voice in the concert of his contemporaries until long after Mozart's death, when these contemporaries were growing older, survivors, like Constanze herself, and possessors of fallible, if not always fallacious, powers of memory. As the wife of the Danish diplomat Georg Nikolaus Nissen, she became stately and sober, a judicious administrator of the heritage; in that capacity she wove her piece of the Mozart legend, quietly but audibly. She not only broadened the Novellos' picture of Mozart in a surprising way, by adding to it new and undreamed-of qualitites (for example, that he ". . . had a superior talent for all the arts . . ."[60] and that he was a great flower and nature lover), but she also supplied the Gymnasium teacher Franz Niemtschek, Mozart's second biographer (after Schlichtegroll), with this kind of material. "The beauty of nature in summer delighted his passionate heart,"[61] he writes. This thought, too, was probably culled from Constanze.

Her sons lived far away; one was a high official in Milan, the other, whom she had exhorted not to disgrace her and his deceased father by becoming a mediocre musician, had become a mediocre musician, in Lemberg. Both honored their dead father, as was seemly, were moderately attached to their mother, not unfriendly to their stepfather. We find them unremarkable, though various documents reveal that they knew quite well what their limits would have to be; neither considered himself capable of attaining a stature even remotely equal to that of his great father.

The older son, Carl Thomas, died in Milan in 1858, at the age of seventy-four, respectable, generous, and retired from public service. He could well afford his generosity, for he had become rich: from the proceeds of only three performances of

Figaro in Paris around the middle of the nineteenth century he was able to acquire a country estate north of Milan. What would his father have said to that?

The younger son, Franz Xaver Wolfgang (his first two names were later suppressed; they were Süssmayr's Christian names), died in Karlsbad, in 1844, at fifty-three, like his brother, unmarried. If we can believe the gossip the Novellos heard from Constanze in Salzburg, and noted almost reluctantly, he had had an affair with an aristocratic lady. It would probably have been Josephine von Baroni-Cavalcabò; at any rate, he left the Mozart autographs in his possession to a woman of that name. According to some sources, Carl Thomas had an illegitimate daughter in Milan: Constanze, who died of smallpox in 1833; thus, the Mozart line was not continued here, either. Franz Xaver Wolfgang was said to have been a talented but frail child, since his mother, Constanze, had been in poor health both before and after his conception. That is what Streicher related to the Novellos. But he probably did not go so far as to suspect that Mozart may not even have been the father.

Constanze gave out the smaller autographs with a rather free hand; several people who had helped further the reputation of her late husband, or who had promised to do so, received something, only a line perhaps, but a line nevertheless. She was strict and exact with these dispensations, carried on active dealings with publishers, as was her right, and eventually became prosperous. She supported her second husband's efforts to write the biography of her first, became a worthy widow for the second time, received the visits of admirers with grace and dignified propriety, and had cards printed on which she called herself the "widow of the state counselor von Nissen, formerly the widow Mozart." Nissen died in 1826, an upright public servant, without having finished his book; so Constanze had ample time to manipulate it more in her own favor. She continued her visits to spas until the end of her life and died at eighty, on March 6, 1842. Whatever her complaint was, the spas seem to have done her no harm. When Mozart was alive she went to Baden, afterward to Bad Gastein, closer to Salzburg and probably more elegant; there she spent many weeks each year, vegetating mindlessly. From her diaries we learn the kind of thing that moved her:

> Today the 19th of September 1829 I arose, thanks be to God, hale and hearty, said Good morning to all mankind, took coffee in my room, washed my mouth and face as always, had breakfast, read aloud in the *Hours of Piety* until the time for the baths, but did not arrive at my 8 o'clock bath until 9 o'clock, because the stranger, who will take my letters with him to London and whose name I still do not know, bathes in the nude and I cannot therefore as a respectable woman, bathe with him. And so I spent the time until 10 o'clock. Then I lay down for a quarter of an hour, dressed to the noise of little Caroline and her dog. Afterwards I knitted until dinner, dined quite well, with a good appetite, and sit here now and write, since it is raining; otherwise I would go for a walk, as usual.

When we read this record, we cannot help wishing that Constanze had been this thorough while her first husband was alive. But perhaps it was the petty complacency of her second widowhood that awakened her powers of articulation. In a certain way she even became religious:

> Today on September 23, 1829, I had the good fortune, with the help and blessing of my heavenly Father, to take my twelfth bath.

Thus the widow. As Mozart's wife she has to be reconstructed painstakingly, and ultimately unsuccessfully, from her husband's letters. Only very sporadically do they reveal what she did and what she neglected to do. They cannot bring her into clear focus, first because they document only those periods when the two were apart. Without doubt, Mozart suffered more than she did from these separations; Constanze was better able than he to find erotic substitutes when he was on his journeys, with their continual duties and disappointments and the increasingly gloomy mood that developed as a result. The letters from the last two trips, to Berlin with Lichnowsky in 1789 and the completely unsuccessful, indeed degrading, trip to Frankfurt in 1790 with his brother-in-law Hofer, reveal that he missed her physical presence; but this was only one of many things he missed. In the last summer of his life even the desire for her presence in Vienna faded. He did not want her to witness the growing confusion of his outer life; he no longer missed anyone; his involvement with his social circle became a hectic treadmill. Rather untouched by it all, Constanze continued taking the waters in Baden, more or less fulfilling her objective in these extended visits, vague as it seems to us. But diseases at the time were ill-defined; chronic illnesses even more so, and imaginary complaints were not defined at all. We do know of Montaigne that he lost a kidney stone now and then on his Swiss journey, so his medical history is supported, as it were, by substance. Constanze's suffering remains imaginary; only on a single occasion can we gather anything precise from Mozart's comments and advice, namely that she complained of constipation. He prescribed an electuary. Clearly her letters were not sent off with anything like the same frequency as his, and not one of them has been preserved. Today it is still disconcerting, if not positively eerie, to leaf through a correspondence in which one side speaks and the other remains as silent as the tomb. Sometimes we feel as if Mozart were addressing a partner who never existed. Because of this, Constanze's image has a kind of puzzling aura around it, a touch of mystery, which was surely not part of her personality. Of course, we do not have to see her as transfigured. We can scarcely reproach her for having no idea of her husband's mental life; only rarely did he let her guess at it, and even more rarely did he consciously speak of it. Instead, he usually (and splendidly) made light of it, with the bearing worthy of a great man, but which only a few great men have ever mustered. She had no idea of any of this, but that is not her fault. Nothing is her fault, least of all that she was not exceptional.

To say that she had a hard time of it with him would be to mistake the relationship two lives can have to each other. Let us leave Constanze in peace. In a certain connection she is laughing at us posthumously, as Goethe's wife, Christiane, does. One of the most human sides of their husbands belonged nearly exclusively to them, and posterity has not the slightest share in it. This is one curtain that will not be lifted.

The evaluation of contemporary reports requires as much care as that of the primary sources. Our faculty of semantic discrimination can no longer focus clearly on the language of either. At times there is a change of meaning within one word alone. When Mozart wrote of his lied "Verdankt sei es dem Glanz," K. 392/340a, one of the three lieder to poems from Hermes' *Sophiens Reise*, that it should be sung *"gleich-gültig und zufrieden," "gleichgültig"* did not mean what we understand by the word (i.e., "indifferently"). And he surely meant something other than what we mean when he wrote of a pupil that she had "genius." It was a term he applied too generously, even in its reduced meaning, as he himself later came to see. When Haydn praises Mozart's "taste" as his greatest gift next to his supreme "knowledge of composition" (letter of Leopold Mozart, February 14–16, 1785), he is not speaking of that same aesthetic concept about which we are so ambivalent today.

The majority of intimates' eyewitness reports are also unreliable in an even wider sense. Less important than their subject, these authors are subjective in taking sides, and especially in describing their own relation to the object of their devotion. And yet here, too, we must differentiate: there are some reports whose grudging truth begins with the information they give about the reporter; then, filtered through his unconscious patterns of articulation, we gain a view of the figure he is describing. These reports are not credible because their authors are especially honest or honorable, serene or objective, or because they have earned our trust in other areas, but simply because we cannot credit them with the ability to invent freely, for either positive or negative reasons. These are the peripheral, shadowy figures, usually people of limited imagination, totally lacking a sense of what might have been, but who, on the other hand, strike us as truthful rather than loquacious. Loyalty orders them to be discreet to an appropriate degree; only when asked by someone they acknowledge as an authority do they sometimes consent to depict the darker side of the man they admire—the things that seem less than natural, the embarrassing, unpleasant things, or qualities they themselves deem undesirable or incomprehensible.

Sophie Weber, Constanze Mozart's sister, is a witness of this kind. Born either in 1763, 1767, or 1769, at any rate still a child when Mozart was in Mannheim, she enters his life late. As the youngest of the four "Weber girls," she, too, was living in Vienna, with her mother, Cäcilie, when Mozart and Constanze were there, and she visited them often. Mozart seems to have esteemed her and, to a degree, confided in her. Although she is the only source for this assumption, we need not doubt it, for he liked many people—which is not to say that they penetrated very far into the sphere of his interest since he tolerated nearly everyone. She remained single until 1807, when she married Petrus Jakob Haibl, a member of Schikaneder's troupe for a while, and later a choir director and composer. His opera *Der Tyroler Wastl* (libretto by Schikaneder) was in its time more successful than Mozart's operas, and was also repeatedly on the program of the Weimar Court Theater, managed by Goethe (though we do not know if we should hold Goethe responsible for this).

In 1826, after the deaths of Haibl and Nissen (on the same day!), Sophie moved to Salzburg, to live with her sister Constanze. She died in 1846, four years after Constanze, the last one remaining from the circle around Mozart. Mediocre and, ultimately, as lusterless as her sister, she, too, was probably uneducated except in the rudiments of music; she seems more reliable and good-natured than her three sisters, less egotistic and calculating. But we always find it hard to attribute any life of their own to these secondary figures. In critical situations she was there to help; she cared for Constanze during at least three of her six confinements and assisted with some devotion during the night of Mozart's death (December 5, 1791). She kept her head at that time, in contrast to Constanze, who was of course harder hit. The Novellos met her in Salzburg at her sister's, but neither wasted any words on her appearance. Taking advantage of Constanze's momentary absence, she related to them that Mozart died in her (Sophie's) arms. Thus, each witness insists to the end on his or her share of immortality.

In 1825 Nissen asked her to relate the events of this night for his biography, and her report turns a secondary character in Mozart's life into a key figure. Since the report was not written down until thirty-four years after the event, the borders between fact and legend are permanently blurred—which is to say that legend probably won the day. The conditions necessary for credibility are absent from the outset because, as we all know, even the most reliable witness's view of a major event changes over the course of decades. Sophie may well have been honest, but she certainly was not self-critical enough to submit her memory or the degree of her objectivity to a test later on. Constanze never explicitly confirmed Sophie's report, but neither did she challenge it. She comes off well in it. Her overt expression of grief accords with what would be in order. She seems to have mastered her last scene as wife and the transition to widow of a husband subsequently declared great. As we said, after Nissen's death, she supervised the publication of his biography of Mozart.

Nissen's book was published in 1828, two years after his death. Its complete lack of system is reinforced by Constanze's later inclusion of apparently arbitrary interpolations and addenda; she does not indicate them as such, and scatters them indiscriminately throughout the book. Nevertheless, here and there we have a brief disclosure, an attempt at an interpretation of Mozart's personality, as for example:

> Sophie, his sister-in-law, who is still alive, confirms his continual mental activity, as she describes him and his last years: He was always in good spirits, but very reflective, even at the best of times. He looked at everyone with a piercing glance, giving balanced answers to everything, whether he was merry or sad, and yet he seemed at the same time to be lost in thought about something entirely different. Even when he washed his hands in the morning he walked up and down, never stood still, knocked one heel against the other, and was always reflective. At the table he often took a corner of his napkin, twisted it up and rubbed it back and forth under his nose, seeming, because of his reflections, not to notice, and often he grimaced at the same time. He was always enthusiastic about new entertainments, riding and billiards for example. His patient wife did everything she could to keep him from bad company. He was always moving his hands and feet, always playing with something, e.g. his hat, pockets, watch chain, tables, chairs, as if they were pianos. As a child, his youngest son was just like him.

Obviously neither Nissen nor Constanze took the trouble, and probably did not possess the ability, to put this report into any kind of logical or even chronological order. On the contrary, they have weakened its descriptive power by adding irrelevancies; that was probably Constanze's doing. The hint of the son's heredity does not belong here, unless she was trying, as if in an aside, to remove any doubt about his legitimacy, and to keep Süssmayr, whose role in all of this we will consider later, out of the picture. Nor do we know which image to believe—the one about Mozart's permanent "good spirits" or the following dependent clause, "whether he was merry or sad." According to this, his sadness would not have impaired his good spirits—a rare state of affairs, we have to admit. And over everything, his "continual mental activity," his "reflectiveness" supposedly prevailed, though he was also quick to jump at the chance of riding or billiards or any new kind of entertainment. Whatever the case, the mental activity attributed to the hero was not the strong point of the author of the biography: his methodology belongs in a grade-school essay.

Although Mozart's passion for billiards has often been confirmed, we do not know whether his ability equaled his enthusiasm. The musician Franz von Destouches claims he played badly, but his information comes through a third party, the art collector Sulpiz Boisserée; the details are incorrect, and on the whole his information is as unreliable as Michael Kelly's, who claims Mozart played well. The biographer Niemtschek thinks billiards served Mozart primarily as "physical conditioning," and that he liked most to play alone, talking with his wife—but he gets his information, as we noted, from the wife herself. Mozart did own the equipment, and the "green-covered billiard table with 5 balls and 12 cues, a lantern and 4 candelabra" was, next to the "fortepiano with pedal," the most valuable object in the catalogue of his estate. It is not completely out of the question that he lost money playing billiards, but it is improbable. In that case, neither Nissen nor Constanze would have mentioned the "passion" at all. They either avoided ticklish topics or mentioned them only if the erring behavior could be used to call attention to Constanze's salutary or forgiving countermeasures.

It has also been verified that Mozart went for a horseback ride every morning, beginning in 1787. Dr. Barisani had prescribed riding to compensate for his sedentary life—probably the only sound advice Mozart ever received in his life. He kept a horse, which he sold "for 14 ducats" two months before his death, not because he was by then too sick to ride (on the contrary, at this time he felt perfectly well), but probably because he needed the 14 ducats. Mozart on a horse is only one, though an especially striking one, of the many images from his daily life which we find hard to visualize. He probably did not resemble the equestrian statue of the Commendatore.

"His patient wife did everything she could to keep him from bad company." This assertion, too, most likely comes not from Sophie but from Constanze, who apparently could not refrain from recording evidence of her patience. We will not accept it, however, and see in this remark, rather, an attempt to exculpate her own guilt. In this connection, "company" suddenly acquires a rather sinister nuance, to be examined later. What the "everything" was that she claims to have tried unfortunately remains obscure. We could not even begin to guess at it.

Of course, the report is valuable only when it records behavior. When it tries to interpret, it reveals the mind of the scribe more than the mind described. It is influenced, indeed dictated, by Mozart's subsequent fame and acknowledged greatness. The "piercing glance," the "balanced answers," the "deep thoughts"—all this is less authentic than tendentious, designed to demonstrate the alleged characteristics of Mozart the Important Man, which he became as soon as he was dead. The wish not only to have him appear great, but also to appear to have recognized his greatness early on, affected the witnesses of the past; the wish merged with their subjective views and convictions. Above all, it also influenced the future, by setting up the cliché on which the whole nineteenth century based its image of Mozart.

But there is more valuable evidence, in a different idiom. At the time it would hardly have supported Sophie's statement, but because our distance from it enables us to see behind words and deduce their objective meaning, this report works as a complement, confirming the objective truth:

From his conversations and actions, it was hardest to recognize that Mozart was a great man when he was busy with an important work. Then his speech was not only confused and muddled, but he also occasionally made jokes of a kind unusual for him; indeed, he even deliberately neglected his manners. But he did not seem to be mulling over or thinking about anything in particular. Either he was intentionally hiding his inner exertion by being frivolous on the outside, for inexplicable reasons, or else he liked to contrast the divine ideas of his music with inspirations of a common kind, taking delight in a kind of self-irony. I can understand that such a sublime artist, out of deep respect for his art, might degrade and neglect his own person, as if mocking it.

A spirit different from Nissen's speaks to us from these lines. It is already the spirit of Romanticism, but, beyond that, a spirit of superior insight and an almost complete objectivity. It is from the autobiography of the actor and painter Joseph Lange,[62] who married the woman Mozart once adored, Aloysia Weber. Aloysia later claimed that Mozart continued to love her throughout his life (and how many other women, who rejected him when he was alive, would have liked to claim the same thing). But as far as we know, Mozart never resented his victorious rival, who was favored, if not fortunate. On the contrary, he did not begrudge the "jealous fool" (as he called him in one of his frequent uncharitable moments) this victory—although it may have been a case of sour grapes. At any rate, Mozart maintained his connection with the Lange couple until the time when all his connections dissolved.

Joseph Lange, born in Würzburg in 1751, trained as an actor and painter, was the first Hamlet and the first Clavigo at the Vienna Burgtheater. As his notes (especially his discussion of the role of Hamlet) show, he was a serious, sober artist, nothing like Schikaneder, for example, who was an adventurer all his life and, in the last analysis, no more than a strolling player. Lange was one of the few people of his time and place who had read Shakespeare in the original,[63] and the only one of Mozart's nondescript circle of friends who had some education and was obviously highly intelligent. He also had the sensibility, the feeling for nature of a Romantic painter, although his technique left a lot to be desired. He, too, had traveled; in 1784 he met Klopstock in Hamburg and Moses Mendelssohn in Berlin. His testimony renders an essential facet of Mozart's personality visible and credible; here one of Mozart's intimates has made an effort to be objective and seems (however reluctantly) to have realized that a genius might manifest himself to the outside world as unpredictable and irritating; that Mozart could not express his inner greatness in outer dignity, but rather, as if in unrestrained reaction to his greatness, had to embarrass outsiders by his behavior. Lange may have been the only person close to Mozart to have recognized the need for this behavior, that desire for self-exposure, for a radical letting go—the vent for everything he denied himself in his music. For his *music* does not communicate his momentary state of mind but rather the creative process of his self-control. In his music he is not the bearer of a will (like Beethoven) but rather the will itself, unaware of the imperative it is obeying. "A want of consciousness"? As far as the concept applies to abstract thought, perhaps. Pursuing the inner or outer sources of his motivation was the last thing on his mind; he was selective, not in choosing his opportunities, but in applying his phenomenal range of expression. No one manipulated it more consciously than he. Lange must have intuited all this, the only one of his time to do so.

Sophie, more primitive, struggles in vain against her own observations. After the fact, she would have liked her dear brother-in-law Mozart to have been different, quiet and sublime and just the way one wants to read about in books. This is also the way those others, his first biographers, would have liked to see him: as a prototype for the dawning Romantic period, whose children they were or whose representatives they became.

In vain. The frivolous, eccentric Mozart, who on top of everything kept "bad company," is the Mozart we find real, at the expense of that other Mozart, the one who supposedly demonstrated his greatness to his inferiors, housemates, and drinking companions with piercing glance and deep thoughts. For his balancing acts, jester's gags, and juggling tricks are none other than reflexes of gesture and mimicry. They are physical necessities, automatic compensation for a transcending mind, its inevitable counterpoint, and as such only too easy to imagine. They are the results, as well as the reflection, of mental distraction. It has been claimed that there was no horizontal surface, no table, no "window cushion" which he did not immediately play on, as on a piano. Here we have him, the mercurial, restless little man capable of driving us mad. Furthermore, the pacing back and forth while washing his hands, the knocking his heels together, the grimaces, gesticulations—neither Nissen nor Constanze nor Sophie would have had the equipment to dream up this kind of behavior for their hero. Why should they have wanted to? They meant well, after all; they revered him, or at least they revered him after the fact, and they wanted posterity to think of them as reverent, and as indulgent, understanding human beings. Let us not take it amiss if they were at a loss before the habits and norms of the exceptional man, if they tried to counter his apparent foolishness with different behavior which they, less favored by the muses, took as the signs of greatness.

So we must ask ourselves how Mozart might have struck those who were not prepared for his strange behavior and abnormal conduct, whatever it was, those who did not know him or who had no means of knowing how to take him. Someone, for example, who sat across from the creator of *Don Giovanni* for the first time and searched for even one of those qualities with which he had endowed the characters in his operas.

Karoline Pichler, a "prolific" writer, author of historical novels in several volumes, and for a time the center of the literary circle in Vienna, corroborates the picture:

> Once I was sitting at the piano, playing "Non più andrai" from *Figaro*; Mozart, who happened to be present, came up behind me, and my playing must have pleased him, for he hummed the melody with me, and beat time on my shoulders; suddenly, however, he pulled up a chair, sat down, told me to keep playing the bass and began to improvise variations so beautifully that everyone present held his breath, listening to the music of the German Orpheus. But all at once he had had enough; he jumped up and, as he often did in his foolish moods, began to leap over table and chairs, miaowing like a cat, and turning somersaults like an unruly boy . . .[64]

This sketch, too, was written more than half a century after the event, and yet one senses its objective truth. Not only does the picture coincide with Sophie's and Lange's, it is also the kind of testimony which cannot be invented. Frau Pichler has no purpose other than to portray a curiosity; she neither exalts nor degrades her subject, but has obviously found it a source of astonishment and mild disapproval throughout her life. Besides, everything she writes is very easy to imagine. True, leaping over tables and chairs requires a certain amount of acrobatic agility, but we can see it happening, can hear the "German Orpheus" miaowing like a cat.

Frau Pichler was a sedate lady of upper-middle-class background with a bourgeois sense of what was proper, of how things ought to be. Where the actor Lange tries to interpret (and does well at it), she censures, with gentle indulgence, but strictly nevertheless:

> Mozart and Haydn, whom I knew well, never demonstrated in their personal intercourse any unusual intellectual power at all, and scarcely any learning or higher culture. In society they displayed only a common temperament, insipid jests, and in the case of the former, a thoughtless way of life; and yet what depths, what worlds of fantasy, harmony, melody

and feeling lay hidden behind these unpromising exteriors! What inner revelations gave them the understanding they had to have to bring forth such powerful effects and to express feelings, thoughts and passions in musical tones, so that every listener must perforce share those feelings, his soul touched to its depths?[65]

It is a rhetorical question. Frau Pichler was not able to arrive at Lange's realization and recognize the apparent discrepancy for what it is: loss of contact resulting from transcendent intellectual achievement and compensation for the loss in ways and places society finds unexpected and undesirable.

In reality Mozart had a well-developed sense of the tedious and ludicrous nature of banality. In his postscripts to letters to his father from Paris in 1778 we noticed his sometimes fierce displeasure at keeping to the routine of traditional forms and formulas. A pleasure in parodying them runs through his life, a constant itch to break the power of convention, at least verbal convention. His entries in Nannerl's diary express the boredom of the last Salzburg years. On May 27, 1780, he writes:

> . . . on the 27th at 7:30 Mass, or some such thing, then at Lodron's or some such person, but not at the Mayrs'—stayed home instead. In the afternoon at first to Countess Wicka, played tresette or some such thing, then home with Katherl, she deloused me a bit—ended the day with a game of Tarot cards.

Or in September of the same year:

> . . . on the 26th at 9 o'clock to Mass. To Lodron. In the afternoon, Eberlin Waberl and Schachtner at our house. Altmann came, too. Rain in the morning, turning warm weather in the afternoon. O warm! O weather! O turning! O afternoon. O rain. O morning.

And a few months before his death he still takes pleasure in his displeasure at everyday banalities. In a letter to the schoolmaster and choir director Anton Stoll in Baden, Mozart plods through the dreariest routine: Constanze wants to visit the spa again and Mozart asks him to reserve her rooms there. In stubborn and fussy detail he plays through all the variants and priorities of his or her wishes. Fully aware of this triviality, he adds a postscript at the bottom: "This is the silliest letter I have ever written in my life; but it is just the very thing for you" (end of May 1791). Not very kind, but we can assume that Stoll was used to these moods in Mozart. Besides, Mozart rewarded him for his favors by acceding, almost casually, to his request and writing a short piece for him. He himself probably did not realize, let alone comment, on the fact that it turned out to be one of his most glorious works; perhaps he forgot it entirely after copying it out. It was the motet "Ave verum Corpus" in D, K. 618 (June 17, 1791).

Ave, verum corpus, natum de Maria virgine:
Vere passum, immolatum in cruce pro homine;
Cujus latus perforatum unda fluxit et sanguine.
Esto nobis praegustatum in mortis examine.

For those who do not regard Church Latin as prayer and exempt, therefore, from stylistic criticism, this is strange language, with its deficiencies of sound and its uneven metrics. To be sure, for Mozart it was familiar, but it still seems at the very least risky to regard this work as a sign of religious fervor. We know that nothing was easier for him than to throw himself into the spirit of the subject at hand. If we were to judge the degree of his emotional involvement from the appearance of the manuscript, we might say that it testifies to unqualified objectivity, the control of someone not involved. This is grandiose music, proof of an unerring dramatic mind and understanding of the subject matter. The music, as always, takes life from its theme: it is an interlinear interpretation of sacred material. For the sake of declamation the meter is sacrificed, as is the (impure) rhyme, assonant only in the last two unaccented syllables. Once again, a small assignment has been mastered in a great way.

Mozart's life is made up of roles to which he unconsciously adapts himself, giving his best to whatever subject is posed for him. In this case, too, role and incarnation and ego have become one. These two splendid pages, then, a present for the schoolmaster Stoll, in a flawless, vertical script, with no corrections of any kind, perhaps the work of less than an hour, a sublime evocation *"sotto voce,"* intended as reparation for the "silliest letter I have ever written in my life"—these disparate factors reveal Mozart's myriad facets most characteristically; a mysterious double life, and yet only apparently so.

We who are more experienced than were Mozart's contemporaries in interpreting the outer manifestations of psychological anomalies, who know their origins, or at least think we can guess at them, believe we can also respond with understanding to the extreme symptom. We no longer try to extenuate or mitigate it in retrospect, as biographers, in their efforts to "redeem" Mozart's image and behavior for posterity, have done to excess. We cannot reach him with fantasies; it is, in fact, hard to imagine that this excitable and unstable figure did not have a metaphysical aura, as did Beethoven, who, knowing that he did, cultivated and exploited it. Mozart, not knowing that he had it, exaggerated his physical presence with continual diversionary tactics, which became routine. His personality must have been irritating, at times daemonic (not in a grandiose way, but rather clownish), a presence not even "intellectuals" like Karoline Pichler could fathom, though a man like Lange could, capable as he was of distinguishing life from acting. Many must have found it irritating, for they gradually began to avoid him. But, in contrast to Beethoven's, Mozart's image is set up in such a way that its peculiar manner and effect resist definition. He is the stranger who did not intend to be seen that way, who never understood the nature of his strangeness, a man who did not give himself away. And when we think a figure is beginning to take shape out of the incomplete testimony, we, too, still find its inner essence, the element that joins the creative self and the outer self, obscure and puzzling.

His biographers have had a harder time making their peace with this puzzle than did his contemporaries. For the latter he was either strange or commonplace or incomprehensible, but they soon adopted the phrase coined by his pale sister, Nannerl, apparently for all time: except in his music, he remained a child all his life. Of course, for the last seven years of his life (a fifth of it) she had not seen him. Her statement haunts the entire literature, condescendingly friendly, insinuating as a gentle poison; it will always be associated with him. This view seems to have lessened somewhat the confusion that arose after his death as to how a man, now recognized as great, could have acted so contrarily to his greatness, with such extremely eccentric behavior. Not everyone was as gifted in analyzing Mozart's outward appearance as his brother-in-law, Lange.

I have cited three accounts that are in harmony with each other. The writers themselves recede behind the figure they are describing. Accounts by others whose intention (more or less overt) it is to bring themselves into the picture are less reliable. For example, some of his pupils, and others who claimed to be or were said to have been his pupils, say that their playing pleased the "maestro." That there exists a large number of such uniformly favorable reports is probably due to the reluctance of those whom Mozart judged more harshly to make it known; or perhaps it is because he was inclined to judge benevolently, probably less for pedagogical reasons than out of the friendly apathy of the great man. His real opinion of pupils and colleagues was far less kind, as his *Musikalischer Spass* tells us. And conversely, we often hear in a pupil's work exactly the deficiencies that Mozart in the *Spass* satirizes in grand style, and yet with a polite restraint known to be lacking in his verbal statements. Even Michael Kelly claims that Mozart praised his compositions. Very possibly: the creator of

Figaro was careful to keep his performers in good spirits. Privately, he probably had a different opinion.

Michael Kelly, actually O'Kelly, ultimately became a wine merchant in London. The sign outside his house read, MICHAEL KELLY, IMPORTER OF WINES, COMPOSER OF MUSIC. The playwright Sheridan, however, thought the reverse wording would be more apt: Composer of Wines, Importer of Music. Even his contemporaries, then, doubted Kelly's seriousness as a composer. Some booty of Mozart's provenance was probably smuggled in along with the other imported articles, but Mozart would not have taken it amiss; he was used to that kind of thing from Vienna, from the large circle of amateur composers to which singers, instrumentalists, and music publishers belonged. He himself corrected a few compositions for the tenor Benedikt Schack; and even the publisher Hoffmeister, who thought Mozart's piano quartets too difficult, produced a few paltry, botched Mozartean ideas in his woodwind music.

The banker von Henickstein, apparently rather a gossip, told the Novellos that Mozart had been in love with all his pupils. This may well have been the case with a few, beginning with Rose Cannabich, who in 1777 earned a moderate place of tender interest on the scale of his affections in Mannheim. It is especially true of Therese von Trattner, whose mysterious aura is primarily due to the fact that we have no word or picture as testimony to their possibly important relationship. It certainly was not true of his first pupil in Vienna, Josepha Auernhammer, whose appearance, really not very attractive, Mozart described with a concise lack of charity (letter of August 22, 1781). Unfortunately, her compositions also show that she could not make up musically for her apparently dismaying lack of charm.

Mozart as a teacher is only one more image in that series of images we find it hard to visualize. True, he had mastered the material to be taught as no one else had, and he certainly had a store of didactic methodology, thanks to his father, his only teacher. He applied it at least twice, with Barbara Ployer and, especially, with the Englishman Thomas Attwood, Mozart's pupil from fall 1785 to August 1786. Both must have learned a good deal, assuming they mastered the workload imposed systematically by Mozart. Unfortunately, neither made any statement about the instruction, as to whether Mozart was able to educate by his personal presence in addition to his written assignments. How did he take to the role of teacher? It was probably a burden to him, since the regular hours would keep him from composing. Not one of his pupils attests to his phenomenal mental orderliness, which might indicate that he was not able to apply it when teaching. As far as we can form any kind of idea about it, we would expect a certain arbitrariness and unpredictability, unpunctuality and impatience. In addition, both pupils and friends testify to the chaotic state of his papers and music. Sometimes he had to copy his compositions from memory, unable to find the originals. It was much more of a bother to look for them than to write them out again—which is saying a lot. Scores would pile up under the piano or lie around the house; potential copyists could help themselves as they wished, and did so. He lost many things; he himself, as we have seen, literally forgot some of his works.

However much we search the reservoir of our imagination for an image whereby Mozart becomes real to us, we find it, strangely enough, only in the reports of his eccentricities. It is easier to visualize him making faces than walking in the door. I think only someone with no imagination can imagine him. Only a person without fantasy, and unable therefore to go beyond fitting the hero out with his own characteristics, drawing on his own familiar emotions, will think he has a flesh-and-blood image of Mozart. We (*pluralis concordiae*) cannot visualize him even in his "normal" functions; we cannot even imagine him sleeping.

Perhaps it is easier to see him at something actively biological—eating, for example. Of course, Mozart was not the sort of man to dine in the cultivated, discriminating way we imagine Goethe dining, in the formal course of his day; his meals certainly cannot be compared to Goethe's. Although Mozart himself often mentions his "good appetite," we do not know if he was a big eater. We tend to imagine him gulping things down, talking with his mouth full, too interested in his talk to notice whether or not his food tastes good.

Leopold Mozart calls the meals in his son's home in 1785 "economical," whether with disapproval or respect we cannot say for sure; he was probably just noting the fact. Possibly Constanze was unwilling to serve anything special for him. Mozart's son Franz Xaver Wolfgang told the Novellos that Mozart liked trout: this predilection must have come down in anecdotal form, for the son never knew his father. Now and then Mozart, stimulated by the appropriate odors, described his desire for this or the other dish; but the descriptions are of secondary importance. We know that his favorite dish as a youth was liver dumplings with sauerkraut. It is mentioned for the last time on January 5, 1771; perhaps he never touched it after that. None of this goes beyond the bounds of the imaginable; we can picture him providing himself with modest comforts.

It is less easy to visualize him in his peripheral activities, riding or fencing (he learned to fence in Olmütz in 1767). He was an enthusiastic dancer. Can we visualize him with a partner on his hand or in his arms? Can we visualize him conducting? At rehearsals he sometimes kept his hat on, stamped out the beat with his foot, and vented his impatience by exclaiming: "*Sapperlot!*" Can we hear him? His voice is said to have been soft (he was a tenor). He was said to have been an acceptable violinist, a better violist. Can we hear him?

Can we hear Mozart playing the piano? We have little conception of the technique and style and presentation of his time; we are not even sure about the tempi. Nevertheless, this is where his physical presence seems most tangible, for in this regard, fortunately, the witnesses agree. Contemporaries report that when he was playing the piano, especially when improvising, he became that other human being they would have liked him to be in his daily life. His expression changed; he seemed to become serene.* Many contemporaries vouch for the fact that he played very simply, without stretching the rhythm, without exaggerated *rubati,* without extravagant dynamics; he sat calmly, hardly moving his body, showing no feelings. These must have been the moments (often hours) when he reveled in blissful self-forgetfulness, when he severed his connection with the outside world; here he was the unadorned Mozart, who needed no intermediary in order to communicate—no singers, no instrumentalists or fellow musicians, and no bothersome score, either. Here, and perhaps only here, he achieved true pleasure in his own genius; here he transcended himself, becoming the absolute Mozart.

We are not able to put ourselves in the place of someone from the past; but we always try to do so. Since our attempts are never rewarded (or tested) by the eventual appearance of the person in question, they proliferate boundlessly, nourished on their own unfulfilled hopes. We recapitulate only what we already know or think we know, changing the sequence, hoping that somewhere in all these facts a sudden illumination will offer itself, an inspiration be given us. An important condition for visualizing Mozart's physical presence is his historical time and place—but, be it noted, not the

---

* "When playing, however, he appeared completely different. His countenance changed, his eye settled at once into a steady calm gaze, and every movement of his muscles conveyed the sentiment expressed in his playing." Quoted in Grove's *Dictionary of Music and Musicians,* Fifth edition, edited by Eric Blom (London, 1954). This is a summary of what a great many contemporaries have confirmed, too many for it not to be true.

cliché, not only what is called the "age," not just the metaphorical space, but the actual place, today become a museum.
We must consider his circumscribed field of action: the moves
and countermoves of the allies and opponents of this genius,
the people who coined the commonplaces and voiced the objections, the people he answered, the mute and muted listeners
who heard not only his music but his words as well, the banal
words and the outrageous ones, too. Everyone who loved him
or hated him or had no opinion about him is part of it,
everyone who received him or avoided him or sought him out.
Also part of his time and place were the rooms he walked
through, disarranged, or left untouched, their acoustics, ac-
coutrements, their furniture, all the matter that helped give
him shape, even the most concrete: the wood of a violin or a
table he leaped over or threw his hat on before sitting down at
the piano, and the sound of the piano. The figure of Mozart is
only imaginable, if at all, in his own milieu. For the transitory
Mozart was bound to transitory objects, and his senses were
stimulated by the most concrete things; the other sources of
stimulation evade us. His conscious life was, as we know, tied
to matter, to physicality, sometimes to excess. Eating and
drinking were part of it, unsublimated physical contentment,
right down to the voiding of his intestines, which, as he left
ample evidence, not only stimulated his fantasy, but also provided him with a kind of animal satisfaction. Every prosaic
function to which he gave expression is part of it, and as we
know, even the most prosaic ones were sources of inspiration.
Of course, we will never really be able to comprehend the
dimensions of his experiential range. We lack the key to the
driving force that kept this temporally short-lived being in
motion. If we want, despite all our reservations, to see him as a
static figure, we can construct the following picture of his outer
form.

Mozart's appearance was "unassuming." In the last years
of his life he became physically unattractive. His face was

pockmarked, the skin grew yellowish and puffy; toward the end he developed a double chin. His head was too big for his body. His nose was outsized; a newspaper once called him the "great-nosed Mozart." His eyes protruded more and more; he grew stout. He tried always to have a hairstyle which hid the strange malformation of his ears. Whether they ever caused a shock of self-awareness in his childhood or youth we do not know, since we know nothing about the traumas of a prepsychological time. He was surely not manic-depressive in a clinical sense, but he did incline more and more in his later years to one of the two extremes, becoming irritable and unstable. The increasing mental exhaustion of his last two years must have exacerbated anomalous behavior, whatever "tics" he had, which were perhaps hard for others to tolerate. It is possible that there was some reciprocity between his conduct and his growing isolation, that he reacted morbidly to his isolation and his reaction deepened it. Even Constanze clearly no longer wanted to be in his presence, and left him finally to that "bad company" she claims to have kept him from. And it seems as if his former circle of friends no longer felt comfortable with him; the cast of characters is almost completely different from that of his glorious period. Mozart, then, was left to an inferior society we can no longer trace, one we encounter only in sinister intimations from certain survivors. He was happy to dine often at other people's houses, but we no longer know who, in the last months, was still happy to invite him or where he invited himself. For he no longer wanted to be alone; he needed society, even if it no longer needed him.

We should ask ourselves if we would have felt comfortable in his company. Would his extremely, indeed often violently disorderly behavior have helped us to relax with him, or hindered us? Would we perhaps have been brought up short by the outward manifestation of his indefinable strangeness? Would that peculiar quality of our guest, ultimately disturbed and disturbing ("unstable and distracted" [Niemtschek]), have brought dinner-table conversation to a halt? Perhaps other things were more noticeable, obtrusive signs of a self-neglect that had gone too far to be changed, even if he had been aware of it. Perhaps he did not even wash his hands anymore in the morning. Perhaps he had dirty fingernails, unpleasant table manners, or perhaps he spat when he talked. Who knows if we would not have said, "Sure, the fellow's a genius, but isn't he unbearable?" Perhaps we would have avoided him, not invited him to dinner, even refused to have anything to do with him. A denial is on the tip of our tongue, but we can save ourselves the trouble: as he escapes us, so we escape him, by taking our winnings and leaving him to his documented historical destiny. Although the tragic nature of his life is an essential component of our admiration for him, we repress the fact that we owe the purifying effect of his music solely to his objectifying mastery of this tragedy, its extreme and unique sublimation.

The culmination of the tragedy is generally thought to be his untimely death, toward which his life rushed as if to its destination. Biographers even constructed a kind of *stretto* around the end of his life, out of objective evidence and sub-jective guesses. We will take up both the evidence and the guesses, which, we are convinced, do not overlap (Mozart never communicated to outsiders either his plans for the fu-ture or any decision to renounce them). But let us note here that Mozart's death was not all that premature. We can save ourselves the trouble of listing all the other great men who died young: every reader has his favorite. But since music seems to us the highest non-verbal expression of subjective feel-ings, feelings that are thought to be the composer's, and since it has a direct effect on our own feelings, we think we are hear-ing the composer's own voice when we hear his music. Death, then, stays in the listener's ear, the omnipresent destination of a life that fulfills itself in its work. The fact that Pascal never reached forty, that Spinoza lived only a little longer than that, is less fruitful biographically, for their intellectual achieve-ments are now independent entities. We think of them as works detached from the thinkers. Mozart's Requiem, on the other hand, or Pergolesi's *Stabat Mater*, or Schubert's A-flat Mass are forever the works of masters whose premature deaths made them "young geniuses"; we hear their works with this in mind. In the andante of Schubert's B-flat Sonata we think we hear the grief of a doomed man. The personal tragedy "sings along," adding another emotional element, which, naturally, would not withstand definition.

But this is not what we understand by "the tragic"; tragic, rather, is the increasing lack of recognition, ever more rarely alleviated by a connoisseur, the nearly consistent neglect that Mozart had to bear and did indeed bear with unexampled dignity and self-control. That it broke him is self-evident; though he repressed the realization, he could not avoid its destructive consequences. As far as we know, he never mentioned the various humiliations but seems to have passed over them with all the lightness he was still capable of. He resigned himself to the fact that lesser men were preferred for the great occasions, while he had to provide dance music for fancy-dress balls, toward the end his only commissions aside from music for musical clocks and glass harmonicas. The composition of *Die Zauberflöte* was a game of chance, in which he shared the risk with a gambler; he won, but too late, unfortunately. The commission for *Tito* did not come from the upper classes of Bohemia themselves but from a hired opera director, and it was a failure. And the last, dark commission, that of the Requiem, although it came from a member of the nobility, had to be handled strictly in secret, since the customer, Count Walsegg-Stuppach, intended to—and did—pass the composition off as his own work. It seems at the least doubtful that he would have approached Mozart with his shabby proposal, even through mysterious anonymous middlemen, if Mozart had still been the well-known and sought-after musician of 1784. Thus, even the circumstances surrounding his last great works are lost in dim obscurity, except for the growing plaudits for *Die Zauberflöte*, the last modest joy of the neglected dying man.

These at least are our deductions, as drawn from the moments in the chronicle we know something about. There are other, probably essential factors we do not know about, in particular Mozart's own share of guilt in his ruin, as far as one can speak at all of "guilt" in a process of self-destruction. For we suspect that is what it was, albeit involuntary. Undesired and ultimately unloved, he ended up in unrespectable company that, for us, is veiled in darkness. There is no more light to be shed on the mystery of the last months. What he did in Constanze's absence, and with whom, remains obscure; all the reports and memoirs we have confine themselves to what was respectable. That he was a gambler who lost his meager earnings playing the popular card games faro or tresette, that society rejected him because he did not pay his debts and thus offended the code of honor[66]—this seems unlikely. He could hardly then have afforded to protest his innocence in his petitions. His indictment of Vienna would have been wrong, those he appealed to would have been informed about his vice, Puchberg would not have repeated his loans, no one would have advanced him anything. No Hofdemel would have accepted his note, and the businessman Heinrich Lackenbacher would presumably have found out about Mozart's character before loaning him 1,000 gulden on October 1, 1790. His "lapses" must have been in another area. But not one of his contemporaries was prepared to state anything about the weeks of his last summer. Friends, relatives, former pupils, and admirers, all grew mute when asked for information. Perhaps we should be grateful to them for that; we are spared the apologetic commentaries and helpful reconstructions of intermediaries who wish to see their hero cleansed of everything they consider a stain. By applying their moral standards, they would have exposed the genius of a millennium to further indignities.

The gradual change in his social circle began two years before his death. The evidence no longer shows the familiar names; new ones crop up. Haydn is still there; Puchberg is present and important. Yet Mozart invites only these two men to a rehearsal of *Così*; why not Jacquin, for example, or van Swieten (though the latter was probably not interested in opera)? How ought we to imagine such a rehearsal? A private gathering, reduced circumstances, in a bachelor's household, even though Constanze was not away in Baden. Did the singers come to the house? And did the performance make Mozart forget his misery? Probably.

Così fan tutte: this title could just as accurately be changed to *Così fan tutti*. For the lack of "female constancy," the theme of the libretto (one of the most popular clichés of the time, one that *Don Giovanni* forcefully opposes), is far exceeded by the lack of male morality, which brings the women's fallibility to light. Actually, the women are victims of a miserable intrigue, which ends well only because the men are unfairly put in the position of being permitted to forgive the women, when it really ought to be the other way around. Guglielmo and Ferrando, those two fine officers, whose hearts are more or less in their swords, are not virile, instinctual characters, like Don Giovanni. They are simply concerned about their honor, though they scarcely know the meaning of the word. They represent the epitome of masculine baseness, even more so than the man who incites them to their deed, cynical, sly Don Alfonso, the "old philosopher." We would like to be able to chalk up an error of judgment against him, for deluding himself about his two young friends' willingness to play along with the intrigue (for, one would think, it can't be in their interest to play out their roles to the end). But he is proven right, at the cost of all verisimilitude. The two young men play their roles so perfectly and perfidiously, one would think they *wanted* to prove their ladies' infidelity and take advantage of it, as they undoubtedly will after their marriage. That alone, one might say, goes beyond everything that is humanly possible or believable. But listing the dramatic transgressions is not the way to get at this peculiar work.

Goethe never made any statement about *Così*, but Wagner and Beethoven did; negatively, of course. They evaluated it on moral grounds, and therefore did not distinguish between form and content, something even lesser contemporaries had managed. Wagner thought that Mozart would necessarily be unable to conceive any good music for such material, and, in Wagner's judgment, this was so, to Mozart's credit. Beethoven would have nothing to do with the work, which however did not stop him from using the rondo "Per pietà" (No. 25), with the two *obbligato* horn parts, as a model for his great *Fidelio* aria, right down to the identical key (E major).

But neither Mozart nor Da Ponte was thinking of moral judgments. Their intention was to write an opera. It was claimed (and still is) that the plot is based on a true incident. Emperor Joseph is said to have related it to Da Ponte, and commissioned him to write a libretto about it. Of course, that is legend, a way to overcome the general antipathy to the libretto, and excuse Mozart's complicity in it. At this time, in the autumn and winter of 1789, the Emperor was already dangerously ill. Only the uncommon name Guglielmo seems to point to a character who might well have been originally Wilhelm.

All attempts at a psychological approach to the text founder on its extreme improbability, which, as is usual in *opera buffa*, culminates in the failure to recognize what is near at hand. The women do not perceive one another's lover in their exotic swains (who present themselves as Albanians, Albania being here what Illyria, in actual fact a neighbor of Albania, is to Shakespeare: a land geographically remote so that its inhabitants may be portrayed without any regional characteristics). Neither do they recognize the doctor and the notary as their own lady's maid, Despina. In addition, both men remain as nameless to the ladies as Lohengrin is to Elsa.

The temporal sequence is as undefined as in *Don Giovanni*; changes of heart take place, if possible, even more abruptly. In fact, *Figaro* is Mozart's only opera that upholds the unity of time; at least everything in it proceeds sequentially in such a way that single moments of action are in a definable relationship to one another.

But these improbabilities are not the issue, either. It is, rather, the acceptance of a drama in which marionettes function as personified ideas, having no existence outside the ideas they incorporate. It would, of course, be foolish to impute moral intentions to Da Ponte (much as we would like to), i.e., that he might have wanted to save the honor of the two women and thereby of women in general, at the expense of the men's dubious morals. Neither Da Ponte nor Mozart posed the idle question of whether these two pairs will later be happy with one another. Eighteenth-century artifacts do not answer questions about the future. Going from an unhappy heart to a happy vice was a characteristic feature of the rococo. But the question is valid in general for what we call, to oversimplify, a "comedy." It is an ambiguous word. Can Shakespeare's Orsino, in *Twelfth Night*, be happy with Viola after he has loved Olivia for four acts and taken Viola for Cesario, who in that form is loved by Olivia, who now, for better or worse, decides on Sebastian? And does it damage the play? Whether it is a question of Albanians or Illyrians, the issue is not the probability of the configurations; what counts is the emotional relationship and its proper expression. No matter if the event is improbable as long as its participants experience it as true and true to life. Logic is neither a quality of the human soul nor its yardstick. Orsino's music, as "the food of love," becomes reality in *Così*, a reality in Kierkegaard's sense of the "erotic nature of music," and especially in the case of the unfortunate Fiordiligi. What is a comedy for the others becomes a tragedy for her, although she does not know it. With the temperament of a character from *opera seria*, she grows far beyond it in her fatal entanglement. No doubt about it: she is in love for the first time in her life, and unfortunately, because she is completely without experience, with a puppet whom she does not recognize as such. He is the lover of her friend or sister, disguised as an absurd foreigner. That cannot end happily, and does not. In every sense she is the "prima donna"; Da Ponte took a special interest in her part, for the singer of the role, Adriana del Bene, was Da Ponte's mistress at this time, and incidentally, the real-life sister of Louise Villeneuve, who sang Dorabella. As in the opera, both ladies were from Ferrara, which is why del Bene (a prima donna offstage as well, by the way) was called Ferrarese del Bene.

The libretto is based on Ovid, Ariosto, and Cervantes.[67] Nevertheless, we may consider it Da Ponte's own, for apart from the prearranged infamy of the game, apart from the intentional coolness of what presents itself as warmth, he invented two essential characters to add to the quartet of ladies and gentlemen. Despina and Don Alfonso only belong to the *buffa* form in appearance, and superficially. Despina, a far cry from the chambermaid with a silvery laugh, neither "saucy" nor "roguish," is a woman of the world, experienced, inclined to realism, terse to the point of coarseness. She has her own opinions; not only does she know what she thinks about the opposite sex, she also has views on the injustice of the prevailing social structure, though admittedly she opposes it only by secretly nibbling sweets. No one looked for subversion in this character; her nature escaped Joseph II's censor and his cultural watchdogs, as Da Ponte knew it would. He was free to use her as a vent for his social criticism, which he did, with no one the wiser. *Figaro* takes place almost entirely in the world of the servants, and deals, so to speak, with problems with the hired help, which here consists only of one person. She is thus in the minority; no one expects her to strike a blow against the other five. Her two ladies have no reason to desire social upheaval nor any reason to fear it; on the contrary, they are materially well off, in fact too well off. All the others are rich, even Don Alfonso, the *"vecchio filosofo,"* who has nothing better to do than take the threads of other people's destinies into his own hands and watch them interact, not according to chance, but according to convictions derived from his personal insights; he is a "de-mythologized divinity" (Kramer), rational and enlightened. In his disillusioned premeditation he, like his inventor, is a disciple of Rousseau. His wicked side (it is revealed in a hypocritical minor [F] in the aria "Vorrei dir" [No. 5]) is somewhat mitigated, though not canceled out, by his C major aria (No. 30) "Tutti accusan le donne." That's the way things are, and the less we deceive ourselves about them, the better for all of us, even for those who are injured; let's keep our feet on the ground. He is right, it's just that he chose the wrong case to illustrate his point—that is, he designed it himself.

We can be certain that Mozart, entering into the spirit of his material, adopted the reality of the opera and its thesis "Thus do they all." The two officers' hearty exclamation, provoked by Don Alfonso, "Così fan tutte!" is not in the libretto; Mozart added it himself, not because he was persuaded of the fact, but because he had assumed his heroes' newly won conviction. He probably wasted no time pondering the plausibility of the thesis, unless his experience (with Constanze, for example) had already taught him something about it. This thesis stands in blatant contrast to those of his other operas and the characters who represent them, especially Constanze in *Die Entführung* and the women in *Figaro*. The Countess, whose grandeur lies precisely in her moral nature; Susanna, who resists the Count; and even the fatal attachment of Donna Elvira in *Don Giovanni* would tend to indicate the opposite thesis; they prove that Mozart fused himself with these characters, too, and in doing so forgot about objectivity.

The social criticism concealed in the libretto did not escape Mozart. On the contrary, he tried to stress it. *Così* was written at a time when his eyes had already been opened and he perceived the inequities that he had previously ignored; his view of the world had become more bitter. In this opera only Despina is socially inferior, and thus less involved in the continuity of the music. Although she does not oppose the voluptuous, recurrently elegiac flow of the music with any rebellious contrast (on the contrary, her solo numbers are the most conventional of all), Mozart devoted himself to her in another way. He gave her a special comic character; she is an artful minx rather than a rogue. We gather from the divergence of score and libretto that Mozart took an especially lively interest in her part. To Don Alfonso's "Ti vo fare del ben" (I want to help you), Da Ponte has her answer, "Non n'ho bisogno, un uomo come lei non può far nulla," which is to say, "An old fellow like you can't do much anymore." Mozart changed the retort, and even rhymed it: "A una fanciulla, un uomo come lei non può far nulla," which is to say, "An old fellow like you can't do anything for a girl anymore." The big magnet, with which she pretends, in her doctor's disguise, to draw the poison from the bodies of the two supposedly love-crazed Albanians, is not Da Ponte's invention; he was not familiar with Mesmer's treatments. But Mozart had met Franz Anton Mesmer when he was twelve; *Bastien und Bastienne* is said to have been performed in Mesmer's garden. Mozart was familiar with the cure by magnet. Here he disposes of it as quackery. Because he did not want to attribute any genuine knowledge to Despinetta, he has her mumble incorrect Latin, changing the vocative from "bonae puellae" to "bones puelles." This was unfair; for Despina is clever, and if she had learned something by heart, she would have learned it correctly. Don Alfonso, on the other hand, is given correct Latin to speak; Mozart changed Da Ponte's slurred "isso fatto" back to "ipso facto." No doubt about it, he was having fun.

The triumph of rationalism, which Don Alfonso and Despina both embody, though on different planes, shows that true love and its sentimental manifestation are lost forever, not only for the two couples, but for everyone. In the future we shall act according to reason. Thus, a covert melancholy governs this glorious music, and love and the mockery of love become one. Mozart was uniquely successful here at something he never tried before or after. His *accompagnati* attain the meaning they had in his early *opere serie*, and become the direct expression of feeling, living apart from the schematic form of the arias and ensembles. They are free in their changing tempi and expressive dynamics. Whether they express feeling or only its counterfeit is unclear. Einstein considers Fiordiligi's B-flat aria "Come scoglio" (No. 14) a parody; Abert considers it ridicule; both are wrong. Fiordiligi's conflict is genuine from the beginning; from the very start she is a victim of the evil game. The phrase "Così ognor" is, by the way, a note-for-note quotation from the "Kyrie" of the Coronation Mass, K. 317. Although no connection can be drawn between the two texts, the musical motive speaks against any notion of parody. But when, shortly before, in the first act, the two disguised officers interrupt their *secco* to give objectively passionate expression to their subjectively dishonest passion ("Amor . . ." bar 28 of the recitative "Che susurro"), when first Ferrando and then Guglielmo sings his way from D minor through G minor, when the violins and the violas complete the surging upheaval with a mighty ascending crescendo— here we have sublime parody. It is parody as a discipline, reflecting its subject in a unique beauty, a splendor *sui generis*, in a way no one, not even Mozart, ever imagined before or since. Again we see that morality is not the source of music.

It is evident that there is simulated emotion here. But now and then we ask ourselves to whom are the two men referring in their protestations of love, such as Ferrando's B-flat aria "Ah, lo veggio" (No. 24), which he is to sing *"lietissimo"* (most happily)? Is it about his new conquest, who comes to him so easily? Or is it for his former lady, now in danger of being forgotten? Does the music tell us? It does not. Although we have here and there an apparent indication, we are never fully certain what it is meant to indicate: is it the playacting or the play within the play? The text of Guglielmo's G major aria "Non siate ritrovi" (No. 15) strikes us as unusually silly. We can hardly imagine that these women could be taken in by such a coarse and obvious approach. Musically, too, the aria falls short (significantly, the theme is stated by the flutes, instruments that often get short shrift from Mozart). Originally he had planned to use a different aria, "Rivolgete a lui lo sguardo," K. 584, in D major, whose text is scarcely less silly but whose music belongs with the most important *buffo* arias he ever wrote; another case where the music goes beyond the text and makes a ludicrous swain into a real man. Why did he exchange this aria for an inferior one? Biographers say it was Mozart's sense of proportion, which would not allow him to include an aria of such dimensions at this point; it would have burst out of the light, satirical framework. This does not seem very illuminating, especially since it is not true. Obviously critics were hard pressed to find an answer to this question, which was, perhaps, the result of casting problems. Guglielmo does step out of character here, in that the extraordinary frivolity of his material, the praise of women's most external charms, would probably scare off sensitive ladies, especially those momentarily in an extremely unstable state. We find it incomprehensible that a girl like Dorabella, even if she is less serious than her sister, could yield to a man who cannot present himself as anything better than a *"papagallo."* One could argue that he does not want her to like him, so that he may win his bet by acting contrary to Don Alfonso's orders. But this is speculation; it remains an open question.

In the F major quintet "Di scrivermi ogni giorno" (No. 9), beneath the continuous sixteenth-note *ostinato* of the strings, the dissimulating men and grieving women are given vocal lines of precisely the same emotional intensity; even Don Alfonso's aside, "Io crepo se non rido," despite its contrasting counterpoint, does not seem like parody. Mozart usually used interval leaps like the two officers' sevenths to portray genuine emotional upheaval in his characters. Nevertheless, this ensemble, representative of others, does have an element of play, conveyed by the staccato quarter notes of the two ladies as they ask the men to write every day. Who is laughing at whom? The men at the women? Or all the players at us? Or are we laughing at the players? In the trio in E major, "Soave sia il vento" (No. 10), which, like several other numbers in this opera, is a poetic as well as a musical masterpiece, even Don Alfonso joins in the wish for a prosperous sea voyage; with their sixteenth notes, the muted strings suggest it so realistically that the voyage (on a lightly swelling ocean) might really be taking place. Nothing here seems to indicate that Don Alfonso is dissimulating, for he seems to have become an unwitting participant in the game, as everyone is, ultimately. Mozart himself slips deep into the fiction, carried away by its illusive magic. The music "does not take part in the deception, but neither does it realize only the outward situation and the sorrow of farewell. Rather, Mozart's music makes it clear, although the characters do not know it, that this parting, with its epilogue, the terzettino, is a farewell to something that cannot be restored."[68] Later the quotation marks are lifted, even instrumentally; the deceptive quality fades. The introduction to the duet "Secondate aurete amiche" (No. 21) seems like an andante from earlier wind serenades, and its key of F-flat anticipates *Die Zauberflöte*. The wicked joke always threatens to turn serious; this quality of "almost" pervades the entire opera, especially in the many ensembles, against which the dramatic accentuation of the arias is almost startling. As individual numbers, they often stand in contrast to the flowing melancholy surrounding a world where baseness may reign, but which, draped in beauty, still gives us pleasure. Mozart takes Don Alfonso's position in this world, and gives his vote to realism and alleged reality; he is in Fiordiligi, who becomes the pitiable victim; he is in Despina, who makes the best of this world; he is, in short, in every subjectively experienced moment, even when it contains an utterly base action. But *he* is not being expressed by the music. For, as so often, the music is used here, too, as a deception; it confuses the "beautiful" with the "good," and is therefore a harbinger of an imminent decadence—the bitter lesson we are to learn from it.

Mozart liked this work. Perhaps it served him as an escape from his misery, which at the time was taking on ominous proportions; it was an escape into art and artificiality, into his characters, his marionettes. He wanted to let others play, too, so he invited his friends to rehearsals. We have no proof that he did this for any of his other operas.

Let us remember once again that music lays down its own logic, the logic of "musicality," in Kierkegaard's sense of the word. But opera has not only its own specific logic but also (when it expresses an extramusical will) its own morality, separate from the text. Beethoven would have had something to say about that—and he did say it in *Fidelio*. But we mean something different, not the untransposed expression of an ethical stance, not a moral manifesto. The moral component in opera (we could conclude) lies in the fact that music reflects the distance from its object, defines it and, in doing so, lays itself open to our evaluations. In this regard *Così* does, in fact, pose greater riddles than all Mozart's other operas. And if the music of this opera seems not only to sanction the diabolical ideas of its characters but also to stud them with jewels, we must assume that Mozart wants to be seen as a *diabolus ex machina*, meting out deceit as beauty and watching our reaction from the vantage point of eternity.

Così fan tutte was more or less successful in Vienna. Mozart himself tells us nothing about its reception. He entered the work into his catalogue along with the first four measures of the overture; with that the affair was closed, at least as far as we can tell from his own documentation.

The series of pleading, begging letters to Puchberg was by no means curtailed as a result; now and then they reached the point of embarrassing self-degradation, as when he wrote on

April 18, 1790: "You are right, dearest friend, not to honor me with a reply! My importunity is too great." In the same letter, however, he still asks for money to "extricate" himself from a "temporary embarrassment." It was actually not so temporary, and lasted until his death.

Not only does the list of his friends contract during these last two years of his life; it also shifts over to mean, indeed shabby, company. The patrons have long since left the scene (not that there had been nothing shabby about some of them); lodge brothers represent the honest-bourgeois element; stage "artistes" predominate, and chief among them Schikaneder, the theater director. Two members of Schikaneder's ensemble are also identifiable as friends, the bass Franz Xaver Gerl, the first Sarastro, and the tenor Benedikt Schack, the first Tamino. In addition, Franz Hofer, a rather sorry violinist, the husband of Mozart's sister-in-law Josepha (the first Queen of the Night), accompanies him on his last trip to Frankfurt, making the journey even more unhappy by his presence. And of course there was Süssmayr, his last pupil and assistant, already indispensable as a target for Mozart's last mocking jibes and desperate sarcasm. The friends from the upper middle class turned away, and the nobility to an even greater degree, although it is not impossible that many of them were literally on the battlefield: from 1788 to 1790 the last (so-called little) Turkish War took place, a straggler of a war, which, though no longer "storming" or "raging," may nevertheless have required its supply of Viennese aristocrats. The Emperor himself spent nine months at headquarters, and returned, not wounded, but fatally ill. The war was large enough to necessitate taking measures of thrift which particularly affected the theatrical and musical life of Vienna. In this case, too, Mozart was one of the first victims, at a disadvantage, as ultimately he always was in Vienna. Even during his brilliant period, in 1785, he received for court performances of his works only half the amount Salieri got for his.

Of course, some of his former patrons were no longer alive. Only van Swieten seems to have remained faithful, in his usual limited way; but Mozart could not buy anything with this kind of faithfulness. Jacquin seems to have disappeared; the splendid evenings at his house were in the distant past. Baron Wetzlar is mentioned once again later on: he invites Mozart to dinner. The name Lichnowsky no longer appears (until it is mentioned in connection with Beethoven). His esteemed friend Haydn is in England, celebrating triumphs and receiving the degree of honorary doctor at Oxford. Perhaps Mozart missed him more than anyone.

The friendship between Haydn and Mozart is covered by a veil of mythmaking idealization; behind it, the real facts of the relationship are hard to make out. Like the friendship of Goethe and Schiller, it has been enriched and ornamented by cultural history. But there are some unshakable points of reference. Mozart probably respected no contemporary and certainly no figure of the past as much as he did Haydn; and it is remarkable that the human relationship, however close it may have been, had its source in artistic admiration. Thus, Mozart made him what was tantamount to an offering of six of his important quartets, K. 387, 421/417b, 428/421b, 458, 464, 465, along with a stylized, respectful dedication, in which, however, he also very decidedly demanded respect and recognition from the recipient; for these works were the "fruit of a long and laborious effort" (*"il frutto di una lunga e laboriosa fatica"*). Mozart never said the like about any of his other works. We cannot hear the effort involved, but we can see the intensity and mighty concentration of the process of composition in the manuscript scores. Nowhere else does Mozart make so many corrections; they are strewn above crossed-out tempi and dynamic markings; he even corrected on the engraver's plates, necessarily in mirror writing: an additional *"fatica."* For he wanted the man he admired to admire him, and we note with satisfaction that his wish was fulfilled. Leopold Mozart, who was visiting his son in Vienna in 1785, informed his daughter, this time with unabashed pride, of the famous statement Haydn made to him at an evening of chamber music in Mozart's house (letter of February 16, 1785):

> Before God and as an honest man I tell you that your son is the greatest composer known to me either in person or by name. He has taste and, what is more, the most profound knowledge of composition.

A nice observation, within Haydn's somewhat limited powers of articulation. It speaks for his generosity and kindness that he did not add, "But, you know, without me and my quartets your good son would never have been able to accomplish anything like that." He would have been right, in essence.

The last three of the six quartets to Haydn were performed that evening, among them the one in C major, K. 465, completed shortly before January 14, 1785. Because of its bold harmonies in the adagio introduction, it has been foolishly called the "Dissonant." Before their inner logic was understood, the first twenty-two measures confounded an entire generation of critics and listeners. At that soiree, however, no one seems to have objected to it; that is, we do not know what the two other guests—who were lodge brothers, the Barons von Tinti—thought about it; Leopold found the quartet "excellently composed" (it is to Leopold Mozart's eternal credit that he was the first connoisseur and the first admirer of the composer Wolfgang Amadè Mozart); and the great inspiring figure, Haydn, was not unfamiliar with boldness himself.

Haydn and Mozart met again in the apartment of Stephen and Nancy Storace, where music was also performed. Haydn played first violin, Dittersdorf second, Mozart viola, and the composer Vanhal cello. If we count the host, Stephen Storace, five professional composers played together in an uncompetitive joint concert. Michael Kelly, who was among the guests, reported that the four played well enough, but by no means extraordinarily. The moderation of his verdict makes it all the more credible. Nevertheless, we would like to have been present.

We have no other evidence of meetings between the great men except for a farewell dinner on the eve of Haydn's voyage to England, on December 14, 1790. Mozart is said to have counseled him urgently not to make the journey, because Haydn was too old (he was fifty-eight at the time) and spoke no English. Since we cannot assume that Haydn asked his younger friend for advice about the trip, we must wonder what Mozart's motives were; he must certainly have identified unconsciously with Haydn. He himself would have dearly liked to go to England, and must also have wanted to force his own renunciation of the wish onto his friend, whom he would sorely miss. Without doubt, Mozart loved Haydn; in the beginning he thought of him as his superior; later as his equal, the only one. The fatal term "Papa Haydn" is unfortunately his doing; and we can only hope that he would have regretted it if he had known what he had done: with this phrase the "papa" gets back at the "eternal child."

Haydn, a stranger to pettiness, who envied no one and had no need to, was not only the third important musician (after Handel and Gluck) who lived to experience fame during his lifetime, he was also a man who knew how to carry it with equanimity and self-control. He soon recognized Mozart's universal superiority and made no secret of it. After Mozart's death he told his London publisher Francis Broderip, "Friends have flattered me that I have genius. But he [Mozart] surpassed me." He also tried actively (if unsuccessfully) to intercede on Mozart's behalf. We have a letter dated December 1787, when he was fifty-five, to one Herr Franz Rott (or Roth), chief commissary director for the province of Prague. He was a music lover and a patron of the arts who could afford to order an opera from Haydn.

You ask me for an *opera buffa*. Gladly, if you wish to possess one of my vocal compositions for yourself alone. But

I cannot serve you if you want to produce it on the stage in Prague, because all my operas are too much connected with our company (in Esterhazy in Hungary); moreover they would not produce the proper effect, which I have calculated to suit this locality. It would be something quite different if I had the inestimable good fortune to compose an entirely new libretto for your theater there. But that too would be a daring thing to do, in that hardly anyone can risk being compared to the great Mozart.

For if I could impress upon the hearts of music lovers, especially the great ones, how inimitable are Mozart's works, how profound, how musically intelligent, how sensitive (for this is how I understand and feel them), then nations would compete to possess such a jewel within their walls. Prague should hold on to the precious man—and reward him, too. Without that, the fate of great geniuses is sad indeed, and gives posterity but little encouragement to strive further; unfortunately, this is why so many promising talents succumb. I am angered that this unique man Mozart has still not been engaged at any royal or imperial court. Forgive me if I have gotten off the track; I love the man too much.

I am, etc.

Joseph Haydn

This letter seems almost too fine and its lesson too correct to be genuine. Unfortunately, the original has not been preserved. We do not like to doubt its authenticity and we hope we are wrong in doing so. Such glorification is easy to invent, of course, but who, we wonder, would take on glorification either as duty or amusement? Let's consider the letter genuine. After all, no one profited from it. Nissen is the first to cite the text after Niemtschek. Niemtschek was a Gymnasium professor, so we can assume that he corrected the orthography (not Haydn's strong point). Here we have the letter of a great man, great enough to argue passionately and persuasively for the greatness of another great man. Nothing of the "common temperament" of which Karoline Pichler accused him is betrayed here. Of course, he was less skilled with words than was Mozart; unlike him, he was no rhapsodist, no letter writer at all. His style was usually dry and clumsy; only rarely, and almost bashfully, does he strike an emotional note. On May 30, 1790, he wrote from Esterhazy to a friend, Frau von Genzinger:

> . . . this time, too, will pass away and that day will come again, when I will have the inestimable pleasure of sitting beside you at the piano, hearing Mozart's masterpieces being played and kissing your hands for so many beautiful things.

What all the other "beautiful things" (apart from Mozart's) might have been, we do not know. But one should assume that something of Haydn's own was included among them. Probably Frau von Genzinger played them substantially better than he did.

When Haydn was again sitting alongside Frau von Genzinger at the piano, and "this time, too" had passed away, when he was playing "Mozart's masterpieces" with her, the master was dead. While Haydn was celebrating, and being celebrated, in London, Mozart was completing the phenomenal productions of his final year, uncelebrated, though not, as legend stubbornly maintains, in poverty. Besides the contractual items for the court, he fulfilled large and small commissions for occasional works and for two operas, the first of which was a failure, the second of which earned him nothing. He also wrote his last two works for solo and orchestra, the Clarinet Concerto in A, K. 622, for his friend Stadler, and, for himself, the Piano Concerto in B-flat, K. 595, which is thought to have the quality of a transfigured farewell. Perhaps it does and perhaps not: we will continue to refrain from definitions of even the greatest masterpieces, and this concerto is one of them.

Mozart was not given the chance to perform this concerto at his own academy concert, the brilliant context of his early years in Vienna. He had sunk to a single number on the program. We can see the level to which he had descended from the announcement of the première:

ANNOUNCEMENT
Herr Bähr, Chamber Musician presently in
the service of His Imperial Russian Majesty,
will have the honor of being heard
playing several pieces on the clarinet,
at a grand musical concert on Friday next,
the 4th of March, in Herr Jahn's hall; at which
Mme Lange will sing and Herr Kapellmeister Mozart
will play a concerto on the fortepiano.
Those still wishing to subscribe can obtain
their tickets any day from Herr Jahn.
The concert begins at 7 o'clock.

Herr Jahn was a restaurateur whose establishment happened
to be very near Mozart's apartment; Mozart only had to go
around the corner for his last performance as a soloist, on
March 4, 1791, overshadowed by the artistry of Herr Bähr
(Joseph Beer). His very last official appearance was as conductor of the first two performances of *Die Zauberflöte* on September 30 and October 1, 1791; but that was not in the city center
and did not count as a first-class event in the imperial city's
musical life. It was only acknowledged as such after Mozart's
death. It is probable, though not certain, that he himself conducted the première of *Tito*, on September 6, in Prague. And
thus it is also probable that, as he stood there, his back to the
audience of disapproving aristocrats, his agony growing, he
experienced the fiasco at first hand. He never recovered from it
during the little that remained of his life. The fact that *Tito*
"did not meet with the hoped-for success" was due less to what
we find objectionable in this opera today than to the conditions of the performance and the audience's obstinate personal
reservations about the composer.

In a sense *La Clemenza di Tito*, K. 621, was already a
relic at the time of its composition. The opera became popular
at the end of the eighteenth and the beginning of the nineteenth centuries because the classicist taste of the age inclined

to high-minded heroic allegory. Metastasio's libretto was already sixty years old at the time of the Prague première and had been set by twenty composers, including Gluck. The "poet laureate of Saxony," Caterino Mazzolà, tightened it up and reduced the number of characters, but he remained true to the plot, and therefore to the invariable format of *opera seria*: the use of fiction to expand and embroider ancient, usually Roman, history, displaying the noble nature of a ruling figure (historically documented, it was claimed) in his private, as it were unofficial, life. These operas were symbolic acts, humble offerings, usually produced for coronations, official visits, and other ceremonial occasions, an obeisance to the ruler or prince being honored. His legendary surrogate, the personified wisdom and kindness of his theatrical counterpart, demonstrated how superior he was to his subjects. (When we read the stilted strophes of *opera seria* today, we realize how revolutionary must have been the *opera buffa*, where a man like Figaro suddenly began conversing in the vernacular.) This pervasive aristocratic magnanimity detracts from all psychological verisimilitude in *Tito*, particularly since the hero himself draws attention to it time and time again. Mozart cut one of these self-righteous arias completely: no doubt he thought "virtue" had gone too far. In addition, he must have realized that the age of *opera seria* was over. There is evidence that after *Figaro* and *Don Giovanni* he could no longer do much with such material. It was assumed from the entry in his catalogue of compositions, which says that Signore Mazzolà had "reworked" the libretto "into a real opera" (*"ridotta a vera opera dal Signore Mazzolà"*), that he was satisfied with it. But we think this unlikely; he must have meant something else. More likely, if he could have afforded to, he would have rejected this libretto as he had so many others.

But he could not afford to. Although it would have been a matter of relative indifference to him that the Bohemian nobility needed an *opera seria* for Emperor Leopold II's coronation as King of Bohemia in Prague, and the commission meant interrupting work on two more important assignments, *Die*

Zauberflöte and the Requiem, he needed the renown, and most of all the money. He got the money, but not the renown. *"Una porcheria tedesca"* ("German hogwash") was the verdict of the Empress and newly crowned Queen of Bohemia, Maria Louisa of Spain. Obviously Her Majesty was a severe and pithy judge.

In vain do we seek through the entire history of response to music for a single apt judgment from a single one of the princes to whom works were dedicated or who were present at performances, either as patrons or simply as members of the audience. We find nothing, not a truthful sentence, let alone a direct hit; not even a *bon mot*. But despite that, they had the presumption to have the last word, as if the arts, too, were part of their domain. "So many notes!" said the Emperor to Mozart after a performance of *Die Entführung*. Mozart is said to have replied, "Exactly as many as necessary, your Majesty!" But we can confidently consign this retort to the realm of anecdote.

The harsh words of the evidently anti-German Empress were no more than a summary of the general feeling about *Tito*. This was probably due less to its artistic quality than to its creator, no longer *persona grata* with the great lords, indeed already held to be a man of dubious reputation, and perhaps even a potential rabble-rouser. He was no longer the honest court composer; nor was he appearing in that role, for he had not received the commission directly. It was given to the Prague impresario Guardasoni, who procured it for Mozart, remembering the popular successes of *Figaro* and *Don Giovanni*, and forgetting perhaps the difference in this assignment. It was earnest dignity, not popularity, which was desired.

There are two versions of the story of how *Tito* was composed. Legend has it that Mozart wrote the score in the eighteen days between commission and performance. Like all stories that have hardened into legend, this one has been challenged by recent scholarship, which goes to the other extreme and claims that Mozart took up the work repeatedly over several years. Four years before its première, after the success of *Don Giovanni*, he did, in fact, write to his friend Gottfried von Jacquin (November 4, 1787): "People here are doing their best to persuade me to remain on for a couple of months and write another one. But I cannot accept this proposal, however flattering it may be." This passage is somewhat puzzling. We cannot make it out. Mozart loved Prague; he enjoyed his greatest successes there; nowhere did he feel as good as among his friends in Prague. He preferred composing operas to anything else. He would not be missing out on anything in Vienna. From what we know of him, he would willingly—indeed, gladly and cold-bloodedly—have sacrificed the few pupils he may still have had there to a more gratifying activity. Aside from them, no one in Vienna would have missed him. Why, then, could he not accept the commission? Perhaps his plan to go to London had become a more real possibility. But then surely the wording of this passage would not have been so melancholy. Mozart's verbal statements are always most mysterious when he is refusing something, when he writes "I cannot . . ." For, as far as we know, he never wrote *why* he could not, unless the letter of refusal to Da Ponte is genuine.

How, for example, might he have answered the London entrepreneur Robert O'Reilly, who on October 26, 1790 invited him to London to write two operas there for £300? What kept him in Vienna? England had been his dream kingdom; Vienna closed the door on him, refused his petitions, put him off, as if awaiting his death. Can "gloomy intuition" really have been the reason? It cannot have been the "mysterious magic" of Vienna. Or did the letter perhaps never reach him? Did rivals destroy it? Did Constanze keep it hidden from him? We do not know.

It is unlikely, however, that the earlier offer in Prague referred to *La Clemenza di Tito*. As we have noted, he would have tossed such a libretto into the wastebasket, accustomed as he was by now to protagonists like Don Giovanni and Figaro. We tend, therefore, to believe the version of legend, without insisting, however, on the eighteen days, though it was probably not much more than that. He did not need much more time. The *secco* recitatives were assigned to Süssmayr, who accompanied him to Prague. He reserved the *accompagnati* for himself, as we can tell not only from their quality but also from the autograph of the score. The usual smears and blots are there, but the hand that glides over the pages is his own: controlled, steady, light. It is in no way the hand of a sick man, as biographers claim, basing their assumption on vague and dubious sources, and looking ahead to his death three months later.

Nowhere does the manuscript show signs of haste. Strangely enough, Mozart's hand never seems rushed, even when the facts and dates indicate that he was pressed for time; even the beams of his thirty-second notes are never crooked. The rondo of the D minor Piano Concerto, K. 466 (February 10, 1785), written in great haste, so that he "did not even have time to play [it] through, as he had to supervise the copying" (Leopold Mozart to his daughter, February 14–16, 1785), is a calligraphic (but not simply a calligraphic!) masterpiece. The manuscript of the C minor Concerto, K. 491, is sketchy only where Mozart the pianist wanted to keep open possibilities for improvisation. True, two autographs that we could have used for corroboration have been lost: the Serenade for winds, K. 388/384a, mentioned earlier, a composition for eight instruments written in two days; and the C major Symphony, K. 425, "Linz," which Mozart wrote "at breakneck speed." He was to give a concert in Linz at "old Count Thun's" on his return journey from Salzburg to Vienna at the end of October 1783 and, because he had nothing with him, wrote and rehearsed the symphony in three days. However these manuscripts may have looked, the works themselves do not reflect the extreme pressure of time under which they were composed.

We do not mean to minimize the importance of *Tito*, but we invariably find ourselves lapsing into apologia when we assert that this or that aria is of the quality of *Così*, or even anticipates *Die Zauberflöte*. We are already assuming there will be an argument to the contrary.* Only a few of the arias can be compared, strictly speaking, to the highest standard of Mozart's dramatic music, the three Da Ponte operas. Seldom do we enjoy here the deep satisfaction of a dramatic action conveyed by music. Most of its arias revert to the Neapolitan style of the early operas, although they are shorter and do not have *ritornellos*: in this respect, the pressure of time seems to have had a beneficial effect. And, however grateful we may be for the absence of long coloratura passages, the repetitions of isolated, thematically unconnected word sequences are still rather hard to appreciate. But Mozart obviously did not care: this is the last, not wholly successful, of those familiar exercises written "with the left hand."

Characteristically, Mozart was most successful in the *accompagnati*, as in the early *opere serie*. Here we have exciting inner drama again, or rather, only here do the stereotypical characters take on an inner life of their own, with their own language, beyond words, detached from the plot and independent of its insignificant events. Of course, in opera we cannot separate the music from the subject it is expressing (much as we would sometimes like to), but here the text is so completely abstruse, the individual motivations so totally undetermined, that in comparison even *Die Zauberflöte* could be called a

* For Ernst Bloch, neither *Tito* nor *Idomeneo* are "proper Mozart operas; rather than in apotheoses, the elysium of this spirit lies in the garden music of *Figaro*; but *Die Zauberflöte*, too . . . ends on a triumphant note, in the land of triumph, which Baroque opera had foresworn." Ernst Bloch, *Das Prinzip Hoffnung* (Frankfurt, 1959), p. 271. The negative apotheosis of *Don Giovanni*, of course, cannot be encompassed by the principle of hope.

psychological drama. In order to do absolute justice to the music, we would have to take the text seriously, and though Mozart was obliged to, we cannot. Mozart was, of course, familiar with this kind of subject and its problems of expression; besides, he had heard Hasse's *Clemenza di Tito* in 1770 in Cremona, so he knew how to approach the material. There is a kind of genius in the way he opens up the static tableau of these scenes and the hollow rhetoric of these puppets, the way he thaws the frozen quality, giving it life and breathing into it a refreshing *buffo* spirit (which never left him after the Da Ponte operas); his is the optimal solution. Nevertheless, this music does not give us total pleasure; of necessity it lacks that interpretive character which gives his other stage creations their value and their presence. Characters like those of *La Clemenza di Tito*, stragglers within their genre, really seem designed to carry the *opera seria ad absurdum*. The borderline between the sublime and the ridiculous is almost completely blurred.

What, for example, could the composer have made of the bravura role of Sesto, who, although he loves his bosom friend and lord, Tito, is ready to murder him, since his (Sesto's) beloved Vitellia desires it, for she does not love him (Sesto) but is in love with that very Tito whose death she desires, because he does not love her? The answer is, of course, that Mozart could make nothing of Sesto, for he is unreal, a stillborn artifact, existing only in the emotional situation of the moment, with no dramatic continuity. Mozart interpreted this character, who deserves to be thrown to the wolves, with tenderness and delicacy, making him into a susceptible and overly devoted lover, who voices his sorrow in a voluptuous bel canto, as long as his pangs of conscience do not require him (with good reason) to break out into passionate outbursts in C minor. At every opportunity, however unworthy, he gives vent to the whole gamut of his irresolute feelings; when, in the trio of the second act (No. 18), he sings "Di sudore mi sento, o Dio bagnar" ("I am bathed, O God, in perspiration") the beautiful E-flat motive does seem rather unsuited to this kind of indisposition. From several sketches we can see that Mozart intended the role for a tenor, but the impresario Guardasoni had imported a first-class castrato from Italy (probably, incidentally, the last one in the history of opera, Domenico Bedini). Mozart changed the concept, probably without much protest—ever the threatrical pragmatist, taking things as they came. And, given this particular commission, it may not have been too hard to relinquish his own ideas.

Bedini, then, was one of the last castrati, and this opera was probably the last *seria* in music history—the end, long overdue, of a stillborn dramatic form, which by its very nature flies in the face of all thematic verisimilitude and dramatic vitality; for the theatrical nature of its characters lends itself to plans and reflections, but not to action. Certainly, its great themes are love and death, but these are watered down by secondary ones, like generosity and renunciation, and they are robbed of all their drama. No one draws a dagger or embraces anybody onstage, unless the director invents such business on his own. True, in *Tito* we see Rome going up in flames, but none of the stage figures is really distressed about it. Even the music seems unconcerned; in E-flat major it accompanies the prayer (beautiful, to be sure) of the arsonist, who entreats the gods that no harm may come to Tito, his friend and enemy.

In any artistic discipline, a work whose form is already outmoded at the time of its creation can never make up for it over the centuries. If it is not forgotten entirely, it vegetates on, forever old-fashioned, forever a lifeless anachronism. *Tito* has none of the impetus and freshness, and therefore none of the explosive validity, of *Idomeneo*, written ten years before it. Mozart himself felt that he never surpassed *Idomeneo*, the only example of *opera seria* which has survived into our time, and indeed is just beginning to experience a renaissance. We must realize, however, that, at best, the *seria* as a genre has only a museum-piece kind of beauty today. Since we cannot recognize ourselves in its characters, we hear it, in a sense, in quotation marks. Thus, *Tito* remains a special case: both unproduceable and yet worth producing, forever the object of experiment, music worth redeeming, its tendrils twining around a worthless monument of paper, unable in the end to hide it entirely.

"Mann und Weib, und Weib und Mann reichen an die Gottheit an" and "Ein Weib tut wenig, plaudert viel" ("Man and wife, wife and man attain the godhead" and "Woman does little, talks too much"). These two quotations, the first from two very dissimilar partners, Pamina and Papageno, the second from (no less than) a priest in the temple of wisdom, give only a small idea of the wide variety of views represented in *Die Zauberflöte*, not to mention the range of its themes. The concept of the godhead is not defined any more exactly than in the rather puzzling wording of the first quotation, and yet the entire opera is pervaded by it. It has also been the basis of countless speculative studies, which usually like to point out the ethos lying deep within the opera. The second quotation is not only an out-and-out lie; it also represents, in a special way, the essential untruthfulness, the totally unexamined, indeed foolish language of the work. Nevertheless, hardly any of the commentators seem to have objected to this lack of truthfulness, the shallow meaning of such obscure language. In this case the meaning is misogyny, a motif that recurs strikingly throughout the libretto. Surely, however, neither Schikaneder nor Mozart was seized by this idea: perhaps Giesecke, the third collaborator, was responsible for it.

Despite the immediate popular success of the opera, objections to the text were heard at once. The *Musikalisches Wochenblatt* in Berlin wrote in December 1791:

The new comedy with machines, *Die Zauberflöte*, with music by our Kapellmeister *Mozart*, which has been produced at great expense and with much magnificence in the scenery, has not met with the hoped-for success, the content and language of the piece being altogether too low.

And Count Zinzendorf entered into his diary on November 6, 1791: *"La musique et les decorations sont jolies, le reste une farce incroyable."* It is probably untrue that the work was a critical failure, and the verdict of the count (who was anything but a discerning critic—a philistine, rather) was perhaps influenced by the out-of-the-way location of Schikaneder's theater. It had at its disposal a considerable orchestra, but not the musical powers of the Italian vocal ensemble. How did Mozart's sister-in-law Josepha Hofer (whom Wolfgang, incidentally, did not like very much) manage the coloratura of the Queen of the Night? And how was Nannina Gottlieb, now seventeen, in the role of Pamina? Let us hope, at least, that the singers did not look the way they do in contemporary illustrations.

No other opera of Mozart's has stimulated biographers' wishful thinking in such rich measure as *Die Zauberflöte*. It is considered his swan song, a concluding apotheosis, a return to divine simplicity. Actually, nowhere are Mozart's extramusical ambitions as clear as in *Die Zauberflöte*. Sentimental Mozart interpreters cannot reconcile themselves to the fact that although he sets markers beside each stage of his musical style (or styles), he does not scatter them throughout his life so that we may gauge his world view. Thus, critics in search of a reconciled rounding off to his life, a harmonious dying away, have succeeded in forcing upon *Die Zauberflöte* the marks of transfigured wisdom, the qualities of a late work, as in, for example, the duality of Tamino–Papageno. According to Abert, "This text corresponds so perfectly to his views on opera that we have no qualms in assuming that the composer had a great share in it."[69] Here again is that desire for a correspondence between life and work, the same one that led to the idea that

Shakespeare is embodied in Prospero, the protagonist of the "late work" *The Tempest* (although he was only forty-seven years old when he wrote it). For us the work on *Die Zauberflöte* is a last, energetic attempt to achieve solvency, even if it meant a concession to "popular" taste. There is ample evidence that Mozart had long ago stopped caring about "pleasing," as such. But how else can we explain his birdcatcher, except to conclude that this carefree, merry fellow was meant to be profitable for his creator?

Because, to the sorrow of many, nothing authentic is known about the collaboration of librettist and composer, there are countless insidious legends about the creation of *Die Zauberflöte*. Schikaneder is said to have locked Mozart in a wooden summerhouse (later transported to Salzburg, where it can still be visited) and kept him there for more than a week. Of course, he supplied him with adequate bodily refreshment, including, according to legend, Barbara Gerl (the first Papagena and wife of the first Sarastro), so that the maestro should lack for nothing and devote himself, in contented enjoyment of wine and women, to song. The disseminators of this trivial story obviously did not consider that it is more a proof of Mozart's flagging spirit than of his joy in his work. There would have been no need for such embellishments in the case of the Da Ponte operas, where his mighty inner drive needed no stimulation.

Biographers claim that this work, in particular, was an inner necessity for him, that here, more than in any other opera, Mozart was able to realize his humanitarian ideals. But, in fact, there is absolutely no verifiable basis for this view, nor for the idea that here at last he could seize the welcome opportunity of writing a German opera. True, in some early letters to his father he had championed things *"Teutsche"*; this apparent attachment culminates in a letter of 1785 to the librettist Anton Klein in Mannheim, in which he complained about the *"directeurs des theaters"*:

Were there but one good patriot in charge—things would take a different turn. But then, perhaps, the German national theater which is sprouting so vigorously would actually begin to flower; and of course that would be an everlasting blot on Germany, if we Germans were seriously to begin to think as Germans, to act as Germans, to speak German and, Heaven help us, to sing in German!!

Naturally, this passage was a happy find for every nationalistic and patriotic cultural history; "Mozart's German way" (Alfred Orel) seemed assured and proven once and for all. In reality, of course, this is another passage that should also be in quotation marks, a momentary fit of patriotic chest thumping. His real purpose was to use pretty speeches to shake off Herr Klein, who had sent him a libretto entitled *Kaiser Rudolf von Habsburg*. We must admit that the thought of Mozart composing an opera by this name is not without a certain absurd charm.

How little these sporadic wishes to compose to German texts reflect his patriotism is evident from the fact that, as early as 1783, he imagined a suitable text for a "German" opera to be a translation of *Servitore di due padroni* by Goldoni (we, too, think it would be suitable). No one has ever been able to accept the idea that all the intentions or desires he expresses in his letters are literally of the moment, his behavioral response to a particular fleeting stimulus, and often also an unconscious desire to adapt to the situation. He wanted to please the addressee.

Those passages, however, in which he tells his father of his intentions as a composer, and exhorts him urgently to support him in their realization, are always truthful and significant. On February 4, 1778, he wrote to him from Paris: "Do not forget how much I desire to write operas. I envy anyone who is composing one. I could really weep for vexation when I hear or see an aria. But Italian, not German; seriosa, not buffa." A few days before, on the other hand, on January 11, 1778, he had written to his father in a postscript: "If the Emperor will give me a thousand gulden, I will write a German opera for him." One could not say that a national ideal was paramount here. Mozart cannot be pinned down by his written wishes or opinions; his artistic will was expressed only after the fact, in each respective work. In the last analysis, he was interested exclusively in the works themselves, and not in the realization of a "mission."

Schikaneder was actually named Johann Joseph, but he called himself Emanuel (as if Da Ponte had bequeathed his original name Emanuele to the next librettist). He was a true man of the theater, and exclusively that. His aesthetic taste went exactly as far as that of his public, his artistic views were governed exclusively by what the potential audience did or did not want to see or hear. He did not strive for "higher things," something we do not hold against him. He was not cut out for "higher things," for he was profoundly ignorant. Although he had read a few of the classics (among them Lessing, whom he adapted for his own plays), it was only for the sake of their possible economic value and their useful effects. It is entirely possible that he was a popular Hamlet; it is unlikely that he was a great Hamlet, as his apologists repeatedly assert. His greatest successes were plays that displayed an impressive theatrical apparatus, flashy machinery, lighting, fireworks, explosions, or in which he and his actors could personally appeal to the emotions of his audience, to whose wishes he was always very sensitive. He usually succeeded, though not always. Schikaneder's play *Rache für Rache (Vengeance for Vengeance)*, either his own work or the joint effort of his "team," was touted as "the finest of all character plays" in his official announcement, "seasoned with the best comical salt, so that my honored patrons need digest neither tasteless nor warmed-over food (*of which, unfortunately, there is so much*)." As we can see, language was not his element. In Nannerl's letter to her brother on November 30, 1780, we read that the play was such a failure in Salzburg that its author had to leave the city soon after. Schikaneder undoubtedly makes a fruitful topic for cultural history; he was undoubtedly a refreshing and unique personality, but it is senseless to try, as biographers do, to raise this man from the hurly-burly of itinerant theatrical life and place him at Mozart's side as an equal. "Two geniuses had found each other, the musician with a theatrical sense, and the man of the theater who was also a musician."[70] This assertion by the authoritative biographer of Schikaneder, Egon Komorzynski, who, of course, does not mention the Salzburg debacle, again points up the habit of wishful thinking, the governing motive of a self-imposed task, which is to save the honor of a figure whose honor really does not need to be saved. After all, Schikaneder is no negative character, either, no "adversary."

Since we know nothing about Mozart's share in producing the libretto, we cannot judge if the Freemasonry implicitly advocated in it reflected his active intention or even his particular wish. The image of Mozart the Freemason has often been idealized; he certainly was caught up in a new wave of interest when in December 1784 he joined the lodge *Zur Wohltätigkeit* (Benevolence), to which Karl Ludwig Giesecke, the other poet of *Die Zauberflöte*, also later belonged (Schikaneder did not belong to any lodge). The lodge *Zur Wohltätigkeit* was less important than *Zur gekrönten Hoffnung* (Crowned Hope); it was considered a "gorging and boozing lodge," though it is not certain who coined this phrase.

The Masonic ideal of human brotherhood, though undoubtedly praiseworthy for the time (although it actually had more to do with *male* brotherhood), indeed revolutionary in its moral goals and general ethical concepts, was expressed only in vague proclamations. More a matter of words than deeds, much sung about—and always badly—Freemasonry never led to any real theory, nor would Mozart have been interested if there had been one. The "meaning of life," man's task on earth—these were not things he wondered about consciously. On the other hand, he needed company, and he found it in the lodge. When his duty as a composing lodge brother ordained that he write music for celebrations or funerals, he wrote it. He used his own sacred style, the solemn stance, which usually miscarried when he had to keep to the texts. Heavy, well-meaning but ineffectual, they were written by gentlemen such as Ziegenhagen, Ratschky, or Petran (honorable men, but amateur poets)—or by Herr Giesecke. The essence of the work lay in the text; it could not be generalized musically. The message had to be kept intact; at most, Mozart could use pathos to accentuate it. These compositions have the forced quality of required exercises. It was much harder for Mozart than for Beethoven to set the word "mankind" to music.

The non-verbal Masonic music is a different matter. Apart from the marches of *Die Zauberflöte*, we have only the splendid and unique Masonic Funeral Music, K 477/479a, of November 10, 1785, commissioned after the death of two members of *Zur gekrönten Hoffnung*, the Duke of Mecklenburg and Count Esterhazy. This piece, like the *Ave verum Corpus*, is one of those wonderful occasional works ordered and delivered punctually and in perfect condition by the great man, himself as little involved as a painter who paints a burial scene. Two illustrious lodge brothers have died; Mozart has to paint the picture and he paints it. He brings it forth at a majestic distance, a painting of grief, grand and controlled, perfect from the beginning, with its huge sighing motifs in C minor and the *cantus firmus* in E-flat major, to the final cadence in C major, like a signature at which he withdraws with a bow, leaving his work behind. We can no more see it as a "personal expression of Mozartean feelings about death" (whatever that may be) than as his "surrender to death."[71]

But *Die Zauberflöte* is not a Masonic cantata, however much the main plot may be infused with the strange, secretive Masonic ethos. It is a German *Singspiel*, originally an entertainment for the theaters of the outer city, a "comedy with machines" (today we would say a "musical"), with harsh, gaudy stage illusions laid on lavishly by Schikaneder. Yet, in the serious sections, Masonic symbolism and morality form the essential theme, the theoretical components underlying the ostensible action, which is a cipher destined for a flood of interpretations.

There is no relation between the literary value of the libretto and these numerous interpretations, and that is precisely what they convey. There is usually a defensive element to the various mythmakings and analyses, which are apologetic, sometimes aggressively so, as if the author had to defend his views against the attack of incompetents. "Schikaneder's genius" (William Mann) is hurled at us categorically; in a discussion during a Bayreuth master class in 1960, the renowned director Walter Felsenstein said, "I would not want to force anyone to share my opinion, but if we were to talk about it in another context, I could prove to you that *Die Zauberflöte* is a quite exceptional piece of work on Schikaneder's part, too. In collaboration with Mozart's music, it is, for its time, a very revolutionary, indeed, a dangerous manifesto in the form—or better, in the guise—of a fairy tale."[72] At the time, however, no listener, and no censor either, seems to have noticed this dangerous element.

Goethe's remark to Eckermann on April 13, 1823, that *Die Zauberflöte* is full of "improbabilities and jokes, which not everyone is capable of understanding and appreciating," does, it is true, have something of the nature of a defense against expected attacks. But it was none other than Goethe who laid the cornerstone for the positive evaluation of the text, with an assertion that Schikaneder admirers wear like a badge; it legitimizes them and vindicates them. Goethe declared, "It takes more education to appreciate the worth of this libretto than to deny it." There we have it. So defenders of the libretto usually begin, "No less a man than Goethe . . ." etc. Since Goethe, there has been a pious tradition of explaining away the opera's meaningless action by invoking its "higher meaning" (Goethe). Those with a "loftier consciousness" feel like "initiates" in the sense of the text; like Tamino and Pamina, they have passed the tests, while we uninitiated skeptics, unable to get beyond the nonsense, have to stick to the low level of Papageno, who would not exchange the tangible material world for a vague promise of an ideal world, sight unseen. The sacraments are withheld from the ineducable, and so we stand and ask, for example, in whose service the Three Boys are bound, or why the Queen of the Night did not take up the magic flute herself to prevent her daughter's abduction. Did she have trouble playing the instrument, when even the foreign prince Tamino, to whom she presents it, can master it at once? And these are merely questions selected at random.

We do not know what Mozart thought of the libretto, despite all claims to the contrary. It is unlikely that his driving motivation was the Masonic subject matter. He needed money; he had to make do. Since magic operas, especially with spectacular stage devices and fireworks, were fashionable in Vienna, and well attended, this job promised to earn him something. And after Mozart's death, it did make money for Schikaneder. Mozart himself, in his last days, could rejoice only in its apparent success, and in the fact that he seemed to have hit upon the proper tone for something that until then had not been in his line.

Significantly, this work was immediately a great hit; it might throw some light on the taste of the audience at the première if we consider which numbers had to be encored. They were, in fact, the most accessible ones, the duet "Bei Männern, welche Liebe fühlen" (No. 7) and the glockenspiel passage "Das klinget so herrlich . . ." (first finale), which tells us something about performance practices: a number could be interrupted by applause at any time, regardless of the fact that continuity was thereby destroyed, as, in this instance, when the glockenspiel leads directly and unexpectedly into a duet between Papageno and Pamina. Also encored was the trio of the Three Boys in the second act (No. 16), "Seid uns zum zweiten Mal willkommen," and we are almost compelled to assume that this piece, whose true magic is subtle and hidden, was accompanied by a technical gimmick, perhaps a stage machine in which the Three Boys glided down to earth.

Of course, not even a Mozart could come up with a device to correct a lack of logic, especially the fatal want of continuity in the action. He could not give it the consistent musical line of the Da Ponte operas, the breathlessly surging power of *Don Giovanni* or the ironic sovereignty of *Così fan tutte*—these were libretti in which he almost literally guided the action. In addition, the *secco* recitatives and, especially, the *accompagnati* of Italian opera were able to create a harmonic and dynamic logic in the sequence of arias (and did so in Mozart's work in a truly unique way). The spoken dialogue of the *Singspiel* works against logic; at each such break our bubble is suddenly burst, not least because opera singers can seldom handle these speeches. It is hard enough to sing Tamino, and even harder to act the role, to master, for example, the mime with which, like Orpheus, he has to gesture rejection to his sweetheart, Pamina, much against his will. And what member of the audience does not shudder at the exaggerated diction, the Christmas-pageant solemnity, the strained hollow laughter of the men or the tinkly laughter and teasing ingénue mannerisms of the women? (A rhetorical question. The answer is that hardly anyone does, unfortunately.)

Because of the arbitrariness with which the characters represent now this, now that abstract principle, and their need to articulate these inconsistent views, the composer was unable to control their conception and development. He had to take each number as it came, determine its relative value and momentary significance, and adapt his music both to the character's particular change in situation and to his change in attitude. Thus, the representative of the negative principle, the Queen of the Night, is introduced in G minor as a tragically bereft mother; after rehearsing her grief (No. 4), she promises her daughter to the hero, Tamino, but in the very same aria, in the key of B-flat, she is transformed into a resolute demon; she is no longer the same woman. In the second act she becomes a larger-than-life villain in D minor ("Der Hölle Rache kocht in meinem Herzen," No. 14), the enemy of the son-in-law she had selected, and confederate of the evil Moor, Monostatos, to whom she promises her daughter in marriage, the same daughter for whose sake she has allegedly been grieving. There is no thematic or personal resemblance between the birdcatcher Papageno, who calls "heisa-hopsasa" in G major (No. 2), and the meditative E-flat major Papageno of the duet with Pamina (No. 7). We conclude that in between he has begun to think, and this does not suit him. We do not quite understand how love "rules in Nature's own way." Even Monostatos, the Moor, undergoes his transformations: "as a human" he is different from his role as the lowest of the low. Probably Johann Nouseul, whose task it was to portray this cowardly, single-minded spoilsport, Osmin's dull brother, wanted an aria too. And he got one: "Alles fühlt der Liebe Freuden" (No. 13), a musically undemanding allegro in C major, above which Mozart wrote in the score: "To be played and sung as softly as if the music were a great way off." What might that mean? Perhaps it is the great distance from the Moor's native land. We do, in fact, seem to hear the echoes of janissaries in the distance: the piccolo, in unison with the flute, and the first violins (an octave below) produce a strange sound; at any moment a shift to A minor seems imminent, but it doesn't happen. No panorama opens up; rather everything remains one-dimensional in this lascivious yet flat tone behind which the Moor is certainly concealing his true intentions vis-à-vis the white maiden Pamina. We don't believe he just wants to kiss her; after all, he orders the moon to hide its face. This sad Moor is excluded from all good will; even the generous Masonic ethos won't go that far. For a moment he is granted mercy, but the next minute it is withdrawn.

The preoccupation with "females" (in *Così fan tutte* still an acceptable slight, because both sexes receive the same treatment) gets on our nerves in *Die Zauberflöte*. Nowadays this convention seems comic only in moderation; and in this case, too, no one has benefited from experience in life. We cannot assume that women's promiscuity at that time was any worse than men's, although, unlike men's, it was not sanctioned. And in *Die Zauberflöte* women are always presented, annoyingly, as "little pigeons." Mozart certainly never addressed his Constanze by that name, nor did Schikaneder use it for his various ladies, and we do not know if Giesecke was in the habit of addressing ladies at all. Probably not, since he is most likely the one responsible for the misogyny. As we have mentioned, neither Mozart nor Schikaneder had misogynist inclinations, and their insistent advocacy of the Masonic ideal of male supremacy is therefore surprising. Under these circumstances, it is amazing that Pamina is allowed to incorporate the positive principle, that she, too, is deemed worthy of initiation, and is, in fact, initiated. Only Papagena, like her dear little husband, has to remain on a lower plane, but she feels quite at home there. Even noble Tamino, a kind of Parsifal figure, is infected with this attitude: "Silly nonsense, spread by women," he answers his companion when Papageno requests an explanation. The Queen of the Night is "a woman, has a woman's mind," and a few hours (as far as one can speak of a time sequence) after the Three Ladies save his life, he calls them "common rabble." He quickly learned from Sarastro's priests that man is superior to woman; he has it hammered into him continually, as, for example, in the two priests' duet "Bewahret euch vor Weibertücken" ("Beware of women's wiles") (No. 11). In a light, apparently gay C major the two moralize to him, treating the case of a man who did not follow their advice and met a horrible end: "Tod und Verzweiflung war sein Lohn" ("Death and despair were his reward"). The fact that this would be a post mortem despair is not the only inconsistency in their teaching. But Mozart could not do anything with the inconsistency; he was a keen, a brilliant musical thinker; a verbal message stimulated him immediately to its interpretive possibilities. Consider how he might have interpreted "death and despair," and how he actually did so before: Don Giovanni's descent into hell, and the exaltation of Donna Anna. That it is in this case merely a report and not action changes nothing; we have seen that Mozart can often make an experience described in a ballad or a messenger's report the equal of stage action itself, for example, in Basilio's jackass aria or Figaro's wicked depiction of Cherubino's future life as a soldier. But in this instance the music tells us that it has to do with a completely hypothetical case. The bad end of the "wise man" who let himself "be ensnared" is portrayed neither in the *sotto voce* of the two voices nor in the strangely alienated staccato of the trombones. On the contrary, just where the text would seem to prescribe solemnity, the music becomes positively merry; the four-measure postlude turns into a jolly march. As so often in *Die Zauberflöte*, Mozart was here composing against the text. Or does this alienation reflect an intention we can no longer recognize?

(If we consider the passage "Das ist der Teufel sicherlich!" ["That surely is the devil"] from the G major trio [No. 6], we see that the comic nature of this sudden fright, this reciprocal confusion, is not exploited musically, and instead, Mozart varies only what has gone before; he was probably not concentrating.)

Nevertheless, the message of the two priests seems to have stayed with Mozart in a strange way. At the end of a letter of June 11, 1791, to Constanze in Baden, he writes: "Adieu—my love! I am lunching today with Puchberg. I kiss you a thousand times and say with you in thought: 'Death and despair were his reward!'" Obviously this line had pursued him into his private life, but whatever it might mean here will always remain obscure: could he be making light of a presentiment?

A stylistic analysis (insofar as it is applicable in this case) would show that the libretto of *Die Zauberflöte* had several authors; the exact number, of course, cannot be determined. In Mozart's time and in Schikaneder's workshop, "teamwork" was quite common; many of the members of an ensemble of this kind were also active "creatively," if the need arose. The singers Benedikt Schack and Franz Xaver Gerl could also compose, if they had to; everyone lent a hand where it was needed, even as prompter. And besides Schikaneder there was at least one other member, a relatively lowly one, who was also active "as a poet": Karl Ludwig Giesecke. He appeared in *Die Zauberflöte* only as a subordinate Moor, and possibly assisted as prompter; otherwise he served as the troupe factotum, and, evidently, often took up a pen, if only to plagiarize something that was needed, for no one was too particular about "intellectual property."

Karl Ludwig Giesecke (actually Johann Georg Metzler)* was born in Augsburg in 1761, and at first studied law in Göttingen. But he was drawn to the theater, and toward the end of the 1780s he ended up in Schikaneder's troupe, which he supplied with texts, usually adaptations of existing material. In 1794 his passion was spent, perhaps because he hadn't gotten too far, and he left the theater, went to Freiberg, and there studied mineralogy. After 1800 he traveled through Denmark and Sweden, doing research, and founded a school of mineralogy in Copenhagen. In 1806 the Danish King sent him to explore Greenland. He remained there for more than seven years, then returned to Denmark via Scotland and England to evaluate his results. In 1814, in competition with three other highly qualified mineralogists, he was elected, by a large major-

* I could not rely on German and Austrian sources for this digression; because of their attachment to well-established legends and subjective wishful thinking, they claim Schikaneder's sole authorship of the work to be an irrefutable fact. The will to mythologize one single figure, rather than to distribute the myth among several, is as old as monotheism. My sources are Henry F. Berry, *A History of the Royal Dublin Society* (London, 1915); Edward J. Dent, *Mozart's Operas* (London, 1922); and the *Enciclopedia dello spettacolo*, Vol. 5 (Rome, 1958).

ity, to the chair of mineralogy at the Royal Dublin Society. He remained in Dublin until his death in 1833. He was probably elevated to a knighthood: Sir Henry Raeburn, a prominent portrait painter whose clientele and subjects were members of the nobility or the intellectual elite, painted him in Dublin as "Sir Charles L. Giesecke." In his portrait he cuts a confident and elegant figure, a man of intellect with an air of importance. Giesecke was, in fact, considered extremely charming and witty in Dublin society, and he was greatly respected in scientific circles. The 1905 edition of Meyer's *Grosses Konversations-Lexikon* still lists him as an explorer of Greenland and mentions his publications (written in Danish), as well as a stone named for him, gieseckite.

In 1818 he stopped in Vienna, probably for the last time, and took the opportunity to confide privately that he was the author of most of the libretto of *Die Zauberflöte*. We should by no means consider this a boast, but rather the admission of a youthful folly, a wistful memory of a life far in the past; for at this time the *Zauberflöte* libretto was not highly regarded. At a performance in 1801 in the Kärntnertortheater the name Schikaneder was omitted entirely: it had become Mozart's work. Giesecke's claim neither improves the text nor makes the author into a true poet, something he presumably no longer wanted to be and, as an eminent scientist no longer needed to be. Thus it would be dishonest to try to label Giesecke an adventurer or a confidence man. He is surrounded by mystery, a romantic aura created, perhaps, by that break in his life: an emotionally impressionable, unstable "youth," who, in the nineteenth century, would even be seen as the model for Wilhelm Meister, who admired great scholars and collected their signatures in his overflowing poetry album, who had become the researcher who could spend seven years in Greenland's isolation with stoic self-control, and who then surfaced again, an eminent scholar and authoritative mineralogist who corresponded in that capacity with Goethe. A letter to Goethe about barometric observations had still been preserved up to the Second World War.

Perhaps an early interest in mineralogy brought him to Vienna, for Ignaz von Born, an outstanding mineralogist, was active there. Perhaps the contact between these two men led Giesecke to become a Freemason: Ignaz von Born was president of the Viennese lodges, and master of the lodge *Zur wahren Eintracht* (True Harmony). Nothing authentic is known about their relationship, however; there was a nearly two decade difference in their ages. In 1786 Born gave up his membership and activities as a Freemason and left the lodge, for what mysterious reason we do not know. When *Die Zauberflöte* was being written, he was already dangerously ill, and he died at the age of forty-eight on July 24, 1791. His death, too, is shrouded in mystery, and seems to have passed without comment, like his departure from the lodge. There is no report of his death, no ceremony, no mention in the gazettes. If Born is truly the model for Sarastro, as is generally claimed, it can be only because Giesecke wanted to commemorate his honored teacher, in spite of whatever trouble there might have been. If this is true, the symbolic significance of *Die Zauberflöte* was not the work of Schikaneder, who, after he had been ejected from his Regensburg lodge for reasons unknown, never joined another lodge again. Thus, Giesecke would be not only the "creator of Sarastro" (Edward Dent) but also the inventor of Pamina; and although it is Mozart alone who gives her a unique, sublime soul, she is also, with her ever-constant love and her longing for death, relatively the most consistent character in the libretto.

Another indication of Giesecke's decisive participation in the libretto is the existence of his own personal interleaved copy of it (preserved in the Austrian Nationalbibliothek). As "First Slave," which the opening-night program lists as his role, he would scarcely have needed his own copy; it must be a proof copy of his work. Might he have been proud of it at first? Whatever the case, Giesecke seems to be trustworthy. We do not doubt that he is the inventor of Sarastro and Sarastro's sphere in *Die Zauberflöte*. More doubtful is the contention that Sarastro is "one of the most attractive and distinctive stage creations in the history of music drama" (Dent). We would contend, on the contrary, that he is a perfect cardboard cut-out, the protagonist in a kind of spurious initiation rite. He is a memorial, and as such inconsistent; even as an ideal of humanitarianism he is unbelievable and unreal. "Vengeance is unknown" within his "hallowed halls"; nevertheless, immediately upon his first entrance he orders seventy-seven bastinados for his bad black slave, whom the good man keeps specifically to guard the sweet stolen maiden, because this slave had lustfully approached her, though we know that she cannot "be forced to love." (Might Monostatos once have been an alter ego of the originally ambivalent, symbolic figure of Sarastro in a rejected version of the material?) This punishment is a bad falling-off from Sarastro's otherwise virtually inert goodness, a goodness that discloses his total lack of history, however, for he did not work for it but was born to be the "leader of mankind" (or better, "of men"). Sarastro certainly did not correspond to Mozart's idea of a stage character; even Mozart needed at least a little "flesh and blood" in the libretto, so he could enrich it with some emotional content and give it a destiny and a life of its own. As we see from the Masonic cantatas, he himself did not object to the proclamation of abstract teachings, but something *in him* objected. The categorical imperative of the Freemason texts probably left him colder than he knew himself. Sarastro does not sing about inner experience, but about morality; no one carries this out, however, since it cannot be transformed into stage action. Thus, the role can neither be acted convincingly nor sung without being involuntarily comic. No bass is capable of managing the E major aria, "In diesen heil'gen Hallen" (No. 15), without audible exertion, for in its lowest notes ("Dann wandelt er an Freundes Hand") it seems to support the contrabasses from below, as if it were man's function to underpin the expressive power of the instrument. With the exception of Osmin, none of Mozart's other basses has to sing so low, not even the Commendatore. But Osmin is known to have a different nature; he represents the opposing principle. His low notes are meant ironically, and serve to characterize the comic side of a wicked character. Sarastro, on the other hand, is good; we are meant to take him seriously, but it is usually hard for us to do so. It is likewise hard to understand why, in the B-flat trio, "Soll ich dich, Teurer, nicht mehr sehn . . ." (No. 19), he has to be present at all, since his only function is to support Tamino verbally and harmonically (and morally); he is Tamino's literal echo.

We know Mozart contributed actively to the libretto for *Die Entführung*. At that time he apparently was not able to decide totally in favor of the "German *Singspiel*": the glorious D minor *accompagnato* between Constanze and Belmonte, "Welch ein Geschick!" (No. 20), with string accompaniment, was taken from his own treasure store of *opera seria*, and worked to this opera's advantage. Another dimension is opened up—this, too, is already music drama. He preferred to have his Bassa Selim, who almost competes with Sarastro in the realm of goodness, speak rather than sing. Mozart no doubt had his reasons: virtue is expressed better in speech. Pure, absolute "goodness" is hard to master musically or vocally; we are moved by it only within limits. To be sure, Sarastro, too, appears against a subdued orchestral background; the music of the priests breathes renunciation, voluntary restrictions, a certain musical puritanism, which others have called "divine simplicity"; it is "cleansed" of all sensuality. If we compare the March of the Priests (No. 9) with the very similar one (No. 25) in *Idomeneo* (same key [F major], same tempo, both *"sempre sotto voce"*), we see that the latter is immeasurably richer. It is a felicitous inspiration within a closed whole. Everything about it has a glorious spontaneous strength, which in *Die Zauberflöte* would overshadow the tight restraint of the male choral music. Fortunately, things look different with the "females," the Three Ladies and Pamina especially.

The *Singspiel* never was a satisfactory formal structure. The spoken text, which must further the action, also furthers the collapse of the musical continuity. A number can be no more than a number. And the diversity of action in *Die Zauberflöte* cannot render the opera's vague claims more consistent. The declamatory, hallowed quality forced Mozart (we would not want to impute an ulterior motive to him) into bad prosody, wrong phrasing. "Du bist un*schuld*ig, weise, fr*ooo*mm" (quarter note), sings the Queen of the Night. "O Isis und Osi*risschen*ket," sings Sarastro with his male chorus. In the wonderful *andante a tempo* of the first finale the words "Pamina lebet *noch*!" ("Pamina is *still* alive") are squeezed in, giving the false sense that soon she will not be. In passages like these, Mozart had separated himself from the text. That some of these rough spots resulted in grandiose music is another matter. One could list other such incongruities, but the connoisseur of *Die Zauberflöte* already has them at his fingertips; even lovers of the libretto know the offending places. Some of Papageno's spoken texts are relatively successful and often refreshingly funny. This is to Schikaneder's credit, for they are certainly his work.

The importance of *Die Zauberflöte* within Mozart's *oeuvre* has always been overestimated. The sacred, monumental quality—the waving of palm branches, the long robes, the pious processions—is strange and un-Mozartean; it seems as if they were forced upon him. The prosodic recitatives of the priests and near-priests, these strophic arias ("song-like structures" [Paul Nettl])—all this makes the opera into a work *sui generis* and inimitable, to be sure, but not something complete and successful within itself. To be sure, Mozart's music is for long stretches at its highest level. But it was conceived as an unpretentious entertainment, and is not equal to the pretentious claims made for it later.

There are errors in criticism of the opera which stem, not from the experience of the work itself, but from extraneous theoretical factors: the importance of the creator, the choice of a subject in accordance with an ethos (an essential element of *Fidelio*), the atmosphere and conditions of the composition. These factors tend to replace one's judgment about the thing itself, or at least they prejudice it, and their influence grows ever greater as each new judge adopts some of the existing opinions. The thing itself *has* to be good, for geniuses, even in the service of lesser minds, have to be great, right up to their dying day, which, in the case of the composer of *Die Zauber-flöte*, was not far off. Without doubt, this apotheosizing vision plays a role in judging the opera.

Again and again we have been made aware of the pathos of creativity, the "wrestling with one's genius," especially in the case of Beethoven, where even his (traditional) physiognomy suggests it. This has necessarily led to critical errors. Paradoxically, the composer is thought to be greatest not where his music sublimates the situation in life giving rise to it (both as a problem and as a work) but where the music seems to portray the act of mastering, either positively or negatively, these conditions. And, moreover, the triumph is to be represented thematically, as a final catharsis. In almost every program note, the concert public is asked to rate the degree of the creator's nobility in defying fate with his works. But we know nothing of how Mozart experienced his fate. He did know how to control it and compensate for it like no one else. And in his operas he was not just in his own company, but in that of his creations, their concerns, their laws (assuming they had them), laws which made it possible for him to penetrate their characters. It would be an injustice to the greatest of all musical geniuses to declare *Die Zauberflöte*—a work that did not offer him this opportunity—the sum total of his creative work, or his earthly swan song. It is rather a final demonstration of his tremendous ability to objectify, the brilliant response to a last challenge; but it is not his last will and testament.

It almost seems as if Mozart unconsciously wanted to avenge himself on the Masonic rule of male dominance by taking a special, fond interest in the female roles. The Three Ladies, for example, are a unique creation, a musical entity in and of themselves, which, however, never becomes purely instrument-like but remains always human and feminine. As they feast their eyes on Tamino in the A-flat major section of the introduction (No. 1), their quite unplatonic observation of masculine beauty draws its magic from the radical musical stylization of what Mozart had always rejected per se: stage asides, used continually and consistently. We remember the letter to his father from Munich on November 8, 1780, in which, discussing dramatic problems in *Idomeneo*, he wrote about "spoken asides." "In a dialogue all these things are quite natural, for a few words can be spoken aside hurriedly; but in an aria where the words have to be repeated, it has a bad effect . . ." In the case of the Three Ladies, it is not an aria but a trio; but Mozart surely wanted his remark in the letter (an instruction for the librettist Varesco about the way to write an opera text) to be understood as the contrast between recitative or spoken text and a musical number. The Three Ladies do not interact, so to speak, with each other. When they are not imparting directions they speak in "asides," first about the discovery of the "beautiful youth," then each about the other two ("Sie wären gern bei ihm allein"— "They'd gladly be alone with him . . ."). Again, Mozart is composing in quotation marks and obviously enjoying it. He ignored the insoluble problem of the "asides" (like all the insoluble problems of *Die Zauberflöte*) and composed a delightful rivalry scene for three girls, who here, compared with later scenes, still have a thoroughly fairylike quality.

"Pamina presents the sweetest form of all dream sweethearts, and because of the music with which she manifests herself, she is also the most significant" (Ernst Bloch). But not even to Pamina, his glorious musical creation, could Mozart give a logical dramatic line to accompany her on her way, as he had to the Countess Almaviva, whom she sometimes resembles in her music. Of course, she makes up for what she lacks in psychological individuality by the way she expresses general human feelings; in her, love and sadness and happiness are expressed directly. Her music is among the most sublime Mozart ever wrote. Her embodiment of objectified emotion is ultimately his doing; textually she is laid out as the most naïve person imaginable. Even if she corresponds to a pre-existing role model, she still remains the invention of Giesecke the mineralogist, a man who, unlike Da Ponte, knew nothing about women.

Although they tell us nothing about his condition per se, two tiny passages in the letters relating to Mozart's intellectual and emotional involvement in *Die Zauberflöte*, and his general frame of mind at the time, are characteristic of the relationship between his life and his work. On July 7, 1791, he wrote to Constanze, who was taking the waters in Baden with Süssmayr:

> Even my work gives me no pleasure, because I am accustomed to stop working now and then and exchange a few words with you. Alas! this pleasure is no longer possible. If I go to the piano and sing something out of my opera, I have to stop at once, for this stirs my emotions too deeply.

Such remarks are so rare for Mozart that they assume a special importance. Without doubt he was at this point aware of the futility of his life (from his own point of view) and, psychologically at least, in an unstable condition. Every attempt at success had foundered; we may say that he had given up. It is tempting, therefore, to assume that this "something out of my opera" was Pamina's G minor aria "Ach, ich fühl's . . ." (No. 17), with its longing for death; for it "stirs [our] emotions," too, if we want to put it that way. We seem to sense, in the heartbeat of this 6/8 andante, steady and stately, in these chromatic alterations of the *arpeggios*, that a human life is longing for exhaustion. In the four-bar postlude it rises once again to a crescendo and then, in one last measure, acquiesces and disappears. Of course, it is Pamina's life, her death wish, not her creator's. Once again we have that eternal mystery: is there an element of identification here or not? The key is G minor: it is here again, too, this apparent clue, this last resort of the critic. But do we really need it? If we call to mind the predecessor of this aria, Constanze's aria (No. 10) from *Die Entführung*, in which the key of G minor literally expresses *"Traurigkeit"* (sadness), we seem to be getting at the character of this key: "poignant pessimism." And our deduction would then be that because Mozart intended it for the sad mood of some of his female characters, it must therefore also have been used in the same way in his absolute music, especially in the G minor Symphony, K. 550, and the Quintet, K. 516. Most critics seem to have decided that this is a valid assumption. But as listeners we cannot go along with this kind of scheme. We must remember, for example, that someone like Osmin in *Die Entführung* also claims the key of G minor to represent the opposite principle: "Wer ein Liebchen hat gefunden" (No. 2), sung by this *miglior fratello* of Monostatos, is a less sublime use of the key perhaps, and yet in its way no less brilliant. One could list many such antitheses, but do we really need them?

Pamina: "Fühlst du nicht der Liebe Sehnen . . . so wird Ruh' im Tode sein" ("If you do not feel love, I will find peace in death"). This foggy thought, too, acquires a meaning only through the music, a meaning, in fact, so deep that it cannot be transposed back into words: it is a non-verbal existential statement. This is true music drama. Even if Pamina sang her musical line on one single vowel, the meaning would still be clear. It is the overwhelming subjective reality of the character, not of her creator. Any attempt to prove that he identified with her, even when his death six months later seems to give us the right, is a sentimental if seductive reading. Mozart betrays himself neither in words nor in music. Where the music seems to be a key, seems even to offer itself in that capacity, he erases the clues to its composition. Throughout his life, Mozart preferred whenever possible to act the part of a joker, in the unconscious desire that the things that moved him not be expressed in his extramusical or unmeditated life. He handled everyday relationships in a different way (to say he "cultivated" them would be too much). In the hours spent away from the world of music he was usually, almost until the end, determined not to be serious. He knew neither sentimentality nor self-pity; he was not a complainer, and in contrast to so many great artists, he was no hypochondriac. Of course, he often took advantage of an illness for his own purposes. Humor was a compulsion and a mask; the two could not be separated. At the time of his work on *Die Zauberflöte*, of course, he often had to let the mask fall. Not that he lacked a group of friends that would have assigned him, even then, the joker's role, and would have relied on his playing it until the bitter end: Schikaneder's clique, if we assess it correctly, was probably ready at any time to keep him in a good mood and to accept his caprices into the bargain. But he probably lacked the inner impulse, the initiative, the strength to jest in the old, free way. And yet his letters, up to two months before his death, reveal that he was still in the habit of making light of himself, his moods, and, especially, his situation. Thus, it is just as possible that a passage from an earlier letter refers to Pamina's aria: "From sheer boredom I composed today an aria for my opera," wrote Mozart on June 11, 1791, to Constanze. And perhaps the aria that "stirred his emotions" was "Der Vogelfänger bin ich ja, stets lustig, heisa hopsasa" ("The birdcatcher am I, merry always, heisa hopsasa").

Around this time, six months before his death, some enigmatic allusions in his letters to Constanze in Baden begin to suggest that he was for the first time deliberately making light of something; a mysterious, indefinable element appears between the lines. We have already mentioned the end of his letter of June 11, 1791, "I kiss you a thousand times and say with you in thought: 'Death and despair were his reward!'" Was Mozart using parody to make light of death? On July 5, he becomes clearer, his thought sadder:

> As soon as my business here is over, I shall be with you, for I mean to take a long rest in your arms; and indeed I shall need it, for this mental worry and anxiety and all the running about connected with it is really exhausting me.

Even here we cannot bring ourselves to conclude that he is referring to some knowledge of his fatal illness; the facts are too uncertain. *"Sono in procinto di spiràre"* ("I am on the point of death"): the letter to Da Ponte (if it is genuine) would not have been written until September, closer to his death. It would, of course, be compelling proof of his foreboding. A long rest in Constanze's arms: perhaps that was only a symbolic image for a longing he could no longer quiet, a longing for something indefinite and undefinable. If, perhaps, he did not want to live anymore, that does not necessarily imply the knowledge that soon he really *would* not live anymore. Some of the lines from his letters to Constanze, restless, excited, with inserted passages, digressions, intuitions tossed aside—all seem to point to something that must have been present unconsciously. Nothing in Mozart's early letters reveals passive surrender, indolence, or sloth. The phrase about death as man's dearest friend, in the letter to his father, is un-Mozartean in its speculative self-appeasement. The word "destiny" belonged neither to his vocabulary nor to his conceptual storehouse.

Up to the turning point of the Paris journey, Mozart's communications were direct, if one-sided, indications of his intense experience of life, vivid, unselfconscious comments about every kind of event, however commonplace. Later, however, Mozart tried, whenever possible, not without grim and bitter resentment, to perceive all of life as comic. Though not always successful, he often did succeed. In these late letters, he could do it no longer. The letters still report his apparently undiminished activity, visits to the opera, dinners at the inn Zur Krone; they mention rising at 5 a.m., regular music-making at gatherings or at dinners with friends, surprise morning visits, participation in a procession with "a candle in the hand" (pure hypocrisy, for he wanted to send his son Carl to the Piarists' seminary, the destination of the procession). Less than two months before his death, he writes of taking walks, of treating himself to magnificent cutlets (*"che gusto!"*) and eating them to Constanze's good health. After two rounds of billiards, he sells his horse, sends for black coffee, and drinks it while smoking "a splendid pipe of tobacco." Afterward he quickly orchestrates the third movement of the Clarinet Concerto for Stadler. Or he dines on "a delicious slice of sturgeon" and other delicacies, but is not satisfied, and since he has a "rather voracious appetite" he sends the valet for second helpings.

Is he diverting her from his real condition? We think that Constanze cannot have been too concerned, for Mozart was not ill, and anyway, she never was too concerned about what was going on in his mind.

Stretching the facts to feign a will to live? Perhaps. Possibly he needed to convince himself of it. Between some lines one senses the effort. Nevertheless, he certainly did indulge in these physical pleasures and thought that they were worth mentioning to Constanze; indeed, he was showing her, in a strange way, that he could get along even without her.

On the other hand, these letters often testify to his low spirits, especially when he had again not received a letter from Constanze (she probably hadn't written) or when a potential creditor had left him in the lurch. Among his jests, which now usually sound strained, we find brief insights into his inner turmoil, moments of depression he notices himself for the first time, and even comments on: "It is not at all good for me to be alone, when I have something on my mind." What does he mean by "on his mind"? Debts or music? For the first time he perceives that mysterious longing, though he does not know its object nor pursue it very far. His melancholy is as clear as his resolve to overcome it. His repeated wish that Constanze should not worry, that she be merry and cheerful, ultimately refers as much to himself; he is trying to cheer himself up, with varying degrees of success. In between, he warns her to conduct herself properly; we cannot measure to what degree he was identifying with her here, either. Was this also self-admonition? The constantly reappearing cause of these admonitions is the unknown factor, a figure, a man: N.N. As puzzling as a palimpsest, but ever-present, the initials were crossed out of the manuscripts by Nissen, stubbornly and consistently, especially when they obviously had something to do with Süssmayr (for this mysterious N.N. is by no means always the same person). Nissen was not able to erase all traces of these apparent lapses; here and there he forgot to, and then Süssmayr appears. Thus, for example, in Mozart's very last letter, in the postscript to Constanze on October 14, 1791, we find: ". . Do what you like with N.N. Adieu." Mozart's last extant written statement! Constanze seems to have followed his instructions, at least as far as was in her power.

N.N. *Nomen Nescio* (name unknown) or *Notetur Nomen* (let the name be noted), or however one chooses to interpret it (perhaps originally *Numerius Negidius*, name of the defendant), this abbreviation is found strewn throughout Mozart's letters to Constanze during the last years. Besides Süssmayr, the main figure, we can also identify a creditor, a suspicious individual, and a chance acquaintance. Now and then we find two N.N.s in one line, each a different one, as is clear from the context. Thus, we do not know who entered into a new financial deal with Mozart when Puchberg came up with too little; we do not know whose attentions Mozart is warning his wife against, or who it was who had a "taste" for her. "N.N. (you know whom I mean) is a cad." Who might that be? "In my opinion you are too free and easy with N.N. . . . and it was the same with N.N. when he was still at Baden. Now please remember that N.N. are not half so familiar with other women . . . as they are with you." Who are these two? Could Constanze keep them straight? Did she know at once who was meant? Did she remember all these different people when, many years later, she and Nissen put the correspondence in order? And what about the missing letters? Did Constanze destroy them before Nissen saw them, or did they read through them together, saying here and there, "Not this one!"? In any event, for both of them the name Süssmayr was taboo.

Constanze had frequented the baths in Baden since 1789, for a week at a time, but irregularly. She was usually in the company of Süssmayr, who was Mozart's pupil, but also (as Constanze emphasized meaningfully to the Novellos) the sometime pupil of Mozart's more fortunate rival Salieri. What Süssmayr had to do in Baden can no longer be determined. Did Mozart really prefer him to "protect" Constanze rather than have him near at hand, to copy out the parts for *Die Zauberflöte*, or to prepare the recitatives for *Tito*? Whatever the reason, scores had to be sent back and forth between Vienna and Baden, which cost time and money.

On July 26, 1791, Constanze gave birth to a son, Franz Xaver (Süssmayr's names) Wolfgang. What role had Süssmayr played since August 1789? Had he been obliged to watch over the ailing woman? How ailing was she? We know she was well enough for Mozart to admonish her in the above-mentioned letter of August 1789:

A woman must always make herself respected, or else people will begin to talk about her. My love! Forgive me for being so frank, but my peace of mind demands it as well as our mutual happiness. Remember that you yourself once admitted to me that you were inclined to *comply too easily*. You know the consequences of that. Remember too the promise you gave to me. Oh, God, do try, my love! Be merry

and happy and charming to me. Do not torment yourself
and me with unnecessary jealousy. Believe in my love, for
surely you have proofs of it, and you will see how happy
we shall be. Rest assured that it is only by her prudent behavior that a wife can enchain her husband. Adieu.

A strange letter. Guilt and accusations seem intermingled, and
both probably have a certain justification. What makes us prick
up our ears is this "enchain her husband." Does it mean that
he felt (as things stood) that he was free of chains?

But let us stay first with Constanze. Why would she and
Nissen consistently make Süssmayr's name illegible, whether it
was spelled out or implied, but, on the other hand, retain and
make public a passage like this one? Constanze's role, of course,
can concern us only secondarily, and yet an examination of
her behavior leads us to a central question: what moved Constanze to entrust the unfinished Requiem not to Süssmayr, as
Mozart had specifically ordered, according to her own statement of January 1, 1826, but rather to a different pupil,
Joseph Eybler? Only when the latter refused (we are not completely sure that he did not first have a go at it) was she
forced to give it to Süssmayr, for she needed the money. Later
in 1826, when asked about it again after Nissen's death, she
wrote, "I offered it to Eybler to complete because I was angry
(why, I do not know) with Süssmayr." Constanze, then, who
remembers so much, most of it unimportant, claims not to
remember why, in this critical period of her life, she was angry
with Süssmayr. We cannot believe it.

On the other hand, we cannot answer the question, either.
It is possible (let us be cautious) that she was having a love
affair with Süssmayr. It is also possible that she wanted to
marry him after Mozart's death, and that the younger man
rejected her. The theory has been advanced that Franz Xaver
Wolfgang was Süssmayr's son.[73] We can deduce nothing from
Hansen's portrait of the two surviving Mozart sons in 1798. If
Franz Xaver Wolfgang was indeed Mozart's child, he was born
at least seventeen days too early: nine months before his birth,
in October 1790, Mozart was away on a journey, and returned

only on November 10. Mozart's crude, toward the end positively taunting, heartiness vis-à-vis Süssmayr leaves open many possibilities for a relationship improper in some way we can no longer understand, a relationship of submissiveness, perhaps, or indifference, of understanding or even complicity. Perhaps Constanze had had no love affair with Süssmayr; perhaps she was "angry with him" because he informed his friend and teacher Mozart about her overly free ways and her affairs with those other N.N.s. Perhaps he was not the object of the husband's repeated reproaches, but had provoked them as his informant. To whom, then, had she been "inclined to comply too easily"? And above all, what were "the consequences of that"? A year later, Mozart writes: "Do what you will with N.N. Adieu." Does that mean "I don't care"?

We do not want to become attorneys in a *chronique scandaleuse*. As far as Constanze is concerned, the puzzle is unimportant and trivial. But we would like to know more about Mozart's stolid tolerance of what he must at least have suspected, more about the reasons for his remaining tolerant under all circumstances, and for his suffering that which pained him.

Or toward the end of his life did it no longer pain him? Did he, in the last months of life, not even have to be so tolerant? Did he, in the end, not want to let himself be "enchained"?

On July 7, 1791, Mozart writes to Constanze in Baden:

> You cannot imagine how I have been aching for you all this long while. I can't describe what I have been feeling—a kind of emptiness, which hurts me dreadfully—a kind of longing, which is never satisfied, which never ceases, and which persists, nay rather increases daily.

This is perhaps the most moving passage in all his letters. It is so rare and appears so unexpectedly, and he dwells with intensity on something he had never expressed before. All at once, and very late, we witness this deep insight into his soul, an insight he himself would have found horrifying in earlier times. And yet he betrays nothing to us about the kind of emptiness he feels, nothing about the longing which is never satisfied and therefore never abates. Constanze cannot satisfy it; she is not even a substitute satisfaction, and he refrains from appealing to her. He is writing about himself, without considering what it is he longs for. Yet two days later (July 9) he writes:

> At the same time I do think that in this fine weather Baden must be very pleasant for you and most beneficial to your health, as there are such glorious walks there. You yourself must feel this more than anyone. So if you find that the air and exercise thoroughly agree with you, stay a little longer. I shall come and fetch you or, if you like, spend a few days with you.

This is quite a different tone, more resolute than that of two days before. It is probably only a coincidence that the *"du"* in the original letter is no longer capitalized, and yet we suddenly have the impression that Mozart is not unhappy to have his wife in Baden. He can do all right in Vienna without her. On October 8, too, less than two months before his death, he writes:

> I hope that these baths will help you to keep well during the winter. For only the desire to see you in good health made me urge you to go to Baden.

That sounds like a bad conscience. Apparently he had been the motivating factor this time; he had been the one to suggest the trip. Did Mozart, who could not bear solitude, want to be rid of her? Was he, when he was "alone," not alone? His wish for his wife to build up her health in Baden for the winter would lead us to conclude that at this time, less than two months before his death, he was still not thinking of dying, or at least that he did not share this thought with Constanze. There are none of the forebodings which he seems to have harbored three months earlier.

The darkness surrounding Mozart's last months can hardly be cleared up now. We are dependent on his intimations and on the cryptic remarks of some of his companions. In his own writing there are certain omissions, like isolated unconscious bits of information, less the distortion of the truth than a purposeful concealment through circumlocution. Where, on the journey to Frankfurt in September 1790, did he "on three occasions rest a little at night," he, who was so used to traveling by coach? The carriage was so "splendid" that he "wanted to give it a kiss." He was not ill: in Regensburg he "lunched magnificently to the accompaniment of divine music; we had angelic cooking and some glorious Moselle wine." He was indeed traveling with his brother-in-law Hofer, but he surely joined in everything himself. The two had even taken along a servant; they were spared all inconvenience. On his trip to Berlin with Lichnowsky in 1789, he wrote to Constanze from Dresden that he had received on the previous day "a very handsome snuff box" from the Elector of Saxony. He jokingly imitated the Saxon dialect to cover the fact that the box had contained 100 ducats. We do not know what he did with the money. Nor do we know whether Constanze believed his story that the box had been empty.

In 1791, however, cheerful accounts like this one gradually cease. He declines to a lower level of existence. His former patrons do not notice his descent. As far as the people who shared in his splendid Viennese period are concerned, his "dearest, most beloved friends," he no longer seems to exist. Thus, documentation of his decline comes only in subsequent commentaries. After Mozart's death, the rumors of his reckless living spread, but they were always vague. What does Friedrich Schlichtegroll, Mozart's first biographer, mean when he speaks of his "marked sensuality"?[74] And Karoline Pichler must have heard about Mozart's "thoughtless way of life" somewhere; there was an element of Biedermeier prudery involved, no doubt, but she must have had some reason to say what she did.

The rumor about Mozart's dissolute life endured stubbornly. Even in 1827, thirty-six years after Mozart's death, Carl Friedrich Zelter wrote on August 19 to Goethe:

> Mozart was born two years before me, and we remember only too well the circumstances of his death. Mozart, who had been so soundly taught that he could compose easily enough to still have time for hundreds of things besides— dallying with women and the like—had thereby run his good natural disposition into the ground.

We have good reason to ask what Zelter might have understood by Mozart's "good natural disposition." And when he follows "women" with "the like" he makes himself a narrow-minded prig rather than the subject of his comments a degenerate. Of course, where anecdotes abound, it is hard to determine the truth. It is common knowledge that the number of ladies who did not leave Mozart entirely cold is legion. But there is probably no longer anything authentic to be learned about Mozart's very last, perhaps desperate search for diversion during the time of his deepest solitude. No one wanted to talk about it, and the honest Novellos were not only too tactful to explore in this direction but even cut off their informants, as we have seen, as soon as they threatened to touch on baser topics.

"And where did I sleep? At home, of course," wrote Mozart rather casually, in a later letter (June 25, 1791) to Constanze in Baden. We must remember that he never paid too much attention to the literal truth, unless it could be expressed in conventional forms. Nevertheless, Constanze seems to have inquired about his daily (and nightly) activities. She knew little about the company he kept when she was away and did not have much contact with Schikaneder's group, either; it was thought to be dissolute. There is, incidentally, a strange message from Schikaneder to Mozart on September 5, 1790. It reads, "Dear Wolfgang, I am sending you back your pa pa pa. It will be all right . . . This evening we will see each other at the usual—places. Your Schikaneder."[75] The "pa pa pa" probably refers to a discussion between the composer and the librettist about the effectiveness of stuttering, which Michael Kelly had already introduced in *Figaro*. But we can hardly imagine what the "usual—places" could be. The dash suggests a surrogate term for a locale that could not so easily be mentioned by name, or perhaps an ironic code name Mozart and Schikaneder had agreed upon. As mentioned before, Schikaneder was concerned about Mozart's well-being, because he had to keep him artistically productive. Possibly, in addition to "gluttony," he offered him "lechery" as well.

The letters of the last months are highly suggestive, yet we do not always understand what they are saying. Written during weeks of extreme, often hectic activity, both in his work and in his daily life, they reflect an exceedingly tense frame of mind, sometimes an almost hysterical energy. Crammed full of minute diary-like reports, they are strangely overarticulate. Sometimes we find the most prosaic news presented with fierce precision and embellished with a kind of humor that grows more violent and vigorous the more intensely Mozart is involved with his last great works, and the closer he is to death. He becomes more and more exact in specifying the petty details that are intended to elicit laughter in the recipient, who is usually Constanze. It is as if he himself had need of them, so he might laugh, too. Although the verbal wit has become duller, he consciously makes fun of the dullness; sometimes we find a surly aggressiveness indicating a deeper turmoil, as if his aggression were concealing, in a man who had given up, a desperate need to laugh. Thus, he wrote to Constanze two months before his death (October 7 and 8, 1791):

Give Süssmayr a few sound boxes on the ear from me, and I ask Sophie H., whom I kiss a thousand times, to give him a couple too. For Heaven's sake do not let him starve in this respect. The last thing in the world I could wish would be his reproach that you had not treated or looked after him properly. Rather give him too many blows than too few.

An outburst of unnerving facetiousness; he seems furious in some deeply hidden, inadmissible way. Again we must ask about Süssmayr's guilt and trespasses. Did he really deserve this obvious, almost rhapsodic aggression? Or had Mozart's gallows humor gone too far?

In the letters of the last months we find, closely juxtaposed, expressiveness followed by outbursts, calmness followed by emotion that can only be explained as the sign of a deep disturbance. Even if we examine the letters dispassionately, even if we disallow the questionable letter to Da Ponte, we cannot fight off the impression that Mozart did in the last analysis see death coming nearer, and not as "man's dearest friend," but as a tremendous irritant, a destructive spoilsport. But does that make him a sick man?

If we assume that "being healthy" is an absolute state in which the objective condition is in accord with subjective feeling, and does not exist solely in relation to the particular individual who enjoys or does not enjoy good health, then one would have to say that Mozart was never, in our sense of the word, healthy. Geniuses are rarely healthy (Goethe is an exception), for their creativity is determined by a constitutional anomaly.

If it is really the mind that builds the body, it is no coincidence that great minds have almost never considered it useful to develop their physique. They have always preferred to have sickly, delicate, unassuming bodies, so they might confront their physical weakness and overcome it again and again. Let it be noted, we are speaking here of *great* minds, not of *healthy* minds. The healthy mind may well develop a healthy body, but no one is interested in that, except philistines, whose ideal, whose collective wish fulfillment is expressed in the words "*mens sana in corpore sano.*"

Mozart had no ailment that might have kept him from completing his workload, however heavy it was, however unstructured and unpredictable, even chaotic. Except for a brief period in 1790, when his productivity lessened both qualitatively and quantitatively, we know of no setbacks due to illness. As an adult, Mozart canceled no trips because of sickness; no concert obligations, no commissions went unfulfilled because of the state of his health. It is said that on his last journey, from August 28 to September 25, 1791, he was sick in Prague and had even been ill when he set out, that he took medicine constantly and that his condition forced him to gloomy premonitions. But Constanze is the only source for this information: Nissen and Niemtschek got it from her, and set about constructing the legend of Mozart's death. During the eighteen days of this sojourn he copied out the last third of *Tito*, part of it in inns during the journey, part in the Duscheks' villa, and wherever else he had the opportunity. He conducted *Don Giovanni* on September 2, and *Tito* four days later on September 6; four days after that, on September 10, he visited the Freemason lodge *Zur Wahrheit und Einigkeit* (Truth and Unity), where his cantata "Die Maurerfreude," K. 471, was performed (we do not know whether he himself conducted); and shortly before his departure he composed, like a bonus, the bass aria in E-flat "Io ti lascio, o cara, addio," K. Anh. 245/621a. Constanze challenged its authenticity energetically, but in vain, which leads us to wonder who this "cara" may have been: perhaps no one more mysterious than Josepha Duschek. Be that as it may, this schedule does not seem like that of a sick man. It seems probable that he took the failure of *Tito* ("German hogwash") to heart and that it may have had an effect on his productivity, if indeed we can dare to compare our own nervous system (or the typical nervous system of today's creative artists) with his.

Mozart himself probably paid no attention to his health, insofar as it did not directly influence his musical activities. Although he never went hungry, either as a child or as an adult, he certainly did not plan his diet along principles of good health. Nor did any of his contemporaries. Later, his eating patterns grew more and more irregular, but perhaps he was no exception in that regard, either. Indeed, we cannot judge to what degree, if at all, the physical well-being of a man of that period and in that situation was influenced by his eating (or living) habits, assuming he was not taking (or being given) poison.

Two months before his death, after he had sold his horse, his only exercise was the "favorite walk" he took daily, whenever he could, until he began to die. So he did not do much for his physical well-being. It was not his style, nor was it the style of the age; nor had his father, however much he liked to play the doctor in acute cases, taught him to watch his health. But Mozart was certainly never conscious of his self-neglect; at least, no remark to that effect has been discovered. We never find even the hint of a thought that he should do or stop doing this or that for the sake of his physical health—and incidentally, not for the sake of his spiritual health, either. Now and then in his letters we find evidence of momentary, sometimes serious ill health, or sudden pains, but no conscious indication of the symptoms of a disease. Of course, he may have kept back any kind of presentiment. But *we* cannot help having the impression that he usually felt well physically. Not until the day after the performance of the "Kleine Freimaurerkantate," K. 623, which he conducted himself in the lodge *Zur neugekrönten Hoffnung* on November 18, 1791, did he feel that he would "soon have played himself out." Suddenly he no longer wants to drink his wine in the inn *Zur silbernen Schlange*. He asks the factotum, Joseph Deiner, who is always at his service, to finish his glass for him, and he lies down for the last time. Even if the actions and the wording of this report are not purely anecdotal, the manifold embroideries on his lying down "never to rise again" certainly are. We need not concern ourselves with them.

In some of his letters we are not sure whether Mozart is deliberately making his condition sound worse than it is or whether he is using his illness as an unconscious means to an end. On August 14, 1790, he wrote to Puchberg:

Dearest Friend and Brother,

Whereas I felt tolerably well yesterday, I am absolutely wretched today. I could not sleep all night for pain. I must have got overheated yesterday from walking so much and then without knowing it have caught a chill. Picture to yourself my condition—ill and consumed with worries and anxieties. Such a state quite definitely prevents me from recovering. In a week or a fortnight I shall be better off—certainly—but at present I am in want! Can you not help me out with a trifle? The *smallest* sum would be very welcome just now. You would, for the moment at least, bring peace of mind to your true friend, servant and brother

W. A. Mozart

Puchberg sent him ten gulden—too little, of course. But the letter is not convincing as a depiction of illness, and also suggests, incidentally, that Mozart did not connect his ill health with a recurrent disease but saw it more as an effect of his poverty, whether deserved or not. Even if pain caused by a chill is an amateur's diagnosis, during these summer months he probably really was sick enough at times to have to stay in bed, and was therefore physically handicapped. His limited productivity attests to this: he wrote a few piano sonata movements, mostly fragments, and an adaptation of Handel's oratorio "Alexander's Feast," K. 591, probably a commission from van Swieten, which was to make him better off "in a week or a fortnight." Immediately after the letter, he wrote a "comical [!] duet for soprano and bass" in F, "Nun, liebes Weibchen, ziehst mit mir," K. 625/592a, so distressingly weak that we would like to doubt its authorship, unless in this case illness really is to blame.

But until the crisis (which some like to call an apotheosis) of the last year and a half, Mozart rarely complained about the state of his health. Perhaps he was ill during the times when he did not write letters, but the fact that his musical productivity was so constant also makes any lengthy illness unlikely.

As an adolescent, on the Italian journeys, he complained about being indisposed. We are not surprised, for he had to master huge programs and his capacity to absorb had undoubtedly worn thin. And not only his body suffered from the exigencies of travel; they affected his spirit as well, and he was often ill humored, as at the departure from Salzburg in December 1769 in icy cold weather. It was an unhappy winter's journey of several days to Bolzano ("that pigsty"); there followed the wearisome trip by coach from Rome to Naples, the obligatory return journey back to Rome, twenty-seven hours without interruption. Still, travel in the south did him good: his postscripts to his sister reveal a mind stimulated and sharpened by new experiences; his keen powers of observation are seasoned with a critical outlook, by skepticism and doubts about the quality of his own impressions. Sometimes he complains about lack of sleep and fatigue. Probably his physical maturation and creative overactivity combined to produce an inner compulsiveness. He may have been obliged to fulfill his assignments, but he also wanted to, independently of the discipline imposed upon him by his father.

Although Mozart as a child was seriously, perhaps even dangerously ill on two occasions, it was in both cases the result of an epidemic: typhus in The Hague in 1765 and smallpox in Olmütz in 1767. There has been no convincing proof that the journeys permanently damaged his health. His powers of resistance were great enough to withstand them, just as, to our amazement, he withstood other grave situations later.

We can detect in Mozart's life no illness, recognizable as such, that builds up and then stays latent for long periods. True, the descriptive vocabulary of his time would not extend far enough to give us any coherent picture of a disease; we find even the terms for symptoms strangely vague, if not absurd: an "alteration" can mean practically anything; what was called a "catarrh" is only in part what we understand by the word today. We usually get the impression that sicknesses took other forms in those days, or vice versa, that different illnesses hid behind the recognizable symptoms. Mozart's first son died at the age of two months (August 21, 1783) from *Gedärmfrais*, (intestinal cramp); Nannerl's son fell ill with *Mehlhund* (thrush) (September 1785); and we can no longer reliably tell the cause of Mozart's mother's death, even from the extensive medical report (June 28, 1778). Mozart himself died, we are told, of a "severe miliary fever." We are happy to acknowledge modern diagnoses of his diseases (there are at least three divergent ones) as examples of scientific diligence; we only object to the categorical certainty with which they have sometimes been presented, for they are ultimately proof only of their own fallibility. We cannot succeed in integrating the idea of Mozart as a sick man into our consciousness. We see him neither as "ailing" nor as "suffering" nor as "rallying," not even before his death. We would be tempted to assert that his dignity and self-control forbade him to attribute any of these conditions to himself or to characterize himself by them, although such an interpretation would be dictated by wishful thinking. It really does seem impossible to imagine his having any attributes which do not spring from his own world of thought. Here lies the central riddle: how did Mozart experience himself? One can objectify oneself in one's work, but one cannot entirely shut out all mental and physical experiences. Even if he was able often enough to forget his suffering (if he suffered!) through work, it must have come over him again when he stopped working. What kind of pains did he experience then, what forebodings did they trigger? Did his feelings go beyond the direct sensations of the moment? And in what way did he fear for the future of his body?

The wealth of documentation, primarily from Mozart himself, and secondarily and less weightily from contemporaries, has seduced us into thinking that we "know about Mozart." But we must remember that his self-documentation, which he, of course, never thought of as such, is, almost to the end, no conscious reflection of his emotional state. On the contrary, it is discretion passing for communication. As far as we can determine, it is devastating proof of a self-control the like of which great men rarely display. Except for the "bread and butter" letters to Puchberg, as terse as they are tragic, or the almost parenthetically brief revelations to Constanze in the last months, what he felt most deeply can be read only between the lines or, if he was composing at the time, not at all. His diversionary vocabulary, whether conscious or unconscious, is designed not to expose his real attitude (or his real intentions) except where the exposure will help him attain his own ends. Many of his communications, the letters to Puchberg included, are true compositions in this dodging counterpoint.

But we must also remember that there were long silent periods, periods for which we have only very scanty information and even scantier documentation, years in which the Mozart family remained together or in which, after his father's death, Constanze's presence or that of other potential correspondents made writing superfluous. We cannot even guess what went on in Mozart's extramusical life during these periods. His music gives us no more and no less information about it than does a novel about the inner life of its author. It stimulates us to guess, but never gives us answers.

It is, therefore, not impossible that he often felt worse than the documents would indicate. Nevertheless, we do not find it easy to subscribe to the thesis that Mozart went through life a sick man, predestined for an early end. Many of his "dearest, most beloved friends" did not live to be so old: Barisani, Therese von Trattner, Hatzfeld, Jacquin, Stephen Storace, Sigmund Haffner the younger. Many of his circle died not much older than he: Hunczowsky, Hofer, Marianne Kirchgässner, Süssmayr—we must not think of Haydn as typical. If Mozart really was ill, his complaint must have been in remission for years at a time. Medicine does know of such cases; perhaps it did not know of them at that time, but they must have existed. Then there would be a tremendous difference between objective findings (insofar as they were clear) and subjective feelings, which were clear only to Mozart himself. Perhaps his maladies were more grave than he himself admitted. He refrains from mentioning them in his letters. Mozart did not complain, nor did he make accusations, unless his honor was at stake. Even if we do not think his self-control is conscious, let alone intentional, and even if he seems rather to be unconsciously suppressing that part of his physical being which he did not deem worthy of mention (in contrast to that other part, about which he made merry until late in his life), the mysterious element in the figure of Mozart remains not least his ability to objectify what he, too, must have experienced as nearly unbearable: his physical decay.

If he had been given the posts he strove for, let alone the ones he dreamed of, if he had been granted a regulated existence like Haydn's, for example, would Mozart then have lived longer? The question is unanswerable, since we cannot imagine the "late" Mozart in royal service; we can visualize him engaged as an artist, but not as a servant. We are tied not only to the image of a Mozart who sought security but, if we look a little deeper, we are forced to accept the image of a Mozart who finally rejected any offer of security. Of course, he was galled by his insecurity, but who can say whether he could have borne the restrictions an exacting service might have imposed. It is unimaginable that he might have remained with the Archbishop Colloredo, for example, as his father had done, even though—aside from his unsatisfactory professional career—the twenty-four-year-old must have been quite happy there in his private life; at least, he had it a good deal easier than he did later during his "free" life in Vienna.

Ultimately, however, he did not want to have it easy. The vague thoughts of the "splendid life" he wanted to lead with

Constanze would have been dearly bought. "I will work—
work so hard—that no unforeseen accidents shall ever reduce
us to such desperate straits again," he wrote to his wife on
September 28, 1790, from Frankfurt. And he did work. But the
"desperate straits" continued. How desperate were they, really,
and of what did their desperation consist? The "accidents"
recurred and can have been "unforeseen" only in his own
view. Employees like Haydn and Salieri did not need to slave
away as he did. Of course, they drew in more than 800 gulden a year; they were Kapellmeisters, not mere "chamber
composers." The claim that "the most pleasant thing of all is
to have a mind at peace" (October 8, 1791) was a halfhearted,
already hopeless attempt to buck himself up; as an insight it
came too late. Even as a wish-fulfillment dream, in his case it
probably could never have been realized: Mozart was not made
for a peaceful life. His inner motor did not permit him passive
contemplation; he was not in control of his mobility, or even
of his physical reflexes. He never would have rested; he could
not rest even in Constanze's arms, only in death. At the time of
this insight, he knew that he could no longer buy himself "a
pleasant life," even if he took on the most artistically unac-
ceptable commissions, for nothing he was offered could bring
in enough to pay his debts.

Among the unsatisfactory commissions of this period
are three works for an instrument that certainly cannot have
sounded much better than a hurdy-gurdy: the "Adagio und
Allegro für ein Orgelwerk in einer Uhr," K. 594, begun in
October, on the Frankfurt journey, and completed in Vienna
in December 1790; the "Orgelstück für eine Uhr" (allegro and
adagio, K. 608, March 3, 1791); and the "Andante für eine
Walze in eine kleine Orgel," K. 616 (May 4, 1791). From
these clumsy entries in his catalogue of works we see that
Mozart himself did not know exactly what to call the mechanical instrument, which he found extremely unsympathetic and
"childish"-sounding. These pieces were commissioned by

Count Deym for the wax museum he had created, a collection of fanciful monuments to recently deceased men of note. The first two of the three works are masterpieces, not just as the supreme mastery of a disagreeable task, composing program fodder for a discordant automatic music box no bigger than a baby's bassinet, but also as integral pieces of absolute music. Indeed, their absolute quality gives them life, for in this case nothing could be expressed by instrumental timbre. The first two pieces are in a profoundly serious, almost intimidating F minor (the third, K. 616, in F major, is weaker and more conventional); they are high points of Mozartean achievement, of a unique logical power, which in K. 608 culminates in an exciting double fugue. This is funeral music written to order, a perfect fulfillment of the customer's request, like the Masonic Funeral Music, but in this case not for instruments of his own choosing but rather for a music box that played the music automatically on the hour. Profound music for a mechanical box, an almost tragicomic configuration, at the very least a "triumph of mind over matter."*

In addition, there were the miscellaneous works written as favors for this or that instrumentalist. At least we cannot imagine that the Adagio and Rondo for armonica (or musical glasses), flute, oboe, viola, and cello, K. 617 (May 23, 1791), grew out of an inner urgency. Rather, the blind virtuoso Marianne Kirchgässner had asked him for it, and he wrote what she desired, a beautiful "sensitive" C minor adagio, flowing into (in our opinion) a really dull rondo, which hardly conveys any inner involvement on his part. In the final analysis, the concert audience in the Burgtheater on June 10, 1791, had really come to observe the dexterity of a blind woman.

His last instrumental work, and his last great completed work of any kind, the Clarinet Concerto, K. 622, composed in October 1791, a few weeks before his death, is a different

---

* "In spite, however, of the distasteful nature of the task, Mozart's integrity rose superior to the artificial medium, thus achieving in both this piece [K. 594] and K. 608 a notable triumph of mind over matter." A. Hyatt King, *Mozart in Retrospect* (Oxford, 1970).

matter. It, too, was written as a favor, for Anton Stadler, his friend and inspiration until the end. We have the impression that Stadler had said to himself, "I have to get something good out of this Mozart before he's finished; let him sing one more time, even if it should be his swan song."

The basset clarinet, for which the concerto is written, is now obsolete; it died out like the basset horn. Its range is lower than the clarinet's; when played on it, the concerto achieves a different effect due to its "unbroken" intervals; it becomes heavier, more momentous, less agreeable, but more transparent. In addition, however, it becomes a definitive Mozartean statement: let me show you (for the last time) what a wind concerto should be—*cantabile*, free of virtuoso decorations, dense, but never thick. Of course Mozart would never have said this in so many words, nor would he ever have reflected on his unique contribution to wind music. He never thought, "No one else has ever done anything like this." Therefore, it is for us to assert, not only that no composer in the genre before or after him ever even approximated the quality of Mozart wind concerti, but also that his treatment of the woodwinds has never been surpassed. They are combined with a precision that never hardens into a pattern; pure melody and *cantabile* style are differentiated to achieve enormous suggestivity in instrumental timbre (think of the woodwinds' role in the great piano concerti). Only two composers ever matched him in this: Berlioz and Mahler.

The autograph of the Clarinet Concerto has been lost. His good friend Stadler may not be entirely innocent in the matter; he probably allowed some of Mozart's works to vanish, and published some smaller ones as his own. Thus, the last Mozart manuscripts we have are for the Masonic Cantata, K. 623, of November 15, 1791, which he himself conducted in the lodge *Zur neugekrönten Hoffnung* two weeks before his death; the entries of the beginning bars of his last works into his thematic catalogue; and, last of all, the torso of the Requiem.

In contrast to the handwriting of his letters, which betrays a depressive state of mind not least in the increasing downward slope of the lines, the music is written clearly, as vital as ever, legible down to every note stem and head, the beams as straight as arrows. Nothing is hasty, everything is even and controlled: thoughts from a clear mind, undistorted by illness or confusion. Nothing here, at any rate, would suggest that Mozart, twenty days before his death, was even frail. We are inclined to believe Constanze when she tells the Novellos that he died of a sudden fever ("that fever which kills him suddenly"), thus supporting the theory that Mozart's earlier illnesses had nothing to do with his death.[76]

For physicians, analysis of a medical history of the past is a seductive game with many possibilities. Yet it can only be speculation, of course. Since nothing can be demonstrated any longer, let alone proven, the researcher can proceed to improve upon or refute the competing theories, according to his evaluation of the material. The result certainly makes informative, often fascinating reading, but no interpretation can be bent into a conclusive whole. Too many factors in the life and death, not only of Mozart, but also of other figures from before the age of scientific diagnoses, justify the assumption that not only the mind but also the body changes over the centuries, at least in reaction to varying conditions of life, its rules and irregularities. As mentioned before, a sixteen-hour journey in a badly sprung coach over cobblestones, or a banquet of fourteen overseasoned courses, would do us in. Can we imagine the constitution and resistance of a man like Cervantes, for example, whose left hand was maimed in the battle of Lepanto, who nevertheless remained a soldier until he was taken into captivity in Algeria, where he vegetated for five years, who then became a bank official in Spain, spent another five years in prison for embezzlement, and in his last impoverished years wrote a literary masterpiece? Or in the non-creative sphere: how do we visualize a Mary Stuart, who sits through nineteen cold winters in the icy, stinking, filthy rooms of her prison, increasingly eaten away by illness, and plans a Catholic revolution, writing flattering letters to her aunt (commonly called her cousin), Queen Elizabeth, while plotting her murder and embroidering anagrams on doilies? In these cases our imagination balks, both at such hearts and at such bodies. Perhaps it has been proven that medical practice in the past had other forces to combat; but it has not been proven that the body itself is subject to changes determined by time, as well as by environment. Perhaps it can no longer be proven, but if we consider the histories of diseases of the past, it is hard to find any other explanation.

Mozart's late but rapid decline, after long periods of intensive work rarely interrupted by illness or indisposition; his brief, almost breathless act of dying, his sudden death after a coma of only two hours—all this seems to demand a better explanation than the one furnished by traditional medicine (although we do not wish to suggest that some other kind of medicine would be able to furnish it). Only ten hours before his death, Mozart attempted to rehearse the Requiem with his friends, but the claim, originating with Constanze, that he actually worked on it on his deathbed is mistaken. One look at the autograph belies it: we have before us the script of a man who is to all intents and purposes healthy, a man with a clear mind, showing no trace of exhaustion, no slackening or sign of trembling (the unavoidable reflex of the moribund). He clearly did not write one note lying down.

"A severe miliary fever." This absurd-sounding diagnosis of Mozart's illness strikes us, first of all, as coming closer to the truth, the grim truth, than any other. Pustules was the name for the eruption of the skin that befell Mozart in the final stage of his mortal illness; today the concept refers to an inconsequential skin disease. It describes symptoms more than a cause. A severe miliary fever—that was the cause of death in the official version of the facts, in the coroner's records and on the death roll of the parish. It seems to have been one of those illnesses whose treatment was confined essentially to bloodletting. Carl Bär states that in his last twelve days Mozart was bled of two to three liters of blood; he does not exclude the possibility that he actually died from loss of blood. Mozart would not have been the only one. In our opinion, this hypothesis is more than clear. We are horrified when we read about treatments of the time—the dispensing of emetics as cure-alls, or that "black powder," of which Mozart, too, must have swallowed more than was good for him.

The scantiness and imprecision of all information from both Mozart and his contemporaries lead us to assume that he did die of an acute illness and not from a prolonged complaint. Thus, whatever the genesis of his earlier indispositions and discomforts, he did not go through life a sick man. From this point of view, Bär's theory of rheumatic fever seems more acceptable than the others, though on condition that Mozart did not die of the treatment, from the application of these radical, apparently arbitrary methods; to the detriment of his general state, they gave the sick man momentary relief.

Also coming under the heading of death by treatment is the gradually disappearing theory of mercury poisoning.[77] It cannot be sustained in its present form: even late into our own century the theory was expanded in certain obscure but eloquent quarters (which we need not investigate here) into a legend of murder by poison. Theory and legend have since become inseparable. Later mystifications are not solely to blame: the rumor of poisoning had been spread even among Mozart's contemporaries, though in an oddly restrained, almost indifferent way, as if nothing could be done about it. We have noted that the contemporaries of a genius can seldom be believed without qualification, since their memory begins to blossom only when it promises to bear fruit. They hope that a glimmer of the remembered man's immortality will likewise descend upon them. But although no one could expect reflected glory from deliberately misrepresenting the circumstances of Mozart's death, not one eyewitness describes the conditions of any illness known to us or to them. A uremic coma, about which various posthumous diagnoses agree, is the final stage of several diseases, including mercury poisoning.

In his last weeks, according to Constanze, Mozart several times expressed the suspicion that he was being poisoned. "I know I must die; someone has given me aqua tofana," he told her, or at least this is what she told Mary Novello in 1829. Aqua tofana was a slow-working arsenic poison, common in the seventeenth and eighteenth centuries. It was named after its inventor and first dispenser, Teofania di Adamo (a strange claim to immortality), who not only prepared and marketed it but, before her execution, left the formula to her daughter, who carried on the business. Mozart must have known about this popular method of disposal; even if he did make such a remark, however, it demonstrates nothing more than an already sick imagination and a disturbed psyche. It has been asserted that Salieri admitted on his deathbed (May 1825) that he killed Mozart. This, of course, is extremely unlikely, unless he died insane, which does not seem to have been the case. That Salieri is said to have been one of the few people who accompanied Mozart's body to its grave would not necessarily speak against murder; what does is the fact that the rumored rivalry between Mozart and Salieri is a product of the literature, and has in turn furthered this literature: only through the envious rival's antagonism does the hero acquire complete and true virtue. This is a very typical sort of legend. It is undoubtedly based in part on Mozart's great and not entirely inexplicable emotional impact. Salieri was a sociable and apparently altogether conciliatory man, a serious practicing musician and teacher, whose pupils included Beethoven, Schubert, and Liszt.

Poisoning with mercury, especially if it had to be dispensed in several doses over a period of weeks, was no way to kill anyone. On the other hand, mercury was available, since at this time people began to treat venereal diseases with an oral sublimate: the noted Dutch doctor Gerard van Swieten, personal physician to Maria Theresa, was the first to use it, though presumably not on his imperial patient. His son Gottfried, a diplomat and high state official, and a self-appointed, dilettantish, but respected *arbiter musicae*, was Mozart's patron. However, one should not assume that Mozart brought anything home from the concerts in his house apart from the music of Bach and Handel—certainly not mercury.

We would only have to think a little further in this direction to arrive at the suspicion that the mercury treatment was intended not for murder but for the cure of syphilis. Syphilis can take the form of several illnesses, a fact, by the way, that some biographers have used to veil or gloss over the illness of their respective heroes.

From the biographer's vantage point, at a distance of two hundred years, Mozart did not gradually languish but was suddenly extinguished; he was not slowly worn away, but suddenly torn away; no final apotheosis, no "last glow," but rather the interruption of a mighty creative act of many years' duration by a precipitous death. This does not exclude the possibility that he sensed death approaching. Perhaps in the last months of his life he was more and more aware of his inexorable destiny. With his days and nights now numbered, he turned into a Dionysian figure and lost his footing; he became a man who thought of himself as ruined. Plagued intermittently by depressions, he craved distraction, seeking his pleasure in places where the bourgeois imagination does not want to follow him. As one of the great syphilitics, he would at least be in the company of no less than the greatest intellects of the eighteenth and nineteenth centuries. Nor would this necessarily imply promiscuity. Although in Mozart's case nothing is known, it does not seem out of the question (for these aspects, especially, were subject to the great historical whitewashing of the nineteenth century). Sometimes, as in Nietzsche's case, one single impulse was enough to ruin a man. Beethoven's truly gruesome (and hushed-up) post-mortem examination would also lead us to ask what terrible course of physical destruction must have preceded his death. We do not know, and cannot even guess, at the kind of impulses.

The final state in Mozart's case, then, would have been a uremic coma. A third medical source, it is true, describes the coma as the final stage of a different disease: nephrosclerosis,[78] the result of a kidney ailment that had been latent in Mozart since his early Italian journeys and had gradually impaired his condition. We do not have the authority to dismiss a theory founded on serious examination of the primary literature, but it seems in our opinion insufficiently verified. Although this primary literature, Leopold's and Wolfgang's letters, provides extensive information about complaints and dosages of various medications, it is not of much value for determining the illness or for defining its cure. If, in this confusion, we decide to eliminate all factors based on speculation, we are inclined (I am inclined) to believe that Mozart died suddenly of an acute illness, perhaps in an epidemic.

The last hours and the death of a genius are also subject to aesthetic censure: they must provide at least some undisputed beauty for reverent generations to come; they must also have the stuff of tradition, "last words," last gestures. Today we know that Goethe did not say *"Mehr Licht"* (more light) on his deathbed. He apparently was asking to have the windows opened; that would have been enough. The physician Dr. Vogel's report of "searing pain" and a "painful urge to urinate" struck biographers as too radical a diminution of his immortal side. The dying Mozart who puffs out his cheeks to imitate the timpani (other sources say the trombone) of the Requiem will, of course, outlast any objective discussion about his death; this Mozart will be the victor. We are only too happy to avoid imagining the necessarily unpleasant smell of any deathbed (I admit I have often wondered how it could be tolerated); but however Mozart's death may have taken place, whichever death it was, it is easier for us to imagine than his life, which, despite all the records and interpretations, is shrouded in mystery and always will be. The evidence is massive, but we will find Mozart forever puzzling and unapproachable. The almost continual creative activity of an intellect who towered so far above his society, and yet continually communicated with it and seemed to adapt to it, but who lived in it as a stranger, a condition neither he nor his circle could encompass; who grew ever more deeply estranged, never suspecting it himself until the end of his life, and making light of it until the very end—our imagination cannot accommodate such a phenomenon.

We know nothing more precise about Mozart's death than what Sophie Haibl reported, thirty-three years later. The simplemindedness with which this distance in time is ignored reveals the anomaly of would-be biographical documentation, which passes, for a while at least, as fact. Nissen took Sophie's report for hard currency. Constanze, the last to edit it, probably made corrections as she saw fit, and added the finishing touches. According to other incomplete and unauthorized reports, a few friends were also there—Schack, Gerl, and Hofer. Joseph Deiner, the factotum, also claims to have been present. But Sophie mentions only Süssmayr, with whom the dying man, exerting his last strength, rehearsed the Requiem. That is what she told Nissen; that is what he wrote, and that is what Constanze released to the outside world. Fearing that the commission would remain uncompleted, she presumably wanted to salvage as much of the authenticity of the work as she could. Count Walsegg should not receive a Requiem by Süssmayr, whom she was "angry with" anyway. In any event, she did nothing to counteract the legend that Mozart kept working to the end. Both the Novellos left her in 1829 firmly convinced that the pen literally dropped from his limp hand. (Vincent: "The pen dropped from his weak hand." Mary:

"The pen dropped from his hand.") Dr. Closset, the physician, came as soon as he could leave the theater. This is believable. It took Sophie, so she wrote, a long time to round up a priest who was ready to administer the last rites. This is fairly believable. Other details have been handed down, the removal of the canary, for example, whose song the dying man could no longer tolerate. This is an arresting detail, the kind that cannot be invented. We are only surprised that he could ever have tolerated it at all.

We do not know whether the priest whom Sophie went to find ever came or not. Probably not, for no one mentions him. If he had come, Sophie probably would have used a more conciliatory term than "reverend monster." Nor can we judge whether Mozart cared about the priest's visit or if he would have cared had he been fully conscious. We think not. Arthur Schurig, whose very decided views seem to give him the right to the most daring insights, writes: "Wolfgang Amadeus, deeply religious like every Germanic artist, did not need the pitiable comforts of Christianity."[79] Annette Kolb, on the other hand, propounds a different theory: "Thus died the glory of Catholicism."[80] We, who have no such categorical insights to work with, wonder, at this late stage, whether Mozart really was a believer—a much more complex question than the one Gretchen, anticipating an unambiguous response, asks Faust.

On the surface, and seen in retrospect, Mozart was a "Catholic phenomenon," raised in an area in which (atmospherically, geographically, and philosophically) faith ruled life, or at least religion represented an omnipresent voice in the score of life's activities. Or are we in error about this, too? Do we overestimate the power of customs peculiar to certain historical periods? Probably. The "rococo man," who experienced his age aesthetically, is a product of wishful thinking, especially where it concerns his religiosity. A typical example: "The festive, colorful, visually appealing ceremony of the Catholic church, which finds its appropriate context in the joyous architectural diversity of Austrian and Southern German houses of worship, was in harmony with the open nature of the young artist."[81] Really? It certainly was in harmony with the author's nature and his identification with Mozart. Still, today we find it as hard to imagine Mozart a dissenter as to imagine Bach a Catholic. Of course, those unverified characteristics that we find easy to imagine still have little to do with fact, since they are based on a tradition of subjectivity. Generations have painted on the picture and laid on the signs of piety like so many coats of glaze. Bach's life consists of dates, facts, and didactic kitsch. His personal documents (requests, applications, advice, proposals, complaints) have no language of their own. Their pious style, their stylized flourishes stifle any response. Unfortunately, the man underneath never gave himself away.

Certainly Mozart was a believer, in that his mental life was never given over to the critical examination of God, to doubts or denials. Like his society, and like his father, whose relative enlightenment never went so far as to include agnostic ideas, he too believed in God as a figure of authority, a ruler of man's fate, and, of course (conveniently for him), the destroyer of individual free will. We have seen that "God's will" often provided a good opportunity for him to change a touchy or tiresome subject. But it never occurred to him to doubt God: he had other things to do. He did not know any agnostics or atheists who might have influenced him. Of course, he did not know anyone who affected piety, either, except Frau Hagenauer; but she soon disappeared from view, and her bigotry was, in fact, scorned in Salzburg circles. Mozart probably never perceived Protestants as such; at least he never uses that term. Among the small number of Jews he knew were Baron Wetzlar and Da Ponte, both converts who were hardly recognizable as Jews; he does call the former "a rich Jew" in a letter to his father (January 22, 1783), but in this context it is probably not meant as a value judgment. His expression "a sow of the first order" is a value judgment, however. He used it to describe the "Jewess Eskeles," whose alleged espionage activities were a topic of conversation in Vienna. At his father's request he wrote to him extensively about her (September 11, 1782). But we know his philistine lapses, by now, his habit of adopting generally held opinions in order to please his father. Apart from these instances, he never uses the word "Jew," in contrast to his father, who had anti-Semitic tendencies, which did, however, subside as soon as a Jew was converted. In London Leopold claimed that he himself converted a Jewish cellist, who thereafter apparently became a respectable person.

No one in Mozart's circles spoke of the Church as an institution; as a building the church was for him less a holy site than the place where an organ stood. It was not his favorite instrument, but one could play on it. If he was in the mood, he heedlessly disrupted the devotional atmosphere of the Mass by joking with cadenzas and extemporaneous embellishments, and reduced potential worshippers to laughter (Mannheim, November 13, 1777). He wrote in the prayerbook of his fiancée Constanze, "Do not be too devout . . ." (Vienna, 1781).

There is no indication that Mozart ever went to church at all after 1782, except for a performance of his own liturgical work. The Mass had always been a function he had to get over before he could go bowling or play Tarot cards. As early as his Italian journeys he had expressed critical, satirical ideas about priests: in his circle, too, they were always regarded with disapproval. Except when he reached back into his stock of commonly held edifying thoughts for letters of condolence, he was not moved by clerical or religious matters. They had no place in his mental world. The frequent exclamation *"O Gott!"* in his letters has nothing to do with God.

The non-literary genius, as a type, is usually monomaniacal and possessed by one thing, his own work (except for the Renaissance genius, about whose inner life we know only that his intellectual drive was nourished by a new view of the world and correspondingly enlarged perceptions). Mozart was a musician and a dramatist; his music provides no answer to the question of his belief. His Masses may evoke religious fervor in believers, and that is their conscious intention; but they are infused not with belief but with the will to portray it. In them we usually hear, as well, the dramatist's desire to write opera. This is not meant as a diminution of their quality; certain of his sacred works approach greatness. Certainly we experience moments that make it hard to regard Mozart as anything but inspired by the theme of his text. Everyone has his own examples; for me, the shift from G minor to E-flat major at the end of the "Qui tollis" of the C minor Mass or the soft *ostinato* of the double chorus "Salve nos" in the "Rex tremendae" of the Requiem are breathtaking passages (I take the liberty of the non-professional: I have my favorite "beautiful parts"). And yet I never visualize Mozart as "fervent." For "fervor" is the feeling he empathizes with, the *result* of the creator's efforts. It is what he has evoked, but it is not his frame of mind during the creative process. To evoke it he must be in control, he cannot himself be carried away. By and large, we think that Mozart, when writing his sacred music, did not have his mind on the job (if one can call the creative expression of religious faith a "job"). There are perhaps some exceptions, phrases in the text which may have moved him deeply, beyond the mere liturgical context; some of us, of course, may think of the unfinished "Lacrymosa" of the Requiem, perhaps the last notes he ever wrote down. One wonders if even an utterly perfect portrayal of a theme implies belief in it, or whether it may really be nothing more than magnificent drama. He probably died holding the Requiem. A strange note: he predated it: "Requiem. di me[!] W:A: Mozart mpr. [*manu propria*] 792" he wrote on the score. 1792. As if he knew that he would not finish the work in 1791 but thought he would surely complete it the following year, when he was once again restored to health. Or is he being bitterly ironic? We do not know. Until today no one has been able to explain why he never finished his C minor Mass. Did he not want to?

It is said that the priest stayed away from the dying man's bed because Mozart was known to be a Freemason and an apostate. The latter is possible, if one chooses to see apostasy as a way of life, amoral, according to the Church, and if one does not connect it with Freemasonry; for in reality these two allegiances did not overlap. Many people, Mozart's father included, had been able to combine Freemasonry and religiosity, moderately observed. The truth is probably that Mozart was not interested in the Church as an institution; it represented a habit he had given up. It is unlikely, therefore, that he would have missed a priest at his deathbed, even if his fading consciousness had been aware of his absence.

We do not know exactly who was present. Constanze and Sophie, of course. And Süssmayr's presence has been vouched for satisfactorily. This would suggest that Mozart's disapproval of the relationship between his pupil and his wife, whatever it was, had not gone too far. Constanze did not report any last words directed at herself, nor did she invent any. The last person on the scene was the doctor, Thomas Franz Closset. It is possible that he was a theater doctor; otherwise he might have come sooner, for as Mozart's family physician he must have known the condition of his patient. Of course, he also knew that nothing more could be done. This is why the apparently spontaneous order "cold poultices on his burning head" (Sophie Haibl) seems so incomprehensible. Anyone today would understand that such a shock not only would be of no use to the dying man but would also necessarily hasten his death, which it did, so that "he became unconscious and remained so until he died" (Sophie Haibl). But let us leave judgments of medical expertise to those better qualified. Perhaps we are unfair to let a minor actor enter the last act of this drama as a villain. Surely he did what he could. But what could he do?

Thus died Mozart, perhaps the greatest genius in recorded human history. We feel no qualms in using the sentimental cliché. This is the exemplary coincidence of reality with its overused notation. His was not an unusually premature death, it is true, but he was on the threshold of the years that are usually called "the prime of life." Impoverished, broken (our examination obliges us to retain this cliché, too), he "leaned his head against the wall" (a dubious recollection of the factotum Joseph Deiner, whose presence has not been verified) and left his world, which, to the end, consisted only of his city, the scene of his futile efforts. It had scorned what he offered, quashed his aspirations, and rejected his applications. And yet in an inexplicable way he had remained true to it, no doubt bound by debts and miserable obligations. Here and there the city remembered him, but then again failed to appreciate him; it favored inferior musicians, who surpassed him. His operas ran in Berlin and Hamburg, Frankfurt and Mannheim; Hungary and Holland offered him honorary awards; but he never knew about them. True to the rules of tragedy, the rescue came too late.

The names of the potential rescuers have not been handed down; we would have liked to list them—a handful of just men in a world full of indolence and ignorance, in which a last, paltry, and powerless few (not even a "hard core") had remained loyal to Mozart, but yielded to the inevitability of his fate and acknowledged it without indignation. It simply had to be that way.

In all likelihood, the caesura of his death did not even disturb Mozart's most intimate circle, and no one suspected, on December 6, 1791, when the fragile, burned-out body was lowered into a shabby grave, that the mortal remains of an inconceivably great mind were being laid to rest—an unearned gift to humanity, nature's unique, unmatched, and probably unmatchable work of art.

Notes
Chronology
Index of Works
Index of Names

NOTES

As in the original German edition of this book, all sources are cited in the original language of publication, except for two sources (see notes 10 and 51), for which the author cites German translations

1 Bruno Walter, *Vom Mozart der Zauberflöte* (Frankfurt, 1956), pp. 7, 16.

2 Bernhard Paumgartner, *Mozart* (Freiburg and Zurich, 1945), p. 263.

3 Alfred Orel, *Mozart in Wien* (Vienna, 1944), p. 5.

4 Quoted in H. H. Stuckenschmidt, *Mozart als Europäer*, in the program for the Mozart Week of the Deutsche Oper am Rhein (Düsseldorf, 1970), p. 11.

5 *Mozart: Briefe und Aufzeichnungen.* Complete edition, edited by the Internationalen Stiftung Mozarteum Salzburg. Vols. I–IV, *Briefe*, collected and annotated by Wilhelm A. Bauer and Otto Erich Deutsch; Vols. V, VI, *Kommentar* by Joseph Heinz Eibl, based on Bauer and Deutsch's preliminary work; Vol. VII, *Register*, assembled by Joseph Heinz Eibl (Kassel, Basel, London, New York, Tours, 1962–75). All quotations from Mozart's letters in the original German text of this book are from this edition. The English translations given here are—with the exception of some letters and passages unavailable in her edition—by Emily Anderson, *The Letters of Mozart and His Family*. Three volumes (London, 1938).

6 Alfred Einstein, *Mozart: Sein Charakter, sein Werk* (Zurich, Stuttgart, 1953), p. 41.

7 Karl Barth, *Wolfgang Amadeus Mozart* (Zollikon, 1956), p. 13.

8 Quoted in Kurt Pahlen, "Dem Angedenken Joseph Krips," in the

program for the 1975–76 concert season, Gesellschaft der Musik-
freunde, Vienna.

9   *A Mozart Pilgrimage: Being the Travel Diaries of Vincent and
    Mary Novello in the Year 1829*, transcribed and completed by
    Nerina Medici di Marignano, edited by Rosemary Hughes (Lon-
    don, 1955), p. 5.

10 Søren Kierkegaard, *Entweder–Oder* (Munich, 1975), p. 59.

11 "Spare a thought for Mozart himself, who was weak for want
    of food as he wrote this music for us." R. B. Moberly, *Three
    Mozart Operas: Figaro, Don Giovanni, The Magic Flute. An
    Altogether New Approach to Mozart's Scores* (London, 1967),
    p. 274.

12 Théodore de Wyzewa and Georges de Saint-Foix, *Wolfgang
    Amédée Mozart: Sa vie musicale et son oeuvre. Essay de bio-
    graphie critique*, Vol. I (Paris, 1936), p. 526.

13 Sigmund Freud, *Das Ich und das Es (Studienausgabe der Gesam-
    melten Werke)*, Vol. III, p. 290.

14 Hermann Abert, *W. A. Mozart*, revised and expanded edition of
    Otto Jahn's *Mozart*. Two volumes, with an index volume, pre-
    pared by Erich Kapst (Leipzig, 1973), Vol. I, p. 836.

15 Ernst Bloch, *Geist der Utopie* (Frankfurt, 1964), pp. 68ff.

16 Ibid., p. 84.

17 Ulrich Dibelius, *Mozart-Aspekte* (Munich, 1971), p. 9.

18 Abert, op. cit., Vol. II, p. 147.

19 Arthur Schurig, *Wolfgang Amadeus Mozart: Sein Leben und sein
    Werk*, two volumes (Leipzig, 1913), Vol. II, pp. 330f.

20 Hanns Dennerlein, *Der unbekannte Mozart: Die Welt seiner
    Klavierwerke* (Leipzig, 1955), pp. 75f.

21 K. R. Eissler, "Prinzipielles zur Psychoanalyse des Genies," in
    Jahrbuch der Psychoanalyse (Bern, 1975), VIII, p. 24.

22 Abert, op. cit., Vol. I, p. 610.

23 Einstein, op. cit., p. 283.

24 Quoted in Dennerlein, op. cit., p. 101.

25 Ibid., p. 96.

26 See note 9.

27 Novello, op. cit., pp. 149ff.

28 *Biographie des Joseph Lange, K. K. Hofschauspielers, Wien*
    (1808).

29 Unpublished letter, quoted in Johannes Cremerius, "Stefan
    Zweigs Beziehung zu Sigmund Freud, eine 'heroische Identi-

fizierung,' " in *Jahrbuch der Psychoanalyse* (Bern, 1975), VIII, p. 77.

30 Erich Schenk, *Mozart: Sein Leben, seine Welt* (Vienna, Munich, 1975), p. 282.

31 Robert Münster, "Mozart . . . 'beym Herzoge Clemens . . . ,' " in *Mozart-Jahrbuch*, 1965/66, p. 136.

32 Abert, op. cit., Vol. II, p. 123.

33 Einstein, op. cit., p. 379.

34 William G. Niederland, "Klinische Aspekte der Kreativität," in *Psyche*, XXXII, 12, p. 913.

35 Richard Wagner, "Die Oper und das Wesen der Musik," in *Gesammelte Schriften und Dichtungen* (Leipzig, undated), Vol. III, p. 246.

36 Novello, op. cit., p. 115.

37 Ludwig Finscher, Foreword to the miniature score of the quartet (derived from the *Neue Mozart-Ausgabe*) (Kassel, Paris, London, New York, 1962), p. v.

38 Aloys Greither, *Wolfgang Amadé Mozart* (Reinbek bei Hamburg, 1962), p. 109.

39 Werner Lüthy, *Mozart und die Tonartencharakteristik* (Strassburg, 1931), p. 79.

40 Abert, op. cit., Vol. I, p. 741.

41 Leo Schrade, *W. A. Mozart* (Bern and Munich, 1964), p. 23.

42 Uwe Kraemer, "Wer hat Mozart verhungern lassen?" in *Musica*, 30th series, no. 3.

43 Michael Kelly, *Reminiscences* (London, 1826). Quoted in Otto Erich Deutsch, *Mozart: Die Dokumente seines Lebens* (Kassel, Basel, London, New York, 1961), p. 457.

44 Abert, op. cit., Vol. I, p. 319.

45 Ibid., p. 206.

46 Einstein, op. cit., pp. 226f.

47 English translation from Marcia Davenport's *Mozart* (New York, 1932, 1956), p. 273.

48 Abert, op. cit., Vol. II, pp. 326–30.

49 Paolo Lecaldaro, Introduction to *Lorenzo Da Ponte: Tre libretti per Mozart* (Milan, 1956).

50 *Memorie di Lorenzo Da Ponte, da Ceneda. Scritte da esso* (New York, 1829–30). The edition used here is *Memorie e i libretti mozartiani*, edited by Giuseppe Armani (Milan, 1976).

51 Hector Berlioz, *Lebenserinnerungen* (Munich, undated), p. 68.

52 Theodor W. Adorno, "Huldigung an Zerlina," in *Moments musicaux* (Frankfurt, 1964), pp. 37ff.

53 Quoted in Greither, op. cit., p. 142.

54 Adorno, "Klemperers *Don Giovanni*," in *Süddeutsche Zeitung*, February 24, 1967.

55 Wolfgang Plath and Wolfgang Rehm, "Einführung und Revisionsbericht zur Partitur des *Don Giovanni*," in *Neue Mozart-Ausgabe* (Kassel, Basel, Tours, London, 1975), p. xi.

56 Georg Nikolaus Nissen, *Biographie W. A. Mozarts*, second unrevised printing of the 1828 edition (Hildesheim, New York, 1972), p. 415.

57 Novello, op. cit., p. 187.

58 Ludwig Schiedermair, *Die Briefe W. A. Mozarts und seiner Familie*. First critical edition, five volumes (Munich, Leipzig, 1914).

59 Paumgartner, op. cit., p. 276.

60 Novello, op. cit., p. 80.

61 Franz Niemtschek, *Leben des K. K. Kapellmeisters Wolfgang Gottlieb Mozart* (Prague, 1798), p. 79.

62 Lange, op. cit., p. 46.

63 Emil Karl Blümml, *Aus Mozarts Freundes- und Familien-Kreis* (Vienna, Prague, Leipzig, 1923), p. 40.

64 Karoline Pichler, *Denkwürdigkeiten aus meinem Leben* (1843–44), edited by Emil Karl Blümml (Munich, 1915). Quoted in Deutsch, op. cit., p. 472.

65 Ibid., p. 473.

66 Kraemer, op. cit., p. 210.

67 Kurt Kramer, "Da Pontes *Così fan tutte*," in *Nachrichten der Akademie der Wissenschaften* (Göttingen, 1973).

68 Stefan Kunze, "Über das Verhältnis von musikalisch autonomer Struktur und Textbau in Mozarts Opern: Das Terzettino 'Soave sia il vento' (No. 10) aus *Così fan tutte*," in *Mozart-Jahrbuch*, 1973/74, p. 270.

69 Abert, Introduction to the miniature score of *Die Zauberflöte* (London, Zurich, New York, undated).

70 Egon Komorzynski, *Der Vater der Zauberflöte* (Vienna, 1948), p. 82.

71 Both quotations from Horst Goerges, *Das Klangsymbol des Todes im dramatischen Werk Mozarts* (Munich, 1969), p. 162.

72 Quoted in the transcript of the master class, in the program

for the Mozart Week of the Deutsche Oper am Rhein (Düsseldorf, 1970), p. 15.

73 Dieter Schickling, "W. A. Mozarts Requiem," in *Mozart-Jahrbuch*, 1976/77, pp. 265–76.

74 Friedrich Schlichtegroll, *Mozarts Leben* (Graz, 1794). Facsimile reprint of the original edition (Kassel, Basel, Tours, London, 1974).

75 Quoted in Komorzynski, op. cit., p. 137.

76 Carl Bär, *Mozart: Krankheit–Tod–Begräbnis*. Second, expanded edition (Salzburg, 1972).

77 Dieter Kerner, *Krankheiten grosser Musiker* (Stuttgart, 1963), pp. 9–51.

78 Greither, "Die Todeskrankheit Mozarts," in *Deutsche Medizinische Wochenschrift* (Stuttgart, 1967), 92, pp. 723–26. Also *Die sieben grossen Opern Mozarts, mit einer Pathographie Mozarts* (Heidelberg, 1970).

79 Schurig, op. cit., Vol. II, p. 280.

80 Annette Kolb, *Mozart* (Erlenbach-Zurich and Stuttgart, 5th edition, 1970), p. 308.

81 Roland Tenschert, "Mozart und die Kirche," in Paul Nettl, *W. A. Mozart* (Frankfurt and Hamburg, 1955), p. 67.

CHRONOLOGY

1756

January 27 Joannes Chrysostomus Wolfgangus Theophilus (Lat. Amadeus) Mozart born in Salzburg, the youngest (seventh and second surviving) child of Johann Georg Leopold Mozart and his wife, Anna Maria (née Pertl).

The Seven Years' War begins.

1757

Death of Domenico Scarlatti.
Death of Johann Stamitz.

1759

Haydn's First Symphony (D major).
Publication of Voltaire's *Candide* (Voltaire raises his cry *"Ecrasez l'infame"* against the Catholic Church).
Birth of Friedrich Schiller.
Death of George Frederick Handel.

1760

George III becomes King of England (until 1820).
Birth of Luigi Cherubini.

1761

First composition: Minuet and Trio for piano in G, K. 1/1e.

Haydn Kapellmeister to Prince Esterhazy (until 1790).
Publication of Rousseau's *La nouvelle Héloise*.

1762

January 12 Leopold Mozart and his two children travel to Munich (for three weeks).

September 18 The Mozart family leaves for Vienna. Stay in Passau for six days; on September 26 from there by boat along the Danube to Linz. On October 4 the river journey continues via Mauthausen, Ybbs, and Stein.

October 6 Arrival of the Mozart family in Vienna, where they remain until December 31. An interlude (December 11 to 24) in Pressburg.

End of October Mozart ill for approximately ten days (*Erythema nodosum*).

Première of Gluck's *Orfeo ed Euridice* (Vienna).

Publication of Rousseau's *Emile* and *Du contrat social*.

Catherine II (the Great) Empress of Russia (until 1796).

1763

January Mozart ill for a week (rheumatism of the joints).

June 9 The Mozart family leaves on its grand European tour.

June 12 Arrival in Munich.

June 22–July 6 Augsburg. Leopold Mozart buys a portable keyboard instrument.

Beginning of July–beginning of August Journey continues via Ulm, Ludwigsburg, Bruchsal, Schwetzingen, Heidelberg, Mannheim, Worms, Mainz to Frankfurt.

August 10–31 Frankfurt. The fourteen-year-old Goethe hears the Mozart children in a concert.

Until mid-September Second stay in Mainz.

September 17–27 In Koblenz.

End of September–beginning of October Journey via Bonn, Brühl, Cologne, Aachen, Lüttich, Tirlemont to Brussels.

October 5–November 15 Stay in Brussels.

November 15–18 Journey via Mons, Bonavis, Gournay to Paris.

November 18 Arrival in Paris, where the Mozart family remains five months.

First sonatas for violin and piano.

Peace of Hubertusburg ends the Seven Years' War.
Birth of Jean Paul.

1764

April 10 Departure from Paris for London (via Calais).

April 23 Arrival of the Mozart family in London, for a stay of fifteen months. Meeting with Karl Friedrich Abel and Johann Christian Bach.

After various compositions for the piano, Mozart writes his first symphony (E-flat, K. 16) at the end of the year (or 1765?).

Publication of Winckelmann's *History of Ancient Art*.
Death of Jean-Philippe Rameau.

1765

Further compositions for piano, two and four hands (e.g., Sonata in C, K. 19d), which Mozart (sometimes with his sister) performs publicly. Further symphonies.

July 24 Mozart family leaves London. Journey via Canterbury, Dover, Calais, Dunkirk to Lille, where first Wolfgang, then Leopold fall ill with angina. The family remains a month in Lille.

September 4 Departure from Lille to Ghent and via Antwerp, Moerdijk, Rotterdam to The Hague.

September 10 Arrival in The Hague, where the Mozart family remains six and a half months. Piano compositions, symphonics (among others Symphony in B-flat, K. 22).

September 12 Mozart's sister, Nannerl, falls ill with typhus of the stomach. On October 21 she receives the last rites (recovery beginning of November).

November 15 Mozart falls ill with typhus of the stomach, and is not fully recovered until spring 1766.

August 18 Death of Emperor Franz I in Innsbruck.
Joseph II becomes Emperor (until 1790).

1766

End of January Removal of the Mozart family from The Hague to Amsterdam, where they remain until the beginning of March.

Piano and violin sonatas.

Beginning of March Back to The Hague.

End of March Departure of the Mozart family from The Hague to Haarlem. Via Amsterdam, Utrecht, Antwerp, Mechlin, Brussels, Valenciennes, Cambrai to Paris.

May 10 Arrival in Paris. Stay until mid-July. An interlude (May 28 to June 1) in Versailles.

July 9 Departure from Paris. Via Dijon (two weeks), Lyons (almost four weeks), Geneva, Lausanne (five days), Bern (eight days), Zürich (two weeks), Winterthur, Schaffhausen (four days), Donaueschingen (eleven days), Messkirch, Ulm, Günzburg, Dillingen, Augsburg to Munich.

November 8 Arrival in Munich.

November 12–21 Mozart ill (rheumatism of the joints).

November 29 Mozart family returns to Salzburg after a journey of three and a half years.

Piano sonatas, various works, fragments.

Publication of Lessing's *Laokoön, oder Über die Grenzen der Malerei und Poesie.*

Publication of Wieland's prose translation of Shakespeare.

1767

March 12 Performance of *Die Schuldigkeit des ersten Gebotes* (first part of a sacred *Singspiel*, K. 35) in Salzburg.

May 13 Performance of *Apollo et Hyacinthus seu Hyacinthi Metamorphosis* (Latin comedy for music, K. 38) in Salzburg.

Symphonies, sacred cantatas, first piano concerti (adaptations of isolated sonata movements).

September 11–15 The Mozart family travels to Vienna.

October 23 To avoid a smallpox epidemic in Vienna, the Mozarts travel to Brünn, where they remain until October 26.

October 26 Journey to Olmütz (stay until December 23).

Mozart falls ill with smallpox.

November 10 Wolfgang recovered. Nannerl falls ill.

December 24 Mozart family again in Brünn.

Première of Gluck's *Alceste*.

Publication of Lessing's *Minna von Barnhelm* and *Hamburgische Dramaturgie.*

Publication of Moses Mendelssohn's *Phädon, oder Über die Unsterblichkeit der Seele.*

Publication of Rousseau's *Dictionnaire de musique.*

Death of Georg Philipp Telemann.

1768

January 9–10 Return journey of the Mozart family from Brünn via Poysdorf to Vienna.

January 19 Audience with Maria Theresa and Emperor Joseph II.

April–July Composition of the *opera buffa La finta semplice,* K. 51/46a.

Late summer Composition of the *Singspiel Bastien und Bastienne,* K. 50/46b.

Autumn Performance of the *Singspiel* in the garden theater of Dr. Franz Anton Mesmer (?).

End of December Departure of the Mozart family from Vienna. Via Melk, Linz to Salzburg.

Cook's first sea journey around the world.

Death of Lawrence Sterne.

Murder of Johann Joachim Winckelmann.

1769

January 5 Return of the Mozart family to Salzburg after an absence of fifteen months.

May 1 Première of *La finta semplice* in Salzburg.

August 6 Performance of the Serenade in D, K. 100/62a, in Salzburg.

Other serenades and cassations. Sacred compositions.

November 14 Mozart is named third (unremunerated) Konzertmeister of the Hofkapelle in Salzburg.

December 13 Start of Mozart's first Italian journey, accompanied by his father. Via Lofer, Wörgl, Innsbruck, Steinach, Brixen, Bolzano, Egna, Rovereto to Verona.

December 27 Arrival in Verona.

Birth of Napoleon Bonaparte.

1770

January 5 Mozart's first concert in Italy, at the Verona Accademia Filarmonica.

January 10 Continuation of the journey to Mantua.

January 19 Departure from Mantua. Via Bozzolo, Cremona to Milan.

January 23 Arrival in Milan.

February 15 The English scientist Daines Barrington reads his report on Mozart in the London Royal Society.

March 15 Departure of the two Mozarts from Milan.

Stay in Lodi, where Mozart's first String Quartet in G, K. 80/73f, is written.

Continuation of the journey via Piacenza, Parma, Modena to Bologna.

March 24 Arrival in Bologna. First meeting with Padre Martini.

March 29 The travelers leave Bologna and reach Florence on March 30.

April 3 and 4 Meeting with the English violinist Thomas Linley, also fourteen years old (died in 1778). Playing music together, important friendship.

April 6 Departure from Florence. Via Siena, Orvieto, Viterbo to Rome.

April 11 Arrival in Rome; stay until May 8.

May 8 to 14 Journey via Terracina, Sessa, Capua to Naples.

May 14–June 25 The two Mozarts stay in Naples. Private concerts in the homes of aristocrats and diplomats. Excursions to Pompeii, Herculaneum, Vesuvius, etc.

June 26 Again in Rome, after a coach journey (express post) of twenty-seven hours and a coach accident in which the father is injured.

July 5 Mozart receives the insignia of the papal order: a golden cross on a red ribbon, sword and spurs.

July 8 Father and son are received by the Pope in a private audience.

Composition of several symphonies.

July 10 Departure from Rome. Via Terni, Spoleto, Foligno, Loreto, Ancona, Senigallia, Pesaro, Rimini, Forlì, Faenza, Imola to Bologna.

July 20 Arrival in Bologna.

August 10 to October 1 Stay at the country estate of Field Marshal Pallavicini near Bologna (Leopold Mozart still suffering from the consequences of the accident). Mozart begins to compose his *opera seria Mitridate, Rè di Ponto*.

October Daily instruction with Padre Martini, the most noted contrapuntist of his time. Canon exercises, K. Anh. 109d/73x, Symphony in G, K. 74.

October 10 Mozart receives the diploma of the Bologna Accademia Filarmonica.

October 12 Certificate from Padre Martini.

October 13 Departure from Bologna. Via Parma and Piacenza to Milan.

October 18 Arrival in Milan.

December 26 Première of the *opera seria Mitridate, Rè di Ponto*, K. 87/74a, in Milan. Mozart conducts from the harpsichord (the first three performances!). Length (with three balletic interludes): six hours!

The Great Provincial Lodge of the Freemasons of Germany founded in Berlin.

Birth of Ludwig van Beethoven.

Birth of Georg Wilhelm Friedrich Hegel.

Birth of Friedrich Hölderlin.

Death of Giuseppe Tartini.

1771

January 5 Mozart is named Honorary Kapellmeister of the Verona Accademia Filarmonica.

January 14–30 The two Mozarts stay in Turin.

January 31–February 4 Again in Milan.

February 4 Departure from Milan. Via Brescia, Verona, Vicenza, Padua to Venice.

February 11 Arrival in Venice.

March 5 Mozart gives a concert (academy) in Venice.

March 12 Departure from Venice. Via Padua, Vicenza, Verona, Rovereto, Bolzano, Brixen, Innsbruck to Salzburg.

March 28 Arrival in Salzburg.

Early summer Work on the sacred *Singspiel (Azione sacra in due parti) La Betulia liberata*, K. 118/74c.

Sacred works, symphonies.

August 13 Beginning of the second Italian journey with his father. Via Innsbruck, Bolzano, Trento, Ala, Verona, Brescia to Milan.

August 21 Arrival in Milan.

August, September Work on the opera *(Serenata teatrale in due atti) Ascanio in Alba*, K. 111.

October 17   Première of *Ascanio in Alba* in Milan, in the presence of the Archduke Ferdinand on the celebration of his marriage.

November 22 (23?)   Mozart gives an academy concert in Milan.

November 30   The Mozarts are received by Archduke Ferdinand.

December 5   Departure from Milan. Via Brescia, Verona, Trento, Bolzano, Bressanone, Innsbruck to Salzburg.

December 15   Arrival in Salzburg.

Haydn's "Sun" quartets.

Publication of Klopstock's *Odes*.

1772

Symphonies, sacred sonatas, lieder.

Work on the opera (*Serenata drammatica*) *Il sogno di Scipione*, K. 126.

March 14   Hieronymus Count Colloredo becomes Prince Archbishop of Salzburg.

Beginning of May   *Il sogno di Scipione* is performed in the Salzburg Residenz (in honor of Colloredo).

August 21   Mozart is named Konzertmeister (salaried).

October   Beginning of work on the *opera seria Lucio Silla*, K. 135.

October 24   Father and son embark on the third Italian journey. Via Innsbruck, Bressanone, ˙Bolzano, Ala, Verona, Brescia to Milan.

November 4   Arrival in Milan.

December 26   Première of the *opera seria (Dramma per musica in tre atti) Lucio Silla* in Milan.

Cook's second journey around the world.

The Göttinger Hain poetry group.

Wieland goes to the Weimar court.

Publication of Lessing's *Emilia Galotti*.

Publication of Wieland's *Der Goldene Spiegel*.

1773

January 17   Performance of the motet *Exsultate, jubilate*, K. 165/ 158a, at the Theatiners in Milan.

March 4 (?)   Departure from Milan. Via Brescia, Verona, Ala, Trento, Bressanone, Innsbruck to Salzburg.

March 13   Arrival in Salzburg.

July 14 Mozart travels with his father to Vienna (for more than two months). Contact with Dr. Mesmer. Concerts in the latter's garden.

August 5 The Mozarts are received in an audience with the Empress.

August 12 Audience with the Archbishop.

September 24 Departure from Vienna. Via St. Pölten and Linz to Salzburg.

September 26 Arrival in Salzburg.

String quartets, divertimenti, wind divertimenti, symphonies, among which is Symphony in G minor, K. 183/173dB.

December First independent piano concerto (D major, K. 175).

Publication of Goethe's *Götz* and *Urfaust.*
Completion of Klopstock's *The Messiah.*

1774

Piano sonatas, symphonies, sacred music.

October Work on the *opera buffa La finta giardiniera,* K. 196.

December 6 Mozart leaves with his father via Wasserburg to Munich (for stay of three months).

December 16–22 Mozart has a mild illness.

Première of Gluck's *Iphigénie en Aulide* in Paris, April 19. On October 18 Gluck becomes "true royal and imperial court composer" in Vienna. Salary: 2,000 florins a year.

Publication of Goethe's *Werther* and *Clavigo.*

Publication of Wieland's *Die Abderiten.*

Birth of Caspar David Friedrich.

1775

January 13 Première of the *opera buffa La finta giardiniera* in Munich, in the presence of the Elector Maximilian III.

March 6–7 Return to Salzburg with father and sister (who had come to the Munich première on January 4).

April 23 Performance of the opera *Il Rè pastore* in Salzburg. *Finalmusiken,* piano sonatas (among them K. 284/205b, "Dürnitz," in D). Serenades. Missa brevis in G, K. 220/196b, "Sparrow."

September–December Violin concerti.

Goethe at the Weimar court.
Première of Beaumarchais's *Le Barbier de Seville*.
Birth of William Turner.

1776

June 18 Performance of the Divertimento in F, K. 247 (the first Lodron *Nachtmusik*) in Salzburg.
July 21 Performance of the Serenade in D, K. 250/248b, "Haffner," in Salzburg.
Church sonatas. Divertimenti.

American Declaration of Independence.
Cook's third journey around the world.
Torture abolished in Austria.
Birth of E. T. A. Hoffmann.

1777

January Composition of the E-flat Piano Concerto, K. 271, "Jeune-homme."
February Composition of the Divertimento in B-flat, K. 287/271H.
September 23 Beginning of the Paris journey with his mother. Via Wasserburg to Munich.
September 24 Arrival in Munich. Stay there until October 11. Several vain petitions and audiences, small private concerts.
October 11 Departure with his mother from Munich and arrival in Augsburg. Academy concerts in Augsburg. Time spent with his "Bäsle."
October 26 Departure from Augsburg. Via Donauwörth to Hohen-Altheim.
October 28 Continuation of the journey via Nördlingen, Ellwangen, Bruchsal, Schwetzingen to Mannheim.
October 30 Arrival in Mannheim. Stay of four and a half months. Contact with the Mannheim court musicians: Ramm, Wendling, especially Cannabich, for whose daughter Rose Mozart writes the C major Piano Sonata, K. 309/284b; meeting with the Abbé Vogler.
Petitions to the court and audiences unsuccessful.
December 21 Performance of the Missa brevis in B-flat, K. 275/272b, in St. Peter's Collegiate Church.

December 30 Death of Elector Maximilian III of Bavaria in Munich.

Première of Gluck's *Armida*.

Performance of *Hamlet* (In F. L. Schröder's translation) in Hamburg.

Birth of Heinrich von Kleist.

1778

January 23 Mozart makes a detour to Kirchheimbolanden without his mother, in the company of Fridolin Weber and his daughter Aloysia. They spend several days there at the court of the Princess Caroline von Nassau-Weilburg, where Aloysia sings and Mozart plays.

January 29 Return via Worms, where they remain until February 2, before returning to Mannheim.

February 13 Academy concert in Cannabich's home.

February 20 Mozart ill briefly.

March 14 Mozart and his mother leave Mannheim. Via Metz to Paris.

March 23 Arrival of the two Mozarts in Paris.

May 17 Performance by Leopold Mozart of the Missa brevis in C ("Organ solo" Mass, K. 259) in Salzburg for the consecration of Colloredo.

June 11 Mozart's mother falls ill and remains in bed from June 19 on.

June 18 Performance of the "Paris" Symphony, K. 297/300a, with great success.

July 3 Death of his mother.

Flute concerti; the Oboe Concerto, K. 314/285d; sonatas, among them the Sonata in A minor for piano, K. 310/300d, and the E minor Sonata for piano and violin, K. 304/300c.

August 15 Repeat performance of the "Paris" Symphony with a new andante.

August 19 Stay in Saint-Germain (until the end of August).

September 26 Mozart leaves Paris. Slow journey via Nancy (October 3) to Strasbourg (October 14 to November 3).

October 6 Arrival in Mannheim, where Mozart lives at Frau Cannabich's (Cannabich has moved with the Mannheim court Kapelle to Munich, where the Elector of the Pfalz has succeeded the Bavarian Elector).

December 9 Mozart leaves Mannheim. Journey via Heidelberg,

Schwäbisch Hall, Crailsheim, Dinkelsbühl, Wallerstein, Nörd-lingen.

December 13 Arrival at Kaisheim monastery near Donauwörth (as guest of the imperial prelate Angelsprugger).

December 24 Continuation of the journey via Neuburg and Ingolstadt to Munich.

December 25 Arrival in Munich, where Mozart lives with the Weber family.

First opening of La Scala in Milan and the National Singspiel in Vienna.
Death of Jean-Jacques Rousseau.
Death of Voltaire.

1779

Beginning of January Aloysia Weber, now engaged to sing in Munich, rejects Mozart's marriage proposal.

January 13 Departure from Munich, probably in the company of Bäsle.

January 15 Arrival in Salzburg. Again in the service of the Archbishop as Konzertmeister and court organist.

March 23 Completion of the Mass in C, K. 317, "Coronation Mass."
Church sonatas, divertimenti, sonatas.

Summer Sinfornia Concertante for violin and viola with orchestra in E-flat, K. 364/320d. Sacred music (some of it unfinished). The *Singspiel Zaide*, K. 344/336b.

In September Aloysia Weber is engaged to sing in Vienna.

National Theater of Mannheim founded.
Première of Gluck's *Iphigénie en Tauride*.
Publication of Goethe's *Iphigenie auf Tauris* (first version).
Publication of Lessing's *Nathan der Weise*.
Death of Jean-Baptiste Siméon Chardin.

1780

May 1 Performance of *La finta giardiniera* in Augsburg.

August Symphony in C, K. 338. *Vesperae solennes de confessore*, K. 339.

September 2–4 Concerts at the court of the Archbishop.

September 6–7 Leopold Mozart goes with Wolfgang and Nannerl to St. Zeno and Bad Reichenhall.

September Schikaneder and his troupe come to Salzburg.

October 31 Aloysia marries the actor Joseph Lange.

November 5 Mozart travels to Munich (stay of four months) to rehearse *Idomeneo*. On December 1 the first rehearsal with the orchestra.

Death of Maria Theresa (November 29), succeeded by Joseph II.

Publication of Wieland's *Oberon*.

Publication of Lessing's *Über die Erziehung des Menschengeschlechts*.

1781

January 26 Leopold Mozart and his daughter arrive in Munich.

January 29 Première of *Idomeneo, Rè di Creta ossia Ilia ed Idamante (Opera seria in tre atti)*, K. 366, in Munich.

March Kyrie in D minor, K. 341/368a. Wind Serenade in B-flat, K. 361/370a, "Gran Partita."

March 7–10 The three Mozarts visit Augsburg.

March 12 By command of the Archbishop Colloredo, who is visiting Vienna, Mozart travels directly to Vienna.

March 16 Arrival in Vienna and participation in a concert on the same day.

April 27 Last Salzburg concert in Vienna, before the Archbishop.

Beginning of May Mozart moves to the home of Frau Cäcilie Weber.

May 9 Break with the Archbishop.

May 10 Mozart petitions for release from service.

June 8 Mozart receives his release, with a kick from Count Arco.

Violin sonatas, Wind Serenade in E-flat, K. 375.

Summer First pupils: Countess Rumbeke, Countess Thun, Josepha Auernhammer, Therese von Trattner.

Academy concerts and soirées in the homes of the nobility.

Beginning of September Mozart takes a room on the Graben, Inner City, No. 1175.

Háydn's "Russian" quartets.

Reforms of Emperor Joseph II: Freedom of religion, abolition of serfdom (Edict of Tolerance).

Publication of Kant's *Critique of Pure Reason*.
Death of Gotthold Ephraim Lessing.

1782

Work on *Die Entführung aus dem Serail*, K. 384.
Fugues (mainly fragments), canons.
March 3   Mozart gives an academy concert in Vienna.
April 2   Performance of *La finta giardiniera* in Frankfurt.
July 16   Première of *Die Entführung aus dem Serail (Komisches Singspiel in drei Akten)* in the Burgtheater.
July 23   Mozart moves from the Graben to the inn Roten Säbel by the Hohe Brücke.
August 4   Marriage to Constanze Weber.
Wind serenade *(Nacht-Musique)* in C minor, K. 388/384a.
Symphony in D, K. 385, "Haffner." Fugues.
Beginning of the great series of piano concerti.
String Quartet in G, K. 387.
November 11   Mozart postpones his planned journey with Constanze to Salzburg.
December   Change of quarters. Mozarts now living near the Hohe Brücke, No. 412, third floor.

Première of Schiller's *Die Räuber* in Mannheim.
Posthumous publication of Rousseau's *Confessions*.
Birth of Niccolò Paganini.
Death of Johann Christian Bach.
Death of Pietro Antonio Metastasio.

1783

February   Change of quarters. Mozarts living temporarily on the Kohlmarkt, No. 1179, in the house Zum englischen Gruss.
Concerts and performances.
Meeting with Gluck.
April 24   Change of quarters. Mozarts now living on the Judenplatz, No. 244, first floor, in the Burghischen Hause.
June 17   Birth of the first child, Raimund Leopold.
Summer   Work on the C minor Mass, K. 427/417a.
String Quartet in D minor, K. 421/417b.
End of July   Mozart travels with Constanze (without their child) to Salzburg.

August 19 Raimund Leopold dies of *"Gedärmfrais"* (intestinal cramp).

October 26 (?) Performance of the C minor Mass in St. Peter's Church. The Mass is incomplete. The missing movements are supplemented with parts of earlier Masses (undocumented).

October 27 Departure of Mozart and his wife from Salzburg. Via Vöcklabruck and Lambach to Linz.

October 30 Arrival in Linz. Quarters at Count Thun-Hohenstein. Mozart writes a symphony "hastily" (C major, "Linz," K. 425).

November 4 Performance of the symphony in Linz.

Beginning of December Mozart and Constanze again in Vienna. String Quartet in E-flat, K. 428/421b, *Notturni*.

Birth of Stendhal.
Death of Jean le Rond D'Alembert.
Death of J. A. Hasse.

1784

January Yet another move. Mozarts living in the Trattnerhof, Am Graben, No. 591–596, second entrance, third floor.

February 9 Mozart begins his catalogue of works. First entry: Piano Concerto in E-flat, K. 449.

Spring/summer Concerts in aristocratic houses, public academies, Wednesday concerts in the Trattnerhof.

August 23 Nannerl marries Johann Baptist Franz von Berchtold zu Sonnenburg, Prefect of St. Gilgen.

Piano concerti, Wind Quintet in E-flat, K. 452, piano music for his pupils.

String Quartet in B-flat, K. 458, "Hunt" quartet.

August 23–mid-September Mozart ill (kidney ailment? cold?).

September 21 Birth of Mozart's second child, Carl Thomas. (Died October 31, 1858, in Milan.)

September 29 Change of quarters. New address: Grosse Schuler-strasse, No. 846, first floor (very spacious).

December 14 Mozart is accepted into the Freemason lodge *Zur Wohltätigkeit* (first rank: apprentice).

Première of Beaumarchais's *Le mariage de Figaro*.
Publication of Schiller's *Kabale und Liebe*.
Death of Denis Diderot.

1785

January 7   Mozart attains second rank in the Freemason hierarchy: journeyman.

String Quartets in A, K. 464, and C, K. 465.

February/March   Piano Concertos in D minor, K. 466, and C, K. 467.

February 11   Leopold Mozart arrives in Vienna, lives with his son.

Active social life. Concerts, academies.

Meeting with Haydn.

Masonic music.

Fantasie in C minor for piano, K. 475.

March 10   A concert of Mozart's music in the Burgtheater.

April 6   Leopold Mozart accepted into the Lodge *Zur Wohltätig-keit*.

April 24   Mozart's father departs from Vienna.

August 24   After two petitions on his part (February 11 and March 15, 1785), Mozart receives word that the decision to accept him into the Society of Composers has been deferred (Mozart was never accepted!).

September 1   Six String Quartets, K. 387, 421/417b, 428/421b, 458, 464, 465, printed. Composed for and dedicated to Haydn.

October   Beginning of work on *Figaro*. Piano Quartet in G minor, K. 478. *Masonic Funeral Music*, K. 477, Piano concerto in E-flat, K. 482. "Das Veilchen" (text by Goethe), K. 476.

Thomas Attwood becomes Mozart's pupil.

1786

Work on *Figaro*. Meanwhile, work on the *Schauspieldirektor*, K. 486.

March   Piano Concerti in A, K. 488, and C minor, K. 491.

April 7   Mozart's last academy concert in the Burgtheater.

End of April   *Figaro* completed.

May 1   Première of the *Le Nozze di Figaro* (*Opera buffa* in 4 acts), K. 492, in the Burgtheater.

Piano Quartet in E-flat, K. 493, String Quartet in D, K. 499.

October 18   Birth of Mozart's third child, Johann Thomas Leopold.

November 15   Johann Thomas Leopold dies of *"Stickfrais"* (choking catarrh).

Autumn   Plan for a journey to England.

Piano concerto in C, K. 503, Symphony in D, K. 504, "Prague."

Haydn: six Paris symphonies.

Social self-help for musicians: Founding of the fund for pensioners, widows and orphans in Vienna and Leipzig.

Birth of Carl Maria von Weber.

Death of Frederick the Great.

Death of Moses Mendelssohn.

1787

January 8 Departure of the Mozarts with Constanze (and servant) to Prague. The violinist Franz Hofer and the clarinetist Anton Stadler accompany them.

January 11 Arrival in Prague.

January 17 Performance of *Figaro*, with great success, in Prague, in Mozart's presence.

January 18–19 Academy concert in the Prague Theater. Collaboration in further concerts.

January 22 Mozart conducts a performance of *Figaro*.

February 18 Departure from Prague, mid-February again in Vienna.

February 23 Nancy Storace's farewell concert. Mozart participates.

Rondo in A minor for piano, K. 511.

String Quintets in C, K. 515, and G minor, K. 516.

April 4 Last (extant) letter of Mozart's to his father.

April 7 The sixteen-year-old Beethoven is in Vienna, but returns on April 20 to Bonn, as his mother lies dying.

Lieder, among them "Das Lied der Trennung," K. 519, and "Abendempfindung," K. 523.

April 24 The Mozart family moves. New address: Hauptstrasse in the suburb Landstrasse, No. 224, garden wing.

May 28 Leopold Mozart dies in Salzburg, aged sixty-eight.

Ein musikalischer Spass, K. 522; *Eine kleine Nachtmusik*, K. 525; Violin Sonata in A, K. 526.

June 4 Mozart buries his starling.

October 1 Mozart travels with Constanze to Prague.

October 14 Mozart conducts *Figaro* in the presence of the Archduke.

October 29 Première of *Il dissoluto punito ossia il Don Giovanni* (*Dramma giocoso in due atti*), K. 527, in Prague. Further performances in November.

November 13 Departure from Prague, and in mid-November Mozart and Constanze are again in Vienna. Beginning of December, the Mozart family changes quarters. New address: Inner City, No. 281, Unter den Tuchlauben.

December 7 Mozart named royal and imperial chamber musician.

December 27 Mozart's fourth child, Theresa, born.

Boccherini court composer in Berlin.

Publication of Goethe's *Iphigenie*.

Publication of Schiller's *Don Carlos*.

Death of Christoph Willibald Gluck.

1788

February 24 Mozart completes the Piano Concerto in D, K. 537, "Coronation."

May 7 Viennese première of *Don Giovanni* in the National-Hof-theater.

June 17 Change of quarters. The Mozart family moves into an apartment in the suburb Alsergrund, No. 135, Währingerstrasse, Zu den drei Sternen, garden side. Material difficulties increase.

June 29 Daughter Theresa dies of *"Gedärmfrais"* (intestinal cramp).

Symphonies in E-flat, K. 543, G minor, K. 550; C, K. 551, "Jupiter."

Canons, dances for the court.

The second (so-called, little) Turkish War necessitates economy measures in the cultural life of Vienna. Thus, the Kärntnertor Theater is closed for nearly a year.

Publication of Goethe's *Egmont*.

Birth of Schopenhauer.

Death of Carl Philipp Emanuel Bach.

1789

Beginning of the year Change of quarters: New address: Inner city, No. 245, Judenplatz, Zur Mutter Gottes.

April 8 Beginning of the journey with Prince Karl Lichnowsky. Via Zanim, Mährisch-Budwitz, Iglau to Prague.

April 10 Arrival in Prague. Contract with the impresario Guardasoni for a new opera.

April 12 Arrival in Dresden.

April 14 Mozart plays before the Elector Friedrich August III.

April 18 Departure from Dresden. Via Meissen, Hubertusburg, and Wurzen to Leipzig.

April 20   Arrival in Leipzig.

April 23   Trip to Potsdam.

May 8   Mozart and Lichnowsky again in Leipzig.

May 12   A concert of Mozart's music in the Gewandhaus.

Lichnowsky leaves Leipzig. Mozart remains until May 17.

May 19   Mozart arrives alone in Berlin.

May 26   Concert at the court of Friedrich Wilhelm II.

May 28   Departure from Berlin. Via Leipzig and Dresden to Prague, where he stays from May 31 to June 2.

June 4   Arrival in Vienna.

Summer   Financial worries. Constanze's first visit to the spa in Baden. In mid-August, Mozart visits her there.

String Quartet in D, K. 575; Clarinet Quintet in A, K. 581.

November 16   Mozart's fifth child, Anna Maria, born, dies one hour later.

Autumn and winter   Work on *Così fan tutte*, K. 588.

Beginning of the French Revolution.

Publication of Goethe's *Torquato Tasso*.

1790

Financial worries.

January 26   Première of the *opera buffa Così fan tutte* at the Burgtheater.

February 20   Emperor Joseph II dies, succeeded by Leopold II.

May   Constanze in Baden.

Mozart looks for pupils and tries to pay off his debts, both efforts in vain.

String Quartets in B-flat, K. 589, and F, K. 590.

Beginning of June   Mozart with Constanze for a few weeks in Baden (occasional day trips to Vienna?).

September 23   Setting out on his last big journey. In his own coach, in the company of his brother-in-law Franz Hofer (and servant), via Eferding, Regensburg, Nuremburg, Würzburg, Aschaffenburg to Frankfurt.

September 28   Mozart and Hofer arrive in Frankfurt.

September 30   In Wolfgang's absence, the Mozart family moves to new quarters: Rauhensteingasse, No. 970, first floor.

October 9   Coronation of Leopold II as German Emperor in Frankfurt. Mozart is ignored at the ceremonies.

October 15 At an academy concert in Frankfurt, Mozart plays his Piano Concertos in F, K. 459, and D, K. 537, and conducts his own works.

October 16 By market boat to Mainz.

October 20 Mozart plays before the Elector in the palace at Mainz.

October 22 Departure from Mainz to Mannheim.

October 24 In Mannheim the first German performance of *Figaro* in Mozart's presence.

October 25 Beginning of the return journey. From Mannheim via Bruchsal, Bad Cannstatt, Göppingen, Ulm, Günzburg to Augsburg.

October 29 Arrival in Munich. Stay until the beginning of November.

November 4 (5?) Participation in a Royal Academy concert.

November 10 Mozart again in Vienna.

December 14 Farewell dinner for Joseph Haydn before his first journey to London.

String Quintet in D, K. 593; Adagio and Allegro "für ein Orgelwerk in einer Uhr," K. 594.

Publication of Goethe's *Römische Elegien*.

1791

January Piano Concerto in B-flat, K. 595, minuets, German dances.

Beginning of March "Orgelstück für eine Uhr," K. 608.

March 4 Mozart's last appearance: in an academy concert of the clarinetist Bähr (or Beer), he plays the Piano Concerto, K. 595.

May Mozart begins the composition of *Die Zauberflöte*, K. 620.

June 4 Constanze and her son Carl go to the spa in Baden, where she remains until mid-July. Mozart visits her several times.

June 17 Composition of the motet "Ave verum corpus," K. 618, in Baden.

Mid-July Mozart brings his wife and son back from Baden.

July 26 Birth of his sixth child, Franz Xaver Wolfgang. (Died July 29, 1844, in Karlsbad.)

End of July Interruption of work on *Die Zauberflöte* to write the commissioned work *La Clemenza di Tito*, K. 621.

Middle or end of August Mozart travels with Constanze and Süssmayr to Prague to rehearse *Tito*.

September 2 Mozart conducts the festival performance of *Don Giovanni* in Prague.

September 6 Première of the *opera seria La Clemenza di Tito* as the coronation opera in the National Theater in Prague in the presence of the Emperor Leopold II and his consort. Mozart conducting.

Mid-September Mozart, Constanze, and Süssmayr return to Vienna.

September 30 Première of the "German opera" *Die Zauberflöte* in the Freihaus Theater auf der Wieden in Vienna. Mozart conducting.

Beginning of October Constanze goes again to the spa at Baden.

Clarinet concerto in A, K. 622, for Anton Stadler.

Work on the Requiem (?).

October 15 Mozart goes with Carl to Baden, to bring Constanze home.

October 17 Return of the Mozart family to Vienna.

November 18 Mozart conducts his "Kleine Freimaurer Kantate," K. 623, for the dedication of the new temple of the lodge *Zur gekrönten Hoffnung.*

November 20 Mozart ill, takes to bed.

December 4 Rehearsal of the still unfinished Requiem, K. 626, at Mozart's bedside.

December Hungarian noblemen offer Mozart a yearly honorary donation of 1,000 florins. Dutch music lovers make an even better offer, immediately after his death.

December 5 Mozart dies at one o'clock in the morning.

Haydn's "Drumroll" Symphony.
Birth of Giacomo Meyerbeer.

INDEX OF WORKS

INDEX OF NAMES